LANGUAGE OF POLITICS

studies in quantitative semantics

**by Harold D. Lasswell,
Nathan Leites
and Associates**

Raymond Fadner

Joseph M. Goldsen

Alan Grey

Irving L. Janis

Abraham Kaplan

David Kaplan

Alexander Mintz

I. De Sola Pool

Sergius Yakobson

The M.I.T. Press
Massachusetts Institute of Technology
Cambridge, Massachusetts

320.1

L349

Second printing, September, 1965

PREFACE

THE CENTRAL theme of this book is that political power can be better understood in the degree that language is better understood, and that the language of politics can be usefully studied by quantitative methods. Part of the volume is given over to the technical problems of quantification, but space is taken up with "applications," chiefly to the language of communism since 1918. Specialists on government, diplomatic history and law will find themselves most at home among the "applications," while social psychologists and statisticians, on the other hand, will examine in detail the treatment of reliability, validity and sampling.

Most of the work reported here was done at the University of Chicago or in connection with the War Communications Research Project at the Library of Congress. The Project was financed by a grant from the Rockefeller Foundation as part of a program for the advancement of research in the field of communication initiated by John Marshall and David Stevens of the Foundation. The facilities made available by the University, the Foundation and the Library of Congress (under the librarianship of both Archibald MacLeish and Luther H. Evans) are gratefully acknowledged. The relationship of these studies of political communication to the rapidly expanding field of research on mass communication can be ascertained by consulting the articles and literature in *Propaganda, Communication, and Public Opinion; A Comprehensive Reference Guide,* by Bruce Lannes Smith, Harold D. Lasswell and Ralph D. Casey (Princeton University Press, 1946), and the earlier survey, *Propaganda and Promotional Activities; An Annotated Bibliography,* by Lasswell, Casey and Smith (University of Minnesota Press, 1935).

Acknowledgement is also made of the courtesy of *Psychometrika* and the *Journalism Quarterly* for permitting two research reports, originally appearing in their pages, to be included in this volume.

v

CONTENTS

I
INTRODUCTION

Chapter **1**

THE LANGUAGE OF POWER

THE LANGUAGE of power has been an arresting topic of comment and systematic inquiry from classical times to the present. The speculative minds of Greece were fascinated by the many uses of language, treating language as an instrument of truth, a means of artistic expression, and a tool of persuasion. It was, of course, Aristotle whose ideas had the greatest subsequent effect.[1] However, the most immediate link between the theory of language and power was furnished by the many treatises on oratory that flourished in antiquity. In Athens, where collective action so often depended upon the outcome of debate, the Sophists worked out practical rules of successful speech. Rome continued the Greek tradition, notably Cicero's *De Oratore*.[2] It is known that Pliny wrote a rather long manual called *The Student*.[3]

During the Middle Ages the overwhelming significance of oral communication in practical life is reflected in the number of treatises devoted to the sermon. Since the sermon was often intended to transcend the immediate limits of ceremony or religious instruction, ecclesiastical oratory is not wholly devoid of relevance to the study of politics. We have ample evidence that many sermon-makers had keen insight into the preaching situation. Gregory the Great devotes a chapter to the different kinds of audience that confront the preacher, and Jacques de Vitry enumerates no less than one hundred and twenty categories. A high level of self-awareness is indicated by the notations found on the surviving manuscript of a sermon delivered in 1500 by Oliver Maillard: "Sit down—stand up—mop yourself—ahem! ahem!—now shriek like a devil." [4]

With the rise of the printing press in sixteenth century Europe, the literature of rhetoric gradually became concerned with the use of printed media. In the twentieth century, two inventions, the film and the radio, brought voice and gesture once again into the foreground. During the modern period, the expansion of private business enterprise produced for the first time an enormous literature of salesmanship. Equally typical of our civilization, with its high level of insecurity induced by rapid and erratic change, is the literature of political propaganda. In general, as population multiplies and activities grow more specialized, greater attention is given to the control of what people do. There are manuals for business managers about their relations to stockholders, customers, workers, legislators and other groups. Officials of government, trade unions, trade associations and political parties have their special "how" books. In the later middle ages, there were books about the art of dying; today there are handbooks about how to run a funeral.[5]

Emotional Resistance to Research

Ever since men began to be aware of the effect-getting impact of language—whether the effect is power, gain or composure of mind—there has been resistance to the appraisal of language from an objective point of view. In this connection, we have only to remember the opprobrium that has so long been attached to the term "Sophist," although the Greek Sophists were reputable teachers of rhetoric. Even the term "rhetoric" is given a negative evaluation in addition to the positive one. William Butler Yeats in *Ideas of Good and Evil* called it "the will trying to do the work of the imagination," while less perceptive maladverters use blunt everyday adjectives: to be rhetorical is to be phony, windy and false.

It is not difficult to understand the many factors that contribute to the hostility with which the study of the practical effect of language is regarded. The adult layman is far from looking upon language with the same detached opportunism with which he operates an electric-light switch—words are too closely tied to basic attitudes about the self. To an extraordinary degree our well-being depends directly upon words and gestures. If the proper words of greeting are not forthcoming, we are annoyed; and the intonation must be exactly right. We would be hard put to it to describe the more subtle speech claims that we make upon our neighbors, or that they make on us, but "we know what we like," or at least what we don't like, when we meet it. In short, the status of our personality as a whole is involved in a flow of verbal deference from the environment. If we belong to that unfortunate yet numerous company of those who are somewhat unsure of themselves, we are apt to magnify the details of daily discourse out of all proportion. We are supersensitive to "slights," fancied or real. We re-live every contact, wondering if that half-smile meant friendliness or covert ridicule, or whether the tone was curt because the other fellow was in a hurry or because he was slightly miffed, or whether we had presumed too far in addressing the boss by his first name.[6]

Child Development and Language

The endless internal soliloquies of the neurotic at least reveal the high ego value put on language from the beginning of life. No child is fully adopted into human society unless and until he makes progress in picking his way through the labyrinth of language. Of all the achievements of the infant, none is more commented upon, at least in our civilization, than the first intelligible sounds and the subsequent acquisition of language skill. From the earliest days, our proficiency in speech not only serves the simple utilitarian end of signalling for food or protection; it is a measuring stick constantly applied to our personality as a whole. Language facility usually carries with it a stream of indulgence from members of the home circle and beyond, while failure shrivels the self.

Further complicating our attitude toward language is the resentment experienced in childhood against arbitrariness and secrecy. Speaking faster than we can follow, or using

words longer than we have mastered, adults settle our future
in the pseudo-publicity of conversation. Little wonder that
the child imputes an enormous power to language and to
secrecy. Hence, the energy that so often goes into the invention of a secret language. Half the fun comes from the bewilderment of adults who have the tables turned on their
speech monopoly.[7]

Political Magic and Language

Given these powerful factors conditioning the early development of the individual, we are prepared to understand the
enormous part played by magic, including magical words,
in the political history of man. Societies have had the task
of disciplining the fantasies of a million million childhoods
through the slow conquest of reality. In some cultures, the
advance in this direction has taken but a few halting steps
and adult assumptions are low in reality value; and in periods
of stress, even the more cultivated members of the community revert to primitivism.

According to the magical attitude, inexplicable powers are
imputed to symbols or signs. Conjurers, diviners and medi-
cine men were stock figures in the courts of the ancient
kingdoms and among the simpler peoples. Even when magic
involves material objects and procedures, the total pattern
includes spells and incantations. When occult knowledge is
involved, proper words are expected to swing open the door
of understanding. We have only to examine Pliny's *Natural
History* to recapture examples of the magical outlook. In
Roman history, comets were sometimes viewed as signals of
disaster. Some of the early emperors, fearful of the astrolo-
gers, banished all except their own from Rome or Italy because they had been too free in predicting the death of the
emperor. Some stones were alleged to benefit public speakers
or to admit to the presence of royalty. The blood of the
basilisk was said to procure response to petitions made to
the powerful and answers to prayers addressed to the gods.[8]

So closely interwoven, indeed, have been politics and magic
that the art of politics has frequently been classified with
magic. In a treatise on dreams, written by Philo of Alexan-
dria in the first century A.D., Joseph's "Coat of Many Colors"

is compared to the "much-variegated web of political affairs," where, along with "the smallest possible portion of truth," falsehoods of every shade of plausibility are interwoven. Philo compares politicians and statesmen to augurs, ventriloquists and sorcerers, "men skilled in juggling and in their incantations and tricks of all kinds, from whose treacherous arts it is very difficult to escape." Twelve centuries later, Moses Maimonides made the same associations in his *Guide for the Perplexed*. In some men the imaginative faculty was said to predominate, while the rational faculty was imperfect. "Whence arises the sect of politicians, of legislators, of diviners, of enchanters, of dreamers . . . and of *prestidigiteurs* who work marvels by strange cunning and occult arts." [9]

Linguistics

Whatever resistances there have been to the study of certain phases of language, the science of linguistics as a whole can boast of a long, rich, successful tradition. However, the scientific study of language has been deeply affected by the magical attitude that originally prevailed. In India, under Brahmin influence, the *vedas* came to be invested with such magical power that the slightest error in pronunciation, accent or metre annulled the value of the sacrifice. Phonetics, grammar, etymology and metre originated in the quest for proper understanding and pronunciation of the sacred texts. Musical science arose to enable the *udgatri* to chant the sacred formulae. Mensuration was needed in the construction of altars, and astrology was employed to calculate the right times for sacrifices. Since the eighteenth century, the literature of India has acted directly upon European science; the study of the *rigveda* gave rise to comparative philology.[10]

Most of the laws of scientific linguistics generalize the interaction of parts of a given language structure upon the whole, and the impact of one language structure upon another. A striking example of the predictions made possible by linguistic law is the work of Edward Sapir on the Athabaskan languages of North America. By comparing the basic sound forms of interrelated languages, he inferred the existence in Hupa of an initial *ky*, in spite of the absence of this combination in the records at that time available. In the summer of

1927, however, Sapir carried on independent researches on Hupa and came across the missing, and predicted, form. Other scholars have made and verified similar constructions for other languages, and thus have demonstrated the internal drift in sound patterns. This type of linguistic change must be added to the more obvious types (analogic change, borrowing).[11]

Language Function

Between the laws of comparative grammar and phonetics, and principles of the practical sort guiding the purposive use of language, lies much uncharted territory. The impact of personality factors upon linguistic development is only partly understood. Also, various language functions such as the language of power, have not been studied in detail.[12]

We distinguish the various functions of language according to the intentions of those who use language, and the effects achieved by using it. When the aim is to influence power, and there is some impact upon power, we speak of the political function of language. This conception allows for two marginal cases, of which the first is unintentional effect on power, and the second is total absence of intended impact. Perhaps it is worth noting that political intentions and effects are not necessarily exclusive of economic and other aims and consequences.

When we speak of the science of politics, we mean the science of power. Power is decision-making. A decision is a sanctioned choice, a choice which brings severe deprivations to bear against anyone who flouts it.

Hence, the language of politics is the language of power. It is the language of decision. It registers and modifies decisions. It is battle cry, verdict and sentence, statute, ordinance and rule, oath of office, controversial news, comment and debate.

When we look into any language function, we are exploring the two-way relation between function and language. Our leading questions are: What are the effects of function upon language, and of language upon function? (In the terminology of Charles W. Morris, this is the *pragmatics* of communication.)

When we study the impact of function upon language,

we become concerned with two features of language, one of which is *semantic,* the other *syntactic.* (These terms are also used in the way Charles W. Morris has proposed.) Political semantics examines key terms, slogans and doctrines from the point of view of how they are understood. Political syntactics, on the other hand, has to do with logical and grammatical relations. Historians who report the actual vocabulary of power in a given body politic are supplying the raw material of political semantics. Often historians of political doctrine point out alleged consistencies or inconsistencies among doctrines, and, to this extent, contribute to political syntactics.*

When political semantics are analyzed two preoccupations emerge, one with the *purport* of what is said, the other with the *style* of the saying. The scholarly tradition in political science has valuable hints for the study of purport. There is, however, very little about the arrangement of elements used in making a communication (style). Hence the present chapter, which deals chiefly with political purport, is able to review a number of well-understood categories for the analysis of the language of power. The second chapter, on the contrary, deals with style, and is compelled to blaze a new path.

Political Categories: The Political Myth

The study of language by political scientists has developed several broad categories, notably the *political myth.* "The whole body of beliefs existing in any given age may generally be traced to certain fundamental assumptions which, at the time, whether they be actually true or false, are believed by the mass of the world to be true with such confidence that they hardly appear to bear the character of assumptions." [13] The political myth comprises these "fundamental assumptions" about political affairs. It consists of the symbols invoked, not only to explain, but also to justify specific power practices.

* Morris has used no term to cover semantics and syntactics—both concerned with the content of communication—to parallel pragmatics, which deals with the use and the impact of what is communicated. We have suggested the term *semologics,* which fits into the general science of communication, or semiotics as Morris calls it. See Charles W. Morris, *Signs, Language and Behavior,* New York, Prentice-Hall, 1946.

The term "myth" is not to be interpreted as necessarily imputing a fictional, false or irrational character to the symbols, though such an imputation is often correct.

The present concept is close to a number of others which have played an important part in the classical literature: Plato's "noble lie," Marx's "ideology," Sorel's "myth," Mosca's "political formula," Pareto's "derivations," Mannheim's "ideology" and "utopia," and others.

Political Doctrine: the Miranda

The political doctrine consists of the basic expectations and demands * concerning power relations and practices in the society. Merriam refers to these as "credenda," things to be believed, as distinguished from "miranda," things to be admired. "The credenda of power . . . contain the reasons which oblige the intellect to give assent to the continuance of authority. And this assent may be due to government in general, or to particular holders of power, or to the special system of authority in vogue at any given moment in a particular unit of power." † The political doctrine is authoritatively set forth in constitutions (especially preambles), charters, formal declarations and so on.

Frequently political theory serves chiefly to embody political doctrine. No clear separation is made between the hypotheses of political science and the demands and expectations of political philosophy. The matter is forcefully put by Merriam in the view that theories of the state "have been in large measure justifications or rationalizations of groups in power or seeking power—the special pleadings of races, religions, classes, in behalf of their special situation."[14] Theories of the state have often been, in short, enunciations of political doctrine.

In the same way, legal and economic theories have often served as formulations of political doctrine, apart from whatever scientific purport they may have had. Indeed, scientific

---

* A *demand* is a statement that explicitly commits the statement-maker to a preference or a determination. An *expectation* makes no such commitment. "I vote yes" is a demand; "He voted" is an expectation.

† Merriam, *Political Power*, p. 113. We retain the word "miranda" for symbols of sentiment and identification, but the term "political doctrine" is already familiarly used in the sense of "credenda."

propositions in the strict sense may at the same time be functioning as political symbols, and this is especially true of the social sciences. As Louis Wirth has pointed out, "Every assertion of a 'fact' about the social world touches the interests of some individual or group." [15] This fact need not impugn the objectivity of the assertion, but it does call attention to its possible functioning in the political process, as well as in the process of inquiry.

Another important component of the political myth, embodying (at least in its latent content) many elements of political doctrine, are the various elaborations of social norms, the theories of what is right, good, proper—symbols included in what Pareto calls "derivations." Mill observed, in his essay on liberty that, "wherever there is an ascendant class, a large portion of the morality of the country emanates from its class interests, and its feelings of class superiority." And not only does it "emanate" from the social structure, but it may serve also to formulate fundamental justifications for that structure. A similar relation between standards of taste and the social structure has been emphasized by Veblen and others.

The miranda are the symbols of sentiment and identification in the political myth. They are those whose function is to arouse admiration and enthusiasm, setting forth and strengthening faiths and loyalties. They not only arouse emotions indulgent to the social structure, but also heighten awareness of the sharing of these emotions by others, thereby promoting mutual identification and providing a basis for solidarity. "The emblem or shibboleth," says Giddings, "not only calls the attention of an individual who sees or hears it to the object or fact that it symbolizes, and awakens in him certain feelings; it also fixes his attention upon the feelings that it arouses and the conduct that it incites in others. The emotions and conduct of others, of which he is thus made aware, at once begin to act upon himself as an influence that merges with the original effect of the emblem or shibboleth." [16] Flags and anthems, ceremonials and demonstrations, group heroes and the legends surrounding them—these exemplify the importance of miranda in the political process.

The Political Formula

The *political formula* is the part of the political myth describing and prescribing in detail the social structure. The term is adopted from Mosca, who also uses it, however, as comprising what we have called political doctrine.[17] While the political doctrine is the "philosophy of state and government," the political formula embodies the basic public law of the society. The doctrine constitutes the postulates, so to speak, of the formula; hence, its frequent expression in preambles to constitutions, the latter being an important expression of the formula. The political formula, in other words, elaborates in specific and more or less concrete power patterns the content of the political doctrine. For example, the political doctrine of the divine right of kings may be elaborated in the political formula into a system of royal prerogatives, rules for succession to the throne, power patterns for a subordinate nobility, and so on.

The political formula is both prescriptive and descriptive —it is normatively ambiguous [18] in a characteristic way. It is prescriptive in inducing conformity to its specifications, and providing the symbols invoked in the detailed justification or crimination of particular power practices. But it is also descriptive—actually, in the degree to which there is in fact conformity to its requirements, and purportedly in that the formula is widely accepted as correctly describing power patterns and practices.

Key Symbols and Slogans

In every modern state, at least, there are specialists on the repetition, elaboration and application of the political myth. The chosen province of the political philosopher is the doctrine; lawyers concentrate on the formula; ritualists and artists embellish the miranda. Men of action apply doctrine and formula piecemeal to current issues.

The common man, of course, has only casual interest in the subtleties of the philosopher or the lawyer; or even of many political leaders. There is, however, a common denominator running through the utterances of the common man and the man of thought or of action. All use *key symbols*.

A key symbol is a basic term of the political myth. In the United States, key words are "rights," "freedom," "democracy," "equality." Such terms figure in the recondite treatises of the professors, in the opinions of the courts, and in the arguments heard in the halls of Congress or on the street corners of the nation.

One obvious function performed by the key symbol is that of providing a common experience for everyone in the state, ranging from the most powerful boss to the humblest layman or philosopher. Indeed, one of the few experiences that bind human beings together, irrespective of race, region, occupation, party or religion, is exposure to the same set of key words. Sentiments of loyalty cluster around these terms, and contribute to the unity of the commonwealth.

Akin to the key symbol is the slogan, which mediates between the single word and the full-length propositions of law or philosophy. Characteristically, the slogan or maxim is a terse string of words that gain meaning by repetition and context. "The King never dies" and "The King can do no wrong" are among the most famous maxims of the English Constitution. "Freedom of speech," "Trial by jury," "Bill of Rights" are all phrases that function as slogans.

Identifications, Demands, Expectations

For careful investigation it is convenient to classify symbols and statements according to the relation between the statement-maker and the utterance. Statements that commit the speaker or writer to a preference or a determination are *demands*. Non-demand statements, in turn, can be separated into those delimiting the boundaries of the self of the statement-maker, and other assertions. "I am an American" is an *identification*, since it brackets the "I"—the ego symbol of the statement-maker—with those called "Americans." The total self of any person is composed of all who are included with the primary ego. Typically, this comprises family and friends, neighborhood and occupation, and nation. The non-demand statements that are not identifications are *expectations*. They commit the writer-speaker to nothing more than the making of a reference. (The key symbols that usually function in statements as identifiers, or as designators of demands and acceptances, can be called symbols of identification, demand and expectation.) [19]

Myth Types: Ideology and Utopia

In the total myth of any group, one component is invariably found: the justification and location of authority. For this part of the myth the term "ideology" has come into use. In some groups another element is present, namely, the rejection of ideology. Often the established order is criticized at small points, and piecemeal innovations are proposed. In many cases, however, countercurrents are expressed as a well-developed set of doctrines and constitutional proposals that are revolutionary, not reformist. When the basis of authority in government and the basis of value distribution in society are attacked, a "Utopian" myth stands over against the ideology.*

World Revolutionary Patterns

Some utopian myths refer not to a limited area but to the world as a whole. Demands for the total reconstruction of human society are the "world revolutionary" myths of history. They at once proclaim and instigate drastic changes in the social order. When these myths advocate or forecast drastic upheavals, they are not only world revolutionary but "radical." There were several such major myths in the world of 1939, on the eve of World War II, notably communism, fascism, and national socialism. Liberalism had become "moderate," no longer possessing the verve of 1789. In the Far East, a highly local cult (Japanism) was already on the march.

Restriction and Diffusion

One of the principal problems of political science is the study of the factors making for the restriction or diffusion of political doctrines and formulas. This calls, of course, for the study of historical and contemporary trends in the distribution of political myths, and the analysis of facilitating or retarding factors. The methods of "content analysis" de-

---

* A Utopian myth can therefore be defined as a systematic counter-ideology. Some parts of the counter-ideology are not coalesced into a system.

scribed and applied in this book have been devised as aids to the summarizer of trends and the estimator of significant factors.

More specifically, several studies are reported of the major world revolutionary pattern of our historical epoch, the Russian pattern.[20] There is no mistaking the Russian upheaval of 1917 for anything other than a decisive phase in the expansion of a world revolutionary radical movement. A movement is "revolutionary" when it rapidly transforms the doctrines and institutions of the state; it is "world revolutionary" when these changes are proposed and inaugurated in several states during the same epoch; it is "radical" when the method includes violence. The Communists led a movement that was worldwide—"universal," not "parochial"—in announced *goal*, revolutionary in *scope*, radical in *method*.

If the élite that seized power in Russia had consummated a revolution over the entire globe, we should have an example of "total diffusion" from a territorial center (provided always that key symbols and practices remained the same). Had Communism been liquidated by counter-revolution, the case would have been "total restriction." What gives piquancy to the study of recent world politics is that neither one nor the other "total" process prevailed; the pattern to date has been "partial diffusion" and "partial restriction."

The original Russian pattern can be ascertained by looking into the early months and years following the seizure of power. Key symbols, slogans and doctrines stand out in official decrees, resolutions and speeches; and if it is desired to determine the relative prominence of each word or theme, representative sources can be compared.[21]

While it is relatively simple to map the distribution of symbols, it is not justifiable to infer either diffusion or restriction without further evidence, since interaction is involved in both processes. Without interaction, there is merely "expansion" or "contraction."

Consider from this point of view the term "Socialist" in German National Socialism. Long before the Russian Revolution, "Socialism" was a key term in German politics; this was unquestionably a predisposing factor in the Nazi choice. But, in addition, there is evidence that the incorporation of this symbol was affected by the Russian Revolution, since

Nazi leaders sought deliberately to prevent the Communists from appropriating the term for their exclusive use.

In assessing the stability of political language, representative sources must be chosen. One of the researches reported in this volume surveys the annual May Day slogans of the Russian Communist Party between 1918 and 1943; the other studies report proceedings and publications of the Third International.

From a purely formal point of view, it is convenient to classify whatever modifications occur in the language of politics as "additions," "omissions" and "variations." A more significant way to classify language modifications is in relation to the past: Is there "revival" or "innovation"? At first, successful revolutionary movements tend to eliminate whatever has been associated with the old regime; but, as years pass, the old is at least partially restored.

Once the fact of revival or innovation is established, the question becomes: Is the change "progressive" or "reactionary"? We define a progressive pattern as one that *approximates,* or *contributes* to, a free society. Insofar as the Russian Revolution substituted a more democratic ideology and a more democratic set of institutions for czarism, the revolution is progressive. To the extent that the antidemocratic features are perpetuated or presently revived, the opposite is the case.

In passing, we may note that revivals are not limited to the immediate past, since the old regime may have been preceded by governments having more progressive or more reactionary traits. A further point having to do with classification is this: It is exceptionally difficult to describe situations in which a pattern is partly approximated and partly contributed to. A regime that is largely democratic in form may use antidemocratic means to accomplish ends (ultimately to attain a more perfect freedom). It may be contended that it is progressive to adopt reactionary policies in order to expedite revolt.[22]

History provides no example of the total diffusion of a revolutionary pattern throughout the globe, or even—in recent centuries, at least—throughout Europe. The French revolutionary fountain rose and inundated most of the continent, only to recede; and the Russian wave has been held back thus far. It is not implied, however, that significant features of the revolutionary movement are confined to a single state, even when this state is denied dominion. Indeed, when we separate the "world revolutionary pattern of the *center*" from the "world revolutionary pattern of the *epoch*," it is apparent that the scope of the élite at the center does not settle the fate of the epoch. The élite of France did not attain full and secure mastery of Europe, much less of the globe, and yet the basic transformations manifested in the social structure of France were not confined to the territory ruled by the French. The "bourgeois revolution" went forward in many countries, sometimes by independent paralleling, though often by partial incorporation of the French pattern. It is already evident that many trends in Russia are paralleled or incorporated outside the boundaries of the U.S.S.R. The liquidation of the remnants of feudalism, the decline of the free market, the decline of the business man— these developments are not circumscribed to Russia.

Actually, it appears that the pattern of the "center" must undergo no little modification if it is to approach the pattern of the "epoch." It is already apparent that several institutions of the original Moscow pattern are not part of the common structure toward which all major powers may be moving in our period. One example is money. In the early days of the Russian regime, an effort was made to get on without money; but the attempt was soon abandoned. Manifestly, this is not part of whatever common pattern the present epoch is forging among the major states of the world.

Our studies of the changing language of Communism bear upon certain basic questions: What is the form of society toward which the major powers are moving? More specifically, what attitudes and institutions—and groups—are rising in power? To what extent have the distinctive features of the Russian Revolution already been modified by the revival of reactionary or progressive symbols and practices?

Whatever has transpired in Russia is a function of the changing balance of internal and external power. It must not be assumed that trends will continue to move steadily in the direction they have shown in the first quarter-century of post-revolutionary history, especially since the larger outlines of the world political arena have recently been drastically altered. When, as in World War II, allies are sought among élites who profess different doctrines, doctrinal distinctiveness is no advantage. The time for distinctiveness is when more can be had by appealing to foreign masses than from dickering with foreign élites.

By focusing too narrowly upon events in Russia, we may lose sight of some of the most significant portents of future politics. If the history of past revolutionary waves is a reliable guide, world revolutionary initiatives do not rise in the crater of the latest eruption. The bid of Nazi "racialism" against communist "materialism" rose outside Russia; even more significant movements may be germinating elsewhere, perhaps among those who, following Trotzky, see in Stalinism a "reactionary betrayal" of the "proletariat."

Language as an Instrument of Power

The study of diffusion and restriction processes calls for a general theory of language as a factor in power. Trends provide us with information about the state of power; trends register power. Part of the changes wrought by power are brought about by the use of language, and one of our tasks is to assimilate the special theory of language in politics to the general theory of power.

We understand by power a relationship among people in which choices, if challenged, are implemented by coercion Words are involved in power, since the indexes of power may be largely verbal (ordering-obeying, proposing-endorsing, and the like). Words are also involved in the readjustment of power—in revolutionary agitation, in constitutional innovation.

Our problem may therefore be posed as follows: Under what conditions do words affect power responses? If we let the "power response" in which we are interested be referred to by the letter R, the problem is to find what words in the environment of the responders will affect R in one way rather than in another, given certain predispositions on the part of the audience (other environmental factors being held constant). When will a revolutionary appeal be rejected or endorsed? A reformist appeal? An instigation to radical action? To moderate action?

The general law of power is capable of being formulated in rather plain terms: When men want power, they act according to their expectation of how to maximize power. Hence *symbols (words and images) affect power as they affect expectations of power.*[23]

If we verify or apply these propositions, it is necessary to know certain facts about any given audience. What symbols do they recognize as designating power, and as expressing changes in degrees of power? What media of communication come to their attention, and what attitudes toward these media affect the construction given to symbols appearing in them? What style of statement affects the attitude taken toward the purport of a statement?

For the study of political purport we are well equipped with a number of categories which are widely understood by scholars. Not so, however, when we turn to the examination of political style. Here is an unexplored frontier, yet one of no little interest and importance. In the next chapter we shall outline a theory of style for the guidance of thought and research.

Chapter **2**

STYLE IN THE LANGUAGE OF POLITICS

WHEN WE examine the rhythmic pattern of Winston Churchill's prose, or sentence length in the resounding periods of Daniel Webster or Joseph Choate, we are dealing with style. It is a question of style when we look into the deliberate pace and the conversational tone of Franklin Roosevelt's radio chats, and compare them with the bluster and rant of Hitler.[1] Style, in the language of politics, is the arrangement of the parts of which a political communication is made.

The literature devoted to style is often packed with ambiguity, particularly when an author follows the tradition of attaching a wide and often undefined range of esthetic, practical and scientific meanings to the word. "Style," we are told by Middleton Murray, "is not an isolable quality of writing; it is writing itself." Surely we are no further along the path of understanding when we transfer the problem of style to the definition of "writing itself." In the same vein, Cardinal Newman wrote that "thought and speech are inseparable from each other. Matter and expression are parts of one: style is a thinking out into language. . . . When we can separate light and illumination, life and motion, the convex and the concave of a curve, then will it be conceivable that the intellect should renounce its own double." But nothing is gained by identifying all language with style.

More serviceable is Buffon's definition: "Style is simply the order and movement one gives to one's thoughts." The virtue of "order" and "movement" is that these terms can be made to refer to the arrangement of the elements of which communication is composed.[2]

Communication arranges two elements: symbols and signs. Symbols are meanings; signs are physical devices employed in the dissemination of meaning. The word "Constitution" is a symbol (or, more precisely, a group of symbols), and the black marks on paper when the word is printed are signs. Films, drawings, musical notations, monuments are also signs. Whatever the communication element, it occurs in various patterns concurrently with other elements, or in different time sequences.

Certain distinctions are always useful in analyzing the arrangement of parts. Parts are few or many; we speak of *terseness* or *prolixity* of style. Communication is prolix in the degree that it uses more elements than necessary to achieve a given effect. Prolixity of sign occurs when the number of sign accessories is multiplied in relation to the pure signs. A pure sign is the minimum magnitude that enables a message to be transmitted and understood. Any excess is accessory. When the voice is louder than need be, the extra sound is sign accessory. If the letters on a page are larger and more heavily inked than essential for the reader's comprehension, they are accessories. Symbols are redundant when words are used beyond the minimum needed to convey a message to an attentive audience equipped with relevant knowledge and skill.[3] Another convenient distinction is the amount of *repetitiousness* or *diversity* of elements.

Our analysis of political style will also treat as an element (or pattern of elements) the symbols and signs that resemble the effect sought by the communicator. When the chairman applauds the speaker whom he has introduced, he is *effect-modelling* in order to stimulate the audience. When the fund raiser tosses a ringing dollar into the plate as the usher passes in front of the audience, he too is effect-modelling. The opposite relation is *effect-contrast;* it occurs, for instance, when a holy man blesses the kneeling multitude.

Perhaps it is worth noting that the elements chosen for style analysis may be syntactic or semantic. Syntactic studies (in the sense of Charles W. Morris) deal with internal references. Logical analysis is syntactical, since it considers the statements occurring in a given body of discourse according to consistency, generality and similar criteria. Semantic analysis is a matter of meanings external to the communication, and takes note, for example, whether political objects are referred to. The distribution of inconsistent statements throughout a lengthy argument may be a useful style study, on the hypothesis that inconsistencies which are farthest separated from one another are most acceptable to an audience. A semantic topic also is the use of "static" or "motion" symbols. The posters of the Russian Revolution were full of moving masses, defiant gestures and exclamatory words; later symbols were in more repose.

Once discovered, style differences can be examined to determine effect or cause (pragmatics). With one effect we are not primarily concerned in politics, namely esthetic appreciation (enjoyment). We therefore leave to others the problem of style in the sense of Swift's "proper words in proper places." The language of politics is mainly intended to effect action or evaluation (attention or comprehension are typically not politically ends in themselves). That style is moulded by many socio-personal factors has long been understood. There is the oft-quoted maxim, "Style is the man," or, as Freud rewrote it, "Style est l'histoire de l'homme."[4] Hence, many impressionistic and scientific attempts have been made to correlate style with personality and with position in the social structure. Handwriting, gesture, posture, gait, intonation and speech defects are among the style patterns that have been looked into.[5]

Style in the language of politics varies according to the basic features of the power situation. Political situations can be classified according to the degree of crisis. Another criterion is the degree of despotism or democracy.

Crisis and Style

The most intense crisis involves physical *combat,* and includes battles, uprisings and riots. Many of the occasions on which *policy is enunciated* are exceedingly tense, as when verdicts are announced or sentence passed, or when laws are promulgated, treaties signed and votes taken. As a rule, a relatively lower level of tension characterizes the *formation of policy* through diplomatic negotiation, arbitration, litigation, committee deliberation, parliamentary debate, election speeches (and allied forms of public discussion). Least tense, as a rule, is the *ceremonial occasion* on which partisan differences are played down and symbols of unity are played up (celebration of victory, memorial services, solemn induction into office).

A crisis is a situation in which severe deprivations, such as violence, are inflicted or threatened. Hence, the structure of expectation is the dominant feature of crisis. Despotism or democracy, on the other hand, are primarily matters of demand—in the one case for "power over" and in the other for "power with." We expect to find such basic factors in a situation leaving their mark on the *style,* as we know they do on the *purport,* of language.

Let us first consider the crisis of active combat. The most conspicuous instrument of power is the specialized agency of violence—the weapon or the trained combatant. The weapon that bears the closest functional resemblance to language is the missile, since the missile and the word are both able to inflict damage at a distance. From the history of weapons, we know that projectiles are continually being modified toward standardization and economy. The tendency to standardize is illustrated by the uniform specifications laid down for a given type of shell. The drive toward economy is expressed, for example, in the attempt to cut down the relative weight of shell casing in relation to explosive. Shell design is modified, in order to reduce wind resistance and to increase range and accuracy.

The language of combat is also subject to standardizing and economizing tendencies. The battle cry—to choose the most distinctive example—is highly standardized, and typically is composed of one or at most a few sounds or words repeated in a set pattern. Whether it is a question of the Rebel Yell of the Confederate Armies, or the war cry of the Comache Indians, the basic characteristics of terseness and repetitiousness are promptly displayed.

Symbols and signs, it may be emphasized, undergo similar adaptations. Symbols are typically condensed into key slogans or epithets. The Mohammedan tribesmen who dash into battle shouting the name of Allah are compressing into a single symbol an enormous number of inarticulate demands upon themselves, upon the Unbeliever and upon Allah himself. When an epithet is hurled like a grenade at the enemy, it sums up a number of appeals to his conscience. To call a soldier a "baby-killer" is to use a superterse way of referring to an elaborate indictment of his morals in the conduct of war, and of his national and personal character. In combat, the physical carriers of communication are usually compressed, often conforming to the streamlined pattern of the projectile (as when packages of leaflets are thrown or dropped over enemy lines).

It is also true that language is employed defensively, more in the manner of shield, breastworks and fortress than as a projectile. In this case, repetition of units is a continuing trait, but the number of units may increase. One typical situation is that in which communications are addressed to the self, rather than to the enemy, during these periods in which the defenders are patiently withstanding an enemy assault. Everybody may sing the same song, but more songs are sung than on the offensive.

Besides undergoing stylistic changes that parallel the projectile or shield, language is distinctively modified in active combat. If we expect to frighten the enemy, we may emphasize our own strength by arrogant, boastful words and manners. Obviously, this is the opposite of the response we desire from the enemy: it is effect-contrast. If we surmise that our antagonist is inclined to give up, we may cut short the battle by commanding him to surrender. Perhaps we use effect-modelling, and go through some of the motions of throwing weapons away.

The tactic of effect-modelling is open to certain dangers. Misconstruing our gestures, the enemy may think that we are offering to surrender. He may laugh us to scorn for a supposed display of weakness, and take new courage. This directs attention to a factor that significantly determines when effect-modelling can be used. It is essential that the ego of the person finds it acceptable to depict the self as performing the response which the communication is supposed to elicit from the audience. In deadly combat, we readily think of sticking a dagger into the back of an enemy, and we can therefore response-model for the benefit of a fellow-soldier. But self-esteem will not allow us to appear to confess weakness at the start by seeming to surrender. When the battle is going in our favor and surrender on our part is unthinkable, we may then make use of effect-modelling in order to stimulate the enemy to give up, without running the risk of appearing in a shameful rôle to ourselves or others. In general, we do not hesitate to effect-model for those whom we accept as having a claim upon us for special consideration. We instruct children by performing an act for them to copy; and it is not "beneath our dignity" to do the same for the slow-witted or for persons handicapped by ignorance of our language. We are effect-modelling when we illustrate by gestures how to get somewhere.

One phase of effect-resemblance (whether as copy or contrast) is the use of elements "dynamic" or "static," according to the nature of the expectations entertained about the audience. In addressing the "lower classes" in a country, less restrained gestures and vocal effects may be employed than when one speaks to the "upper classes" of those countries.

The same point applies to "concrete" or "abstract" elements in communication. As a rule, popular groups are expected to respond more readily to "depictive" or "realistic" painting than to the abstract. The opposite may be the case, however, where the "enemy" has been stigmatized as one who is favorable to "banal" styles of expression, and where progress becomes associated with more abstract styles. (During the agitational phases of the Russian Revolution, "modern" art currents were welcomed by the revolutionists.)

Some of the impact of combat on style may be summed up by saying that it makes languages more terse, repetitious and effect-contrasted. This comes about on the basis of the expectations involved in active combat. When antagonists of nearly equal strength are engaged, they are aware of the wisdom of economizing energy. Hence, the signs involved in communication are cut down as much as appears compatible with the effect sought; also, the signs are made more uniform. Symbols are held down by the same criteria. Effect-contrast is indulged in chiefly when it is believed possible to intimidate the enemy.

The foregoing statements imply that *style varies according to the expectations of the communicator about the arrangement of communication elements that will most economically achieve the optimum power effect.* When understood to relate to all political situations, and not only to combat, this proposition is basic for the theory of style in the language of politics.

Where crises are less intense, there is more leeway for prolixity and diversity, and for a wider range of expression of whatever motives are aroused. In situations where policy is enunciated, and when obedience is in doubt, symbol-prolixity is a means of multiplying appeals to acquiesce in the result. The language of the law courts is notoriously intricate; much of this involution comes from uncertainty about obedience. The stakes of litigation are often high, and the tradition-crusted symbols of the law may reduce temptation to defy the verdict. (It is pertinent to observe, in this connection, that in appellate court decisions the "opinion" is often designed to appease the losing party and his counsel).

In the process by which policy is formed, the disciplinary effect of crisis on language is less visible than in the enunciation of policy or in combat. To the extent that the peaceful settlement of a dispute is in doubt, crisis expectations affect style. Prolixity is cultivated in the traditional language of diplomacy—up to the severance of formal relations and the declaration of war. In diplomacy, the function of prolixity is to mask the direct clash of personality, and to prevent "crises of self-respect" or outraged "honour." Similar factors are at stake in the conduct of litigation, as well as in the announcement of verdict and sentence. Although parliamentary debate is less formal, it is hedged around by rules that can be reinvoked when sharp cleavages threaten to disrupt orderly procedure.

Where law-abiding attitudes prevail, simplicity is found in enunciating and forming policy. This applies to the conduct of litigation; clerks may mumble and spectators half rise when the judge enters or leaves the courtroom.

A further factor affecting terseness is the expectation that rational standards will be applied. Language becomes almost exclusively the tool of understanding, and is highly condensed. The language of counsel before appellate courts is less adorned with irrelevancy than in the presence of juries.

When it is assumed that decisions will be reached on non-rational grounds, expectations about personal foibles exert a strong effect on manner of approach. In some instances, the official may make it a point of honour never to admit he has changed his mind. If the aim of a speech or an article is to move the official to change, two courses are open. One is to adopt the pretense that he has not in fact passed on the point as issue, and by circumlocution to obscure the fact that he has. Another approach depends upon expectations concerning another trait. It is possible to precipitate an inner conflict, perhaps, between the demand on the self to appear omniscient and the demand to help the weak and deserving. Attention may be distracted from the change requested, and focussed upon the necessity for the strong and wise to stoop from their great height to succor those who unjustly suffer. If the decision-maker is not only vain, but moralistic, vanity and stubborness may be boldly denounced in the name of justice and humanity.

In most of these examples effect-contrast is involved. But this is not always the device most appropriate to the result-in-view. Trusting to the sentimentality of a lay jury, the defense attorney may himself appear to break down as he considers the tragic consequences of separating the defendant from her child (thus setting a model attitude for the jury). Style, it may be repeated, is a function of expectations about style-effect relations; and this is a matter of drawing rational inferences about the predispositions with which an audience approaches a situation.

We have said that ceremonial occasions have the lowest level of crisis. In fact, we might by strict definition exclude them from "politics," since decision-making is not ceremony-making. In a true ceremony, the pattern of values is not supposed to be affected. It leaves power, respect and other values exactly as before, save insofar as values are modified by allocations of respect springing from the proper performance of ceremonial rites.

Repetitiousness is an essential mark of ceremony, but variations do occur from one time to the next. Among primitive peoples who have lost heart under the impact of Western civilization, ethnologists observe deteriorations of style that range all the way from carelessness to total neglect. There are, however, cultural revivals in which dance forms are made more complex. Sometimes the leading rôles are elaborated by effect-modelling, and the most prominent dances show the community defying outside peoples or forces, and living in peace, quiet and grandeur.

By political ceremonies, we mean occasions on which symbols are borrowed from the arenas of active combat, policy enunciation and policy formation. (Representative occasions are victory celebrations, memorial services for the dead, and days of national humiliation.) The following hypotheses may be propounded to account for certain examples of style change: *When the collective outlook is optimistic, the style becomes more prolix and diversified; when the outlook is pessimistic, styles grow terse and repetitious.* Effect-resemblance depends upon other expectations.

The preceding analysis of crisis and style has underlined the dependence of style on the structure of expectations about crisis. *When the crisis is recognized as serious, and as one in which energy must be conserved, the tendency is for what is communicated to be terse, repetitious and effect-contrasted. In crises in which it is assumed that the outcome can be affected by communication, and more energy can be devoted to it, the style grows more prolix, varied and effect-modelled.* An example of the near-ultimate in terseness and repetitiousness is the chant in the same pitch, like "Aye! Aye! Aye!" or "Rah! Rah! Rah!" It is possible—although this is quite speculative—that the dominant pattern under stress of great crisis may be "scalar" rather than "uniform." By this is meant that the elements of communication may tend to bunch themselves at certain intervals along a hypothetical continuum. An example is the orator who, at the climax of his impassioned speech, swings from short, staccato sentences to long, sweeping periods and back again. He may also leap from a whisper to a shout, and from a shout to a whisper. The same form is observable in some "hot" jazz, when the repetition at one level is suddenly varied by a long leap to a contrasting level.

Democracy, Despotism and Style

In many respects, the most striking correlation between politics and style is with despotism and democracy. The distinguishing mark of a despot is the demand to dominate, regardless of the consent of the community. And the "perfect subject" in a despotism demands to be dominated without being consulted. In a democratic order, on the contrary, leaders and led are united in the demand for shared power, for general participation in the making of collective decisions. Hence, as said before, despotism is characterized by "power over," and democracy by "power with."

Since nondemocratic élites demand superiority, they interpose barriers of "distance" and "height" between themselves and the rank and file. Symbols and signs are among the instruments employed for the purpose of being "remote" and "above." Hence, the outstanding style of despotism is effect-contrasting. "Commands" are issued; "obedience" is compulsory. The words and bearing of the monarch are designed to set him apart and above his subjects. The terms of self-reference on formal public occasions are impersonal, lengthy and stereotyped.

As a reminder of the points in which we are interested, examples may be drawn from the language of the British king and emperor of India. Although the power position of the monarch has diminished, much of the language survives from an earlier era. King George VI until recently was "By the Grace of God, of Great Britain, Ireland, and of the British Dominions beyond the seas, King, defender of the faith, Emperor of India." On the whole, this formula is more modest than the phrases employed by the heads of less potent Powers. The future George VI of the Windsor dynasty was baptized Albert Frederick Arthur George. Later he was made Duke of York, Earl of Inverness and Baron Killarney in the peerage of the United Kingdom. On His Majesty's accession to the throne, he became Duke of Rothesey, Earl of Carrick and Baron of Renfrew in the Peerage of Scotland, Lord of the Isles, and Great Steward of Scotland.

The accession of the preceding George (the Fifth) was marked by a Durbar in India, announced in the idiom of the *Official Gazette* as follows:

The Royal Intention to hold an Imperial Assemblage at Delhi was declared in a Proclamation published in the Gazette Extraordinary of the 22nd March 1911:—

WHEREAS, upon the death of our late Sovereign of happy memory, King Edward, upon the sixth day of May in the year of Our Lord one thousand nine hundred and ten, We did ascend the Throne under the style and title of George the Fifth by the Grace of God, King of the United Kingdom of Great Britain and Ireland and of the British Dominions beyond the seas, Defender of the Faith, Emperor of India; and whereas, by Our Royal Proclamations bearing date the nineteenth day of July and the seventh day of November in the year of Our Lord one thousand nine hundred and ten in the first year of Our Reign We did publish and declare Our Royal intention by the Favour and Blessing of Almighty God to celebrate the solemnity of Our Royal Coronation upon the twenty-second day of June one thousand nine hundred and eleven; and whereas, it is Our wish and desire to make known to all Our loving subjects within Our Indian dominions that the said solemnity has so been celebrated and call to Our presence Our Governors, Lieutenant-Governors and others of Our officers, the Princes, Chiefs and Nobles of the Native States under Our protection and representatives of all the Provinces of Our Indian Empire, now We do by this Royal Proclamation declare Our Royal intention to hold at Delhi, on the twelfth day of December one thousand nine hundred and eleven, an Imperial Durbar for the purpose of making known the said solemnity of Our Coronation and We do hereby charge and command Our right trusted and well-loved counsellor Charles Baron Hardinge of Penshurst, Our Viceroy and Governor-General of India, to take all necessary measures in that behalf.

Given at Our Court at Buckingham Palace, this twenty-second day of March, in the year of Our Lord one thousand nine hundred and eleven, and in the first year of Our Reign.[6]

When nondemocratic attitudes prevail in a community, initiatives from "below" are phrased in somewhat labored language. Elaborate words and gestures are used by a subordinate to show that he is not presuming to transgress the prerogatives of his superior. By contrast with the self-assurance of the superior, he represents himself as somewhat uncertain of judgment. By contrast with the assumed omniscience of the superior, the subordinate portrays himself as one who has slowly and painfully come to entertain provisional ideas. By these means of propitiating the ego of the superior, a subordinate reduces the probability of arousing resentment (a result sought by effect-contrast, not modelling).

Some superiors invite discussion from subordinates, but special forms are needed in a despotism to indicate that this is permissible. Among other deviations from the stereotype of a commanding officer, such a superior adopts an informal tone. Permissiveness may be cultivated to the point where decision-making, though hierarchically organized, is relatively uncomplicated by "caste" attitudes.

One permissive situation familiar in the United States is the press conference of the Chief Executive. The President is "first servant" of the people, but in fact he carries with him much of the "majesty" of the chief of state, some of which survives from the days of hereditary absolutism. In the conference, a self-confident president permits a high degree of fraternal informality. However, the Chief Executive is always in a position to refrain from comment or to protect himself from being pushed further than he wants to go. He does not meet an equal in national prestige, and is not compelled to hear arguments on controversial questions. This may be contrasted with the questioning of a Prime Minister in the British Parliament. The Prime Minister can avoid answering specific queries, but day in and day out he must listen to arguments put forward by the leaders of the opposition, men of prestige in the country who expect some day to step into his shoes. The press conference is a permissive "act of grace"; parliamentary questions and debate, on the other hand, are mandatory.

As communities move toward the democratic end of the scale, effect-modelling takes the place of effect-contrast. Leaders reach out for the common speech, and adopt simple, man-to-man manners. Modern nationalistic movements are equalitarian to the extent that they exalt symbols which all members of the nation have in common, rather than the differences of family, race or religion which divide them from one another. A common trait of nationalism is the language "revival," which usually consists in the revival and enrichment of some vernacular tongue. A recent and important example is India, and the two following quotations reflect the tendencies just referred to. The first is from Mahatma Gandhi:[7]

> . . . But names, as you know, have enormous political and social significance because of their associations, and the name to be given to our common language is therefore very important. So far Urdu has been the only language not confined to a province or a religious community: it has been spoken by Mussalmans all over India, and in the North the number of Hindus speaking it has been larger than the number of Mussalmans. If our common language cannot be called Urdu, it must at least have a name in which the peculiar contribution of the Mussalmans—that of having evolved a language more or less common—is implied. 'Hindustani' may serve the purpose. 'Hindi' cannot. It has been studied by Mussalmans in the past, and they have done as much, if not more, than their Hindu brethren to raise it to the status of a literary language. But it has also religious and cultural associations with which Mussalmans as a whole cannot identify themselves. Besides, it is now evolving a vocabulary that is exclusively its own, and is generally unintelligible to those who know only Urdu.

*   *   *

> I am giving below a number of points which, in my humble opinion, are rational in themselves and provide a sound basis for a common language.

> The points are:

> 1. That our common language shall be called "Hindustani," not "Hindi."

> 2. That Hindustani shall not be considered to have any peculiar association with the religious traditions of any community.

> 3. That the test of "foreign" and "indigenous" shall not be applied to any word, but only the test of currency.

> 4. That all words used by Hindu writers of Urdu and Muslim writers of Hindi shall be deemed current. This, of course, shall not apply to Urdu and Hindi as sectional languages.

5. That in the choice of technical terms, especially political terminology, no preference be given to Sanskrit terms as such, but as much room as possible be allowed for natural selection from among Urdu, Hindi and Sanskrit terms.

6. That the Devanagari and the Arabic scripts shall both be considered current and official, and that in all institutions whose policy is directed by the official promoters of Hindustani, facilities shall be provided for learning both scripts.

The second quotation is from Jawaharlal Nehru:[8]

Our great provincial languages are no dialects or vernaculars, as the ignorant sometimes call them. They are ancient languages with a rich inheritance, each spoken by many millions of persons, each tied up inextricably with the life and culture and ideas of the masses, as well as of the upper classes. It is axiomatic that the masses can only grow educationally and culturally through the medium of their own language. Therefore it is inevitable that we lay stress on the provincial languages and carry on most of our work through them. The use of any other language will result in isolating the educated few from the masses and of retarding the growth of the people. Ever since the Congress took to the use of these provincial languages in carrying on its work, we developed contacts with the masses rapidly and the strength and prestige of the Congress increased all over the country. The Congress message reached the most distant hamlet and the political consciousness of the masses grew. Our system of education and public work must therefore be based on the provincial languages.

*   *   *

And this leads us to the real difference between Urdu and Hindi today—Urdu is the language of the towns, and Hindi the language of the villages. Hindi is, of course, spoken also in the towns, but Urdu is almost entirely an urban language. The problem of bringing Urdu and Hindi nearer to each other thus becomes the much vaster problem of bringing the town and the village nearer to each other. Every other way will be a superficial way without lasting effect. Languages change organically when the people who speak them change.

*   *   *

Our writers therefore must think in terms of a mass audience and clientele, and must deliberately seek to write for them. This will result automatically in the simplification of language, and the stilted and flowery phrases and constructions, which are always signs of decadence in a language, will give place to words of strength and power. We have not yet fully recovered from the notion that culture and literary attainments are the products and accompaniments of courtly circles. If we think in this way, we remain confined in narrow circles and can find no entrance to the hearts and minds of the masses. Culture today must have a wider mass basis, and language, which is one of the embodiments of that culture, must also have that basis.

This approach to the masses is not merely a question of simple words and phrases. It is equally a matter of ideas and of the inner content of those words and phrases. Language which is to make appeal to the masses must deal with the problems of those masses, with their joys and sorrows, their hopes and aspirations. It must represent and mirror the life of the people as a whole, and not that of a small group at the top. Then only will it have its roots in the soil and find sustenance from it.

Another document exemplifies the demand for fraternal conduct on the part of officials in a free society. Not the least notable fact about this particular statement is that it was made by a comparatively unknown public serviant in a circular issued to the civil service of revolutionary France in May, 1794:[9]

The civil servant must above all shed his old dress, and put off that mannered politeness, so inconsistent with the bearing of free men, which is a relic of the time when some men were ministers, and others were their slaves. We know that the old forms of government have already disappeared: We must forget even what they looked like. Simple and natural manners must take the place of the artificial dignity which was often the only virtue of the head of a department or a chief clerk. Decency and unaffected seriousness are all the manners needed by men occupied in public affairs. The essential quality of Man in the order of Nature is to stand upright. The nonsensical jargon of the old ministries must be replaced by a simple style, clear, and yet concise, free from expressions of servility, from

obsequious formulas, stand-offishness, pedantry, or any suggestion that there is an authority superior to that of reason,
or of the order established by law—a style which adopts a
natural attitude toward subordinate authorities. There
must be no conventional phrases, no waste of words.

Although most of our examples of the tendency of democracy to adopt an informal style have been from the realm of
spoken and written discourse, and from manners, the major
point applies to all the expressive arts when they are in the
service of power. The theory applies, for instance, to the most
massive of arts, architecture. Consider the significance of the
accessibility and simplicity of the White House and the Cap-
itol in Washington, in contrast with the Kremlin in Moscow,
a walled city of palaces built by the rulers of old Russia and
neither made accessible nor abandoned by the rulers of the
new. Or think of the grandeur of monarchial Versailles, removed from the crowds and mobs of Paris; or the "away" and
"up" of Hitler's Berchtesgaden.

A further indication of the connection between democracy and effect-modelling is the increased resort to modelling
as despotisms pass into popular and constitutional regimes.
The surviving monarchies of Northern Europe are more ap-
proachable today than in the eras of more absolute authority
and control. Members of dynasties that would once have
been humiliated to resemble the commoner today flaunt
their resemblance to the man in the street.

Even in despotically organized states, the style of public
ceremony carried out under stress of great common danger
tends toward effect-modelling. In victory, the emperor-king-
chief may take advantage of the triumph to elevate himself
even higher above the people; but in moments of grave
danger, the leader dramatises not his dissimilarities but his
similarities. He may provide a model for everyone to follow—
bowing the knee in public to the tribal God or Gods.

Several factors conspire, under many conditons, to drive
the political style of despotism toward repetitiousness. One of
these factors is fear—it is chronic apprehension of revolt. One
of the rudimentary protections of the human being against
insecurity is repetition, and one of the most ubiquitous devices of despotisms is to protect themselves from evidences of
discontent by draining public life of its spontaneity and forc-

ing it into a ceremonial routine. Instead of discussion, there is acclamation; in the place of elections, there are plebiscites; where legislatures might be, there are assemblies.

The stereotyping effect of fear and anxiety on the part of the ruling group may be supported by the community as a whole. In despotically organized societies, compulsive-repetitive modes of behavior are widespread, and enter into the prevailing pattern of character formation. It is probable that recurring waves of insecurity generate two contradictory tendencies: on the one hand, an attempt to drain off anxiety through old or simplified channels; on the other hand, attempts to reduce tension by inventing new drains.

In severe crises, whether revolutionary or interstate, anxiety may cumulate to the point of using all the available capacity for expression. The higher the level of utilized capacity, the less margin is left, the more terse and repetitious the style. Hysterical speakers, for instance, may reach a plateau on which they shout as loud as they can, reiterating a limited repertory of more or less unintelligible cries. Variations in style become impossible as the individual regresses to rather primitive modes of "repetitive-compulsiveness."

Behavior during crises and on the part of despotic leaders has something in common, since language is employed as missile and shield in both cases. Symbols and signs are permanently oriented in space, polarized against the enemy. Today this is true of broadcasts and broadcasting facilities. Under more simple technical conditions, the man with a stentorian voice had an equivalent function, whether he addressed the enemy's army, or spoke to disaffected subjects in the workingman's quarter of the capital. We expect the concentration of instrumentalities to be greatest in the direction from which the gravest threat is known or anticipated. In this way, symbols and signs are employed as instruments of power to nullify the threat value of the environment, enhancing both security and the affirmative projection of power.[10]

We may sum up the theory of style in the language of politics by enumerating some of the basic factors that condition the pattern of symbol and sign in communication. Language is one of the instruments by means of which the value position of a "self" is maintained and improved. In any given case, the self may include the body politic as a whole, or only a part—a locality, class, skill-group or family. Instruments of power are used to advance and protect the demands made by the self on the self and on others. The application of each instrumentality, such as language, is modified according to the expectations that are entertained about its probable effectiveness. Language style reflects the identifications of the language user, together with his demands and expectations.

More concretely, style reflects expectations about the imminence of violent or peaceful settlement of disputes, and estimates of the self as strong or weak in relation to the ends in view. Style also is modified by the nature of the ends sought, notably by the despotic demand for "power over" or the democratic value of "power with."

In situations of intense crisis, the participant recognizes that he has no excess energy and the style of communication, responding to the same conditions that shape projectiles or shields, gains in terse compression and repetitive uniformity. In the face of the enemy, symbols and signs are handled to enhance the contrast between the conduct of the self and the response wanted from the enemy.

As crisis diminishes in intensity, words frequently become the cheapest means of affecting the power situation. Hence, the extreme uniformity of deadly, active combat gives way to a more extensive use of more diversified elements, and to a more varied use of effect-contrast and effect-modelling.

Insofar as the demand for superiority enters into the picture, style is modified into a means of expressing the tendency of the superior to "withdraw" and "ascend" (and of the inferior to "keep his distance" in a lower position). When the demand for equality is found, style is a means of reducing barriers.

That effect-resemblance is one of the most significant dimensions of style in the language of politics should not obscure the fact that resemblances may follow (or contrast with) other prototypes. Style may be affected by what is designated, in addition to the effect desired. The effect-in-view may be comprehension (not action), and the message to be comprehended may be, for example, that X is a tall man.

This may be conveyed, not only by words, but by gestures depicting height, or by drawings and sculptured figures. A third possibility is that style is moulded according to the appraisal of an object by the communicator; and the communicator is aiming at no other effect than enjoyment. An artist may pantomine the dying Gaul, not for the purpose of arousing anybody to revenge, but solely for the audience capable of appreciating the technique of portrayal. Symbols and signs are modelled on the figure of the dying warrior, not as a means of stimulating the audience to die, but as part of "self-expression" for general enjoyment. Style resemblances, therefore, may relate to the effect sought from the audience, the characteristics of an object designated, or an appraisal by a communicator. Since a power situation is, by definition, characterized by the pursuit of power effects, it is clear why style in the language of politics is effect-modelled or contrasted.

The preceding analysis has been chiefly directed toward certain "causal" factors affecting style. Of no less interest is the impact of style on response. The *pragmatics* of style comprises both "cause and effect" (inter-determinative) analysis. The main incentive for studying the speeches of Wilson, Roosevelt or other orators has been to learn more about the technique of effective public discourse. No doubt, this will continue to be the most patiently cultivated part of the field of research on communication.

In the long run, however, the study of style may make its largest contribution in relation to the problem of interpreting significant political trends. Certain changes in style may indicate the gradual decline of democratic feeling, or reveal the ground swell of gathering crisis. Style characteristics may prove to be diagnostic criteria for the disclosure of destructice or creative political personalities. For style is not to be dismissed as ornamentation. The most important thing to be said about style is that it can not be exhausted, since style is an indispensable feature of every configuration of meaning in any process of communication. The analysis of what is communicated—of content—calls for the examination of purport and style. Since style is the arrangement of the symbols and signs which are the elementary units of communication, style is a structural fact about any completed sequence.[11]

The ancient rhetoricians took a different view of style, since they began by separating meaning from form. Hence, as Wimsatt remarks, there remains "an irreducible something that is superficial, a kind of scum—which they call style." [12] Since the seventeenth century, the structural significance of style has been gaining ground until today we are in closer harmony with Buffon's sentence about the "order" and "movement" of expressed thoughts. More generally, style is the arrangement of the parts of communication; and these parts may be simple or complex elements composed of signs, symbols or symbol-signs. These arrangements vary as a function of the situation in which communication is an instrument of power.

Chapter **3**

WHY BE QUANTITATIVE?

THE POINT of view of this book is that the study of politics can be advanced by the quantitative analysis of political discourse. Why be quantitative? In reply, it is perhaps appropriate to bring out the limitations of qualitative analysis in terms of the work of the present writer.

At the end of World War I, research on politically significant communication was almost entirely qualitative, consisting in the discovery and illustration of propaganda themes and their use. When the present writer described the propaganda of World War I in *Propaganda Technique in the World War* (1927)[1] he took note of certain common themes running through the propaganda of all belligerent powers. The themes were:

The enemy is a menace.
(German militarism threatens us all.)

We are protective.
(We protect ourselves and others.)

The enemy is obstructive.
(They block our future aims.)

We are helpful.
(We aid in the achievement of positive goals.)

The enemy is immoral and insolent.
(They violate legal and moral standards and they hold everyone else in contempt.)

We are moral and appreciative.
(We conform to moral and legal standards and we respect others.)

The enemy will be defeated.

We will win.

The book was organized to show the form taken by these themes when domestic, allied or enemy audiences were addressed. The chapter on "The Illusion of Victory" showed what was told the home audience on the themes, "The enemy will be defeated," "We will win." The chapter on "Satanism" described how the self was presented as "moral" and "appreciative" while the enemy was "immoral" and "insolent." The "menacing" and "obstructive" rôle of the enemy and our own "protective" and "helpful" activity were illustrated in the chapter on "War Guilt and War Aims." Special attention was paid to "preserving friendship" (of allies and neutrals) and "demoralizing the enemy." Each chapter was composed of excerpts selected chiefly from the propaganda of the United States, Great Britain, Germany and France.

Although none of the criteria which guided the choice of quotations is stated in the book, it is obvious that some selections were made because they clearly stated a theme or developed a theme in detail. No doubt these criteria justified the citation of the extended account of alleged Entente violations of international law which had been compiled by Dr. Ernst Müller-Meiningen (pp. 85-86). In some cases, the wide dissemination of the material was no doubt a selective factor, notably in the case of *J'accuse!*, an exposé of Germany by Richard Grelling (p. 54). Sometimes the eminence of the speaker appears to have been the deciding factor, as with the Bryce report on alleged atrocities perpetrated by the Germans in Belgium (p. 19). In certain instances, the excerpt was a sample of what was distributed by (or to) a professional, vocational, educational or other special group (pp. 70 ff.).

No evidence is given in the book that all the material studied by the author was examined with the same degree of care. We are not informed whether the author actually read or glanced through all the copies of the principal mass-circulation newspapers, periodicals, books and pamphlets of Germany and other countries; or whether he read British, French and American material as fully as German.

Of course, the study did not purport to be an exhaustive history of propaganda during the war. It was called an essay in technique, and the hope was expressed that it would have some influence in directing professional historians toward the study of propaganda, and that the scheme of classification would prove helpful in the organization of future research. The book was to some extent successful in both objectives. Research on war propaganda, as indeed on every phase of propaganda, went forward with vigor, many monographs growing out of the original essay or attributing some degree of influence to it.[2]

Among the most comprehensive books on the propaganda of World War II were those of Hans Thimme, *Weltkrieg ohne Waffen* (1932)[3], and George G. Bruntz, *Allied Propaganda and the Collapse of the German Empire in 1918* (1938)[4]. Both historians explored archives of newspaper, magazine and other source material, the first relying chiefly upon the Reich archives and the second utilizing the Hoover War Library at Stanford University.

Whenever the propaganda message was described, the method adopted by these writers was similar to that of *Propaganda Technique in the World War*. Excerpts were chosen to illustrate what was circulated to different publics and what themes were used. The authors left unspecified their criteria of choice, although these were obviously similar to those of the earlier work. In many respects these monographs are more satisfactory than the first book, since the authors made use of new source material, and employed to advantage the accumulated results of historical scholarship on the relative importance of persons, channels and symbols in the war.

The results, however, can not be accepted as in all respects satisfactory; many relevant questions remain unanswered. Can we assume that a scholar read his sources with the same degree of care throughout his research? Did he allow his eye to travel over the thousands upon thousands of pages of parliamentary debates, newspapers, magazines and other sources listed in his bibliography or notes? Or did he use a sampling system, scanning some pages superficially, though concentrating upon certain periods? Was the sampling system for the *Frankfurter Zeitung,* if one was employed, comparable with the one for the *Manchester Guardian?* Were the leaflets chosen simply because they were conveniently available to the scholar, or were they genuinely representative of the most widely circulated propaganda leaflets?

The very fact that such questions can be raised at all points to a certain lack of method in presenting and conducting research on the history of war propaganda. In all of the books to which reference has been made no explicit justification was given of most of the excerpts chosen to illustrate a specific theme, to characterize the content of any particular channel, or to describe the propaganda directed toward or reaching any given audience. It is impossible to determine from the final report whether the same number or a comparable number of mass circulation media were read for France as for England or Germany, or whether publications were explored with the same degree of intensity at all dates, or whether certain dates were singled out for intensive note-taking.

The limitations of these monographs are apparent when anyone undertakes to follow a particular theme through various periods, channels and audiences. We know that every belligerent used "war aim" propaganda. But suppose we want to find the degree of emphasis laid upon war aims from period to period. Or assume that we ask how they differed when presented to the upper, middle or lower classes of the home population, or to neutral, ally or enemy. Was the war aim propaganda more prominent in the magazines than in the pamphlets, or the reverse? The same questions apply to every theme.

To some extent, historians of war propaganda have sought to reduce ambiguity by multiplying the number of subperiods described within the whole period. Walter Zimmerman studied the English press from the time of Sarajevo to the entry of England into the war, selecting thirty daily newspapers, eight Sunday papers, nine weeklies, four monthlies and two quarterlies, intending to cover all the important regional and social groups in Great Britain.[5] Even in this period, however, we can not be certain of the criteria used in selecting quotations. It is obvious that Zimmerman does not summarize all thirty daily papers every day, but we are left in the dark about why he quotes one paper one day or week and omits it the next time. Even if we assume that his judgment is good, it is permissible to ask if such arbitrary selection procedures create a properly balanced picture, or whether they result in special pleading based, if not on deliberate deception, then on unconscious bias.

The same problem remains in the detailed monograph by Friederike Recktenwald, in which she restricts herself to a single set of themes having to do with British war aims.[6] Miss Recktenwald divides the course of the war into subperiods, and reproduces or summarizes material from the British press having to do with war aims. Although this procedure gives us a plausible indication of the relative amount of attention paid to war aims at different times, not all reasonable doubts are allayed. She follows no consistent scheme of reporting. During any given subperiod only a few quotations may be reproduced; yet this may not invariably mean that there was less war-aim news or diminished editorial prominence. It may signify no more than that what was said is less interesting to the historian because the style is less vivid and quotable. We can not rely upon Miss Recktenwald's excerpts to be true samples of the total stream of news and comment reaching the British public, or even of any particular newspaper, or group of newspapers. The moment we ask clear questions that call for reliable bases of comparison, the arbitrary and dubious character of the monograph is apparent.

It is possible, however, to find studies of great technical excellence. In matters of systematic definition and historic detail, we can go back half a century to *A Study of Public Opinion and Lord Beaconsfield, 1875-1880,* by George Carslake Thompson (1886).[7] At the beginning of that remarkable work, a series of terms for the analysis of public opinion is carefully defined. These terms are consistently applied throughout the two fact-stuffed volumes. One part of the analytical scheme names the standards applied by the British public on foreign policy questions. Among the standards were "international law," "interest," "morality," and "taste." Thompson pointed out that such standards were applied according to the public's conception of England's rôle in relation to other nations, and that these ranged all the way from "England as an island" to "England as a European or Asiatic great power."

In applying these standards and conceptions, Thompson distinguished certain broad motives—"sentimental" or "diplomatic"—that were operating among the members of the British public in their basic orientation toward foreign policy. At any given time—for instance, at the outbreak of war between Russia and Turkey—these standards, conceptions and motivations (public "notions") were fused into public "views." The views of the British public in 1876 were classified as "Anti-Turkism," "Anti-war," "Order," "Legalism," "Anti-Russianism and Philo-Turkism." Such views in turn were related to corresponding policies. In this way, "Anti-Turkism" was bracketed with "emancipation," "Anti-war" with "isolation." The book described each successive phase of England's reaction to the war between Russia and Turkey, and copiously illustrated every move by excerpts from a list of publications.

Thompson's treatise is noteworthy for the unification of carefully defined abstractions with exhaustive data from the sources. Nevertheless, the outcome of all the admirable intelligence and industry that went into this treatise does not yield maximum results, because of a basic failure: the problem of sampling, recording and summarizing sources was not resolved. Hence, the entire foundation of the work rests on shaky ground. Thompson divides the five years with which he deals into subperiods, according to some predominant characteristic. One such subperiod is the "incubation period, third phase," from the opening of the Parliamentary Session of 1876 to the Servian declaration of war. This is followed by the "atrocity period," which in turn is divided into several parts. For each subperiod, Thompson narrates the stream of events and selects from the sources the quotations that impress him as important not only because they are conspicious, but because they bear some relationship to his systematic scheme of analysis (standards, conceptions, motivations, views and policies). However, the critical reader is still justified in remaining skeptical of the representativeness of the quotations. He can not be sure why they impressed the author when he was reading and making notes on the sources, or organizing his chapters. An excerpt may be the only one that appeared in a given newspaper or magazine on the same subject during the period; or, on the contrary, it may be only one among a tremendous gush of news and editorial items. Thompson does not tell us. The fundamental operation—of source handling—remained highly arbitrary.

If the excellence of the Thompson study lies in system and rich detail, a few recent publications rank above it in the sampling of sources. D. F. Willcox (1900) [8] classified the contents of a single issue of 240 newspapers according to topic (by column inches). Later A. A. Tenney, Jr., at Columbia University, interested a number of students in space measurement and initiated investigations of immediate value to world politics. Julian L. Woodward examined the foreign news published in 40 American morning newspapers and improved the technical state of the subject by showing the effect of different sampling methods upon the result. In general, he found that a small number of issues distributed throughout the year were enough to give a reliable picture of the amount of attention usually given by an American morning newspaper to foreign news (at least during a non-crisis period).[9]

In general, these investigations were not expressly related to political science. They were made by statisticians interested in having something to count, or sociologists who were exploring the general social process. The senior author of the present work undertook to direct research toward the use of objective procedures in gathering the data pertinent to political hypotheses. Schuyler Foster, for example, examined the treatment given European war news in the New York *Times* during definite periods before our participation in the war of 1914-18. He summarized his results in tabular and graphical form, and showed that the crisis that led immediately to our entry into the war was the final one in a series of crises of ever-increasing intensity. He measured these fluctuations by recording the frequency with which different kinds of news or editorial comment were made about the war or America's relation to it. The use of quantitative methods gave precision to part of the history of America's mobilization for war, and opened up a series of questions about the relation between the ups and downs in the New York *Times* and corresponding fluctuations in New York newspapers reaching different social groups, and in newspapers published in cities of different sizes throughout the country.[10]

More exact methods give us a means of clarifying certain categories that have been at the root of many past evils in the work of historians and social scientists. For a century, controversy has raged over the relative weight of "material" and "ideological" factors in the social and political process. This controversy has been sterile of scientific results, though the propaganda resonance of "dialectical materialism" has been enormous.

Insofar as sterility can be attributed to technical factors in the domain of scholarship, the significant factor is failure to deal adequately with "ideological" elements. The usual account of how material and ideological factors interact upon one another leaves the process in a cloud of mystery. It is as though you put people in an environment called material—and presto!—their ideas change in a predictable way; and if they do not, the failure is ascribed to an ideological lag of some kind. But the relations, though assumed, are not demonstrated. So far as the material dimensions are concerned, operational methods have been worked out to describe them; not so with the ideological. We are amply equipped to describe such "material" changes as fluctuations in output or amount of machinery employed in production; but we can not match this part of the description with equally precise ways of describing the ideological. The result is that the historical and social sciences have been making comparisons between patterns, only a few features of which are handled with precision. The other dimensions remain wholly qualitative, impressionistic and conjectural.[11]

We have undertaken to clear up some of the confusion that has long beset the analysis of "environment" by introducing basic distinctions: the first between the "attention frame" and "surroundings," and the second between the "media frame" and the "non-media frame." The attention frame or "milieu" is the part of an environment reaching the focus of attention of a person or group; the surroundings do not reach the focus. The media frame is composed of the signs coming to the focus of attention (the press which is actually read, for instance). The non-media frame includes the features of an environment that, although not signs, reach attention, such as conspicuous buildings, or persons. Whether any given set of surrounding does affect the structure of attention is to be settled by observing the phenomena, not by assumption.

The fundamental nature of these relations is evident when we reflect upon the requirements for a scientific explanation of response. Two sets of factors are involved: the environment and predispositions. R (response) is a function, in the mathematical sense, of E (environment), and P (predisposition); and we have shown that the part of the environment immediately affecting response is what comes to the focus of attention (the attention frame).* Information about surroundings is pertinent only to the degree to which it can be shown that the surroundings determine attention. In deciding whether any feature of the environment comes to the focus, it is necessary to demonstrate that a minimum (the threshold level) has been elicited. We do not consider that radio programs which are blacked out by static have come to the attention of an audience. A threshold level has not been reached. (The threshold is not part of the R in the formula of explanation used above; only changes above the threshold are called "effects"—response to what is brought into the attention field.)

The procedures of "content analysis" of communication are appropriate to the problem of describing the structure of attention in quantitative terms.[12] Before entering upon technicalities, it may be pointed out that quantitative ways of describing attention serve many practical, as well as scientific, purposes. *Anticipating the enemy* is one of the most crucial and tantalizing problems in the conduct of war. The intelligence branch of every staff or operations agency is matching wits with the enemy. The job is to out-guess the enemy, to foretell his military, diplomatic, economic and propaganda moves before he makes them, and to estimate

* Or, synonymously, the milieu, which is divisible into media and non-media frames.

where attack would do him the most harm. A principal source of information is what the enemy disseminates in his media of communication.

The Global War introduced a new source of information about the enemy—radio broadcasts under his supervision. When the enemy speaks to his home population, it is possible to listen in. We overhear what the enemy says to his allies, to neutrals and to his enemies. At the outbreak of the Global War, belligerent governments set monitors to work, listening, recording and summarizing the output of enemy and enemy-controlled stations. In Great Britain a group connected with the British Broadcasting Corporation subjected this enormous body of material to systematic examination and began forecasting Nazi policy. These estimates have since been re-studied.[13] The same procedures have also been applied to the press and to every other channel of communication. The full plan of the enemy often appears only when the entire stream of communication is interpreted as a whole.

As we improve our methods of describing public attention and response, our results become more useful for another practical purpose—the *detecting of political propaganda*. During World War II, the U. S. Department of Justice employed objective propaganda analysis to expose and prosecute enemy agents, like the Transocean Information Service (Nazi-controlled) and "native Fascists." The Federal Communications Commission described in Court the Axis themes recognized by experts who monitored and analyzed short-wave broadcasts emanating from Germany, Japan and Italy. Objective procedures had been applied in discovering these themes. Objective procedures were also used to analyze the periodicals published by the defendants, and to reveal the parallels between them and the themes disseminated by Axis propagandists.[14]

Quite apart from the use of legal action, it is important that members of the public be informed of the behavior of those with access to the channels of communication. In deciding how much we can rely upon a given newspaper, it is important to know if that newspaper ceases to attack Russia when Germany and Russia sign a non-aggression pact, and then returns to the attack as soon as Germany and Russia fall apart. Under these conditions, we have grounds for inferring a pro-German propaganda policy. By studying the news, editorial and feature material in a medium of communication under known German control, we can check on this inference. We may find that the two media distribute praise and blame in the same way among public leaders and the political parties; and that they take the same stand on domestic and foreign issues. If so, our inference is strengthened that the channel is dominated by pro-German policies.[15]

In the preceding paragraphs, we have said that policy may be served by objective procedures used to anticipate the enemy and to detect propaganda. Also, as scientific knowledge increases, the possibility of control improves; hence, a third contribution of objective research to policy is *skill*.[16] Skill is the most economical utilization of available means to attain a goal. Appraisals of skill are among the most difficult judgments to establish on a convincing basis, since they depend upon exhaustive knowledge of concrete circumstances and of scientific relations. To say that A is more skilful than B in a given situation is to allow for all factors being "equal." It is not easy to demonstrate that the two sets of environing and predisposing factors are strictly comparable. The simple fact that the Nazis won out in Germany against the Socialists and other parties does not necessarily warrant the conclusion that the Nazis were more skillful propagandists than their antagonists. Or the failure of the French to hold out against the Germans longer in 1940 was not necessarily because French propagandists were lacking in skill. The "skill" factor can be separated from the others only when a very comprehensive view can be gained of the context. Did the responsible heads of state choose the most suitable personnel to conduct propaganda operations? Were the most effective symbols chosen? The most useful media? In each case, the question must be answered with reference to alternatives available in the original situation.

That content analysis has a direct bearing on the evaluation of skill is evident, since such methods introduce a degree of precise description at many points in the propaganda process. Directives can be described in detail; so, too, can material released through the propaganda agencies and disseminated through various media controlled by, or beyond the control of, the propagandist. Indeed, as we pointed out in our anal-

ysis of the attention factor in world politics,[17] every link in
the chain of communication can be described when suitable
methods are used; quantitative procedures reduce the margin
of uncertainty in the basic data.*

A fourth contribution relates not to policy as a whole, but
to the special objectives of humane politics. The aim of humane politics is a commonwealth in which the dignity of
man is accepted in theory and fact. Whatever *improves our
understanding of attitude* is a potential instrument of humane politics. Up to the present, physical science has not
provided us with means of penetrating the skull of a human
being and directly reading off his experiences. Hence, we
are compelled to rely upon indirect means of piercing the
wall that separates us from him. Words provide us with clues,
but we hesitate to take all phrases at their face value. Apart
from deliberate duplicity, language has shortcomings as a
vehicle for the transmission of thought and feeling. It is important to recognize that we obtain insight into the world
of the other person when we are fully acquainted with what
has come to his attention. Certainly the world of the country
boy is full of the sights and smells and sounds of nature. The
city boy, on the other hand, lives in a labyrinth of streets,
buildings, vehicles and crowds. A Chinese youth of good
family has his ancestors continually thrust upon his notice;
an American youth may vaguely recall his grandparents. The
son of an English ruling family may be reared on the anec-
dotes of centuries of imperial history, while the son of an
American businessman recalls that there was a Revolution
and that Bunker Hill had something to do with it.

The dominant political symbols of an epoch provide part
of the common experience of millions of men. There is some
fascination in the thought of how many human beings are
bound together by a thread no more substantial than the
resonance of a name or the clang of a slogan. In war, men
suffer pain, hunger, sorrow; the specific source of pain, the
specific sensation of one's specific object of sorrow, may be

---

* There is, of course, no implication that non-quantitative methods should
be dropped. On the contrary, there is need of more systematic theory and of
more luminous "hunches" if the full potentialities of precision are to be realized
in practice. As the history of quantification shows (in economics, for instance),
there is never-ending, fruitful interplay between theory, hunch, impression and
precision.

very private. In contrast, the key symbol enters directly into the focus of all men and provides an element of common experience.[18]

It is obvious that a complete survey of mass attention will go far beyond the press, the broadcast or the film. It will cover every medium of mass communication. Further, a complete survey would concentrate upon the most active decision-makers, disclosing the milieu of the heads of states, the chiefs of staff, diplomats and all other groups. An exhaustive inventory would describe the entire intelligence process.[19]

Why, then, be quantitative about communication? Because of the scientific and policy gains that can come of it. The social process is one of *collaboration* and *communication*; and quantitative methods have already demonstrated their usefulness in dealing with the former. Further understanding and control depend upon equalizing our skill in relation to both.

II
TECHNIQUE

Chapter **4**

THE PROBLEM OF VALIDATING
CONTENT ANALYSIS

1. *Introduction*

CONTENT ANALYSIS provides a precise means of describing
the contents of any sort of communication—newspapers,
radio programs, films, everyday conversations, verbalized free
associations, etc. The operations of content analysis consist
in classifying the signs occurring in a communication into a
set of appropriate categories. The results state the frequency
of occurrence of signs for each category in the classification
scheme.

"Content analysis" may be defined as referring to any
technique a) for the *classification* of the *sign-vehicles* b)
which relies solely upon the *judgments* (which, theoretically, may range from perceptual discrimination to sheer
guesses) of an analyst or group of analysts as to which sign-
vehicles fall into which categories, c) on the basis of *explicitly formulated rules,* d) provided that the analyst's
judgments are regarded as the reports of a *scientific observer.**

* Janis, I. L., "Meaning and the Study of Symbolic Behavior," *Psychiatry*
6:425-439, Nov. 1, 1943. The term "sign-vehicle" which occurs in this definition refers to a sign as a physical object without any consideration of its
meaning. In the case of printed communications, for example, each word is
regarded as a sign vehicle on the basis of the shapes of the group of black-

Precise descriptions of the content of communications are of scientific interest insofar as they enable the investigator to determine relationships between a given (content) characteristic of communications and (a) characteristics of the communicator, (b) characteristics of the audience, or (c) some other (content or non-content) characteristic of the communication. In other words, content analysis provides a means for testing three types of hypotheses:

(1) Propositions which state a relationship between (a) a communicator's environment, his position in the social structure, his personality traits, or his intentions and (b) the kinds of signs which occur in his communications.

(2) Propositions which state a relationship between (a) the kinds of signs which occur in communications and (b) the reactions of audiences (such as changes in attitudes) which result from perceiving those signs.

(3) Propositions which state a relationship between (a) one kind of sign in communications and (b) another kind of sign which occurs in the same communications (or some media characteristic of the communications, such as their typography).

The first requirement of any technique which purports to describe any set of characteristics, is that the results have a high degree of reliability, i.e., that different observers report the same thing. In the case of content-analysis results, reliability may be tested by determining the degree of correlation between the frequencies obtained when different analysts independently analyze the same contents.* Unless content-analysis results prove to be fairly reliable, we would not accept them as a description of communication contents. Now let us assume that we have tested the reliability of a content-analysis technique, and have found that the coefficient of correlation is sufficiently high so that the results of one analyst provide, within a small margin of error, an estimate of the results which would be produced by any other

marks-on-white. (Note that elsewhere in the present book the term "symbol" is often used for "sign," and "sign" is used for "sign vehicle." An explicit statement or the context makes evident what is meant.).

* Cf. I. L. Janis, R. H. Fadner, and M. Janowitz, "The Reliability of a Content Analysis Technique," *Public Opinion Quarterly*, 7:293-296, summer 1943.

analyst following the same procedure. One would then say that the content-analysis results were highly reliable and therefore represent a description of some aspect of the contents which were analyzed. The question then arises: *What do the content-analysis results describe?*

A previous article by the author discusses this problem in detail.* Three major types of content analysis were distinguished:

1. *Pragmatical Content Analysis*—procedures which classify signs according to their probable causes or effects (e.g., counting the number of times that something is said which is likely to have the effect of producing favorable attitudes toward Germany in a given audience).

2. *Semantical Content Analysis*—procedures which classify signs according to their meanings (e.g., counting the number of times that Germany is referred to, irrespective of the particular words that may be used to make the reference).

   (a) *designations analysis*—provides the frequency with which certain objects (persons, things, groups or concepts) are referred to, i.e., roughly speaking, subject-matter analysis (e.g., references to German foreign policy).

   (b) *attribution analysis*—provides the frequency with which certain characterizations are referred to (e.g., references to dishonesty).

   (c) *assertions analysis*—provides the frequency with which certain objects are characterized in a particular way, i.e., roughly speaking, thematic analysis (e.g., references to German foreign policy as dishonest).

3. *Sign-vehicle analysis*—procedures which classify content according to the psychophysical properties of the signs (e.g., counting the number of times the word "Germany" appears).

A major part of the discussion in the earlier article was devoted to the thesis that those procedures which take account of *meanings* of signs (semantical content analysis) estimate the semantical signification responses of the sign-

* Janis, I. L., "Meaning and the Study of Symbolic Behavior," *opus cit.*

interpreters who are specified in the hypothesis under investigation. Thus, if one is studying the intentions or any other characteristic of the communicator, in relation to the communications which he produces, the content-analysis operations are based on what the signs signify for that *communicator*. In the case of a hypothesis which relates the reactions of a given audience to the content of communications, the content analyst estimates the signification responses of the *audience* to the signs. For the purposes of content analysis, the main criterion proposed for setting up semantical rules was the following:

> The rules of a content analysis specify which signs are to be classified into which categories. These rules are, in effect, semantical rules for the language of the communication which is to be analyzed. What I am advocating is the use of a *frequency* criterion as the basis for constructing the semantical rules of a content analysis. Semantical significations are to be regarded as meaning habits. Accordingly, the content analyst is restricted to the designata which sign-interpreters most *frequently* take into account by the mediation of signs.*

Any analytic technique—whether it be a means of measuring visual acuity, manual dexerity, "verbal" intelligence, political attitudes or references of a particular type in a communication—is of dubious value until it can be shown that the results obtained by using it describe what they purport to describe. This is the problem of *validation*.

> In nontechnical language—a measuring instrument is said to have *validity* if it measures what it purports to measure; it is said to have *reliability* if it gives the same results consistently.

> *** The validity of a measuring device is usually studied by comparing the results or measures obtained from it with those obtained by another device, the validity of which is already established for measuring the same characteristic. If such a measuring device of established validity is not available—and this is often the case—the problem of establishing validity becomes difficult.

* Janis, I. L., *ibid.*

*** In cases of direct measures, validity is self-evident. In fact, we call those measures direct which unquestionably measure precisely what we intend them to.*

2. *Sources of Errors in Constant-Analysis Procedures*

In the introductory section I have attempted to define what characteristics of communications the various types of content analysis purport to describe. The main purpose of this paper is to consider the means by which evidence may be obtained to demonstrate that content-analysis techniques do in fact describe what they purport to describe.

Pragmatical content analysis will be omitted from the discussion, because it is a generally accepted technological principle that pragmatical categories should be excluded from content analysis—that pragmatical content analysis should not be used. In the earlier article, already referred to, I discussed this technological principle in some detail, and presented what appears to me to be the major grounds for excluding pragmatical content analysis, viz., the prediction that such content analysis procedures will prove to be invalid.

In the case of sign-vehicle analysis, there is little difficulty with respect to validation, because such techniques provide a *direct* measure of physical occurrences. The analyst's operations involve simple perceptual discriminations: determining the presence or absence of a given physical configuration and counting the number which are present. Hence no special validation procedures are necessary. Of course, the reliability of the analyst should be checked, in order to preclude the possibility that he has misunderstood or misapplied the rules of the analysis. This is the only condition necessary to warrant the conclusion that a sign-vehicle analysis measures what it purports to measure: the frequency of occurrence of a given sign-vehicle or of a given set of sign-vehicles.

The problem of validating semantical content analysis, on the other hand, is an extremely difficult one. In designation analysis, attribution analysis and assertion analysis, the operations require judgments of *meaning,* an extremely complex and variable type of human response. In estimating the meaning which would be attributed to the sign-vehicles,

---

* Hagood, Margaret J., Statistics for Sociologists, New York: Reynal and Hitchcock, Inc., 1941. Cf. p. 219.

either by a given audience or by a given communicator, the analyst's judgments are guided to a large extent by the rules of the content analysis. We may expect that such estimates can be made with a fair degree of accuracy for communications which employ everyday discourse, inasmuch as there is a high degree of constant and generally accepted signification for the signs of a language. Nevertheless it is inevitable that borderline cases will arise for which the meaning is not clear-cut, and for which the content analysis rules do not provide a ready answer.

This is especially true when one is classifying characterizors in carrying out an assertions analysis. A typical characterizor category, for example, is "attributions of dishonsty." Consider a statement of the following type: "Political leader X denied that he was negotiating a military alliance, whereas in fact he was doing so." To some people who read this sentence, the words may signify that X was dishonest—he lied to the public; to others the words may signify that X was merely being guided by political expediency. There may be disagreement among audience-members as to what this sentence asserts about X, in terms of dishonesty. Obviously, then, if one classified this sentence one way or the other, it could not be said that this classification would represent the signification which the sentence has for the *entire* audience; one would not even be sure as to which signification this sentence has for the majority of the audience. Moreover, different audiences might show characteristic differences as to what these particular words mean in terms of the moral standard of honesty-dishonesty.

Let us suppose that the content analyst, because he is aware that such borderline cases may arise, sets up a special rule: Assertions to the effect that there is a discrepancy between what is said about one's actions and what is actually done, are to be classified as attributions of dishonesty. In this case, the content analyst would have little difficulty in making a decision—and incidentally there would be high reliability among analysts—because the rule requires that this sentence be classified as an attribution of dishonesty. But following this rule would give an erroneous result in this case if the sentence signifies "expediency" rather than "dishonesty" to the audience.

From the discussion of this example it is seen that there are two main potential sources of error in estimating the significations attributed to signs by an audience:

1. The particular terms may be ambiguous for the audience; several different meanings may be attributed to the signs by different audience members.

2. Different audiences may attribute different meanings to the signs. If the content analysis results are correlated with certain responses of a particular audience, the meanings attributed to the contents by that particular audience may be different from those which the content analyst estimated.

Because content-analysis results attempt to describe meanings attributed to signs by the audience as a whole (or by the overwhelming majority of audience members) difficulties of the first type are unavoidable. If the signs have two different meanings for equally large sections of the audience, either way in which the signs are classified will be incorrect.

In order to minimize such errors, it appears best to weight in some appropriate way assertions which have this sort of ambiguity. In cases where the classification scheme is dichotomous and the hypothesis under investigation deals with the ratio between the two categories (e.g., honesty vs. dishonesty), classifying as *neutral* an assertion for which the audience's signification responses are estimated as split into the two dichotomous categories would appear to be the simplest solution. We might consider this as excluding a fractional occurrence of an assertion from both categories.

In cases like the above example (dishonesty vs. expediency), where only one of the categories is under investigation (dishonesty), not counting a partial occurrence of an assertion in this category is not balanced by not counting the alternative category. Nevertheless, one might still decide to classify such ambiguous assertions as *neutral*, because it would be a more serious error to give them equal weight as clearcut assertions. Moreover, if an approximately equal number of ambiguous cases arises for those categories which are to be compared, the omission of fractional occurrences is balanced and has little effect. This is one of the grounds for the frequent exclusion of the use of rules which require taking account of *implicit* assertions in content analysis, because implicit meanings have a high degree of ambiguity. By requiring the analyst to restrict his categories to occurrences of *explicit* references (manifest meanings), errors of commission are avoided; but some errors of omission are inevitable.

If it appears that errors of omission will not be of negligible frequency, the content analyst can attempt to set up numerical weights to be assigned to assertions which are estimated to be ambiguous. These weights would be fractional values, if unambiguous assertions are counted as unity.*

Another possibility—especially if the content analyst is aware of a high probability of many intra-audience differences in their signification responses to the same assertions— is to narrow down the audience whose significations he is attempting to describe, so that signification responses will be more homogeneous.

The second source of errors—inter-audience differences— is much more likely to occur but, fortunately, is easier to handle. Social scientists are often aware of characteristic differences in meaning which words have for different social groups, usually on the basis of "participant observation." Signification differentials are known to occur for various national, ethnic, regional, occupational and income groups. These differences have not been systemically elaborated—nor is it likely that they will be formulated in the near future, in view of the tedious detail which would be necessary. But content-analysis projects can recruit personnel who are aware of these differences, on the basis of their own experience, to carry out the content-analysis procedures. Obviously, in order to minimize errors arising from the peculiarities of the signification responses of any particular audience, content analysts should at least formulate the purpose of their experiments in terms of *which audience* they are considering. Specification of the audience is, of course, determined by the characteristics of the audience whose non-signification responses are to be correlated with the content-analysis data. Once the audience is defined, the content analyst is unlikely to overlook gross peculiarities in the signification responses of that audience which the content analysis should take into account.

* Cf. section 5, however, for some of the problems of weighting.

The above discussion of errors in estimating signification responses of sign-interpreters is concerned only with those content-analysis experiments which relate content characteristics to pragmatical reactions of the *audience*. For those experiments which relate intentions or other characteristics of the *communicator* to the content characteristics of his communications, the content analyst is concerned with estimating the meanings attributed to the signs by the *communicator*, i.e., the semantical meanings which the communicator is attempting to convey. Sources of error in this case are similar; the sign-classification procedures may require taking into account certain details of the personal history of the communicator, in order to take care of eccentric, personalized meanings.

From this discussion it is clear that there are many sources of errors which affect validity. The extent to which a content-analysis technique provides results which describe the frequency of occurrence of *all* the signs which belong to each class of signs set up in the classification scheme, excluding those which do not belong to the given class, depends on the frequency with which errors occur. *Systematic errors* may arise because of procedural rules which may entail faulty classification. *Spurious errors,* which are attributable to unknown differences in significations or to the observational standpoint of the content analyst, may arise as a result of incorrect judgments of signification responses. The latter type of error is probably even more frequent. One of the chief advantages of precise and detailed definitions of the content analysis categories is the reduction of spurious errors of judgment. Of course, the spurious errors may simply be replaced by systematic errors, but the latter type is more easily eliminated, as will be seen in the discussion below.

In view of the potential errors which may arise in estimating the significations of sign-interpreters, the results of any particular content analysis may be open to question on the grounds that so many systematic and/or spurious errors have been made as to give false frequencies. How does one know whether or not these errors have occurred sufficiently rarely so that the content-analysis results describe what they purport to describe?

It is necessary to discover some procedure by means of

which the validity of a semantical content analysis can be tested. Without such a validation procedure it is impossible to give a rational justification for the operations of semantical content analysis. It would be necessary to rely solely upon the *opinion* of the content analysts themselves that semantical content-analysis techniques estimate signification responses correctly. Thus, when a content analysis reports that a given publication contains 25 references which characterize German foreign policy as dishonest, we would be forced to accept or reject this frequency on the basis of our *a priori* faith in the analyst and in his procedures; we would have no means of knowing, (a) whether each of the 25 references would in fact be interpreted in that way by a given audience, or (b) whether the 25 references were in fact the only references in the publication which would be interpreted in that way. If there were errors of the first sort, the frequency reported (25 references) would be too high; if there were errors of the second sort, the frequency reported would be too low. The purpose of a method of validation is to provide evidence that both sorts of errors occur infrequently.

3. *Productivity and the Problem of Validation*

One possible way to estimate the problem of validation would be to reduce semantical content-analysis to sign-vehicle analysis. This would be a matter of replacing the rules that define the specific kinds of references which are to be counted as falling into a given category with rules which specify sets of sign-vehicles. If this could be done, then designations analysis, attributions analysis and assertions analysis would no longer require the analyst to take account of meanings; such analyses would be sign-vehicle analysis and, accordingly, would constitute direct measures of the frequency of occurrence of a set of sign-vehicles. Thus, validation procedures would be unnecessary.

It appears to me that the reduction of semantical content-analysis to sign-vehicle analysis is totally infeasible.* The main difficulty lies in the fact that the semantical signification of a given sign depends upon the linguistic context. The reduction would require not merely the listing of all sign-

* Cf. Janis, I. L., *ibid* for a detailed discussion of this problem.

vehicles which elicit more or less equivalent significations, but also the listing of the sign-vehicles which make up every possible context in which those sign-vehicles occur. For example, there are thousands of arrangements of sign-vehicles which provide linguistic contexts for the explicit characterization of dishonesty. The magnitude of the task is so great that it is highly improbable that such a reduction will ever be carried out, particularly for any assertions-analysis technique.

Since it is infeasible to reduce semantical content analysis to sign-vehicle analysis, the problem of validation can not be eliminated in this way. There is, however, another possibility to consider, which is quite similar to the first, but which is by no means infeasible. The content analyst might forego the attempt to describe the frequency of occurrence of *all* references which fall within each semantical class. Thus, instead of a designations analysis which purports to describe the frequency of *all* references to Germany, one might simply report the number of times the words "Germany," "Nazis" and "Reich" occur. Inasmuch as the content analyst would not claim to have exhaustive categories, it would be a simple matter to use a set of sign-vehicles in the place of each semantical class.

To be sure, such a *partial* reduction of semantical content analysis to sign-vehicle analysis would eliminate the problem of validation. Unfortunately, it would, at the same time, eliminate most of the scientific value of content analysis. In most cases, the results of such a content analysis would undoubtedly prove to be unproductive.

It is useful at this point to examine the concept of *productivity* as applied to content analysis. To say that a content-analysis technique has a high degree of productivity is to say that the categories of the particular classification system occur as variables in many true empirical propositions. Productivity is a major component of what is vaguely referred to as "scientific significance." It provides an answer to the question which is so often raised whenever a new research technique is presented: "So what?"

A content-analysis procedure is productive insofar as the results it yields are found to be correlated with other variables. Whenever there is a substantial correlation between two variables, one variable may be regarded as an *indicator* of the other, because it is possible to predict, within known limits of error, the value of the second variable from the first. We may say, then, that a technique is productive to the extent that the results it provides serve as *indicators* of other variables. Thus, a content-analysis technique would be highly productive if its results served as indicators of such variables as, (a) intentions of the communicator to produce favorable attitudes toward a foreign country, (b) periods of severe frustration for the political organization with which the communicators are affiliated, (c) "unconscious" guilt feelings on the part of the speaker, (d) changes in attitudes toward democratic practices on the part of an audience, and (e) feelings of insecurity about the future on the part of the audience, etc.

As yet, too few content analysis studies have been made to permit of empirical statements about the relative productivity of the various types of content analysis procedures. One may predict, on the basis of existing knowledge about communicative processes, that sign-vehicle analysis will prove to have a low degree of productivity.*

So far as the political contents are concerned, sign-vehicle analysis will probably be found to be productive in connection with the study of clichés, stereotyped terms and political slogans. For example, the frequency with which terms like "bourgeois," "bosses," "working class," and "dictatorship of the proletariat" occur in a communist publication might be found to co-vary with major changes in the policies of the Third International. In general, we may expect that the productivity of sign-vehicle analysis will be limited to (a) terms which do not have synonyms (in which case, the results will be the same as those of a designations analysis); and (b) terms

---

* Cf. A. Geller, D. Kaplan, and H. D. Lasswell, "The Differential Use of Flexible and Rigid Procedures of Content Analysis," *Experimental Division for the Study of War Time Communications,* Library of Congress, Document No. 12. These authors refer to "rigid" as against "flexible" procedures in distinguishing between what I have called "sign-vehicle" and "semantical content analysis." In their remarks on the advantages of one type as compared to the other, they imply the criterion of productivity: "In general a recurring problem of content analysis is the proper balance to be struck between reliability and significance. We can be completely reliable about the frequency of occurrence of any selected word, but this may be of very trivial importance. * * *" (Chapter VI of the present volume).

which, to speak loosely, have a unique emotional or assertive quality.

Designations analysis may be expected to be more productive than sign-vehicle analysis but nevertheless restricted. In a sense, designations analysis amounts to describing the "exposure-attention" of a communication—that is, the subject matters which are brought to the focus of attention of the audience. We may expect designations analysis to be productive in the study of phenomena related to attention, interests, taboos, preferences with respect to subject matter, and the like. Therefore, designations analysis will probably be productive only in establishing "key symbols" as indicators of relatively nonpersistent, peripheral types of behavior, e.g., correlations with retention rather than with changes in attitude.

Attributions analysis, since it does not provide information about the subject matters to which characterizations are applied, will probably have low productivity, so far as political analysis is concerned. On the other hand, it may be productive in the study of certain aspects of character structure, particularly of deviant-personality types. Evidence of pessimism-optimism, generalized aggressiveness, preferred standards (e.g., use of religious standards as against efficiency in evaluating objects), etc. may be obtained by an attributions analysis of an individual's communications. By indicating which characterizations are most frequently used, attributions analysis should prove useful in determining how an individual perceives his environment.

Assertions analysis will probably be found to be the most productive type of content analysis, inasmuch as the "thematic content" corresponds most nearly to the overall signification of a communication. Thus, the signification-*gestalt* for a magazine article—the answer which most people would give when asked what the article has to say—is in terms of how certain objects are characterized (e.g., "the article says that the war will be over within a year"). The assertions found in a communication are the primary content indicators of the intentions and motives of the communicator. Similarly, the effects which a communication produces on an audience are primarily due to the assertions content. We may expect, therefore, many correlations between the results of assertions analysis and pragmatical responses which are of major political and psychological significance.

Content categories are unlikely to be productive unless they contain homogeneous significations. The grounds for this proposition, which is based on existing knowledge about the communicative process, will be discussed below. This proposition may be formulated as two criteria to be applied in setting up the rules for any content analysis: (1) all sign-vehicles or groups of sign-vehicles which are classified into the same category, refer to the same thing; (2) all sign-vehicles or groups of sign-vehicles which are excluded from a given category, do not refer to the same thing as do the sign-vehicles which are included. In the case of a designations analysis, for example, these criteria would be satisfied if: (a) each term which, according to the rules, is classified as referring to Germany actually does so, and (b) no term which is not classified as referring to Germany actually does so. If the first criterion is violated, errors of *commission* are made; if the second criterion is violated, errors of *omission* are made.

Returning now to the possibility of escaping the problem of validating semantical content by partial reduction to sign-vehicle analysis, it is apparent that this solution of the problem of validation is inadequate. It would require sacrificing high productivity, because those sign-vehicle analysis procedures which are feasible are usually incapable of satisfying the second criterion necessary for high productivity. This is especially true of assertions analysis. It appears to me, therefore, that the problem of validation can not be escaped if content analysis is to be productive.

4. *A Method of Indirect Validation*

In effect, content analysis procedures assume a one-to-one correspondence between certain sign-vehicles and certain signification responses (what is taken account of when the sign-vehicle is perceived). So far as I know, there are no techniques available for the direct measurement of signification response. There are a number of possible ways in which signification responses might be determined—for example, by means of a questionnaire which requires each subject to indicate the (semantical) category which is most appropriate for given sign-vehicles. If such a technique were available it would be possible to make a *direct* test of the validity of content analysis procedures by presenting a representative sample of the contents to a representative sample of the audience or communicator.

But it is not very likely that a direct method of validation will be available in the near future, in view of the enormous difficulties involved in obtaining an unambiguous delineation of the semantical meanings which occur spontaneously when words are perceived. We are impelled, therefore, to look for some *indirect* method of validating content analysis procedures.

Since we can not measure signification responses directly, how are we able to determine the meaning of words? To validate the procedures of semantical content analysis amounts to showing that the definitions used in the content analysis are correct. It appears to me that the same principle which is used in testing definitions in everyday life may be applied as the basis of indirect validation of content analysis procedures. In our day-to-day experience with language, one is rarely aware of the process by which we come to accept a given signification response as the appropriate one for a given sign-vehicle. The meaning of a word is inferred from the wide varieties of behaviors which accompany the use of the word. One infers what is taken account of by the mediation of a sign-vehicle on the basis of the behavioral context in which the sign-vehicle occurs.

When we define a term we specify what is taken into account when that term is perceived by some group of sign-users. Such definitions may be regarded as hypotheses which are to be tested by observing the behavior of those who use the sign. If we find that the stimuli which elicit the use of the term and the responses of those who perceive the term are consistent with our hypothetical definition of that term, we accept that definition as correct. This description of the definitional process, as it operates in everyday life, may be applied to the procedures of semantical content analysis.

Sign-vehicles are classified into different semantical categories on the basis of explicit or implicit definitions. When a sign-vehicle is perceived, it is often possible to observe some particular change in the behavior of the perceiver. These observable modifications in behavior (pragmatical responses) imply an intermediate subjective event, a signification response. Accordingly, the communicative process may be schematized as follows: the communicator's observable reactions to the situation (pragmatical responses of the communicator) ——➤ certain signification responses which he attempts to convey to others ——➤ production of particular sign-vehicles ——➤ particular signification responses of the audience ——➤ observable reactions to the signification responses (pragmatical responses of the audience).

The pragmatical responses of the communicator which lead to the production of sign-vehicles may be regarded as the behavioral *causes* of the communication; the responses of the audience may be regarded as the *effects* of the communication. When similar pragmatical responses are found to be associated with a given sign-vehicle on different occasions, it is assumed that the same signification response to the sign-vehicle has occurred. When different sign-vehicles, in different linguistic contexts, are associated with the same pragmatical responses, the different sign-vehicles are regarded as equivalent (synonymous).

The basic assumption which is used in determining meanings is that relationships among various observable aspects of the communicative process are mediated by signification responses. Different signification responses tend to have different behavioral causes and effects; similar signification responses tend to have similar causes and effects. This is the basis for the two criteria for productivity discussed in the preceding section. Unless the content analyst groups together those sign-vehicles which have common significations, he will not be likely to discover relationships between content characteristics and pragmatical responses. On the other hand, if many relationships are found, it is highly improbable that the content analysis procedures are incorrect in estimating signification responses. On the basis of this view of the communicative process, it appears to me that an indirect method for the validation of semantic content analysis procedures may be derived. This method consists of *inferring validity from productivity*.

If one is able to show that a content analysis procedure provides results which are correlated with many types of pragmatical responses of sign-interpreters, then it may be concluded that the content analysis procedures correctly describe the signification responses of those sign-interpreters. This inference is made on the basis of an assumption derived from the procedures which are used in determining meanings in everyday life: Unless the signs have the significations assigned to them by the content analyst, relationships between the classification frequencies and the responses of the sign-interpreters would not be found. Offhand, this may sound like a rather tenuous assumption. First of all, there is the possibility of spurious correlations. But this offers little difficulty if we recognize that a single correlation provides but a low degree of probability that the content analysis procedure is valid; that the more correlation yielded by the procedure, the higher the probability that it is valid. Secondly, one might argue that a correlation—if it is not spurious—shows only that the sign-vehicles have *some* meaning for the sign-interpreters, but there is no basis for assuming that correlations show that the sign-vehicles have the particular meaning which the content analysis imputes to them.

This argument may be broken down into two questions: (1) How do we know that the sign-vehicles which are grouped together have a common signification for the sign-interpreters? (2) Even if we do know that the content analysis procedures group together sign-vehicles which have a common signification, how do we know that the common signification is correctly specified by the content analyst?

The first question may be answered by considering that the number of possible groupings of sign-vehicles is unlimited. Why should a particular grouping of sign-vehicles be found to co-vary with many of the sign-interpreters' pragmatical responses, unless it is because there is a relationship between *significations* and *pragmatical responses?* If such a relationship exists, then it is likely that there is something common to the significations, because not all significations co-vary with those pragmatical responses. Again, the higher the degree of productivity, the higher the probability that each category of the content analysis is a functional class. That is to say, high productivity indicates that the sign-vehicles which are grouped together elicit significations that have some characteristic in common, and that those sign-vehicles whose significations do not have the common characteristic are excluded.

The second question is concerned with naming the common characteristic of the significations of the sign-vehicles which are grouped together. This problem is not an important one, because so long as it is established that the content analysis categories are functional classes of signs, the classes may be designated by their entire definition as stated in the procedural rules of the content analysis. But, in general, there is no need to resort to this.

There is usually no reason for questioning the ability of the content analyst to name correctly the common characteristic of the significations of the sign-vehicles which fall into the same category. After all, the content analyst knows, when he sets up his content analysis categories, what characteristics of the significations he wants to separate. If his classification scheme is reliable and has proved to be productive, it would be most unlikely that he misinterpreted the meaning of the words which he was classifying.

The assumption therefore appears to me defensible that correlations between content characteristics and pragmatical responses of sign-interpreters imply correct estimation of the signification responses of sign-interpreters. In general, then, the following principle of validation is proposed: *The larger the number of relationships established by use of a content analysis technique, the higher the probability that the procedures estimate signification responses correctly, and hence the higher the degree of validity.*

One further question before we turn to some of the implications of this method of validation: Do correlations between two content characteristics (as against correlations between a content characteristic and a pragmatical response) also provide evidence of descriptive validity? At first sight, one might be inclined to think not, because such a correlation does not directly involve the mediation of signification responses. Thus, a correlatiton between the frequency of references to Germany and the frequency of references to the United States does not seem to offer evidence that the signification responses of sign interpreters were correctly estimated, because the correlated variables do not occur at different stages of the communication process, separated by an intervening stage in which signification responses of sign-interpreters take place. Moreover, it is not even clear at first sight *whose* signification responses are estimated, when one deals with a hypothesis which specifies a relationship among content characteristics.

Yet, it appears to me that this first impression is incorrect, that correlations between content characteristics do imply the mediation of signification responses. Such correlations, whether they are stated in this way or not, deal with relationships among signification responses of the communicator. An hypothesis to the effect that "In publication Z the frequency of references to Germany varies inversely with the frequency of references to the United States" may be translated into "The frequency with which *the writers of publication Z* refer to Germany varies inversely with the frequency with which they refer to the United States." Such a correlation may simply bespeak the usual habit of writing entire articles on one subject (so that an article on Germany would have many references to Germany, few to the United States). But it is a habit exhibited by the writer and, moreover, a habit whose performance requires significations of the writer in response to the signs which he produces.*

It appears to me that correlations among content characteristics may be interpreted as correlations among semantical significations imputed to the sign by the communicator. Such correlations, in turn, may be explained by correlations between signification characteristics and intentions of the communicator. (To return to the same example as above, if the writer *intends* to produce an article which will bring Germany to the focus of attention of his readers, he uses many signs which, for him, signify Germany, few signs which signify the United States. If this is true, then we may apply the same considerations which were adduced to explain correlations between content characteristics and pragmatical responses; correlations between two classes of sign-vehicles can be explained by inferring that each class has a certain

---

* Ordinarily, psychologists and social scientists are interested in relationships over and above those which occur as a result of general language habits. But it should be recognized that language habits are empirical relationships among variables; that the resultant lack of independence among content characteristics is a consequence of *behavior,* not of the methods of analysis.

common signification for the communicator, and that there is a functional relationship between these two classes of significations in the behavior of the communicator. Therefore, correlations among content characteristics, as well as correlations between a content characteristic and a pragmatical response, provide indirect evidence of the validity of a content analysis procedure.*

5. Practical Consequences of Indirect Validation

To date, content analysis has been applied to a relatively limited extent. There is no one set of content analysis procedures which has been applied on a wide scale, and which has proved to be highly productive. Hence, since validity is to be inferred from productivity, it should be recognized that, at the present stage of development, content analysis research has a twofold function: primarily, the scientific function of testing hypotheses about communications, and secondarily, the technical function of increasing the degree of validity of content analysis procedures. In general, these two functions go hand in hand, because the confirmation of hypotheses about content characteristics increases the degree of validity of the procedures. But it is useful to differentiate between the two functions, particularly because the limited extent to which the validation function is fulfilled has definite consequences for designing content analysis researches.

In a sense, every application of content analysis employs a new set of procedures, and the problem of validation begins *de novo*. Even when one content analysis employs classification rules which are identical with those of another, if new personnel performs the classification operations there is the

---

* There is one aspect of correlations among content characteristics which tends to decrease the weight of the evidence. If, for example, we were to correlate references to Germany with references to all designata other than Germany, we would find a perfect negative correlation (if relative frequencies are used, as is the usual practice). But such a correlation is not an empirical one —it is simply a tautologous proposition entailed by the use of *logically exhaustive* categories. No matter how many errors were made in classifying the signs, and no matter how unreliable the content analysis procedure, a perfect correlation would result. Therefore, whenever two content categories which tend toward logical exhaustiveness are correlated, the correlation tends to be nonempirical, and hence irrelevant for the determination of validity. This should be borne in mind in evaluating correlations among content characteristics as evidence of validity.

possibility that the observational standpoints of the new content analysts deviate to such an extent that new *explicit* procedures determine the results to a significant extent. For this reason, among others, it is desirable to make the procedural rules as explicit as possible, in order to reduce spurious errors to a minimum.

In this way, not only is reliability improved but the probability that identical procedures have the same degree of validity is increased. Consequently, the results produced by content analysts who work completely independently—and who have learned the procedures independently—become comparable, even though it may not be feasible to carry out a reliability test. That is to say, the reliability results and the evidence relevant to validity for a given content analysis technique are applicable to other researches in which that technique is used according to the extent to which the classification rules are explicitly stated.

There is an additional reason for reducing spurious errors by stating the procedures as explicitly as possible. It was pointed out above that spurious errors may simply be replaced by systematic ones. But the advantage of such a change is that the determinants of systematic errors may be manipulated. Once a procedural operation has been made explicit by incorporation into the codified rules, it is possible to observe the effect of altering a rule upon the degree of co-variation between content characteristics and pragmatical responses. Hence, it is possible to improve a set of procedures by continually modifying the rules in order to retain those which are the most productive.

By discovering those procedures which tend to provide the largest correlations, a body of technical propositions may be evolved which state the conditions for attaining maximum validity. Such propositions will serve to direct the design of classification rules and to increase the efficiency of content analysis research.

In the same way, the validity of other operations connected with content analysis may be tested. For example, it might be desirable to introduce rating-scales to provide weights for degree of *prominence* by taking account of the page location, size, position and other physical characteristics of the sign-vehicles and their surroundings. It is possible to study the validity of such an additional content analysis operation.

If the frequencies for the semantical content categories are weighted for prominence or some other characteristic, like *generality* (i.e., the extent to which an assertion approximates the degree of generality of the content category), or *intensity of attitude* (i.e., degree of favorableness or unfavorableness), there is involved a special problem which is usually not recognized. Weighted frequencies are the product of unweighted frequencies and their weights. If, for example, there are ten occurrences of assertions which characterize the enemy as dishonest, five of which are given a rating of 3 for prominence, and the other five of which are given a rating of 1 for prominence, the frequency of assertions that the enemy is dishonest, when weighted for prominence, is $5 \times 3 + 5 \times 1 = 20$. Now, the multiplication of frequencies by weights makes the implicit assumption that there are specific transformation formulae which equate a definite number of assertions at one scale-interval of the weighted characteristic to a definite number at each of the other scale-intervals. In the case of the above example, the assumption is that three occurrences of an assertion with the degree of prominence rated as one are identical with one assertion with the degree of prominence rated as three. In practice, however, it is usually possible only to defend giving a *higher* weight to the latter. But one is unable to defend the assigning of a *particular numerical value*. There is usually no justification for the quantitative transformation formulae.

Quantitative transformation formulae assert an identity. With respect to *what* does the identity hold? Presumably, with respect to a variable which is a function of both the content category and the charactersitic for which the weighting is done. The test of the adequacy of weighting is therefore again by inference from the additional productivity obtained by use of the weights. If we find that a set of weights for prominence increases the degree of co-variation between a content characteristic and a pragmatical response, we conclude that the weighting is, at least to some extent, justifiable. The best set of weighting procedures is the one which provides the greatest number of correlations and the largest correlations. Consequently, the adequacy of the quantitative transformation formulae entailed by the use of a weighting procedure may be tested by observing the effects of altering the weighting procedures.

In the same way, the adequacy of indices which combine the frequencies for various content characteristics may be tested. For example, an index to the overall degree of favorableness-unfavorableness (imbalance) may be designed to vary with the total number of *all* assertions in the communications or the total number of *relevant* assertions, or both.* The best choice is the index which provides the largest correlations.

When the procedural rules of a content analysis are modified only slightly, the effect on the classification operations may be considerable. For example, if one has an elaborate set of rules for classifying characterizors as attributions of immorality, the addition of a rule to the effect that attributions of political unskilfulness which result in deprivations to the public (negligence) are also to be classified as "immorality" may make a considerable difference. Two procedures identical in every detail, except that one has this additional rule on "negligence," may provide grossly different frequencies because, in the absence of this particular rule, many assertions were classified only as "unskilful," not as both "unskilful" and "immoral." Thus slight differences in the classification rules, as well as differences in the observational standpoint of the content analysts, may make a considerable difference in the content analysis results.

The consequence of this situation is that it is unsafe to assume that the procedures employed in a particular content analysis have the degree of validity which has been established for similar procedures.*

In the absence of knowledge about the extent to which alterations of the procedures introduce new errors, we are

---

* Cf. Irving L. Janis and Raymond H. Fadner, "A Coefficient of Imbalance for Content Analysis," *Psychometrika 8:* 105-119, June, 1943. (Chapter VIII of the present book).

* The same statement may be made about reliability. Spurious errors tend to decrease reliability; modifications of the classification rules may entail new difficulties in making judgments. It follows, therefore, that reliability should be retested for every application of content analysis which employs new personnel to perform the classification operations or which introduces changes in the rules.

forced to take a position of extreme skepticism. Every content analysis study, therefore, is required to provide some evidence of validity. This means that, for the present, research projects which intend to provide *purely descriptive information* about content—without testing any relationships exhibited by the content data—should be avoided. Content analysis studies in the fields of descriptive sociology and political science are usually intended to provide a description of the contents of communications occurring at a particular historical time and place. The weight of the content analysis data obtained from such studies will be higher if some relationships are shown between these data and pragmatical responses of the communicator and/or the audience.

Each application of content analysis should provide some evidence that the frequencies it reports are not the results of a random grouping together of sign-vehicles. This extreme skepticism is necessary because, (a) the analysts who do the classifying may have been extremely unskilled and/or biased, or (b) the classification rules may have been incorrect in defining the categories which are the content characteristics under investigation. Doubts about the analysts are removed to a considerable extent by showing that interanalyst reliability is high. But a reliable procedure may still be grossly invalid because of faulty rules. Extreme skepticism regarding systematic errors is unnecessary, once it is shown that a set of obtained frequencies for at least one category is related to some other variable in the communicative process. And with each additional relationship into which the content analysis results enter, the probability becomes higher that the particular content analysis technique is valid.

This suggests a general principle for content analysis research: The results obtained from each application of a content analysis technique should be fully exploited by elaborating as many relationships as possible. Some of the relationships which are found may be of little scientific value because they simply confirm the obvious. Nevertheless, such banal results serve to increase the probability that the scientifically interesting relationships established by use of the same procedures are not spurious. Hence, the confirmation of any hypothesis about content characteristics, no matter how obvious, has the technical value of increasing the degree of validity of the procedures which were employed.

Indirect validation has some important consequences in connection with attempts to disconfirm hypotheses. It is obvious that a finding of no relationship between a content characteristic and another variable does not constitute conclusive evidence that a relationship is absent. This limitation is quite aside from the necessity for replication and the difficulties of confirming a null hypothesis which are entailed by the postulates of the probability theory. It is a consequence of relying upon indirect validation that failure to find a relationship may be accounted for by errors of commission or of omission. Even minor errors which do not interfere with the emergence of some relationships, may be sufficient to obscure the particular relationship which is being tested. Hence, negative results are open to question, even if the procedures have a fair degree of validity. Only if the procedures have a very high degree of preëstablished validity are the content analysis results useful in disconfirming hypotheses. Therefore, another principle is suggested for designing content analysis research: Ignore improbable hypotheses, because negative content analysis results will fail to increase substantially the probability that an hypothesis is false.*

Throughout this paper, validity has been discussed in terms of establishing relationships between content characteristics and other variables. It is relevant to consider the various types of relationships and their measurement.

In inferring validity from the confirmation of hypotheses about relationships, the type of relationship specified by the hypothesis affects the *weight* of the evidence of validity. The probability is increased in varying degrees, according to the type of relationship from which the inference is drawn.

In general, the more closely the relationship approximates that of quantitative co-variation between the content characteristic and some pragmatical characteristic which is most directly tied up with semantical signification responses, the

---

* This maxim simply asserts that one should be "opportunistic" about selecting hypotheses to test, because negative results are uninteresting. It should not be interpreted to mean that hunches about subtle hypotheses, which *others* think are improbable, should be ignored.

higher the probability that the content characteristics which enter into that relationship are validly measured. This conclusion is based on the assumption that validity implies a one-to-one correspondence between individual signs and the signification responses of sign-interpreters. The relationship which most closely approximates testing the one-to-one correspondence—the relationship which is least indirect—has the greatest weight as evidence of validity.

This general principle serves to order the varieties of relationships into which content characteristics may enter. It is useful for the investigator to keep this in mind in making decisions between alternative hypotheses the testing of which he may consider. Just to exemplify a few of the implications of this proposition, the following decisions would be indicated in the interest of increasing the degree of validity of content analysis procedures: *

a. Hypotheses involving characteristics of the communicator, rather than characteristics of environmental conditions (e.g., political affiliations of the communicator as against historical political events).

b. Hypotheses involving fluctuating personality traits of the communicator which are altered by immediate changes in the environment, as against highly stable ones (e.g., attitudes as against general intelligence).

c. Hypotheses involving temporally immediate audience reactions, rather than remote ones (e.g., immediate attitude-change as against voting behavior).

d. Hypotheses involving the predispositional characteristics in the immediate social situation in which the communication takes place, rather than predispositional

---

* The statistical types of relationships ranked in order of the highest weight are as follows:

1. Relationships between quantitative values of the content characteristic and one or more other quantitative variables (total, partial and multiple correlation).

2. Relationships between quantitative values of a content characteristic and one or more other nonquantitative variables (analysis of variance).

3. Relationships between the rank order values of a content characteristic and the rank order values of another variable (rank order correlation).

4. Relationships between a nonquantitative content characteristic—evaluated on the basis of content data—and another nonquantitative variable (contingency).

characteristics of the general social milieu (e.g., aggressiveness of public opinion in the United States).

6. *Summary*

The problem of validating semantical content analysis is an extremely serious one, because the operations require judgments of *meanings* which are attributed to the sign-vehicles in a communication by a given audience or by a given communicator. Such judgments may be in error, because the procedural rules may entail faulty classification *(systematic errors)*, or because the content analyst may make incorrect judgments of signification responses in those cases which are not explicitly covered by the rules *(spurious errors)*. Without a validation procedure, it would be necessary to accept or reject content analysis results solely upon the basis of *a priori* faith in the analyst and in his procedures. The purpose of a method of validation is to provide evidence that systematic and spurious errors occur infrequently.

Since there is no available method for testing directly the significations responses to sign-vehicles, an indirect validation procedure is proposed—namely, inferring validity from productivity. The following principle of validation appears to be defensible: The larger the number of relationships established by use of a content analysis technique, the higher the probability that the procedure estimate signification responses correctly, and hence the higher the degree of validity. This indirect method of validation is based on the procedures used for the determination of the meaning of words in everyday life.

The use of this indirect method of validation entails certain consequences for the design of content analysis researches. These may be summarized in the form of technological principles:

1. The classification rules should be as explicit as possible.
2. Content analysis procedures—classification rules, rating-scales for the purpose of weighting, indices, etc.—can be systematically improved by selecting those which provide the largest correlations between content characteristics and other (pragmatical) variables.
3. Every application of a content analysis technique should

present some evidence of validity by showing some relationships between content characteristics and other variables.

4. Content analysis should not be used to disconfirm hypotheses; improbable hypotheses should be ignored.

5. In choosing hypotheses to test by the use of content analysis, the decision should be in favor of those which most closely approximate the following type of relationship: a quantitative co-variation between a content characteristic and a pragmatical response which is directly mediated by the communication.

Chapter 5

THE RELIABILITY OF CONTENT
ANALYSIS CATEGORIES *

A DISTINGUISHING characteristic of content analysis, as contrasted with other techniques of describing communications, is its quantitative aspect. Content analysis aims at a classification of content in more precise, numerical terms than is provided by impressionistic "more or less" judgments of "either-or."

The results of content analysis, like those of other processes of measurement, must meet certain conditions of reliability before they can be accepted as data for hypotheses. By the reliability of a measurement with respect to a given variable is meant the constancy of its results as that variable assumes different values. The variables usually considered are: the measuring event (e.g., the same person using the same ruler in successive measurements of the same object); the measuring instrument (e.g., different "forms" of an intelligence test); the person doing the measuring (e.g., different eyewitnesses of the same event).

The importance of reliability rests on the assurance it provides that the data obtained are independent of the measuring event, instrument or person. Reliable data, by defini-

* Revised from Documents 40 and 41, Experimental Division for the Study of Wartime Communications, Library of Congress.

tion, are data that remain constant throughout variations in the measuring process.

This study is concerned with the reliability of content analysis data obtained by different analysts. In what degree are the results of a content analysis independent of the specific analyst—that is, in what degree would other analysts arrive at the same results?

The reliability may, of course, differ for different types of content, and when different rules of classification are applied. Some of these differences will be examined with a view to determining the conditions for maximum reliability.

For certain investigations it has been found relevant to quantify the content of political communications in terms of two kinds of categories: those of "direction," and those of "standard." The former characterize the content as to favorable or unfavorable presentation of specific referents. The categories of standard describe the content with respect to the kinds of characteristics presented as favorable or unfavorable.

The categories of standard most frequently used are "strength-weakness" and "morality-immorality." "Strength-weakness" includes any property characterizing a referent with respect to its military, economic, diplomatic or ideological power—e.g., its army is winning or losing; its production is increasing or decreasing; it is gaining or losing allies; its policies are being supported or attacked. "Morality-immorality" characterizations are those which indicate the referent's conformity or nonconformity to norms of morality—e.g., the breaking or keeping of promises; heroism or cowardice; patriotism or treason. The categories of direction—"favorable" and "unfavorable," in their ordinary sense, may be used either separately or in conjunction with the above or other categories of standard.

Several studies were undertaken to measure the reliability of the categories of standard and direction, both separately and when applied together, under various conditions of training.

PART A

Reliability of the Categories of Standard

The content analyzed in this study consisted of 500 front-page headlines selected at random from the fifth issue of every other month, throughout 1941, of ten American newspapers.* All headlines on the front page were included; they were not selected, as is usually done, on the basis of the presence of symbols included in a previously prepared list. Approximately 50 headlines were chosen at random from each newspaper, so as to provide a sample of 500 headlines.

To the key categories of "strength" (S) and "morality" (M) were added: a category of the joint occurrence of S and M—"both" (B); a category of the occurrence of neither S nor M—"neither" (N); and a category for the headlines "unintelligible" (U) to the analyst. The following are specimen headlines belonging to each of the categories:

S: RUSSIANS RECAPTURE ROSTOV.
M: HEROISM OF ARMY NURSES EXTOLLED.
B: ATROCITIES CHARGED TO ADVANCING NAZIS.
N: CHURCHILL ADDRESSES PARLIAMENT.
U: D.C. CURRENTS SHOCK INVESTIGATOR.

The 500 headlines were classified independently by eight analysts on two separate occasions, spaced ten weeks apart. In the first classification (hereafter referred to as #I), no explicit rules for the interpretation of the categories were given; the analysts were to reply on their own understanding of the terms, and according to whatever familiarity they had with the procedures of classification previously used. A few general explanations were made, however, such as that a headline could be classified N if it was altogether "non-political" or if it was "political" but concerned neither strength-weakness nor morality-immorality.

In the second classification (#II), the analysts were instructed in the use of an explicit set of rules for the appli-

* The newspapers were: Chicago Daily News, Chicago Tribune, Christian Science Monitor, Cleveland Plain-Dealer, St. Louis Post-Dispatch, Kansas City Star, Louisville Courier-Journal, New York Daily News, New York Times and San Francisco Examiner.

cation of the categories. These rules detailed the kinds of characteristics and presentations to be included under each of the categories, and specified the classification to be made in certain types of borderline cases.[1] The purpose of #II was to gauge the extent to which the level of reliability can be raised by more intensive training and more detailed rules of classification.

The reliability data will be presented in terms of two units: entries and decisions.

Each single classification is an *entry;* the classification of 500 headlines by each of eight analysts yields a total of 4000 entries.

A *decision* is the application of a distinct category by one or more analysts in the classification of each headline. The number of decisions for each headline is the number of different categories applied by the individual analysts to the headline. The minimum number of decisions possible is 500—the result if all the analysts agree on some one category for each of the 500 headlines. The maximum number of decisions possible is 2500—the result if all five categories are applied to each of the 500 headlines. Every decision has a level—i.e., a numerical value—equal to the number of analysts (1 to 8) concurring in the decision. Thus, if four analysts classify a headline as belonging to one category, three analysts to another category, and one analyst to a third category, there are for that headline three decisions, whose levels are 4, 3, and 1, respectively.

1. *Individual Reliabilities*

The reliability of any analyst with respect to the group is the extent of his agreement with the rest of the group. Individual reliability is, then, measured by averaging the levels of the decisions in which the individual concurred—since these levels represent the number of analysts (including the individual himself) who agreed with each of his classifications. This average level is here expressed as a per cent of the maximum level, 8, which represents unanimity and therefore reliability of 100%.

In #I the individual reliabilities averaged 81%, within confidence limits (at .95) of 77% to 85%. In #II the average individual reliability increased significantly to 91%, within confidence limits of 90% to 93%.

It is of interest to observe that, even without a detailed explanation of the categories (#I), a reliability as high as 81% was attained. More important, a specification of detailed rules of classification succeeded in raising the reliability by fully 10%. Thus, even such seemingly vague categories as "strength" and "morality" can be applied to newspaper headlines with over 90% agreement when rules for the classification are provided.

2. *Reliability of the Separate Categories*

An important aspect of the reliability problem is the relative reliability of the categories used in the classification. To what extent was there agreement in the application of each of the categories?

The most direct measure of a category's reliability—hereafter referred to as its *direct reliability*—is the average level of all the decisions in the category expressed as a per cent of the maximum level. Table 1 gives the direct reliabilities.*

TABLE 1

DIRECT RELIABILITIES OF THE CATEGORIES,
IN PER CENT

	S	M	B	N
#I	71	35	40	65
#II	86	41	58	82

As given in Table 1, the order of reliability of the categories was highest for S, followed respectively by N, B, and and M, in both #I and #II.

The difference between the reliabilities of the key categories, S and M, is striking, the reliability of S being more than twice that of M.

As in the case of the individual reliabilities, here again

---

* Since there were so few U entries (2% of all entries in #I and less than 1% in #II), and since U represents a residual category of no independent interest, data concerning this category have been excluded from all computations, unless otherwise specified. The number of U entries fell sharply from 86 in #I to 6 in #II—a partial indication of the success of the rules in clarifying the application of the other categories.

#II showed a marked improvement over #I, for all four categories.

The direct reliability is a composite reliability of the group. That is, it represents the results of no single analyst (nor even of an "average" analyst), but deals with the results of the entire group as though it were a single individual. In so doing, it exaggerates differences but minimizes similarities in the classifications of the analysts. A unanimous agreement is counted once in computing the direct reliability, but each disagreement counts separately. Thus, the direct reliability is lower than that of any individual analyst. Hence this measure may be interpreted as the lowest reliability (by a cumulation of individual deviations) with which a category is applied. As Table 1 shows, this "lower limit" is about 80% for S and N, but no more than about 40% or 50% for B and M.

The reliability which the "average" analyst had in the use of each category may be computed by averaging the *individual reliabilities* in that category. This measure, *the mean reliability,* is given in Table 2.

TABLE 2

MEAN RELIABILITIES OF THE CATEGORIES,
IN PER CENT

	S	M	B	N
#I	87	51	66	79
#II	95	66	77	92

The comparative reliabilities of the categories by this measure conform to those of the direct reliability measure.

It is to be noted, however, that the *mean reliabilities* are about 15% higher in absolute magnitude than the corresponding direct reliabilities. This is due to the fact that the former do not take into account variations among individuals in the *frequencies* with which they applied that category: the reliability of each individual for a specific category enters into the mean reliability for that category with the same weight as the reliability of each of the other individuals. Now, the relation between an individual's reliability in a category and his frequency of entries in that category is this:

when he has a high reliability in a specific category, most other analysts must have applied that category whenever he did, and the frequencies of their entries in that category will therefore be as high as or higher than his. If, on the other hand, his frequency is greater, the others could not have applied the category whenever he did, and therefore his reliability will be lower. Thus, a higher than average frequency of entries by an individual in a specific category is correlated with a low reliability of the individual for that category (as compared with the other individuals), and a lower than average frequency is correlated with a higher reliability.

Consequently, the mean reliability of a category can be taken as a satisfactory measure of its reliability only when the frequencies with which that category is applied are not intrinsically important. This would be true if the category in question were not one of an exhaustive set of categories, so that the omission of doubtful cases would not introduce errors. If, however, as in the present procedure, an item not classified in one category must be classified in another category, frequencies of entries in each category must be taken into account in estimating the reliability of each category. So here a measure must be adopted which is a function of the frequencies of entries made by each individual.

Such a measure, the *weighted reliability*, is obtained by weighting each individual's reliability in the category by the frequency of his entries in that category, with the results given in Table 3.

TABLE 3

WEIGHTED RELIABILITIES OF THE CATEGORIES,
IN PER CENT

	S	M	B	N
#I	79	50	62	78
#II	95	58	76	92

This measure, giving results intermediate between the *direct* and *mean* reliabilities, is the most useful for present purposes, since it neither exaggerates disagreements in classification nor ignores variations in frequency of application of any given category. The *direct reliability* may be regarded as a measure of minimal extent of agreement; the *mean reli-*

ability gives a maximum—relevant when any category is to be applied independently of the others.

By all the measures, and in both #I and #II, the order of the reliability of the categories was: S, N, B, M. Between S and M, the key categories, there was a considerable difference in the reliability of their application.

An illuminating comparison of the reliabilities of the categories, among themselves and from #I to#II, is provided by the distribution by levels of the decisions in each category (Table 4).

TABLE 4

PER CENT OF DECISIONS IN EACH CATEGORY,
BY LEVELS

	S		M		B		N	
Level	I	II	I	II	I	II	I	II
8	46	73	3	5	9	20	30	58
7	8	7	3	0	9	15	15	15
6	7	2	5	8	1	10	9	6
5	5	3	8	0	8	7	8	1
4	6	2	13	18	7	5	8	6
3	7	1	26	3	17	14	8	3
2	6	4	15	5	14	11	9	2
1	15	7	28	61	35	18	12	9
Total	100	99**	101**	100	100	100	99**	100

** Deviations from 100 due to approximations to nearest whole percent.

Table 4 indicates that the improved reliability from #I to #II is in large part accounted for by shifts of the extremes; increases in the proportion of decisions of maximum agreement (levels 7 and 8); and decreases in the proportion of decisions at the levels of minimum agreement (1 and 2). This suggests that the practice provided by #I and the rules supplied in #II served mainly to eliminate erratic judgments. There were still difficulties in classification, but a single analyst differed from the other seven much less often than in #I. The cumulative per cents of decisions at each level are presented graphically in Figure 1, page 91).

The graph shows clearly not only the improved reliability

figure **1**

CUMULATIVE PER CENT OF DECISIONS
BY LEVELS

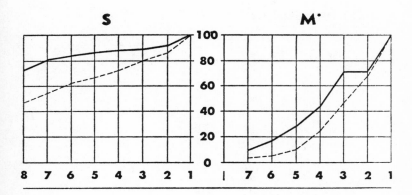

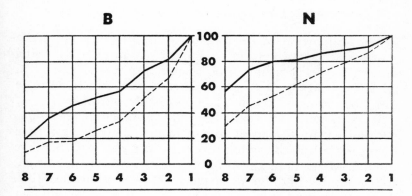

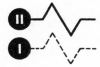

* Based on seven analysts.

from #I to #II, but also the sharp differences which exist between the reliabilities of the categories.

The shifts in the extreme decision-levels exhibited in Table 4, and responsible in large part for the improvement in reliability from #I to #II are made especially striking when the data for the separate categories are combined (Table 5).

TABLE 5

DISTRIBUTION OF ALL DECISIONS * BY LEVELS

Level	Number		Per Cent	
	I	II	I	II
8	262	376	32	59
7	82	62	10	10
6	55	26	7	4
5	48	17	6	3
4	57	29	7	5
3	74	21	9	3
2	71	29	9	5
1	168	80	21	13
Total	817	640	101 **	102 **

* U decisions included.
** Deviations from 100 due to approximations to nearest whole per cent.

The proportion of unanimous decisions (level 8) in the category set as a whole increased 27% from #I to #II. The decisions at level 7 showed no change in proportion; and in all levels below 7 there were decreases, the largest decrease (8%) occurring at the level of minimum agreement.

It is noteworthy that the total number of decisions decreased from 817 in #I to 640 in #II. This decrease is a direct indication of the improvement in reliability, since the number of decisions per headline corresponds, by definition, to the number of different categories applied to the headline. As the total number of decisions approaches 500 (the number of headlines), inter-analyst agreement approaches unanimity. Thus, #II succeeded in eliminating 177, or over half, of the "deviant" decisions (i.e., decisions in excess of 500).

3. Reliability of the Category Set

So far, we have considered individual reliabilities and the reliabilities of the separate categories. It is useful also to analyze the data from the viewpoint of "overall" reliability —the reliability of the category set as applied by the group of analysts as a whole.

Although the individual reliabilities were based on the use of all the categories, the measure was defined by a separate comparison of each individual's results with those of the rest of the group. The results of the group in its entirety provide a basis for the measure of "overall" reliability.

In computing the reliabilities of the individual analysts and of the separate categories, there was no alternative to averaging all the decisions, because for each headline there can be no more than one decision *per analyst* (the decision in which he shared), nor more than one decision *per category* (by definition of "decision"). But for the classification as a whole, there can be, and frequently are, several decisions for each headline. To measure the overall reliability, therefore, we can choose the one decision in each headline to be regarded as expressing the "group-judgment" and compute the average level of this decision. The decision of highest level for each headline was chosen for this purpose.*

Table 6 gives the distribution of headlines by highest decision level.†

Table 6 shows that 52% of the headlines were classified in #I with unanimous agreement, and 75% in #II. These figures deserve emphasis: With additional practice and when detailed rules were provided, all eight analysts agreed on the classification of three-fourths of all the headlines. Six or more of the eight analysts were in agreement in classifying 80% of all the headlines in #1, and 93% in #II. At the other extreme, only 10% of the headlines in #I, and only 5% in

* Since only the level, and not the category, of the decision enters into the measure, headlines where two or more decisions shared the highest level introduce no complication. The criterion of plurality rather than majority was adopted because, in many of the headlines, no decision expressed a concurrence of a majority of the analysts.

† There were no headlines whose highest decision level was 2 to 1. The highest decision level could not possibly have been 1, since there were 8 analysts, and only 5 categories available to them. That no headline was classified in the same way by no more than 2 analysts is, however, an empirical result.

TABLE 6

DISTRIBUTION OF HEADLINES BY HIGHEST
DECISION LEVEL

Highest	Number		Per Cent	
Level	I	II	I	II
8	262	376	52	75
7	82	62	16	12
6	55	26	11	5
5	48	17	10	3
4	41	18	8	4
3	12	1	2	1
Total	500	500	99 *	100

* Deviation from 100 due to approximation to nearest whole per cent.

#II, were classified with less than a majority of the analysts concurring.

Figure 2 (page 95) presents graphically the cumulative per cent of headlines classified at each level of highest decision.

By averaging the highest decision levels and expressing the average as a per cent of the maximum level, an overall reliability of 86% is obtained for #I, and 93.5% for #II, with confidence limits of 84.5%–87.5% and 92%–95%, respectively.*

4. *Conclusions*

The purpose of this study was twofold: (1) to determine the reliability with which newspaper headlines can be classified into the categories of STRENGTH-WEAKNESS and MORALITY-IMMORALITY, and (2) to appraise the effect on this reliability of additional training and the provision of detailed rules of classification. Concerning these questions, the study points to the following conclusions:

1. The mean of the individual analysts' reliabilities was about 90%, having increased from about 80%. The assumption is confirmed, therefore, that the reliability of application

---

* These results are somewhat higher than the average individual reliabilities (81% and 91%), because the measure of overall reliability is based on the decision of maximum agreement for each headline, rather than on the decision in which the given analyst concurred.

figure 2

CUMULATIVE PER CENT OF HEADLINES
BY HIGHEST DECISION LEVEL

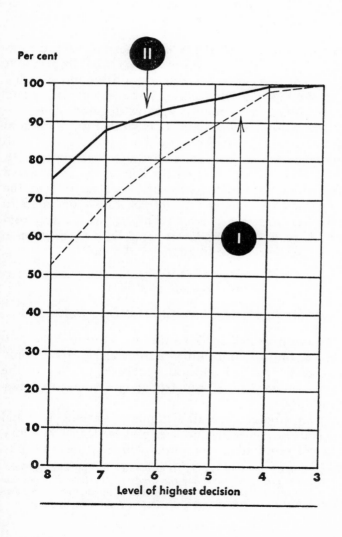

of these content analysis categories to newspaper headlines can be significantly increased by more intensive training of the analysts, and by the provision of more detailed rules of classification.

2. The reliabilities of the categories were about 95% for S, 55% for M, 75% for B, and 90% for N, having increased from about 80%, 50%, 60%, and 75%, respectively. The reliabilities of M and B are thus considerably lower than those of S and N, and point to the need for more elaborate and precise rules for their application than were provided here.

The highest decision level per headline was, on the average, about 93% of the maximum, an increase from about 86%. The high percentage for this overall reliability is due in part to the fact that the most reliable categories, S and N, were also the most frequently applied, together constituting over 80% of all the decisions. Our sample was a random selection of front-page headlines, so that this overall reliability is presumably applicable for analyses of such content. If, however, the method of selecting the content to be analyzed differs from the one used here, in such a way as to alter the relative frequencies of S and N references as compared to M and B references, the overall reliability will differ from that found here, and will be lower roughly in proportion to the decrease in the relative frequencies of S and N.

Part B

Reliability of the Categories of Direction

The content classified in this study to determine the reliability of "favorable" and "unfavorable" categories of presentation consisted of 726 political symbols appearing in the previously used sample of 500 front-page American newspaper headlines.

"Political symbols" were all symbols of nations, national groups, agencies, ideologies, policies and leaders.* The analysts were not required to determine which symbols were to

* The definition of "political symbol" is elaborated in Appendix A, Document No. 41, *Experimental Division for the Study of Wartime Communications*, Library of Congress, p. 23. All such symbols in the sample were classified; but only 348 of the 500 headlines contained any political symbols.

be classified; these were specified for each headline, beforehand.

The presentation of each symbol within the headline was classified into one of the following six categories of direction:

1. *Unqualified Positive* (+ +): Favorable presentation of the symbol, without explicit qualification of its favorable character:

BRITISH ADVANCE IN AFRICA

2. *Qualified Positive* (— +): A basically favorable presentation, with unfavorable aspects clearly involved:

MARINES TAKE TARAWA; CASUALTIES HIGH

3. *Unqualified Negative* (— —): Unqualified unfavorable presentation:

PLANE PRODUCTION IN GERMANY SAGS

4. *Qualified Negative* (+ —): Basically unfavorable, with favorable or ameliorating aspects clearly involved:

NAZIS RETREAT; LINES SHORTENED

5. Balanced (B ±): Both favorable and unfavorable presentations clearly and equally involved:

REDS ADVANCE IN NORTH; WITHDRAW IN SOUTH

6. No Direction (O): Presentations involving neither favorable nor unfavorable aspects:

CONGRESS PASSES TAX BILL

A detailed set of rules for classifying the symbols into the six categories was formulated,* and a group of six analysts was trained in the use of these rules. All the analysts were already familiar with categories of favorable and unfavorable presentation, and in addition were given approximately seven hours of practice and instruction in the use of the specific categories employed in this study.

Each analyst then independently classified the political symbols in the sample into the six categories provided, using one and only one category per symbol.

The study was devised to provide answers to the following questions:

* See Appendix B, Document No. 41, pp. 24-28.

1. What is the level of reliability obtainable for the set of categories as a whole? What is the significance of this level of reliability? Does it indicate a need for additional training, with more precise rules? Or does it indicate that the distinctions between some of the categories themselves are not clear enough for reliable application?

2. Which of the categories are most reliably, and which least reliably, applied: Can the qualified directional categories be applied with as much interanalyst agreement as the categories of unqualified direction? Can analysts reliably distinguish between balanced and nondirectional presentation of political symbols?

3. By combining various of the original ("key") categories (e.g., qualified positive with the unqualified positive) into a "basically positive" category, several new sets of directional categories can be constructed. What are the comparative reliabilities of these sets? More particularly, which combinations of the key categories will result in the highest reliability for the entire set? What light do these results throw on the difficulty of distinguishing reliably between related key categories?

4. With the rules and training involved in this study, what is the highest reliability with which directional categories can be applied when the results are reported in units customarily employed in content analysis investigations? The measures of reliability previously used are based on agreement in the classification of each single symbol occurrence. All that is needed for most studies, however, is agreement in frequencies of groupings of such occurrences; e.g., all occurrences of the symbol GREAT BRITAIN in a certain category per a specified number of issues of a given newspaper. We measure the reliability in these terms by coefficients of correlation—where the frequencies per symbol per category for each analyst are correlated with those of every other analyst. In terms of this measure, we can also judge the effect on reliability of increasing or decreasing the number of issues of a newspaper whose symbol frequencies in the various categories are combined into unit results.

1. Reliability of the Key Set of Categories

Individual reliabilities for the key set of categories averaged 75.3%, with confidence limits fixing a range of 73.0%-77.6%.

It may be noted that the corresponding reliability for the categories of standard was 91% (in #II). Headlines apparently can be less reliably classified according to favorable or unfavorable presentation than according to the characteristics presented as favorable or unfavorable. However, categories of direction less detailed than the key set (to be discussed later) yield reliabilities much closer to those for the categories of standard.

The overall reliability of the key set can be measured, as before (A-3), in terms of the maximum decision-level for each symbol. The overall reliability is 81.0%, with confidence limits of 79.5%-82.5%. In comparison with the corresponding figure of 93.5% for the categories of standard, this appears to be an unsatisfactorily low reliability. The relatively low extent of agreement in the directional classification is brought out in the distribution of symbols by highest decision-level (Table 7).

TABLE 7

DISTRIBUTION OF SYMBOLS BY HIGHEST DECISION-LEVEL

Highest Decision-Level	Per Cent	Cumulative Per Cent
6	45	45
5	18	63
4	17	80
3	17	97
2	3	100

Table 7 shows that not even two-thirds of the symbols were classified in the same category by at least five of the six analysts; and only 80% of the symbols were classified in the same way by a majority of the analysts.

To what is this low level of reliability to be attributed? Could this same set of categories have been applied with a significantly higher reliability if the analysts had been given more intensive training with more precise rules of classification? Or are some of the categories themselves not clear and distinct enough for more reliable application to the sample content? To answer these questions, the comparative reliabilities of the separate categories in the set are next considered.

2. Comparative Reliabilities of the Key Categories

The *weighted reliabilities* of the separate categories (as previously defined, p. 89) are given in Table 8.

TABLE 8

WEIGHTED RELIABILITIES OF THE KEY CATEGORIES, IN PER CENT

$\dfrac{++}{84}$	$\dfrac{-+}{52}$	$\dfrac{O}{75}$	$\dfrac{+-}{40}$	$\dfrac{--}{84}$	$\dfrac{B\pm}{47}$

The order of reliability is, then: the unqualified direction categories highest, the "O" category next, and the qualified and the balanced direction categories lowest.

A more illuminating comparison of the categories is provided by the distribution of the decisions in each category by levels of agreement (Table 9).

TABLE 9

PER CENT OF DECISIONS IN EACH CATEGORY BY LEVELS OF AGREEMENT

Level	++	-+	O	+-	--	B±
6	40	2	24	2	41	3
5	14	6	12	2	12	4
4	12	10	11	5	9	7
3	10	15	14	16	10	11
2	10	24	13	23	11	15
1	15	45	26	51	17	61
Total *	101	102	100	99	100	101

* Deviations from 100 due to approximations to nearest whole per cent.

Table 9 shows a striking difference in the extent of agreement attained in the application of the qualified as compared with the unqualified directional categories. For the qualified categories, at least five of the six analysts agreed in only 8% of the decisions in those categories (sum of the percentages at levels 6 and 5), while the unqualified categories were applied with at least five of the six analysts in agreement in more than 50% of their decisions. For the "O" category the corresponding figure is 36%, and for "B ±" only 7%. Conversely, the decisions at the levels of least agreement (levels 2 and 1) constituted about 70% of all the qualified category decisions, but only about 25% of the decisions in the unqualified categories.

Figure 3 (page 103) depicts the cumulative per cent of decisions in each category by levels of agreement. The graphs clearly show the differences between the categories in their proportions of decisions at each level of agreement.

Both the *weighted reliabilities* (Table 8) and the distribution of decisions (Table 9) make plain that the categories of unqualified direction were far more reliable than the qualified categories. It is of interest to observe that the relatively high reliability of the unqualified categories can not be attributed to their infrequent use—other categories being applied in cases of doubt; on the contrary, the unqualified categories were applied in about twice as many decisions as were the qualified categories. Whether the relatively low reliability of the qualified categories was due to difficulty in distinguishing between qualified positive and qualified negative presentation, will be discussed in the next section.

The sharp difference in reliability between the "O" and the "B ±" categories (75% and 47%) should also be emphasized. Neutral presentations are far more easily recognized as such when favorable and unfavorable aspects are equally present. We shall later consider whether the low reliability of the "B ±" category is due to the confusion of the latter with "O" presentation or with other presentations, e.g., the qualified.

Finally, the symmetry of the favorable and unfavorable categories is worthy of note. The level of reliability depends much more on whether the category is qualified than on whether it is a category of basically favorable or basically

unfavorable presentation. Both the unqualified categories—
"+ +" and "– –" were much closer to each other than those
of the unqualified categories (see Figure 3). Unqualified
deprivation and unqualified indulgence are both equally
easy to classify; qualified deprivation and qualified indulgence are both much more difficult to classify.

3. *Reliability of the Derived Sets*

Each of the "sets" about to be discussed consists of a group
of exhaustive categories, some of which are unaltered key categories and the others of which are derived by combining two
or more of the key categories into one compounded category.
Thus *Set 2,* for example, (regarding the key categories as Set
1) differs from the key set only in that "B ±" and "O" are
combined into a single category, "B,O." It is to be understood that there was no reclassification of the sample content
in terms of *Set 2.* Rather, the results of the original classification were retabulated on the basis of five categories:
"+ +", "– +", "+ –," "– –", and "B,O"; and similarly for
the other sets to be described. For example, if a given symbol
was classified by one analyst as "+ +," by three analysts as
"O," and by two analysts as "B ±," the tabulation for *Set 2*
would be: one entry in "+ +" and five entries in "B,O."

The purpose of considering these derived sets is the following: If a compound category has a significantly higher
reliability than its elements, it follows that the attempt to
distinguish between these elements results in a significantly
lower reliability, and that therefore no such distinction
should be made, so far as reliability is concerned. If, on the
other hand, the compound reliability is not significantly
higher than that of its elements, the distinction between the
elements is justified—again, so far as reliability is concerned.
If the elements have low reliabilities, it can be concluded (in
this case) that this is due to the confusion of the elements
with categories other than each other.

To obtain a single index of reliability for the elements
with which to compare the reliability of the compounded
category, we take the mean of the element-reliabilities, each
weighted by the number of entries in the corresponding
element. This is done because the more frequent element has

figure 3

CUMULATIVE PER CENT OF DECISIONS
BY LEVELS OF AGREEMENT

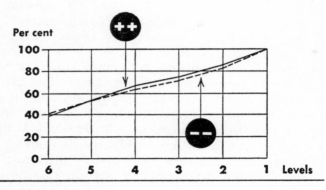

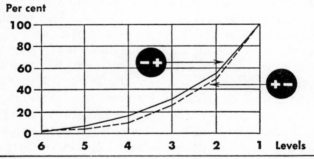

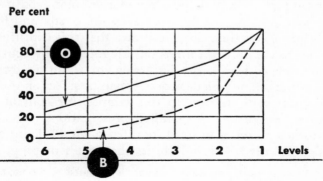

a greater effect on the reliability of the compounded category than does the less frequent element.

Set 2 is defined by the introduction of the compound "B,O." The reliability of the compound does not differ significantly* from that of its elements (97.0% as compared with 71.2%). The reliability of the entire set also differs non-significantly from that of the key set. The results show that the distinction between "B ±" and "O" does not entail any significant lowering of reliability, i.e., the amount of confusion between these categories is slight. This result is somewhat surprising, since the "B ±," and "O" categories are fairly similar, both applying to "neutral" presentations. It can be *partially* explained, however, by the fact that there were more than twice as many "O" decisions as "B ±" decisions, so that there were relatively few cases that afforded an opportunity for compounding split decisions. If the content analyzed had had a more equal distribution of "B ±" and "O" presentations, the reliability of "B,O" might very well have been significantly higher than the elements.

Set 3 differs from the key set by compounding the qualified directional categories "− +" and "+ −". The reliability of the compound is 58.9%, as compared with 48.0% for the elements, a statistically significant difference. The reliability of the entire set, however, is 77.0%, which does not differ significantly from the 75.3% of the key set. Thus, although the compound significantly increases the reliabilities of the element-categories concerned, it has little bearing on the overall result, because both elements together comprise only about one-fourth of all the decisions. It is clear, then, that the two categories of qualified directions *are* often confused with one another; but the fact that even the compound has a reliability of less than 60% indicates that this confusion is by no means the only factor responsible for their low reliabilities. Moreover, although the improvement resulting from compounding the qualified categories had no effect on the overall reliability with respect to this sample, for content with a greater proportion of qualified presentations (e.g., perhaps editorials rather than headlines) Set 3 would definitely have a significantly higher reliability than Set 1 or 2.

---

* Throughout this section, significance is measured by the t-test, .95 level.

Set 4 contains the compounds of both Sets 2 and 3. The reliabilities of these compounds have already been given. The overall reliability of Set 4 is 77.5%—a non-significant increase over the 75.3% of the key set. Thus, even with two compounded categories in the set, and despite the fact that these categories together comprise half of the decisions, the effect on the overall reliability is statistically negligible. The proportion of symbols classified in the same way by at least four analysts is 86%, as compared with 80% for Set 1, but the reliability based on the highest decision levels is only 2% higher than it is for the key set.

Set 5 combines three categories into one compound: "– +, B, + –." This combination was selected for attention because all three of the elements applied to presentations having both favorable and unfavorable aspects to some degree. The reliability of the compound was 64.1%, as compared with only 48.0% for its elements. The difference is clearly a significant one. Comparing this result with that for "– +, + –" alone (Set 3), we find that the addition of the "B ±" to this compound raised the reliability of the compound from 58.9% to 64.1%. These results indicate that the low reliability of the "B ±" category is due more to a confusion with the qualified categories than with "O." If the set of categories used, then, does not contain qualified directional categories, "B ±" might perhaps be combined with "O"; but if qualified categories are used, "B ±" presentations should be combined with them. The reliability of Set 5 as a whole is 78.4%—here we have for the first time a significant increase over the reliability of the key set. But that the reliability of the "– +, B, + –" compound is still so low (64.1%) suggests that the confusion is not basically among these three categories of mixed direction, but between them and the unqualified direction categories (See Set 7).

Set 6 is constructed by adding "O" to the compound of Set 5 which thus consists of all the "middle" categories, as opposed to the extremes of unqualified presentation: "– +, B, + –, O." The reliability of the compound is 74.2%, as compared with 60.0% for its elements, a significant difference of 14%. The addition of the "O" raised the reliability of the compound "– +, B, + –" (Set 5) from 64.1% to 74.2%. Thus, the observations previously made concerning the sources of confusion in the "B" category are also applicable to the "O" category. It is apparently difficult to distinguish reliably between the various "middle" categories. The reliability of Set 6 as a whole is 80.4%—not significantly better than that of Set 5—but here about 90% of the symbols were classified in the same way by at least four of the six analysts.

Set 7 combines the qualified and unqualified favorable categories into a compound of basically favorable direction; and the qualified and unqualified unfavorable categories were similarly compounded. The set thus consists of "+ +, − +", "− −, + −", "B ±", and "O." The reliability of the favorable compound is 87.1%, of the unfavorable compound 86.6%, with 77.9% and 74.4% for their elements, respectively—both significant differences. The reliability of these compounds not only is higher than that of any of the other compounds previously considered, but is even higher than the reliabilities of the unqualified categories themselves. There is little doubt, then, so far as reliability is concerned, that the qualified categories should be combined with the corresponding unqualified categories, rather than with each other and/or with the two "neutral" categories.* The reliability of Set 7 as a whole is 83.8%—significantly higher than that of any of the previous sets.

Set 8 differs from Set 7 only in that "B ±" and "O" are also compounded—yielding the set: "+ +, − +", "− −, + −", and "B,O." The reliabilities of these compounds have already been given. The overall reliability of Set 8, 84.3%, is not significantly higher than that of Set 7, but of course *is* significantly higher than the reliability of any of the other sets. Here, 77% of all the symbols were classified in the same way by at least 5 of the 6 analysts, and 93% by at least 4 of them.

Other sets than the ones chosen could also have been considered. But those discussed here seemed to comprise the most meaningful combinations, since they compound the two "neutral" categories, the two categories of "mixed" direction, and the basically favorable and basically unfavorable categories.

---

* This implies that "double coding"—classifying a presentation as both favorable and unfavorable, with perhaps a weight of .5-frequency for each occurrence—is not nearly as satisfactory in terms of reliability as requiring the analyst to determine which of the two basic directions is dominant in that occurrence.

The data thus far presented may be conveniently summarized in the following two tables.

TABLE 10

RELIABILITIES OF THE DERIVED SETS AND THEIR COMPOUNDS

Set	Compound	Reliability of Compound	Reliability of Elements	Mean of Individual Reliabilities	Reliability by Maximum Decision Level *
1				73-78	80-83
2	B,O	74	71	74-78	80-83
3	− +, + −	59**	48	76-79	81-84
4	B,O	74	71	76-79	82-84
	− +, + −	59**	48		
5	− +, B, + −	64**	48	77-80	82-85
6	− +, B, + −, O	74**	60	79-82	84-86
7	+ +, − +	87**	78	82-85	87-89
	− −, + −	87**	74		
8	+ +, − +	87**	78	83-85	87-90
	− −, + −	87**	74		
	B,O	74	71		

* Given in terms of confidence limits at the 95-level
** Significant increase over the reliability of the elements

TABLE 11

DISTRIBUTION OF SYMBOLS BY HIGHEST DECISION LEVEL, FOR THE DERIVED SETS, IN CUMULATIVE PER CENTS

High Level	\\ Set \\ 1	2	3	4	5	6	7	8
6	45	46	47	47	48	50	60	60
5	63	64	66	67	69	71	77	77
4	80	82	84	86	86	89	91	93
3	97	98	98	99	99	99	99	99
2	100	100	100	100	100	100	100	100

The conclusions to be drawn from the material presented in this section fall under two heads: (1) those concerning the compounded categories, and (2) those concerning the sets.

1. The "B ±" category can not be distinguished reliably

from the "O" nor from the categories of mixed direction. "B ±" had best be combined with either "O" or the two mixed categories, according to the hypotheses being tested by the content analysis. Considerable confusion results from the attempt to distinguish the "O" category from the categories of qualified direction. Standing alone, however, "O" does have a reliability of 75%—a high enough level for many purposes, in view of the stringency of the measure. The categories of qualified direction, though fairly often confused with one another, also tend to be confused with their corresponding unqualified directional categories. If the hypotheses being considered permit, it is more desirable to combine the qualified categories with the corresponding unqualified ones than with each other.

2. As the reader may have noticed, the sets have been numbered in ascending order of reliability, the key set having the lowest and Set 8 the highest reliability. The two most satisfactory sets, from the point of view of "meaningfulness" of their categories, as well as their reliability, are Sets 8 and 6, i.e., basically favorable, basically unfavorable, and neutral; and unqualified favorable, unqualified unfavorable, and the middle categories. Where the interest of the content analysis lies in the degree of imbalance* of the presentation of political symbols, Set 8 is preferable. If the interest is in the "extremism" of the directional presentation, Set 6 yields the highest reliability.

It should be emphasized that the conclusions which have been drawn concerning these sets were based on data obtained by retabulation rather than by reclassification. It may well be that if Set 8, for example, had been applied in the actual classification, its reliability would have been less than that obtained by regrouping the data from the application of the key set. It is a hypothesis worthy of future investigation that the reliability of a given set of categories is improved by the application of a more detailed set and a tabulation of the data in terms of the given set of categories. This point will be touched on in Section 4.

* See Janis, I. L., and Fadner, R. H., Chapter VIII of this book.

4. *Reliability by Grouped Frequencies*

It has been mentioned that the measures of reliability hitherto discussed are more stringent than necessary, in view of the frequency-units customarily employed in content analysis investigations. These strict indices of reliability measure the extent of interanalyst agreement in the classification of each single symbol occurrence. Such indices are particularly suited for determining the reliability of new and untested procedures of content analysis, and for evaluating the adequacy of analysts' training in the application of various sets of categories. For these indices make it possible to locate sources of error by revealing the categories between which it is most difficult for the analysts to distinguish.

The results of actual content analyses are usually reported as frequencies of presentations per specified quantities of content. For example, the analysis might report the fluctuation from month to month in the number of favorable, unfavorable and neutral presentations of the symbol (meaning-unit) GREAT BRITAIN in selected American newspapers. For such purposes, interanalyst reliability can be measured in terms of the agreement among the analysts as to the frequencies of the diverse presentations of given symbols per specified quantities of content. To determine the extent of agreement as to these grouped frequencies, coefficients of correlation may be used.

To this end, 688 of the 726 symbol-occurrences classified in this study, which were occurrences of 18 meaning-units,* were tallied for each analyst under each symbol in terms of the three categories of Set 8—favorable, unfavorable and neutral presentations—and the resulting distributions were correlated by pairing the distribution of each analyst with that of every other analyst.

There were fifteen such paired correlations, which ranged from .94 to .99, and averaged .97.† Clearly, Set 8 yields a very high degree of reliability.

---

* The meaning-units are indicated by the following symbols: Axis, Balkans, British Empire, Democracy, Germany, Great Britain, Hitler, Italy, Japan, Mexico, Near East, Occupied Countries, Roosevelt, United States, U. S. Government Agencies, U. S. Non-Government Agencies, U. S. Policies and Measures, U. S. S. R.

† In all correlations, zero-frequencies were eliminated.

The 688 symbol-occurrences were distributed in 472 front-page newspaper headlines. With approximately 13 headlines on each front page of the newspapers sampled, the frequencies grouped represented total occurrences in approximately 36 front pages, i.e., 36 separate issues. By summing the frequencies for so many issues, considerable opportunity is provided for cancellation of disagreements. We can ask, then, how much the reliability is lessened by grouping the frequencies in terms of one-half or one-fourth as many issues.

On the basis of 18 issues, the 15 paired correlations averaged .95, an insignificant decrease from the value obtained on the basis of 36 issues. Even when only nine issues constituted the frequency-unit, the correlations still were very high, averaging .94.

Samples for content analysis are chosen with two broad considerations in mind: (1) The sample must be representative of the universe from which it is drawn, and (2) it must be large enough to permit of reliable analysis. The results just discussed above bear directly on the second consideration. They clearly indicate that it is unnecessary, from the point of view of reliability, to select more than nine issues for the sample-unit; a larger number of issues would not appreciably increase the reliability of the analysis.

The qualification must be added, however, that this holds only for categories with an initially high reliability. With category sets of lower reliability, there are more disagreements to be cancelled out by combining the frequencies into larger groupings of issues.

PART C

*Reliability of Categories of Direction and Standard
Jointly Applied*

The studies previously discussed dealt with the reliabilities of the categories of standard and of direction applied separately. Content analyses in terms of the categories, however, usually involve their joint application. In these studies, use is made of such conjoint categories as "favorable strength," "unfavorable morality," etc. The reliability of these combined categories was investigated by I. L. Janis, R. H. Fadner and M. Janowitz.*

The material analyzed in their study, as in the preceding ones, consisted of newspaper content, with the difference that editorials were analyzed in addition to front-page headlines, and that foreign newspapers were included in the sample. Thirty-six issues were analyzed for their presentation of sixteen political symbols.†

The categories employed were: "favorable strength," "unfavorable strength" (weakness), "favorable morality," and "unfavorable morality" (immorality). A group of nine analysts, trained in the use of these categories, reported the total frequencies of the political symbol presentations in the 36 issues according to each of the categories. Each issue was then reanalyzed by a different member of the same group so that, in effect, there were obtained the results of two different groups classifying the same content. Reliability was then measured by coefficients of correlation between the results of the two "groups." Reliability of separate categories was not reported.

A retabulation of the data, in terms of categories of direction only, yielded a reliability coefficient of .85. This may be compared with the coefficient of .97 for the direction-categories reported above (p. 109). Several factors may account for this difference.

First, in the previous studies the specific symbol occurrences to be classified were marked beforehand for the analyst. In the study by Janis *et al.*, however, the analysts were required to determine for themselves the presence or absence of the relevant meaning units.‡

Secondly, the categories of direction were applied jointly with categories of standard, but only tabulated separately, whereas in the other study they were applied separately. The conjoint categories multiply opportunities for disagree-

* Reported in Document No. 32, *ibid.*, November 1, 1942. (Also in *Public Opinion Quarterly*, 7:293-296, summer, 1943).

† Both the size of the sample and the symbols classified closely approximated those of the previously discussed studies.

‡ The reliability of this operation in content analysis is reported in "The Differential Use of Flexible and Rigid Procedures of Content Analysis," by A. Geller, D. Kaplan and H. D. Lasswell, *Document No. 12, ibid.,* March 1, 1943. (Chapter VI of the present book).

ment. A presentation classified by one analyst as "favorable strength" might be classified by another as "unfavorable morality" (e.g., NAZIS RAZE RUSS VILLAGE), so that the retabulation shows a disagreement as to direction which, in fact, stems from a disagreement as to standard. If the classification were in terms of direction only, such disagreements could more easily be prevented.

Thirdly, another factor is that suggested as a hypothesis on p. 108—namely, that the reliability of a set of categories is higher when the classification is made in terms of detailed categories, which are then grouped for tabulation so as to reconstitute the original set. This was the procedure which resulted in the .97 correlation in the directional study: the six categories of Set 1 were applied, but the correlation was computed from a retabulation of the results into the three categories of Set 8.

It might be supposed that the difference between the two coefficients is also due to the fact that the Janis study included editorial content in the sample. That study, however, found no significant difference between the reliabilities for headline analysis and editorial analysis (.86 and .84, respectively).

The reliability of the set of conjoint categories as a whole was found to be .75. That this result is so much lower than the reliabilities previously reported for categories of standard and direction separately might be accounted for by the factors just discussed.

Where a correlation of .75 is thought to be an unsatisfactory level of reliability, an increase can be obtained by modifying the procedures of conjoint application so as to take account of these factors.

Chapter **6**

RECORDING AND CONTEXT UNITS:
FOUR WAYS OF CODING
EDITORIAL CONTENT *

DIFFERENT PROCEDURES for measuring newspaper content give somewhat dissimilar results. This report summarizes an experiment designed to compare four alternatitve procedures for the description of editorial matter. Two trained classifiers read the same material four times according to instructions that did not change save for a few selected technicalities.[1]

When the content of a newspaper is carefully read for descriptive purposes it is necessary to proceed as follows:

(1) Select the symbol list. This is made up of the words (unit symbols) or statements (sequence symbols) whose occurrence is to be recorded.

(2) Define the list. If the symbols are to be taken literally by the readers no problem of definition arises. Thus if "Hitler" is to be noted only when explicit mentioned, it is unnecessary to add any explanations. But if the purpose

---

* Appeared originally in the *Journalism Quarterly*, 19 (December 1942), 362-71.

[1] The details are found in Harold D. Lasswell and Associates, "The Politically Significant Content of the Press: Coding Procedures," *Journalism Quarterly*, 19 (March, 1942), p. 12.

113

is broader the classifier may be left free to count as "Hitler" such terms as "Führer," "German Chancellor," "No. 1 Nazi" and so on. The distinction between rigid and flexible lists applies to the use of statements (sequence symbols) as well as unit symbols. The statement "the Germans caused the war" may be applied literally; if so, sentences like "the Nazis caused the war" would be excluded from the count. But the sentence would be included if the purpose is to record all statements consistent with the theme statement.

(3) Select the recording unit and the specified context. The recording unit may be defined as the range of text for which the occurrence of a symbol is tabulated with the unit weight of 1, even if it occurs more than once in the specified text. Thus if the paragraph is selected as the recording unit, one frequency will be recorded for any listed symbol appearing in that paragraph whether the symbol appears once or ten times. The specified context is the range of text which is to be considered in characterizing the presentation of a listed symbol in any given recording unit. Hence it is the portion of text to be read in order to determine whether a given symbol is favorably or unfavorably treated. It is reasonable that the specified context be at least as large as the recording unit. If we are determining the nature of the presentation of the symbol "Britain" in a one-paragraph recording unit, it is relevant to read at least that paragraph before making our decision. We may, of course, use a larger context such as the article as a whole.

(4) Train readers for consistency and reliability.

(5) Collect and process data.

This report is concerned with comparing different recording units applied by readers to the same body of editorial matter. With one exception the specified context is the same as the recording unit, as is shown in the following table:

Method	Recording Unit	Specified Context
I	Symbol	Sentence
II	Paragraph	Paragraph
III	3 sentences	3 sentences
IV	Article	Article

The exception is the first method in which the mention of a symbol counts as 1, but the specified context is the sentence as a whole. Obviously one symbol may occur more than once in a sentence, as in "Germans predominate in all armies in countries occupied by Germans." Strictly speaking, recording units should be named: "unit symbol; symbol-paragraph; symbol-three-sentences; symbol-articles." The word "symbol" is dropped to avoid repetition.

At first glance the paragraph and the three-sentence units are quite similar. But in general we expect that paragraphs are more variable in length than three-sentence units and it is reasonable to ask if this affects the results of content analysis.

It is clear that the principal contrast in the procedures applied in this experiment is between analysis by rather small and by rather large context units. Even larger units might have been investigated. Thus we could have assigned any one symbol according to the net impression left after reading all the editorials appearing in a given issue. On the other hand we could limit the specified context further than was done in this experiment, stipulating that the statement, not the sentence, be the specified context. (A statement is the smallest intelligible sequence of symbols; several statements may be found in one sentence.)

It is evident that the choice of unit depends upon the problem under investigation. Even without detailed research we know that some procedures are inadequate for certain questions. To choose an extreme example: If our problem is to describe the variations in content from one editorial to another, we cannot obtain much information if we record the article as a whole by a procedure that enables us to do no more than say that Britain was mentioned favorably. We may want to know if the whole article was full of references to Britain, or if Britain was referred to but once. We may ask whether the references were overwhelmingly favorable, or whether they were evenly split. If we were examining 100 newspapers in order to find out how many of them paid any attention whatsoever to Great Britain in their editorials, the one-article-one-mention procedure would give us all of the information useful for our purpose.

Whatever the specific question with which we approach the

analysis of content, we need to know how alternative procedures compare with one another in describing different
media of communication in reference to selected problems.
The present report has to do with editorials appearing in the
New York *Times*. This tends to suggest certain limitations
on the results. The *Times* has more—and longer—editorials
than many newspapers. Each editorial is made up of larger
paragraphs than can be found in many more "popular"
publications.

The results of this experiment are further conditioned by
the fact that this is not only a report on the *Times* but a report on politically significant content. For this study a few
symbols were chosen from the list made use of in "The World
Attention Survey." [2] The *Times* is more preoccupied with
politics, especially world politics, than many other newspapers, and this may diminish the applicability of our results.
The specific list (the symbols are listed together with the
numbers used in referring to them):

Symbol No.	Symbol
3	Great Britain
5	China
6	Churchill
9	Germany
10	Hitler
11	Italy
12	Japan
18	Roosevelt
21	United States
22	U.S.S.R.
24	Allies
24.1	Govts. in Exile
24.2	Free French
24.3	Citizens of Occupied Territory
25	Axis
26	Neutrals
27	Vichy
28	Finland

[2] See Lasswell, *op. cit.*, and Harold Lasswell, "The World Attention
Survey," *Public Opinion Quarterly, 5* (1941), p. 456.

Each symbol is characterized according to direction as follows:

1. Presentation in a positive (+) direction is the characterization of a listed symbol in a favorable light.
2. Presentation in a negative(—) direction is the characterization of a symbol in an unfavorable light.
3. Other presentations are neutral (o).[3]

Our experiment deals with weeks whose characteristics are differentiated as follows:

1. December 8–14, 1941; Pearl Harbor—period unfavorable to U.S.
2. April 20–26, 1942: A while after Tokyo Raid—neutral period.
3. June 5–11, 1942: Battle of Midway—period favorable to U.S.

This provides us with a wide range of wartime situations, enabling us to discover whether our methods exhibit distinctive characteristics connected with contrasting periods. As a reminder of the conditions prevailing in our selected weeks, the following sentences may be reproduced:

UNFAVORABLE PERIOD

December 8, 1941, Monday

"Whatever the military and naval strategy which we employ we now go into battle in response to crystal clear aggression and in defense of no far away ideal but of our own U.S. In this crisis we must have unanimity, sacrifice and American patriotism at its best."

December 9, 1941, Tuesday

"Congress has spoken—no, thundered—its answer to the madmen of Japan. . . . This swift and heartening demonstration of American unity meets with a reverberating echo

---

[3] In this experiment multiple coding is used. Thus when a symbol is presented favorably, unfavorably and neutrally, it is coded all three ways, and each entry is given a weight according to the proportion that it represents of all coded meanings of the symbol. The totals of all the weights is 1; in some cases, however, the weights do not add to whole numbers, since fractions like ⅓ cannot be expressed exactly in decimal form. In order to rule out very incidental characterization of a symbol, codings in addition to the first are recorded only when they amount to at least ⅕ of the number of mentions of the first.

outside the halls of Congress. . . . This country has acted in this hour of crisis precisely as those who were most confident of the integrity of democratic institutions knew that it would act. . . ."

December 10, 1941, Wednesday

"Mistakes have been made and losses taken. A hard road lies ahead. But we shall travel that road to victory, because we have a just cause, loyal allies, and a superbly united people. . . ."

December 12, 1941, Friday

"Now Germany and Italy join treacherous Japan in her attack on the U.S.—and the American people go to total war in defense of their lives, their liberties, their very existence as an independent nation. . . . Every faith we hold, and every liberty we cherish calls us into action to defend our own."

NEUTRAL PERIOD

April 21, 1942, Tuesday

"Because the world failed to recognize Adolf Hitler's worth, Adolf Hitler set out to change the world. No one can say he hasn't done so but what did he think about yesterday on his 53rd birthday. . . . An old book says: 'Woe unto the world because of offenses! For it must be that offenses come: But woe unto that man by whom the offense cometh.' There he is."

April 22, 1942, Wednesday

"The resolution adopted by the Republican National Committee at its Chicago meeting cuts cleanly away from those influences within the party which still counsel a 'defensive' war, a war of limited liability, . . . a war in which we concentrate on attack against Japan and give only second thought to Nazi Germany."

April 23, 1942, Thursday

"Slowly but surely, like an ice-bound river in the Spring, Europe is beginning to crack. . . . The occupied countries are not on the verge of revolt; . . . and it is folly to imagine that anything less than assault in superior force . . . can smash the great fighting machine that is now being geared for its supreme test. With these reservations against false hopes of near or easy victory, the signs that Hitler's house is crumbling from within are far too many to ignore."

April 24, 1942, Friday

"Whatever other steps are to be taken in the new inflation program, farm prices and wages, which have been the two openings through which inflation has been forcing its way, must be brought under control."

FAVORABLE PERIOD

June 5, 1942, Friday

"The Japanese raid on Dutch Harbor as a face saving operation to impress the bombed population of Tokyo or a reconnoitering prelude to further attacks. . . . History will mark June 3rd as the date of the first air attack of an alien enemy on the North American continent. We stand between the aggressors to Asia and Europe, and the latest reverberations stir the grass roots of America and blow away the dust of her last illusions."

June 6, 1942, Saturday

"Today marks the end of six months of our active participation in the war. . . . After six months, certainly the country ought to be told how many of our airplanes were destroyed at Pearl Harbor. . . . The record of the past six months has been far from wholly dark. . . ."

June 7, 1942, Sunday

"We failed twenty-three years ago because we did not carry the purposes of the First World War over into the peace, because specifically, we refused the mild commitance of membership in the League of Nations. Our people have seen the fruits of that error."

June 8, 1942, Monday

"The Battle is barely over. The full extent of losses on both sides has not yet been determined, much less told. Yet it is certain that the great sea battle for Midway Island has been a stunning defeat for Japanese sea power."

The experiment reveals, as was anticipated, that consistent differences are obtained in the frequencies recorded by the four methods. The symbol-sentence procedure (I) results in three and one-half times as many entries as the symbol-article Method IV (see Table A, where the weekly averages are shown to be 42 to 12). Method I yields twice as many frequencies as the symbol paragraph Method II. Although much closer to the paragraph procedure than to any other, Method III (the three-sentence unit) results in larger frequencies. This reflects the rather long paragraphs in *Times* editorials.

These results are true of the weeks considered separately, as well as collectively, as can be seen from Tables B, C and D. The neutral week is a little less full of mentions of the symbols on our list than the Pearl Harbor week or the Midway week. Since our list bears especially on foreign relations this is consistent with expectations.

The four methods agree in describing the direction of the editorial treatment of our symbol list during the period as a whole. They are in accord in presenting the period as more positive than negative (Table E).

The data in Table F enable us to compare the four methods in more detail. They report the result of coding a list of four symbols whose presentation by the *Times* is biased in the same direction. "Germany," "Hitler," "Japan" and "Axis" are all presented negatively (with one exception); however, the methods differ in the degree of reported bias. The paragraph and article methods resemble each other in emphasizing the degree of bias. For the entire period the paragraph procedure yields an excess of 38 per cent minus over plus references, and the article procedure gives a 33 per cent excess. The one-sentence and three-sentence methods resemble each other in under-emphasizing the degree of bias (27 per cent and 23 per cent excess, respectively, for the total period).

What factors operate to emphasize the degree of bias recorded by Methods II and IV, and to minimize the degree of bias by Methods I and III? One hypothesis is that the editorial style of the *Times* is reflected in this result. By style we mean the arrangement of the elements of the editorial.[4] The elements are statements—in this case, statements favorable, unfavorable or noncommittal in regard to the symbols listed. It is apparent that qualifications on the over-all bias of any

[4] See Chapter 2 in this book.

editorial (as of any communication) may be arranged in several ways in relation to the whole. They may be evenly distributed throughout the editorial, or concentrated at certain places. In the former case, a small-unit recording procedure would catch qualifying ideas that would elude a larger content method, and diminish the strength of the reported bias.

Table F shows that the number of "neutral" entries diminishes as the size of the recording context increases. For the entire period one-sentence coding gives 25 per cent neutral; paragraph coding, 16 per cent; article coding, 11 per cent. We cannot, however, rely upon this to account for the differences in emphasis by the four methods. There is no sound ground for expecting that the larger the size of the coding unit, the larger the proportion of extreme references; it is always possible that this is a function of the stylistic pattern.

The characteristics of the "zero" category must be revealed in future investigations. At present several kinds of relations are found in this bracket:

a. Characterization in neither a favorable nor unfavorable way; i.e., a "truly neutral" statement, where impartiality is obvious.

b. Ambiguous characterization, where the attitude implied is not clear.

c. Hypothetical import, where the content does not assert a fact but where the underlying attitude is clear, as in rhetorical questions, conditional statements of various kinds, advice, and so on.

d. Coding difficulties—all characterizations which are not otherwise provided for by the rules, or which are of a very complex nature.

In view of the importance of style it may be suggested that samples of the content of any medium of communication be described by more than one coding procedure.

While it is not conclusively established, certain coding peculiarities may influence the result of using different recording units on the same content. Table G reports the proportion of single to multiple coding for each of the four methods. The classifiers made use of multiple coding more often as the context increased. This, of course, is consistent with the common sense expectation that the number of meanings increases with the number of words taken into consideration. More subtle shades of meaning are caught by multiple than by single coding. Does this tend to stress the degree of bias reported in large contexts by giving equal weight to meanings that are omitted when coding is done by small units? In selecting the procedure appropriate to any given content analysis problem, coding speed is a factor to be considered. Table H shows the relative time expended on the four methods. The procedure that corresponds to the obvious structure of the article is the quickest to apply. Article, paragraph or sentence coding outstrips three-sentence coding. Method III is slowed down because of certain anomalies that result when this unit is applied. Often one unit will include sentences from the preceding or following paragraphs. The sentence procedure calls for the largest number of entries, and may be to some degree retarded by the questions that arise in the mind of the classifier who is characterizing a small context.[5]

In conclusion, the present experiment supports the following statements about editorial coding:

1. Sentence, paragraph, three-sentence and article coding of the same editorial content give consistent differences in the count of symbol frequencies.

2. The four methods agree in describing the direction of bias (favorable, unfavorable) though they differ in showing the degree of bias.

3. The degree of bias is emphasized by paragraph and article coding.

4. The degree of bias is minimized by one-sentence and three-sentence coding.

5. In part, these differences may be atributed to the style of the material (the way in which qualifications on the overall bias of the article are arranged within the article).

6. The number of neutral entries diminishes as the size of the context unit increases.

7. The three-sentence method is the slowest procedure, while article coding is the most rapid.

[5] Other factors determining the choice of method are consistency and reliability of coders.

TABLE A

COMPARISON OF FOUR METHODS OF CODING RELA-
TIVE SYMBOL FREQUENCIES

Symbol	Total for All Weeks				Total	
	I	II	III	IV	No.	%
3	39	22	27	12	335.2	100
6	37	20	28	15	64.8	100
9	42	21	24	13	310.5	100
10	41	22	25	12	322.2	100
12	44	19	25	12	572.0	100
18	44	21	23	12	140.7	100
25	37	21	29	13	168.2	100
21	44	17	28	11	1393.1	100
22	46	17	25	12	137.2	100
24	37	21	29	13	232.8	100
5	38	20	26	16	126.0	100
Total	42	20	27	12	3802.7	100

TABLE B

COMPARISON OF FOUR METHODS OF CODING RELA-
TIVE SYMBOL FREQUENCIES

Symbol	Total for Week of June 5–11, 1942				Total	
	I	II	III	IV	No.	%
3	36	20	24	20	87.5	100
6	36	15	30	19	19.8	100
9	47	20	20	13	175.0	100
10	41	22	19	18	36.0	100
12	48	19	19	14	183.0	100
18	46	21	18	15	43.5	100
25	42	19	26	13	31.0	100
21	44	20	24	12	496.0	100
22	38	20	24	18	54.5	100
24	37	22	27	14	116.5	100
5	35	24	25	16	55.0	100
Total	43	20	23	14	1281.3	100

TABLE C

COMPARISON OF FOUR METHODS OF CODING RELA-
TIVE SYMBOL FREQUENCIES

Total for Week of December 8–14, 1941 *Total*

Symbol	I	II	III	IV	No.	%
3	33	26	26	15	105.3	100
6	37	24	25	14	29.5	100
9	36	22	27	15	89.0	100
10	41	20	28	11	91.2	100
12	45	18	27	10	278.9	100
18	36	29	25	10	60.5	100
25	32	21	32	15	84.0	100
21	42	19	32	7	384.1	100
22	52	16	24	8	64.4	100
24	32	26	27	15	62.0	100
5	38	19	24	19	37.0	100
Total	40	20	29	11	1283.4	100

TABLE D

COMPARISON OF FOUR METHODS OF CODING RELA-
TIVE SYMBOL FREQUENCIES

Total for Week of April 20–26, 1942 *Total*

Symbol	I	II	III	IV	No.	%
3	42	20	29	9	148.9	100
6	36	19	32	13	15.5	100
9	35	22	31	12	46.5	100
10	41	23	25	11	195.0	100
12	35	23	29	13	110.2	100
18	46	15	26	13	39.2	100
25	40	22	26	12	53.2	100
21	42	19	28	11	523.0	100
22	47	16	29	8	18.3	100
24	42	12	36	10	54.3	100
5	42	16	29	13	34.0	100
Total	41	20	28	11	1238.1	100

TABLE E

COMPARISON OF FOUR METHODS OF CODING RELATIVE SYMBOL FREQUENCIES BY DIRECTION

Total for All Weeks

	Total No.	Total %	o%	+%	−%
I	1583.5	100	37	34	29
II	758.1	100	24	42	34
III	1010.3	100	30	44	26
IV	450.8	100	20	46	34

TABLE F

COMPARISON OF FOUR METHODS OF CODING RELATIVE SYMBOL FREQUENCIES (SYMBOLS 9, 10, 12, 25) * BY DIRECTION

Totals for Each Week

December		Total No.	Total %	o%	+%	−%	Excess − over +
—	I	223.0	100	51	13	36	23
	II	105.4	100	35	14	51	37
	III	151.1	100	41	11	48	37
	IV	63.6	100	22	23	55	32
April							
0	I	157.0	100	18	25	57	32
	II	90.5	100	7	20	63	43
	III	110.5	100	13	28	59	31
	IV	46.9	100	7	26	67	41
June							
+	I	199.0	100	14	29	57	28
	II	83.0	100	3	39	58	19
	III	84.0	100	10	52	38	−14
	IV	57.5	100	0	34	66	32

Total for All Weeks

	Total No.	Total %	o%	+%	−%	Excess
I	579.0	100	29	22	49	27
II	279.3	100	16	23	61	38
III	345.6	100	25	26	49	23
IV	169.0	100	11	28	61	33

* 9—Germany; 10—Hitler; 12—Japan; 25—Axis.

TABLE G

PROPORTION OF SINGLE TO MULTIPLE CODING FOR EACH OF FOUR METHODS IN A SAMPLE OF THE NEW YORK TIMES

	Single		Multiple	
	No.	%	No.	%
I (Symbol)	500	100	20	4
II (Paragraph)	238	100	111	47
III (3-sentence)	319	100	140	44
IV (Article)	88	100	143	163

TABLE H

RELATIVE AMOUNT OF TIME CONSUMED BY EACH METHOD

(Time of Method I used as base)

Method   I—Recording Unit—Sentence 100.0
Method   II—Recording Unit—paragraph 75.0
Method III—Recording Unit—3 sentences 114.0
Method IV—Recording Unit—article 57.0

Chapter **7**

THE FEASIBILITY OF THE USE OF
SAMPLES IN CONTENT ANALYSIS *

I. *Introduction*

THE CUSTOMARY procedure in content analysis is to classify
the material investigated, such as newspaper headlines or
items on radio news programs, into a number of categories
and to count their number during certain time intervals. If
the material which is being investigated involves a large number of items, the procedure takes much time and labor. This
suggests sampling of the material as a labor-saving device;
instead of classifying and counting all available items, one
may consider using only a part of the material, thus saving
much effort. One might, for example, classify and count only
odd-numbered items on a radio program, or use only newspapers appearing on odd-numbered days of the month or
only during the third week of a month. But can this be done
without invalidating the results?

The answer depends on the degree to which the findings
obtained with samples tend to approximate the findings utilizing the complete available material. This paper reports the
results of an exploratory investigation dealing with the ac-

---

* Revised from Document 49, Experimental Division for the Study of
Wartime Communications, Library of Congress, August 1, 1943.

curracy of content frequencies expressed as percentages derived from samples. A content analysis of headlines appearing in *Pravda* during a six-month period was chosen as material on which the problem of feasibility of sampling was to be explored. The problem had two main parts:

1. How to choose a sampling method, and
2. How to determine the degree to which percentages derived from samples tend to approximate the true percentages utilizing the complete material?

A number of subsidiary problems had to be investigated in conjunction with the above:

What features of the material should determine the choice of the sampling procedure?

By what methods can these features be ascertained?

What modifications of the standard statistical procedures are required, in order to make them applicable to the sampling problem in content analysis?

II. *The Material Utilized* *

The material used for this investigation consisted of newspaper headlines appearing in *Pravda* during the six-month period beginning April 1, 1941, and ending September 30, 1941. Each day's headlines had been classified into ten exhaustive subject-matter categories, as follows:

1. Administration
2. National republics and nationalities
3. Communist Party
4. Red Army
5. Trade unions
6. Soviet economics
7. Soviet cultural life
8. Soviet foreign relations
9. General
10. Foreign news

Tables of frequencies and percentages of headlines falling into the ten categories during weekly and approximately

* I am indebted to Joseph M. Goldsen for the problem which he suggested and for his editorial suggestions in the preparation of this paper. He had also analyzed the original data which was gathered by the Experimental Division for the Study of Wartime Communications, Harold D. Lasswell, Chief. The classification of the *Pravda* content was made by Dr. Sergius Yakobson.

monthly periods, which had been previously computed for other research projects, were made available for this investigation. Since most of the previous research had been conducted in terms of percentages, and since a month was the usual unit of time, the percentages labeled according to the month were selected for treatment as "true" percentages, to be approximated by the samples.

A misunderstanding was unfortunately not discovered until the computations were almost completed: the percentages designated as "monthly" in the table were in reality based on four- to five-week periods rather than actual monthly periods. The errors, however, were small, less than half of one per cent in three quarters of the instances, and only a few of the tables had to be recomputed; other tables were partially recomputed or the approximate errors of the results of computations were estimated; or, if recomputation clearly would not have significantly altered the conclusions, the slight errors were allowed to stand. Which method of dealing with the errors was chosen in the case of the various tables will be pointed out later in the text. The periods designated as months in the table actually were:

> April 1—April 28
> April 29—June 2
> June 3—June 30
> July 1—July 28
> July 29—September 1
> September 2—September 30

A table of the frequencies and percentages for these periods, and for the actual calendar months, is presented as Appendix I.

III. *The Choice of the Sampling Method*

How should the sample be chosen, in order to achieve as close an approximation of the four- to five-week percentages as possible? The following line of reasoning was developed:

The distribution of the *Pravda* headlines in the ten categories varies from day to day. These fluctuations may be of several types. Their nature should determine the choice of the sampling method.

1. Random sampling fluctuations:

Fluctuations of random sampling constitute one kind. Their probable distribution has been investigated in statistical theory. In the case of percentages, the standard deviation of the random sampling fluctuations can be readily estimated, the estimate being a function of the "true" percentage, the size of the sample, and the size of the population from which the sample is drawn.

Random sampling fluctuations can not be eliminated. In order to decrease them, one has to increase the size of the sample. Other features of the way the sample is chosen have little or no effect on the probable size of random sampling fluctuations. If random sampling were the only source of percentage fluctuations, it would not matter how the sample is chosen; this is, however, a most improbable case. Generally there are fluctuations of other types, and their effect on the accuracy of samples is markedly dependent on the method of selecting the sample. If the sample is properly chosen, their influence can be largely eliminated so that only random fluctuations remain.

Three possible kinds of non-random fluctuations were taken into consideration: *primary trends,* both linear and curvilinear; *cyclical* trends; and a tendency towards a *compensatory relationship* between frequencies on adjoining days.

2. Primary trends:

The frequent existence of primary trends in material, such as frequencies of different categories of *Pravda* headlines, may be taken for granted; otherwise, content analysis would serve no research purpose. However, there are trend fluctuations of different types. A trend may be linear, representing a constant rate of increase or decrease of a certain percentage. But it may also be curvilinear, the rate of increase or decrease not being constant during the time interval; for instance, the increase may not continue for a whole month, or may be followed by a decrease after the percentage reaches a maximum. The type of trend functions to be found in any given material can not be taken for granted.

2a. What are the consequences for the accuracy of sampling methods?

A sample consisting of data on several separate nonconsecutive days should largely eliminate the disturbing effects of the different kinds of trends. Consecutive days tend to over-represent a particular part of a trend; if, for example, the trend is linear, either the first or the last week of a month gives a markedly misleading percentage. If a percentage reaches a maximum near the middle of a month, the middle week is just as misleading. If, on the other hand, a sample consists of nonconsecutive days separated by regular intervals —e.g., every second day, every third or every fifth day—a sufficient number of points on the trend line are likely to be represented in the sample.

It seemed purposeless to examine methods for the establishment of the exact nature of primary trends to be found in the *Pravda* headlines. It was considered extremely probable that both linear and curvilnear trends would be found. Hence, a sampling method has to be efficient with both kinds of trends, and the labor involved in the determination of the trend type did not appear justified.

3. Cyclical trends:

The existence of cyclical trends in material such as newspaper headlines appears to be probable. In the United States, Sunday newspapers differ markedly from newspapers published on weekdays, and certain types of events, such as football games, usually take place on weekends. If weekly cycles are present, samples should consist of days carefully chosen from each week; otherwise, high or low portions of cycles may have too much representation.

Are weekly (or other) cycles present in the *Pravda* headline percentages?

In order to determine the presence or absence of cycles, three methods were considered:

(1) A graphic representation of daily frequencies or daily percentages; cycles ought to be visible to the naked eye.

(2) An examination of the variance of the percentages computed for samples of various lengths consisting of successive days; a cycle ought to show itself in lower variance of such samples than predicted from the variance of daily samples.

(3) An examination of the distribution of first differences by the Wallis and Moore method.*

* Wallis and Moore, *A Significance Test for Time Series*. Technical Paper 1, National Bureau of Economic Research.

Actually only the graphic method was used to any extent.

3a. Graphic representation as test for cycles:

Curves representing the frequency of each class and the total number of headlines on different days was plotted, eleven frequency curves in all. Vertical lines were drawn at weekly intervals. The shapes of the curves between adjoining weekly lines were examined. Subsequently, the distances between successive peaks were inspected, the vertical lines being disregarded.

Inspection of the curves failed to reveal anything suggestive of cycles. The shapes of the portions of the curves between adjoining weekly lines were very variable. Disregarding the vertical lines, the succession of rises and falls was found to be irregular, and the distance between peaks fluctuated considerably.

3b. Distribution of first differences:

The Wallis and Moore method (Wallis and Moore, *op. cit.*) was tried out on a few curves.

The authors recently suggested that, in the case of time series, the number of consecutive increases or decreases of the figures may be profitably studied. They computed the probabilities of single increases or decreases, two successive changes in the same direction, three successive changes in the same direction, etc. It is extremely easy to compare the frequencies of observed successive changes to the expected frequencies, and the authors describe their method as a very sensitive indicator of the presence of cycles in time series. Use of this method was planned, but a trial indicated that it was not applicable to most of our material. Wallis and Moore presuppose, in their derivation, that identical measures either do not occur or are rare. On the other hand, certain headline classes were likely to occur either not at all, or only once on any given day during considerable periods. This made consecutive increases or decreases impossible or improbable, thus rendering the Wallis and Moore formulae inappropriate.

The method seems to be applicable to the data in our material involving larger frequencies. Of the counts of the first differences, one seems to be worth reporting, namely, that referring to total numbers of headlines on different days. Here the numbers are sufficiently large, ties are infrequent, and the agreement with the expected numbers is very close. The following table presents the results.

	Observed	Expected
Number of turning points:	115	112.7
Number of "runs of 1" (single increases or decreases)	74	70.0
Number of "runs of 2"	29	30.6
Number of "runs of 3"	9	8.8
Number of "runs" longer than 3	2	2.2

This result further supports the finding that the frequencies of headlines per day in *Pravda* were not subject to cycles, at least not so far as their total number was concerned. Whether this finding holds true for newspapers published in other countries is, of course, an open question.

Since inspection of the curves failed to indicate any features even faintly suggestive of cycles, no attempt was made to test the material by use of computational procedures. If this were desirable, one might reason as follows:

3c. Variance of consecutive day samples as test for cycles.

Given a table of daily percentages for a month, the variance of the percentages may be computed. This can be done by subtracting daily percentages from the monthly percentage squaring the differences, weighting each squared difference in accordance with the total frequency of all categories for the day, adding the products, and dividing the sum by the total frequency for the month. This variance may be viewed as the sum of several component variances attributable, for example, to primary trends, to cycles, and to fluctuations of random sampling. If one computes percentages based on combined frequencies for several consecutive days, one should find that varying the number of days in the interval should have different effects on the various components of the variance of the percentages. Both trend variance and random sampling variance should consistently decrease with the size of the sample—the former slightly, the latter to a marked extent. On the other hand, the variance due to a cycle should be zero when the number of the days in the samples coincides with the duration of the cycle; otherwise it should differ from zero.* Thus, if the cycle variance is considerable, correspondence between durations of samples and cycles should be recognizable in a lower variance of sample percentages than would be expected on the basis of variances of consecutive-day samples consisting of both more and fewer days.

4. Is there a compensatory relationship between frequencies on adjoining days?

It was thought possible, if not probable, that full coverage of a certain type of news on one day might decrease the probability that the same news category would be represented in the headlines the next day. This state of things would have consequences directly opposed to those in the case of trends. The presence of the latter tends to make percentages on adjoining days relatively similar, while a compensatory relationship would tend to produce larger differences between them than could be accounted for in terms of chance factors.

4a. Variances of one-day and two-day samples:

In order to investigate this matter, variances of percentages for single days and for two-day periods were computed. If random sampling were the only source of variability, the expected ratio of the variances would be close to $2 \div 1$ (to be exact, number of days less one over number of two-day intervals less one—see Appendix II). The presence of trends tends to decrease the ratio.

The following table presents the variances of the distributions of the percentages in one-day and two-day samples; the variances were computed for each month for four of the headline classes, numbers 1, 6, 8 and 10. In computing this table, percentages were treated as decimal fractions (e.g., 2% as .02). If percentages had been treated as integers, all variances should have been multiplied by 10,000. The months designate true calendar months, except for the omission of the last day in the case of months with 31 days.

---

* The random variance of percentages in samples of varying size drawn from a population of N elements is proportional to $\dfrac{N-1}{n}$, where n is the size of the sample.

Subject matter category	Variance of	April	May	June	July	Aug.	Sept.
1	1-day samples	.0043	.0056	.0160	.0257	.0267	.0267
	2-day samples	.00095	.0032	.0063	.0106	.0119	.0097
6	1-day samples	.0318	.0237	.0255	.0121.	0058	.0074
	2-day samples	.023	.0117	.0182	.0042	.0037	.0047
8	1-day samples	.0066	.0009	.0023	.0067	.0148	.0045
	2-day samples	.0042	.0004	.0012	.0027	.0118	.0025
10	1-day samples	.0027	0	0	.0459	.0432	.0486
	2-day samples	.00185	0	0	.0143	.0263	.0323

The table has 22 cells with entries different from zero. Of these, 14 have ratios of variance less than 2, indicating that taking adjoining days improves the reliability of the findings rather less than predictable on the basis of random sampling fluctuations; in the remaining 8 cells, the ratios are larger than 2, though in several cases but slightly so. The reliability of these ratios was not investigated as irrelevant, inasmuch as even if a few large ratios should be statistically significant, there still would be no reason generally to consider 2-day samples efficient; the bulk of the findings clearly shows 2-day samples to be inefficient.

5. Consequences:

Trends can be assumed to eixst in any material for content analysis. Cycles were not found. No tendency towards a compensatory relationship between frequencies on adjoining days was discovered. We may conclude that an efficient sample of the *Pravda* headlines should consist of a number of nonconsecutive days, evenly spaced so that different portions of the trend function are represented. The choice of the time interval between the days should not matter, except in terms of the size of the sample obtained. Three kinds of samples were chosen as a result of these considerations: a three-day sample, consisting of the fifth, tenth, and twenty-fifth day of each month; a six-day sample consisting of each fifth day of each month; and a fifteen- to sixteen-day sample consisting of the odd numbered days of each month. The accuracy of these samples was compared with the accuracy of weekly samples and with the theoretically expected accuracy.

IV. *The accuracy of nonconsecutive-day samples compared with that of weekly samples*

Are nonconsecutive-day samples actually superior to consecutive-day samples, as should be the case on the basis of the above discussion? Two methods of comparison were used: ranges of errors of sample percentages were determined for different magnitudes of monthly percentages, and average squared errors were computed.

1. Error ranges:

The following table lists the error ranges (i.e., ranges of deviations from corresponding monthly percentages) for the percentages of the weekly samples, the 3-day samples (5th, 15th, 25th of each month), the 6-day samples (5th, 10th, 15th, 20th, 25th, 30th of each month) and the odd-day samples.

Error ranges (in percentages) of:

Monthly Per Cent	Weekly Samples	3-day Samples	6-day Samples	Odd-day Samples
0	0	0	0	0
.2— 1.0	−1.0 to 2.3	−1.0 to −.2	−.7 to .7	−.7 to .4
1.4— 2.1	−1.8 to 4.0	−2.1 to 1.1	−2.1 to 2.0	−.4 to .9
2.5— 3.1	−3.1 to 6.3	−2.8 to 4.4	−1.9 to .8	−.8 to 1.0
3.2— 5.0	−3.9 to 5.7	−3.9 to 3.5	−3.2 to 2.5	−1.3 to 2.3
5.2— 6.3	−6.3 to 27.0	−5.8 to 4.5	−2.5 to 2.5	−1.6 to 0
6.6— 9.9	−7.6 to 9.6	−5.1 to 3.5	−3.3 to 4.7	−1.9 to 3.3
11.9—16.6	−13.6 to 6.9	−5.3 to 5.5	−7.0 to 2.6	−1.3 to 3.2
16.8—27.7	−11.9 to 10.3	−7.0 to 11.6	−7.3 to 2.3	−4.9 to 3.4
31.6—58.1	−20.1 to 13.1	−17.3 to 17.9	−2.1 to 9.4	−2.4 to 4.6

In terms of the magnitude of the observed errors, the weekly samples are far inferior to the 6-day samples, and even seem to be slightly more inaccurate than the 3-day samples consisting of less than half as many days. The latter finding may be an artifact. Each range of monthly percentages consisted of 6 figures, and each month was represented by 4 or 5 weekly samples, but by only one 3-day sample. Therefore, the error ranges of the weekly samples were based on about 25 errors each, while in the case of 3-day samples the error ranges contained only 6 elements each. A crude computation suggested that an increase from 6 to 25 items should tend to increase the magnitude of the largest error (disregarding the sign) approximately in the ratio of 4.1 to 3; thus, the weekly samples may not be really inferior to the 3-day samples, but nevertheless it is clear that they are not markedly superior (see Appendix III).

2. Average squared errors.

A comparison of the average squared errors indicates slight superiority of the weekly samples over the 3-day samples, the 2 averages being 19.6 and 24.3 respectively. How slight the difference is becomes apparent if one extracts the 2 square roots, thus obtaining approximations of the 2 standard errors of estimate. The 2 square roots are 4.43 and 4.93. Whether the difference is significant was not established; clearly, neither weekly nor 3-day samples are sufficiently accurate, and 6-day samples are superior. No advantage was seen in discovering precisely which of the inefficient sampling methods was the more inefficient one. The 6-day and odd-day samples are far superior, the average squared errors being 8.66 and 2.38. Thus, the expected superiority of nonconsecutive-day samples over the weekly samples was actually demonstrated.

V. *The expected accuracy of the nonconsecutive-day samples and its conformity with the findings*

1. Methodological considerations:

Two types of procedures were considered as affording possible answers to the question of efficiency of the various sampling methods. One might proceed purely empirically, in terms of a tabulation or graphic representation of errors of various magnitudes; or one might deduce the theoretically expected error distribution, and then determine the conformity of the empirical findings to theoretical expectation. The second procedure was chosen.

The principal difficulties with a purely empirical procedure lie in the fact that on the one hand, the distributions of the deviations of the samples from the monthly figures ought to vary with the monthly percentages, while, on the other hand, the number of samples at any percentage level is small. In these circumstances, one can not draw any reasonably precise inferences on the basis of the findings. For example, with one of the sampling methods used, the largest difference between a monthly percentage and the corresponding sample percentage is 9.4. The monthly percentage is between 30 and 58.1. Since there are only 6 samples in this range, we can not be certain that considerably larger deviations might not be found within this range; nor is there any reason to expect similarly large deviations in the case of monthly percentages below 5 where the largest obtained deviation was 3.2%.

Therefore, it was deemed desirable to test the conformity of the sum total of the obtained results with the theoretically expected distribution of the sample deviations. Once conformity is established, a method is available whereby limits of confidence can be computed for different sizes of samples and for different percentage levels.

2. The theoretically expected error distribution.

The form of the expected distribution of random sample percentages is easily determined on the basis of elementary principles of the theory of probability. Let "N" and "F" represent the size of the monthly population and the number of headlines falling into one of the categories; let "n" and "f" represent the corresponding sample statistics. The probability of $f = O$ is

$$\frac{(N - F)\ (N - F - 1)\ \ldots\ (N - F - n + 1).}{N(N - 1)\ \ldots\ (N - n + 1)}$$

For $f = 1$ and $f = 2$, and the probabilities are

$$\frac{n(N - F)\ (N - F - 1)\ \ldots\ (N - F - n + 2)\ F}{N(N - 1)\ \ldots\ (N - n + 1)}$$

and

$$\frac{n(n - 1)\ (N - F)\ (N - F - 1)\ \ldots\ (N - F - n + 3)\ F(F - 1),}{2!\ N(N - 1)\ \ldots\ (N - n + 1)}$$

respectively.

Generally, the probability of $f = K$ (an arbitrary number) is

$$\frac{n(n-1)\ldots(n-K+1)\ (N-F)\ (N-F-1)\ldots(N-F-n+K+1)F(F-1)\ldots(F-K+1)}{K!\ N(N-1)\ \ldots\ (N-n+1)}$$

(See Appendix IV for the derivation)

This distribution differs from the familiar binomial distribution due to the finite numbers of the monthly headlines which are approximated by the samples, the binomial distribution being obtained in samples drawn from infinite populations.

3. The standard error and the estimated variance of sample percentages:

If a monthly percentage is "P," the standard error of the corresponding random sample percentages is

$$\sqrt{\frac{P(100 - P)\,(N - n)}{n(N - 1)}}.$$

In other words, the theoretically expected average squared error of samples of size n is $\frac{P(100 - P)\,(N - n)}{n(N - 1)}$. The expression differs from the familiar $\sqrt{\frac{p(100 - p)}{n - 1}}$ in two ways.

First, the latter formula presupposes that the "true" percentage "P," is unknown and substitutes "p," the sample percentage. Because of this, "n − 1" has to be used instead of "n" in the denominator. In our material, the true monthly percentages were available and were utilized in the computations. Secondly, the conventional formula presupposes that samples are drawn from an infinite population; the formula used here takes into account the finite size of the monthly headline populations. Its derivation is explained in Appendix II. It gives smaller standard errors than the conventional formula; consequently, its use provides a stricter test of the validity of our samples than would have been the case had the conventional formula been used.

3a. The effect of trends on random fluctuations:

If a trend is present during a month, the formula $\frac{P(100 - P)\,(N - n)}{N - 1}$ becomes inexact. It fails to give an exact estimate of the average squared error (the random sampling variance) due to random fluctuations, because "P" is not the true percentage during the whole month. During different parts of the month, the true percentage may be viewed as having different values, "P_1," "P_2," etc., P being their average. The random sampling variance for any part of the month is proportional to $P_k (100 - P_k)$ (assuming constancy of "N" and "n") which is not a linear function of "P_k." The monthly random sampling variance is proportional to the average of the expressions $P_k(100 - P_k)$, which is not the same as $P(100 - P)$; e.g., the average of 10% and 40% is 25%, but the average of 10(100 − 10) and 40(100 − 40), which is 1650, is not equal to 25(100 − 25), which is 1875.

However, the error introduced by the presence of trends is generally small and may be safely disregarded. The matter was only partially investigated, owing to the apparent smallness of the error obtained in a number of selected instances.

VI. *The verification of the theoretical expectations*

The conformity between theoretical expectation and the findings was investigated only in the case of the every-fifth-day and the odd-numbered-day samples. The three-day samples were not investigated, their accuracy being clearly too low for practical uses.

1. Methods:

Three methods were used with the every-fifth-day and odd-numbered-day samples:

First, the squared errors of the samples (i.e., the squared deviations of sample percentages from monthly percentages) were computed, and were compared to the corresponding estimates. The formula $\dfrac{P(1 - P)(N - n)}{n(N - 1)}$ was used. The comparison was made in terms of sums of all obtained squared deviations and the sums of the corresponding estimated variances. This computation was performed in order to discover whether the average size of the deviations agreed with theoretical expectation, i.e., whether effects of trends had been successfully eliminated.

Secondly, similar summations were performed for separate ranges of monthly percentages. This indicated whether there were any consistent discrepancies between expectation and findings.

1a. The chi-square test.

Thirdly, each squared deviation was divided by the corresponding estimated variance, the quotients were added, and the sums were treated as chi-squares; classes belonging to the same month were combined in such a way that no obtained frequency was less than 5. Thus, the formula used was

$$x^2 = \sum \frac{(p - P)^2}{\dfrac{P(100 - P)(N - n)}{n(N - 1)}} = \sum \frac{(p - P)^2 \, n(N - 1)}{P(100P)(N - n)}.$$

The chi-squares were interpreted as indicating whether our samples may be viewed as random samples of monthly populations; essentially, the question was investigated whether the combined probability of differences as large as, or larger than, those obtained was sufficiently considerable so that the differences could be accounted for in terms of random sampling.

The appropriateness of this procedure to our material was not fully established. It would have been appropriate if the samples had been drawn from infinite populations. One of the commonly used definitions of "χ^2" characterizes it as a sum of squared differences between obtained and expected frequencies, each difference being divided by its squared standard error. R. A. Fisher* used this procedure in order to show the degree of agreement between expected and obtained percentages. In effect, he divided squared differences between percentages by their squared standard errors. His own description of the operations is a different one, but the expression he uses is algebraically identical with the description given here. He then designated the sum of such expressions as a modified index of dispersion, appropriate to binomial distributions, and treated it as a chi-square. According to Tippet,† "the chi-square test is an extension of the ordinary method of finding the significance of an ordinary binomial mean, and enables the information given by a number of them to be combined." In view of the similarity between the expression for the binomial distribution and the one expected in the case of our material, the χ^2 test appropriate to binomial distributions was adopted.

It should be repeated that the formula for the standard error used here, taking into account the finite size of the monthly "populations," gives smaller standard errors than the formula assuming an infinite population. Thus, each squared deviation is divided by a smaller number than would have been the case if the finite character of monthly totals had been disregarded, and therefore a larger χ^2 is obtained. Our test of the conformity between the theoretical and the obtained error distributions is stricter than would have been the case if the more conventional formula had been used.

2. The sums of squared errors:

In the case of the every-fifth-day samples, the sum of the

* Statistical Methods for Research Workers, 7 edit., 1938, p. 72.
† The Methods of Statistics, 2d edit., 1938.

obtained squared deviations of the sample percentages from the monthly percentages was found to be 519.87; inasmuch as the data in the table are not true months, this number is probably somewhat larger than would have been the case had true monthly percentages been used. The most probable value of this excess was computed to be 12.06 (see Appendix V), thus giving 507.01 as the most likely value of the sum of the squared differences as found in our material. The theoretically expected sum of squared differences was determined as 524.44; thus, close agreement between the expected and the obtained sums of squared differences was found.

In the case of the odd-day samples, the agreement between the expected sums of squared deviations and those actually obtained was even closer. The obtained sum of squared deviations was 142.89; subtracting 12.06, the most probable value of the excess due to the incorrectly designated table, we obtain 130.83. The expected sum of squared differences was computed as 126.54.

3. Squared errors for different ranges of monthly percentages.

The following table exhibits the obtained and the expected sums of squared deviations for various ranges of monthly percentages. No correction for the mislabeled table was used. Each figure is a sum of five to six squared differences.

Range of monthly per cent	Every-5th-day Samples Expected diff.^{2}	Every-5th-day Samples Obtained diff.^{2}	Every-odd-day Samples Expected diff.^{2}	Every-odd-day Samples Obtained diff.^{2}
.2 — .7	2.06	.91	.51	.72
1.0 — 1.8	10.53	13.7	2.00	1.03
2.1 — 2.9	17.57	11.07	4.71	2.27
3.1 — 4.0	27.08	24.18	5.62	11.31
5.0 — 6.0	29.66	15.70	7.66	5.92
6.3 — 8.5	44.48	29.37	10.76	21.76
8.8 —13.3	54.43	57.62	12.42	6.87
14.1 —17.3	83.35	86.31	20.80	24.77
18.2 —21.6	115.92	71.68	26.35	40.90
31.8 —58.1	139.36	209.34	35.11	27.34

An examination of the table fails to reveal any consistent trend towards large obtained squared errors, on the part of either large or small percentages. The differences between the expected and the obtained squared deviations are in both directions, and appear to be quite irregular. Thus, the computations indicate that, on the average, the obtained squared errors of the sample percentages approximately conform to theoretical expectation.

4. The chi-square test.

Does this mean that the distribution of the sample errors, considered as a whole, contains no unduly great number of large differences, and can be viewed as a product of random sampling? The chi-square obtained for the percentages of every-fifth-day samples was 31.14, the degrees of freedom being 24; the reduction of the degrees of freedom was due to the combining of cells with small frequencies. The corresponding value of P (probability of obtaining as result of random sampling a chi-square as large as, or larger than, the given one) is .15. In spite of the use of the somewhat inaccurate monthly percentages, the error distribution might have readily arisen as a result of random sampling.

In case of the odd-day samples, the chi-square as originally computed was 55.61, giving for 34 degrees of freedom a P of .011. Since it was thought that the factor, other than random sampling, responsible for the errors of the sample percentages was probably the inaccuracy of the table of monthly percentages, new ratios were computed for the cells in which the percentages in the old table deviated from the correct ones by one-half of one per cent, or more. This was done in fourteen cells. Substitution of the new ratios lowered the value of chi-square from 55.61 to 41.05, giving for 34 degrees of freedom P = .192. The error distribution of the odd-day samples is consistent with an interpretation in terms of fluctuations of random sampling.

Summary

By utilizing tabulations of *Pravda* headlines as illustrative material, issues relevant to the determination of reliability of percentages based on samples are discussed. It is inferred that:

1. Generally speaking, samples consisting of consecutive days can be expected to be less accurate than samples consisting of days separated by regular intervals.

2. Cyclical trends, if present, would require samples con-

sisting of days so chosen that representative days of the cycles would be represented.

3. A compensatory relationship between percentages on adjoining days, if present, would require the use of samples consisting of two consecutive days. This, however, does not seem to be a probable state of things.

4. Methods are described whereby it can be determined whether cycles are present, and whether a compensatory relationship between frequencies on adjoining days exists. In connection with this, it is shown how certain procedures utilized in analysis of variance are applicable to percentages.

5. A method of choosing samples of a given size is an efficient one if it gives results deviating from the true monthly percentages by amounts expected of random samples of that size. The theoretically expected form of distribution of percentages obtained in samples drawn from the same distribution of monthly headlines is given. It deviates from the binomial distribution because of the finite number of headlines during the month. The standard deviation is

$$\sqrt{\frac{P\,(100 - P)\,(N - n)}{n\,(N - 1)}}.$$

Thus, the accuracy of samples is a function of the monthly percentage, the size of the sample, and the total number of headlines during the month.

The formula differs from the conventional one because percentages based on finite item frequencies per unit of time are viewed as true data to be approximated.

6. A method was developed to apply the chi-square test to a distribution of percentages, thus enabling one to determine whether the obtained error distribution of sample percentages may be viewed as due to fluctuations of random sampling.

The procedures described here were applied to a tabulation of classified *Pravda* headlines. It was found that:

7. There was no evidence of cyclical trends, and no compensatory relationship between frequencies of adjoining days was found to exist when variances of one-day and two-day percentages were compared. It was concluded that nonconsecutive-day samples were indicated.

8. The accuracy of weekly samples was found to be only

about as good as that of samples consisting of three days (5th, 15th, 25th of each month), neither kind of samples being sufficiently trustworthy for research work.

9. The accuracy of the every-fifth-day and every-second-day samples was found to be distinctly better than that of the weekly samples. The average of the obtained squared errors was found to agree closely with theoretical expectation, and the chi-square test indicated that the error distribution does not reliably differ from chance expectation.

APPENDIX I

Percentages of headlines falling in different subject-matter categories during calendar months and during four to five week periods

Subject Category:	1	2	3	4	5	6	7	8	9	10	No. of Headlines
April	2.1	20.5	9.9	1.6	1.4	31.4	18.3	5.6	7.4	1.8	312
Apr. 1 to Apr. 28	2.1	20.9	9.9	1.6	1.5	31.8	18.2	5.5	6.6	1.8	302
May	5.5	14.2	5.9	3.9	0	47.4	16.3	.3	6.4	0	388
Apr. 29–June 2	5.0	14.1	6.3	4.0	0	46.9	16.6	.7	6.3	0	426
June	5.6	12.1	3.4	3.2	.5	57.1	8.1	1.9	8.2	0	427
June 3–June 30	6.0	11.9	2.9	2.9	.5	58.1	7.1	1.8	8.8	0	399
July	27.3	2.9	.2	3.6	0	12.5	3.2	5.2	12.7	32.8	308
July 1–July 28	27.7	3.2	.2	3.9	0	13.3	3.6	3.9	12.4	31.6	281
August	20.3	2.2	.2	2.8	0	5.5	1.1	4.8	16.9	46.3	272
July 29–Sept. 1	20.6	2.5	.2	2.8	0	5.2	1.0	5.8	16.8	45.6	309
September	18.1	6.8	1.3	3.3	.3	8.2	0	2.6	15.8	43.7	304
Sept. 1–Sept. 30	17.3	6.8	1.4	3.1	.3	8.5	0	2.7	15.6	44.2	294

Appendix II

Standard errors of samples of finite populations and application of analysis of variance to such samples:

The conventional formula for the standard error of a percentage is $\sqrt{\dfrac{p\,(100-p)}{n-1}}$, where "p" is the sample percentage and "n" is the sample size. The meaning of the formula becomes clear if one recognizes that it is a simple application of the formula giving the standard error of a mean, $\sqrt{\dfrac{\sim^{z}}{n-1}}$; a percentage is a mean of a distribution, and p $(100-p)$ is the variance of the distribution in the sample.

The fact that a percentage is a mean is apparent as soon as one assigns the score 100 to f-elements of a sample which possess a trait, the score zero to the $n-f$ elements not possessing it. The arithmetic mean of these scores is the percentage, $\dfrac{100f}{r}=p$. In order to compute the variance of the distribution, we note that the f- elements possessing the trait deviate from the mean by $100-p$, the $n-f$ elements with the score zero by $p-o=p$. Thus the variance is

$$\frac{(100-p)^2\,f + p^2\,(n-f)}{n} = *$$

$$= \frac{(100^2 - 2 \cdot 100\,p + p^2)\,p}{100} + p^2 - \frac{p^3}{100} =$$

$$= 100p - 2p^2 + \frac{p^3}{100} + p^2 - \frac{p^3}{100} =$$

$$= 100p - p^2 = p\,(100-p)$$

The standard error of a mean is generally

$$\sqrt{\frac{\text{population variance}}{n}}$$

or, as an approximation, $\sqrt{\dfrac{\text{sample variance}}{n-1}}$, "$n-1$" being used instead of "n" in order to compensate for the negative bias of the sample variance. Substituting the value of sample

---

* Since $\dfrac{f}{n} = \dfrac{p}{100}$

variance into the latter formula, we obtain $\sqrt{\dfrac{p(100-p)}{n-1}}$.

However, the above expressions are applicable only if the sample is viewed as drawn from an infinite population. The standard error of a mean, in case of samples of a finite population, is $\sqrt{\dfrac{S^2(}{n(}1-\dfrac{n-1)}{N-1)}}$ * $=\sqrt{\dfrac{S^2(N-n)}{n(N-1)}}$ where S^2 is the population variance.

Substituting for S^2 the value of the population variance of a distribution in the above expression, we obtain the equivalent of the standard error of means drawn from a finite population: $\sqrt{\dfrac{P(100-P)(N-n)}{n(N-1)}}$ represents the standard error of a percentage obtained in a sample of a finite population, P representing the population percentage. The square of the standard error represents the best estimate of the average squared error (variance) of sample percentages representing a finite population.

If the samples drawn from a population vary in size, the weighted average of the estimated variances is

$\displaystyle\sum \dfrac{\dfrac{P(100-P)(N-n_k)n_k}{n_k(N-1)}}{\Sigma n_k}$ = (if we assume that the samples exhaust the population and that their number is K, so that

$\Sigma\, n_k = N) = \dfrac{P(100-P)(KN-N)}{(N(N-1)} = \dfrac{P(100-P)(K-1)}{N-1}$

Thus, the ratio of estimated variances of one-day samples and two-day samples may be readily computed. In a thirty-day month, in case of one-day samples, $K = 30$, while in the case of two-day samples, $K = 15$; the ratio is therefore $29 \div 14$.

If only sample percentages, p, are available, one can reason as follows, applying the principles of analysis of variance of a sample, viewing what we called a finite population as a sample, and what we called samples as the classes of the sample. $P(100 - P)$ is then the sample variance, the (s.e. mean)^2 the

---

* Peters and Van Vorhis, *Statistical Procedure and their Mathematical Basis*, p. 131. McGraw-Hill, New York and London, 1940.

estimated interclass variance. In a sample, the estimated interclass and intraclass variance add up to the sample variance. Consequently, the (s.e. mean)^2 plus the estimated intraclass variance, or average value of $p(100 - p)$, equals $P(100 - P)$.

Thus   average $p(100 - p) = \overline{p(100 - p)} = P(100 - P) -$

$$\frac{P(100 - P)\,(N - n)}{n(N - 1)} = \frac{P(100 - P)\,[n(n - 1) - N + n]}{n(N - 1)} =$$

$$\frac{P(100 - P)\,N\,(n - 1)}{(N - 1)n};\quad \text{Then } P(100 - P) =$$

$$\frac{\overline{p(100 - p)}n(N - 1)}{(n - 1)N}, \text{ and } \frac{P(100 - P)\,(N - n)}{n(N - 1)} =$$

$$\frac{\overline{p(100 - p)}\,(N - n)}{(n -)\,N} = \frac{\overline{p(100 - p)}}{n - 1}\left(1 - \frac{1)}{n}\right). \text{ This formula}$$

may be used with $p(100 - p)$, which is then treated as an estimate of $\overline{p(100 - p)}$.

Pursuing similar lines of reasoning further, analysis of variance can be generally applied to percentages.

Appendix III

Estimating the probable largest errors in six tries and in twenty-five tries:

If a monthly percentage is sampled six times, we have six chances to find a large error. The most probable value of the largest error may be defined as one which is surpassed and not reached equally often if six chances are taken an infinite number of times. In other words, the probability of not exceeding the most probable value of the maximal error is .5. What then is P, the probability of not exceeding it in one trial? The combined probability of not exceeding it in 6 trials is evidently P^6; hence $P^6 = .5$, and $P = \sqrt[6]{.5} = .8909$. If we assume, for simplicity's sake, that the error distribution is normal, the size of the critical ratio for which $P = .8909$ * may be determined from the normal probability tables. This

---

* In many tables of the normal probability integral P is not given, but one-half of P is given, designated as .50-q. If this is the case, one has to find .50-q = .4454.

value is 1.6; in other words, the most probable value of the largest error in 6 tries is 1.66 (assuming a normal error distribution).

Similarly, we obtain with 25 tries a value of $P = {}^{25}\sqrt{.5} = .9727$, $(.50 - q) = \dfrac{P}{2} = .4863$ and a critical ratio $= 2.21$. Hence, the ratio of the most probable maximal errors with 25 tries and with 6 tries is $2.21 \div 1.60 = 4.14 \div 3$.

Appendix IV

Derivation of distribution of sample percentages:

A sample of elements is drawn from a population of size N; a certain trait occurs F times, $\dfrac{100F}{N}$ being the percentage P; what is the probability of different f — s, i.e., number of occurrence of the trait in the sample? The answer can readily be given in terms of principles found in most textbooks of algebra for college freshmen.

The total number of samples of n elements is the number of combinations of N elements taken n at a time; the appropriate formula is $_NC_n = \dfrac{N(N - 1) \ldots (N - n + 1)}{n!}$.

The number of samples not containing the trait in question, so that f = 0, is the number of combinations of N — F elements (the number of elements not having the trait), taken n at a time =

$$_{N\text{-}F}C_n = \frac{(N - F)\,(N - F - 1) \ldots (N - F - n + 1)}{n!}$$

The probability of f = 0 is the ratio of the two expressions,

$$\frac{_{N\text{-}F}C_n}{_NC_n} = \frac{(N - F)\,(N - F - 1) \ldots (N - F - n + 1)}{N(N - 1) \ldots (N - n + 1)}$$

Similarly, the number of combinations giving f = 1 is $_{N\text{-}F}C_{n\text{-}1}$ times F, the number of elements possessing the trait, any one of which may be the one occurring in the combination; if f = 2, the number of combinations is $_{N\text{-}F}C_{n\text{-}2} \text{x}_F C_2 =$

$$\frac{(N - F)\,(N - F - 1) \ldots (N - F - n + 3)\,F\,(F - 1)}{(n - 2)!\ \ 2!}$$

If $f = K$, the number of combinations is

$$\frac{(N-F)(N-F-1)\ldots(N-F-n+K+1)\, F\,(F-1)\ldots(F-K+1)}{(N-K)!\ K!}.$$

Dividing these expressions by $_nC_N$ we obtain $\frac{_{n-1}C_{N-F}}{_nC_N} =$

$$\frac{n(N-F)(N-F-1)\ldots(N-F-n+2)\,F}{N(N-1)\ldots(N-n+1)} \quad (\text{since } \frac{n!}{(n-1)!} = n)\,;$$

$$\frac{_{n-2}C_{N-F}\ {_2C_{N-F}}}{_nC_N} = \frac{n(n-1)(N-F)(N-F-1)\ldots(N-F-n+3)\,F\,(F-1)}{2!\,N(N-1)\ldots(N-n+1)};$$

$$\frac{_{n-k}C_{N-F}\ {_kC_{N-F}}}{_nC_N} =$$

$$\frac{n(n-1)\ldots(n-k+1)(N-F)(N-F-1)\ldots(N-F-n+k+1)\,F\,(F-1)\ldots(F-k+1)}{k!\,N(N-1)(N-2)\ldots\ldots\ldots(N-n+1)}$$

As N and F increase, the expression converges towards the term of the binomial expansion,

$$\frac{n(n-1)\ldots(n-1+1)}{k!}\, P^k Q^{n-k}$$

Appendix V

Correcting the sums of the squared sample errors for the inaccurate monthly percentages:

Let us designate a true monthly percentage as P_K and an inaccurate one as P_K^1, and let us assume that there are m samples which exhaust the monthly headlines, as would be the case, for example, with two samples consisting of even days and odd days of a month. Then any deviation from the inaccurate percentage $p - P_K^1 = (p - P_K) - (P_K^1 - P_K)$ and its square, $(p - P_K^1)^2 = (p - P_K)^2 - 2(p - P_K)(P_K^1 - P_K) + (P_K^1 - P_K)^2$. For any given P_K^1 the mean of the squared deviations of the $p - s$ is (using bars above the expressions to indicate means):

$$\overline{(p - P_K^1)^2} = \overline{(p - P_K^2)} - 2(P_K^1 - P_K)\frac{\Sigma(p - P_K)}{m} +$$

$(P_K^1 - P_K)^2$. Since P_K is the mean of the $p - s$, $\Sigma(p - P_K) = 0$, and therefore $\overline{(p - P_K^1)^2} = \overline{(p - P_K)^2} + (P_K^1 - P_K)^2$. This expression holds true for every P_K^1. The sum of these expressions for all values of P_K, from P_1 to P_K is:

$$\underset{K=1}{\overset{K}{\Sigma}}\overline{(p-P_K)^2} = \underset{k=1}{\overset{K}{\Sigma}}\overline{(p-P_K)^2} + \Sigma\overline{(P_K-P)^2}$$

In other words, if five different samples of the same type as our "every fifth day" samples (e.g., a sample consisting of the 1st, 6th, 11th, 16th, 21st, 26th day of each month) had been investigated, the average of their squared deviations might have been computed for each monthly percentage and the averages for all the monthly percentages added. This sum, if incorrect monthly percentages had been used, would have differed from the true sum by $\Sigma(p^1-P)^2$. A computation of $\Sigma(p^1-P)^2$ gave 12.06. The value of the deviation of the sum of squared errors of samples not exhausting the monthly headline frequencies from the true value of the sum is not necessarily 12.06, but this number gives the best estimate of the deviation.

Chapter 8

THE COEFFICIENT OF IMBALANCE *

1. *Introduction* †

AN IMPORTANT aspect of research on interpersonal relationships is the precise statement of relationships between (a) the
symbols found in communications and (b) various other types
of behavior. The development of personality analysis and
propaganda analysis has been brought about primarily by
investigating and inventing situations in which rich interpersonal communications and other behaviors occur together
spontaneously or are elicited. The insights of Freud, for
example, arose from his intensive study of the symbolic communications of his neurotic patients under the special conditions of the psychoanalytic interview. The psychoanalysts,
however, have rarely made explicit the operations involved
in drawing conclusions from interview data. Perhaps because
the data secured by the free association technique were so
immediately suggestive, Freud and his followers have con-
tented themselves with the creation and elaboration of fruitful but ambiguous hypotheses. They have made little advance
in techniques of communications analysis necessary for spec-

* Published in *Psychometrica*, 8(1943), 105-119. Originally Document No.
31, *Experimental Division for the Study of Wartime Communications*, Library
of Congress, Nov. 1, 1942.

† The authors wish to express their appreciation to Mr. Harold Elsten,
Mr. Nathan Leites, and Mr. Ithiel Pool for valuable suggestions and criticisms.

ifying the conditions under which their theories might be confirmed.

Analysis of the spontaneous verbalizations of children in play situations, especially the work of Piaget, has also proved successful in the study of the development of personality. Although the majority of such studies tend to rely upon impressionistic analysis, some investigators of personality structure, such as Rorschach and his followers, have developed precise methods for classifying the symbol data which are elicited in standardized stimulus situations.

Like personality analysts, the investigators in the recently developed field of propaganda and public opinion have tended to rely to a large extent on impressionistic descriptions of communications and of the situations in which communications take place. It is true that these investigators have devised fairly satisfactory quantitative methods for the study of attitudes.* Questionnaires and public opinion polls facilitate quantitative analysis of simple attitudes by restricting the verbal responses of subjects to a choice of one of a few words (e.g., "agree," "disagree," "no opinion"). However, when concerned with mass communications—the press, radio, movies, speeches, etc.—the method of analysis has tended to remain largely impressionistic.

Impressionistic judgments suffice for broad classification of symbol data and description of gross temporal changes in the content of mass communications. Thus, we may report reliably that a certain movie is manifestly anti-Nazi, or that the contents of a certain newspaper changed from pro-isolation to pro-intervention. But if we wish to develop precise hypotheses concerning mass communications, there is a need for quantitative analysis of symbols.

In recent years a number of studies have been reported which are of methodological interest in so far as they have employed quantitative content analysis. In general, the method consists of tabulating the occurrences of content units (subject-predicate, assertion, or group of sentences) and classify-

* For a summary of the outstanding attitude-scales, such as those of L. L. Thurstone and of R. Likert, see Gardner and Lois Barclay Murphy and Theodore M. Newcomb, *Experimental Social Psychology*, New York: Harpers, 1937, Ch. 13.

ing them into such categories as favorable, unfavorable, or neutral presentation.*

The further development of quantitative content analysis requires the development of (a) fruitful and reliable categories for classification of content units, and (b) quantitative methods of expressing the total picture provided by the classified data: i.e., the development of general formulae to serve as definitions of general concepts.

The elaboration of categories has already made considerable progress, especially as a result of the contributions of Dr. Harold D. Lasswell† and Dr. Nathan C. Leites.‡

It is the purpose of this paper to develop a general formula which may be applied to classified content data in order to present an overall estimate of the degree of imbalance; i.e., the extent to which favorable, neutral, or unfavorable treatment is accorded to the topic or symbol under analysis. This Coefficient of Imbalance is intended to be applicable to all types of communications—including mass communications, psychoanalytic interviews, conversations, literary works, cartoons, pictures, etc.—except those in which the communication is arbitrarily restricted to specified symbols, as in multiple-choice or yes-no answers to questionnaires.

Moreover, this Coefficient is intended to apply to any trait

---

* Some of the pioneering studies are the following: Gordon W. Allport and Janet M. Faden, The psychology of newspapers: five tentative laws, *Public Opinion Quarterly*, 1940, 4, 687-703; Thomas S. Green, Jr., Mr. Cameron and the Ford Hour, *Public Opinion Quarterly*, 1939, 3, 669-75; Harold D. Lasswell, The World attention survey, *Public Opinion Quarterly*, 1941, 5, 456-462; David Nelson Rowe, Japanese propaganda in North China, 1937-1938, *Public Opinion Quarterly*, 1939, 3, 564-80; Douglas Waples and Bernard Berelson, *Public Communications and Public Opinion*, Chicago: Univ. Chicago Press, 1941; Quincy Wright and C. J. Nelson, American attitudes toward Japan and China, 1937-1938, *Public Opinion Quarterly*, 1939, 3, 46-62. For a discussion of the methodological problems of content analysis, see N. C. Leites and I. de Sola Pool, On content analysis, Document No. 26, Experimental Division for the Study of War Time Communications, Library of Congress.

† Harold D. Lasswell, A Provisional Classification of Symbol Data, *Psychiatry*, 1938, 1, 197-204;—and Associates, The politically significant content of the press: coding procedures, *Journalism Quarterly*, 1942, 19:1, 12-23;—Communications research and politics, in *Print, Radio, and Film in a Democracy* (edited by Douglas Waples), Chicago: Univ. Chicago Press, 1942, pp. 118-32; —Analyzing the content of mass communication: a brief introduction, Document No. 11, Experimental Division for the Study of War Time Communications, Library of Congress.

‡ Waples and Berelson, *ibid.* Appendix A; and unpublished manuscripts by N. C. Leites and I. de Sola Pool.

for which a communication is analyzed, provided that it is possible to classify units of content according to the occurrence of the trait, occurrence of the opposite trait, and nonoccurrence of the trait. Thus, while the discussion below is in terms of "Favorable" and "Unfavorable" contents, the meaning need not be restricted to pro- and anti-references to a symbol.

It is necessary to have a set of defined terms by which we may refer to those aspects of communications with which we are concerned. A "unit of content" is defined as the unit of meaning selected for analysis. The unit employed in a particular content analysis will depend upon the medium of the communication and the trait under consideration. In analyses of verbal material, the most frequently employed units of content are functional groups of sentences (e.g., newspaper articles), individual sentences, subject-predicate phrases, assertions, and terms.

To designate the entire content of a communication we shall use the term "the total content," which may be expressed quantitatively as the total number of units of content. By "relevant content" we mean the total number of units of content which contain the trait under investigation. The "total content" includes both "relevant content" and "nonrelevant content" (those units of content in which the trait does not occur). The "relevant content" includes the "favorable content" (those units of content which contain favorable occurrences), the "unfavorable content" (those units of content which contain unfavorable occurrences) and the "neutral content" (those units of content which contain occurrences of the trait which are neither favorable nor unfavorable).

To illustrate the use of these terms, let us say that we are investigating the bias in the presentation of Germany in a political pamphlet. We select an assertion as our unit of content. The total content is the total number of assertions on all topics in the pamphlet. (If the pamphlet is long, an estimate of the total content may be made by some short method such as determining the number of assertions on sample pages and multiplying the average per page by the total number of pages.) Only assertions referring to Germany are relevant content and each of these is recorded as either favorable, unfavorable, or neutral. After obtaining the frequency of content units which fall into each of these categories, it is desirable to express the total picture by means of a single numerical value, a Coefficient of Imbalance.

II. *Development of the Coefficient of Imbalance*

A satisfactory Coefficient of Imbalance must meet the requirements set up by a definition of "imbalance" which is consistent with current usage. Such a definition, making explicit the concept of imbalance in communications, is provided by the following ten criteria. In each criterion, the variables not specified as changing are understood to be held constant, with the exception of non-relevant content.* Detailed descriptions of the criteria are to be found in Section III below.

1. The Coefficient should always increase in the positive direction when the frequency of units of favorable content increases.
2. The Coefficient should always increase in the negative direction when the frequency of units of unfavorable content increases.
3. The Coefficient should always decrease in absolute value when the frequency of units of neutral content increases.
4. The Coefficient should always decrease in absolute value when the number of units of total content increases.
5. If there is no relevant content, the Coefficient must be zero.
6. If all the units of relevant content are neutral, the Coefficient must be zero.
7. If the number of units of favorable content is equal to the number of units of unfavorable content, the Coefficient must be zero.
8. If the number of units of favorable and unfavorable content are not equal, the Coefficient must not be zero.
9. If all the relevant content is favorable (or unfavorable), any variation in the frequency of units of favorable (or unfavorable) content should provide a directly proportionate variation in the Coefficient.

* Cf. p. 117.

10. If there is no neutral content, the Coefficient must vary directly as the ratio of the favorable to the unfavorable, whenever the difference between favorable and unfavorable content remains constant.

In developing the Coefficient of Imbalance, let us consider first an analysis of the relevant content. The relevant content may be classified into any number of sub-categories which may be regarded as falling into the main categories: favorable, unfavorable, and neutral content. Analysis into different degrees of favorableness and unfavorableness will determine the number (m) of sub-categories. It is theoretically possible to assign a numerical value to each sub-category (x_i).

Considering the frequency of content units which are in each sub-category as a weight (w_i), we may obtain a weighted average presentation of the relevant content (A); i.e.,

$$A = \frac{x_1 w_1 + x_2 w_2 + x_3 w_3 + \ldots + x_m w_m}{w_1 + w_2 + w_3 + \ldots + w_m} \tag{1}$$

$$= \frac{\sum\limits_{i=1}^{m} x_i w_i}{\sum\limits_{i=1}^{m} w_i}$$

Let us consider next an analysis of the total content. The total content includes all of the sub-categories of the relevant content, and in addition it includes any number (M) of non-relevant sub-categories (N_j). Again, each sub-category of the total content $(x_i$ and $N_j)$ theoretically may be assigned a numerical value and the frequencies of content units in each sub-category (w_j) may be regarded as weights so that a weighted average presentation of the total content (T) is obtainable; i.e.,

$$T = \frac{\sum\limits_{i=1}^{m} x_i w_i + \sum\limits_{j=1}^{M} N_j w_j}{\sum\limits_{i=1}^{m} w_i + \sum\limits_{j=1}^{M} w_j} . \tag{2}$$

In assigning values to the sub-categories of the total content, (x_i and N_j), it is desirable to indicate favorable sub-categories as having a positive direction. Hence all values attached to favorable sub-categories will be positive. Since unfavorable content is the opposite of favorable, it follows that unfavorable sub-categories should be assigned negative values. If there are several sub-categories of favorable content and of unfavorable content, the numerical values assigned to them must be determined by empirical evaluation of the degree or intensity of favorableness or unfavorableness. In the absence of a means of differentiating between degrees of favorableness or unfavorableness, all favorable units of content may be placed in a single category with the value of plus one ($+1$) and all unfavorable units of content may be placed in a single category with the value of minus one (-1).

The neutral category by definition contains relevant content units which are neither favorable nor unfavorable but lie midway between them and so must be assigned the value zero (o). Similarly, non-relevant units of content are neither favorable nor unfavorable and so must also be assigned the value zero. Hence, non-relevant units of content may be considered as being in a single category (which makes $M = 1$) and the weight of this category (w_j) is simply the number of non-relevant units of content, which we may represent by N without a subscript, $w_j = N$. (3)

Let the favorable content be represented by "y" and the unfavorable content by "v" so that

$$y = x > o \qquad (4)$$
$$-v = x < o. \qquad (5)$$

Making these substitutions in the weighted average presentation of relevant content (1) and in the weighted average presentation of the total content (2) and making the appropriate changes in the weight subscripts, we obtain

$$A = \frac{\displaystyle\sum_{i=1}^{m_y} y_i\, w_{y_i} - \sum_{i=1}^{m_v} v_i\, w_{v_i}}{\displaystyle\sum_{1}^{m_y} w_{y_i} + \sum_{1}^{m_v} w_{v_i} + n} \qquad (6)$$

(where $n =$ frequency of units in the neutral category) or

$$A = \frac{\sum_{i=1}^{m_y} y_i\, w_{y_i} - \sum_{i=1}^{m_v} v_i\, w_{v_i}}{r} \tag{7}$$

(where $r =$ total units of relevant content). Also since $N_j = 0$ and $\sum w_j = N$, we obtain from (2)

$$T = \frac{\sum_{i=1}^{m_y} y_i\, w_{y_i} - \sum_{i=1}^{m_v} v_i\, w_{v_i}}{\sum_{i=1}^{m_y} w_{y_i} + \sum_{i=1}^{m_v} w_{v_i} + n + N} \tag{8}$$

$$= \frac{\sum_{i=1}^{m_y} y_i\, w_{y_i} - \sum_{i=1}^{m_v} v_i\, w_{v_i}}{t} \tag{9}$$

(where $t =$ number of units of total content).

To simplify the notation, let $f = \sum_{i=1}^{m_y} y_i\, w_{y_i}$, and $u = \sum_{i=1}^{m_v} v_i\, w_{v_i}$ so that $A = \dfrac{f - u}{r}$ and $T = \dfrac{f - u}{t}$.

(It will be noted that $r = f + u + n$ and that $t = f + u + n + N$, if $m_y = m_v = 1$).

Neither the average of relevant content (A), nor the average of total content (T), will alone serve as an adequate coefficient of imbalance. The former meets all the criteria except 4 and 9; the latter meets all except 3* and 10. We may expect that some combinations of these two averages will meet all of the criteria, for we observe that where one fails the other is successful.

The mathematically inclined reader may demonstrate for himself that none of the combinations resulting from the four fundamental operations of mathematics (addition, subtraction, multiplication, and division†) will give a formula

---

* Since "t" is required to be held constant, an increase of neutral content implies an equal decrease in non-relevant content so that the value of "t" remains unchanged. Cf. p. 117 for a fuller discussion of "t".

† Division provides an index to the attention devoted to the topic or symbol, $\dfrac{r}{t}$.

which will satisfy all ten of the criteria. Nor are the arithmetic, geometric, or harmonic means satisfactory. However, separate formulae for favorable and unfavorable imbalance may be necessary. Thus, one of these procedures may provide a formula which can be broken down into two components: a coefficient of favorable imbalance and a coefficient of unfavorable imbalance. Such a result is obtained by analysis of the product of the two averages.

$$AT = \frac{f - u}{r} \cdot \frac{f - u}{t} \tag{10}$$

$$= \frac{f^2 - fu}{rt} \cdot \frac{fu - u^2}{rt}. \tag{11}$$

Let the first component be called the Coefficient of favorable imbalance, C_f, and the second be called the Coefficient of unfavorable imbalance, C_u. Thus, the combined influence, AT, may be regarded as the difference between the Coefficients of favorable and unfavorable imbalance.

$$AT = C_f - C_u, \tag{12}$$

where

$$C_f = \frac{f^2 - fu}{rt} = \frac{f - u}{r} \cdot \frac{f}{t} \tag{13}$$

and

$$C_u = \frac{uf - u^2}{rt} = \frac{f - u}{r} \cdot \frac{u}{t}. \tag{14}$$

It may observed that the factors making up these Coefficients may be given a rational interpretation in terms of quantitative concepts. The first factor in each, $\frac{f - u}{r}$, is the weighted average presentations of relevant content (A). The second factor, $\frac{f}{t}$ or $\frac{u}{t}$, is the relative frequency of the favorable or unfavorable content. Hence, the second factor represents the extent to which the total content was utilized to present favorable (or unfavorable) content. When the imbalance is favorable, i.e., $f > u$, it is the extent to which the total content was utilized to present favorable content that is the determining factor. Similarly, when he imbalance is unfavorable, i.e., $f < u$, the determining factor is the extent to which the total content was utilized to present unfavorable content. Hence, when $f > u$ the imbalance is favorable and the Coefficient is given by C_f; when $f < u$ the imbalance is favorable and the Coefficient is given by C_u. These two formulae may be used as a Coefficient of Imbalance, which expresses quantitively the imbalance of any communication with respect to the topic or symbol under investigation.

The primary advantage of such a quantitative measure is that hypotheses involving imbalance may be tested by employing statistical techniques. Thus a hypothesis concerning the difference in imbalance between two groups of communications may be confirmed or disconfirmed by testing the significance of the difference between the means of the Coefficients of Imbalance for the two groups. Similarly, the Coefficients of Imbalance for a given symbol in a group of communications may be correlated with (a) the Coefficients for another symbol in the same group, (b) the Coefficients for a related group of communications, or (c) another set of quantitative measures of some non-symbolic event (such as election returns or income of the author).

III. *Demonstration of the Adequacy of the Coefficient of Imbalance*

Criterion 1. *The Coefficient should always increase in the positive direction when the frequency of units of favorable content increases.*

Let df represent a positive increment in the favorable frequency, f. Then, proving that Criterion 1 is satisfied by the formulae requires proving the inequalities:

$$\frac{(f + df)^2 - u(f + df)}{(r + df)t} > \frac{f^2 - fu}{rt} \quad \text{when } f > u$$

and

$$\frac{u(f + df) - u^2}{(r + df)t} > \frac{uf - u^2}{rt} \quad \text{when } f < u.$$

This demonstration may be made algebraically or by using the calculus and differentiating C_f and C_u with respect to f and showing that the slope does not change sign or become zero for positive values of f.

Criterion 2. *The Coefficient should always increase in the negative direction when the frequency of units of unfavorable content increases.*

Let du represent a positive increment in the unfavorable frequency. Then Criterion 2 becomes:

$$\frac{f^2 - (u + du)f}{(r + du)t} < \frac{f^2 - uf}{rt} \quad \text{when } f > u$$

and

$$\frac{f(u + du) - (u + du)^2}{(r + du)t} < \frac{fu - u^2}{rt} \quad \text{when } f < u.$$

This demonstration may also be made algebraically or by using the calculus and differentiating with respect to the independent variable.

Criterion 3. *The Coefficient should always decrease in absolute value when the frequency of units of neutral content increases.*

Since a unit of neutral content is defined as a unit of relevant content which is neither favorable nor unfavorable, but the midpoint between these two, this requirement is essential to making the coefficient consistent with the definition of neutrality.

Let dn represent a positive increment in neutral frequency and this becomes, for $f > u$,

$$\frac{f^2 - fu}{(r + dn)t} < \frac{f^2 - fu}{rt} \quad \text{or} \quad r + dn > r.$$

and for $u > f$:

$$\frac{uf - u^2}{(r + dn)t} < \frac{uf - u^2}{rt} \quad \text{or} \quad r + dn > r.$$

Criterion 4. *The Coefficient should always decrease in absolute value when the number of units of total content increases.*

This requirement means that a communication which uses only a small proportion of its available units of content to present a given number of units of relevant content is less imbalanced than one which uses a large proportion of its available units of content to present the same number of units of relevant content. In other words, if the total units of content increase, the number of units in each component of the relevant content must increase in the same proportion in order that the same degree of imbalance be maintained.

Let dt represent a positive increment in the number of units of total content and the proof is exactly the same as for Criterion 3.

Criterion 5. *If there is no relevant content, the Coefficient must be zero.*

If only non-relevant units of content occur, the communication cannot be imbalanced with respect to the topic or symbol under analysis.

When $f = u = r = 0,$

$$C_f = \frac{f^2 - fu}{rt} = \frac{0}{0}, \text{ which is indeterminate.}$$

With f as the only independent variable,

$$\lim_{f \to 0} \frac{f^2 - fu}{ft} = \lim_{f \to 0} \frac{2f}{t} = 0$$

by differentiation of the numerator and denominator with respect to f.

Also, $C_u = \dfrac{fu - u^2}{rt} = \dfrac{0}{0}$, which is indeterminate.

With u as the independent variable,

$$\lim_{u \to 0} \frac{uf - u^2}{ut} = \lim_{u \to 0} \frac{-2u}{t} = 0.$$

Criterion 6. *If all the units of relevant content are neutral, the Coefficient must be zero.*

If only neutral units occur, the communication cannot be imbalanced.

If

$$f = u = 0, r = n,$$

then
$$C_t = \frac{f^2 - fu}{rt} = 0 \text{ and } C_u = \frac{uf - u^2}{rt} = 0.$$

Criterion 7. *If the number of units of favorable content is equal to the number of units of unfavorable content, the Coefficient must be zero.*

In this case, the communication is exactly balanced. If
$$f = u,$$
then
$$C_f = \frac{f^2 - fu}{rt} = 0 \text{ and } C_u = \frac{uf - u^2}{rt} = 0.$$

Criterion 8. *If the number of units of favorable and unfavorable content are not equal, the Coefficient must not be zero.*

In this case, the communication must be imbalanced. When
$$f > u, f^2 > fu \text{ and } f^2 - fu \neq 0.$$
Therefore
$$C_f = \frac{f^2 - fu}{rt} \neq 0.$$
Similarly when
$$u > f, C_u = \frac{uf - u^2}{rt} \neq 0.$$

Criterion 9. *If all of the relevant content is favorable (or unfavorable), any variation in the favorable (or unfavorable) content should provide a directly proportionate variation in the Coefficient.*

Consider two communications with the same total content, in each of which all of the relevant content is imbalanced in the same direction. If, for example, one publication has twice as many favorable content units as another for the same total content, a rational judgment indicates that the one is twice as imbalanced as the other. (Naturally, cases with unfavorable or neutral content as well as favorable content would make an exact rational comparison of two cases impossible.)

When

$$f = r, u = n = 0, \text{ and } t \text{ is constant;}$$

$$C_f = \frac{f^2 - fu}{rt} = \frac{f}{t} \text{ and } C_u = \frac{uf - u^2}{rt} = 0.$$

Let a be the general factor for relative proportions of favorable content. If one communication with a Coefficient C'_f has "f" units of content, and the other with a Coefficient C''_f has "af" units,

$$C'_f = \frac{f}{t} \text{ and } C''_f = \frac{af}{t} = aC'_f.$$

Similar reasoning demonstrates that the Coefficient satisfies the criterion when $u = r$.*

Criterion 10. *If there is no neutral content, the Coefficient must vary directly as the ratio of the favorable to the unfavorable, whenever the difference between favorable and unfavorable content remains constant.*†

(Thus a communication having no neutral, 6 favorable and 1 unfavorable references is more imbalanced than one having 60 favorable and 55 unfavorable—the former $\dfrac{f}{u}$ ratio being 6:1, the latter 12:11.)

Let "d" represent a positive increment to both the favorable and unfavorable frequency.

If $f > u$, the ratio f/u decreases,

$$\text{i.e., } \frac{f + d}{u + d} < \frac{f}{u}.$$

In this case the criterion states that

---

* It is also true that increasing the total content by the factor "a" decreases the Coefficient by the factor "a" because "t" appears as a single factor in the denominator.

† When there is neutral content ($n \neq 0$), the Coefficient varies directly as the ratio of the favorable to the unfavorable-plus-neutral content ($\dfrac{f}{u + n}$). This is a reasonable relationship since $u + n$ constitute the "non-favorable" relevant content, $(r - f)$, corresponding to the "non-favorable" or unfavorable content in the simpler case stated by the criterion.

$$\frac{f + d - (u + d)}{f + d + u + d} \cdot \frac{f + d}{t} < \frac{f - u}{f + u} \frac{f}{t} \cdot \frac{f}{t},$$

which may be proved.

If $u > f$, the formula for C_u is used and the inequality is also true.

The fact that there is a transition from one formula to the other requires a careful scrutiny of the functions at the point of juncture, $f = u$. The continuity of the Coefficient functions and their derivatives with respect to the variables f and u at the point $f = u$ must be demonstrated before the transition is justifiable.

Continuity of the function itself and its derivatives is questionable only when f or u is the independent variable. If n or t be the independent variable, there is no change from one formula to the other. The matter of considering t as a constant merits some further consideration inasmuch as t is the total units of content in the communication and so is the sum of the units of relevant content and non-relevant content; i.e., $t = f + u + n + N$. Hence variation in f (or any of the other components) would cause a variation in t. A more useful result is obtained by considering N as a balancing component when other variables change. An increase, for example, in f necessitates a corresponding decrease in N, and t would remain constant. If t is to be the only independent variable, only N could change since f, u, and n are to be constant.

Consider first the continuity of the function when f is the independent variable. Inspection of the formulae will reveal the continuity if all variables, except C and f, are held fast. As f approaches u through values less than u, C_u approaches 0, passes through 0, and as f exceeds u, C_f exceeds 0 by continually larger values. That is,

$$\lim_{f \to u} C = C \Big|_{f \to u} = 0.$$

which satisfies the definition of continuity. Similar reasoning demonstrates the continuity of $C = \phi(u)$ when all independent variables except u are held fast.

Continuity of the first derivative may be demonstrated as follows: (Let ∂ be the symbol for partial differentiation.)

Case 1. $C = \phi\,(f,\,u,\,n,\,t)$. Let f be the independent variable.

$$C_f = \frac{f^2 - fu}{(f + u + n)t} \text{ for } f > u \text{ and } C_u = \frac{uf - u^2}{(f + u + n)t} \text{ for } f < u.$$

$$\frac{\partial C_f}{\partial f} = \frac{(f+u+n)t(2f-u)-(f^2-fu)t}{(f+u+n)^2\,t^2}$$

$$= \frac{(f+u+n)\,(2f-u)-(f^2-fu)}{(f+u+n)^2\,t}$$

$$\frac{\partial C_u}{\partial f} = \frac{(f+u+n)t(u)-(uf-u^2)t}{(f+u+n)^2\,t^2}$$

$$= \frac{(f+u+n)u-(uf-u^2)}{(f+u+n)^2\,t}$$

At the point $f = u$,

$$\left.\frac{\partial C_f}{\partial f}\right|_{f=u} = \frac{(2u+n)u-0}{(2u+n)^2\,t} = \frac{u}{rt}$$

At the point $f = u$,

$$\left.\frac{\partial C_u}{\partial f}\right|_{f=u} = \frac{(2u+n)u-0}{(2u+n)^2\,t} = \frac{u}{rt}$$

since $r = f + u + n$,

or more correctly expressed

$$\lim_{\substack{f \to u \\ f > u}} \frac{\partial C_f}{\partial f} = \frac{u}{rt} \text{ and } \lim_{\substack{f \to u \\ f < u}} \frac{\partial C_u}{\partial f} = \frac{u}{rt}$$

Hence, the first derivatives are the same as $f = u$.

Case 2. Let u be the independent variable.

$$\frac{\partial C_f}{\partial u} = -\frac{\partial C_u}{\partial f} \text{ and } \frac{\partial C_u}{\partial u} = -\frac{\partial C_f}{\partial f}.$$

This equality becomes apparent if for u we substitute $-f$ and for f we substitute $-u$. The formulae are symmetrical with respect to f and u except for sign.

Demonstration of the continuity of the higher derivatives would be a more complex problem in the calculus. But the fact that the transition through the critical point, $f = u$, is made in a continuous fashion by the function and that the slope is continuous and equal for both formulae, at this point, is sufficient to insure against rejection of the formula on the grounds of discontinuity.

If the Coefficient is graphed with each of the four variables in turn being considered as the independent variable, it will be observed that the function is continuous as the formulae are interchanged. The relatively constant and low degree of curvature with respect to each variable throughout the range of values to be considered may also be observed, indicating that there are no abnormal ranges in which a small change in one variable results in a much larger change in the Coefficient than occurs in any other equal range.

IV. *Summary*

A Coefficient of Imbalance was developed which may be applied to any type of communication provided that it may be classified into the following categories: favorable content (f), unfavorable content (u), neutral content (n), and non-relevant content (N). The average presentation (A) of relevant content (r) and the average presentation (T) of total content (t) were considered as two main factors involved in the measurement of imbalance. It was shown that the combined influence of these two factors could be reduced to two components, the Coefficient of favorable imbalance and the Coefficient of unfavorable imbalance. These Coefficients are meaningful in that they represent: (a) the average presentation of relevant content $\dfrac{(f - u)}{r}$, and (b) the degree to which the opportunity to present the predominant direction was used $\dfrac{(f \text{ or } u)}{t}$. The formulae provided a precise definition of imbalance:

$$C_f = \frac{f^2 - fu}{rt} \text{ where } f > u$$

and

$$C_u = \frac{fu - u^2}{rt} \text{ where } f < u.$$

This Coefficient of Imbalance was shown to be adequate with respect to ten criteria which together express the concept of imbalance.

III
APPLICATIONS

Chapter 9

DETECTION: PROPAGANDA DETECTION
AND THE COURTS

FACTS OBTAINED by the methods of content analysis have been
admitted in evidence by federal courts. In every instance, the
problem before the court was the detection of propaganda in
a channel of public communication. The Department of
Justice relied in part upon quantitative studies of content in
presenting the government's case.

Litigation first arose in connection with the enforcement
of legislation passed by the Congress designed to disclose to
the American public the identity of persons employed for the
dissemination of antidemocratic propaganda in this country. The McCormack Act provided for the registration of
foreign agents with the State Department, where the list
would be available for inspection.[1]

The disclosure policy of the legislation is exceedingly important for the proper functioning of a democratic system.[2]
Popular government, we well know, depends upon the
morality and the rationality of all who share in the making
of important decisions, and this includes the voters no less
than the legislators, executives, administrators, judges, party
politicians, and pressure-group leaders. If opinions and decisions are to be relatively rational, they must be made on the
basis of full knowledge and, so far as the general public is

concerned, the task of providing the needed body of fact and interpretation is the responsibility of the media of mass communication—chiefly the press, radio and film. We may say that sound decisions always depend upon the proper performance of the *intelligence function*, and that rational public opinion is found only when the mass media perform the intelligence function for the general public by bringing to the focus of general attention what is needed to reach rational judgments.

Few will deny that news and comments are more likely to be evaluated correctly when their source is known. American citizens have had long political experience in evaluating what is said to them by the spokesmen of partisan, economic, sectional, religious and other groups. But no one can expect to make sound judgments when the source of a statement is undivulged.

For several years the Congress has been experimenting with legal measures designed to protect the American citizen from being made a fool of. The aim of such legislation is to disclose the affiliations of all whose statements are disseminated in the press, radio and other channels of communication. The postal registration law requires disclosure of identity of editors, managers and owners of all publications using the mails under the second-class mailing privilege. In addition, the postal law specifies that news and advertising must be separated and the latter plainly labeled. The Federal Corrupt Practices Act and the Hatch Act require full public disclosure of sources and amounts of campaign funds of political parties in federal elections, and committees of the Congress are expected to issue summary reports to the public when an election has been held. The Federal Communications Commission studies and reports the ownership and control of radio stations and broadcasting networks. After the passage of the McCormack Act, another disclosure statute (the Voorhis Act) was enacted to require the registration of certain categories of organizations, whether under foreign or domestic control, with the Department of Justice.[3]

The policy of disclosure is intended to protect the integrity of public opinion, and to provide the citizen with what he needs to know in judging the competence and impartiality of whoever supplies him with "news" and "comment." When the vigilant citizen sees that he depends upon a limited or biased source, he may be expected to look for other sources capable of providing a more balanced picture of reality on the basis of which action may be taken. Hence we may affirm that the policy of disclosure is a special application of the general principle of balance, according to which the probability of a rational judgment is improved when competing reports and interpretations are balanced in relation to one another.

In periods of crisis, it is peculiarly necessary to identify enemies of democracy, and to stimulate the members of the public to be on guard in evaluating what is said. Out of loyalty to their own ideals, democracies are compelled to permit the dissemination of statements hostile to their ideals.[4] This is a source of strength, not of weakness. It makes it necessary for everyone to clarify the primary assumptions of democracy and to keep fresh his devotion to the ideal of human dignity. But this source of strength is sacrificed if democratic leaders do not keep the channels of communication free from unlabeled statements emanating from the enemies of democracy.

Prosecutions that arise under a registration act directed at foreign agents can clarify matters for the public with respect to the identity of such agents, and can expose their operating technique. When the enemy of democracy is a foreign propagandist, his "line" can be identified; thoughtful citizens will examine themselves to see if they have inadvertently been dupes of antidemocratic propaganda. They are enabled to identify fellow-citizens who parallel an enemy line so closely that they provide grounds for presuming deliberate intent to aid the enemy.

The main purpose of a disclosure statute, however, is not served by the publicity that attends whatever prosecutions arise under it. The policy of disclosure is most effective when applied in conjunction with an Instant Reply Plan, which promptly provides a counterstream of prodemocratic news and comment.[5] Unless antidemocratic material is promptly nullified, confidence in democratic aspirations and institutions may go by default. Common sense and science join in testifying to the potent effect of repetition upon sentiment and opinion. Unless we remind ourselves of the facts of history, we forget history; unless we repeat acts of devotion to God, we are in danger of forgetting God. Repetition is essential to the preservation of the good, and re-emphasis is necessary to the prevention of evil.

The balance of what we read, see and hear needs to be strongly tilted on the side of democracy, and this depends upon our vigilance in nullifying antidemocratic material by means of prodemocratic statement. We can not afford to be complacent in the presence of news and comment that undermine our fundamental faith and practice. We must tolerate opinions contrary to ours, but there is no excuse for allowing them to preëmpt the field.

The detection of propagandists is not always a simple task. To some extent we can discover propaganda principals and agents by studying the affiliation of specific individuals. If we find that a lecturer or news correspondent is paid by a foreign power, we have evidence of an entangling commitment. If we find that he disseminates foreign news and interpretations, we have evidence of his "line."

However, it is easy to take statements out of their context and to obtain a distorted picture of what is said. For this reason, in examining parallels between what appears in one channel and what is disseminated in a known propaganda channel, it is important to consider the communication as a whole. It is also important for the analysis to be conducted in a scientific spirit and by means of an objective procedure.

The scientific study of what is said in different channels of communication has a long history and has been carried out for many purposes.[6] One of the most persistent scholarly aims has been to reveal the style of writers and orators.[7] Another purpose has been to show the distributions and trends of popular thought and feeling.[8]

These objective procedures were utilized in connection with certain cases that arose under the McCormack Act and other statutes for the protection of the country. The *Book-niga* case involved a corporation engaged chiefly in the dissemination of books, periodicals and other publications. Although a subsidiary of a foreign government (the U.S.S.R.), *Bookniga* had failed to register. Friedrich Ernest Auhagen was indicted for failure to register as a "publicity agent, agent and representative of the Government of Germany." *Transocean G.m.b.H.*, a news agency, was likewise indicted for failure to register, since it was a "corporation organized and existing under and by virtue of the laws of Germany." The indictment of William Dudley Pelley was on wholly different grounds, namely, sedition.[9]

The government asked the writer to analyze certain materials, in each case, and to be prepared to testify concerning what was said in them. The results of this research were fully presented to the court in the *Bookniga, Transocean* and *Pelley* cases.[10]

The *Bookniga* and *Transocean* cases involved great quantities of printed and unprinted matter. Four periodicals, 76 books in the English language, and 132 books in the Russian language were examined in connection with the *Bookniga* prosecution. Particularly detailed analyses were made of the periodicals. Four kinds of material were relevant to the *Transocean* proceedings: "cables" to Germany from America; "transmissions" to South America from America; English news service to Americans; and German news service to Americans. Samples were taken of each type for selected months.

The *Auhagen* case involved a very limited number of issues of two magazines (*Today's Challenge* and *The Forum Observer*). The *Pelley* prosecution involved intensive study of eleven issues of a periodical, *The Galilean*. For purposes of comparison, certain studies were made of American publications in the *Transocean* and *Auhagen* cases.

Certain standards were used for the detection of propaganda. The term "propaganda," when it appears in this discussion, should be understood to mean the manipulation of symbols as a means of influencing attitudes on controversial matters.[11]

The following standards of propaganda detection may be briefly summarized.[12] The meaning of each will be thoroughly demonstrated when applied to specific situations. (No significance is to be attached to the order of mention.)

1. *The Avowal Test.* Explicit identification with one side of a controversy.
2. *The Parallel Test.* The content of a given channel is compared with the content of a known propaganda channel. Content is classified according to themes.

3. *The Consistency Test.* The consistency of a stream of communication with the declared propaganda aims of a party to a controversy. The aims may be official declarations or propaganda instructions.
4. *The Presentation Test.* The balance of favorable and unfavorable treatment given to each symbol (and statement) in controversy.
5. *The Source Test.* Relatively heavy reliance upone one party to a controversy for material.
6. *The Concealed Source Test.* The use of one party to a controversy as a source, without disclosure.
7. *The Distinctiveness Test.* The use of vocabulary peculiar to one side of a controversy.
8. *The Distortion Test.* Persistent modification of statements on a common topic in a direction favorable to one side of a controversy. Statements may be omitted, added, or over- or under-emphasized (for example).

In the *Bookniga* case most of these tests were utilized. The consistency (with Nazi aim) test was applied to the *Auhagen* and *Transocean* material. The paralleling of Nazi themes figured in the *Pelley* case, and the distortion test was used in the preparation of *Transocean* data.[13]

1. *The Avowal Test*

In examining any given content for the detection of propaganda, the simplest test is, of course, the avowal test. There may be out-and-out declarations that the channel is an authoritative medium of propaganda for one side or another. Even this test can not be taken too literally, however, since other indications may show that the assertion is false.

In the court cases here summarized, the only use made of the avowal test was in the *Bookniga* litigation, when attention was called to the results of analyzing the self-advertisements published in the *Moscow News*. A record was made of the frequency with which the publication described itself to be "authoritative" in what it had to say about the USSR.

The following quotations, selected from these advertisements, show what is meant by authoritative references:

(1) Indispensable to all who want to keep track of latest developments in Soviet industry (etc.). July 5, 1932, p. 5.

(2) It is indispensable for the reader and student of Soviet affairs desiring authentic information about the Soviet Union. August 25, 1932, p. 8.

(3) MOSCOW NEWS, packed with exclusive stories, pictures and authoritative articles, tells you about the Soviet Union as no other English publication can. July 7, 1934, p. 11; July 21, 1934, p. 10.

(4) You will find information . . . that is available nowhere else in English.

. . . 'Moscow News' has attracted a group of contributors who give you authoritative information on every phase of Soviet life. They write of successes and difficulties, plans and problems, with that intimate knowledge which comes from day-to-day participation in the events they describe. June 20, 1935, p. 11.

(5) Soviet news that's STRAIGHT from the USSR. July 11, 1935, p. 9.

(6) Outstanding Soviet writers and specialists in many fields give you an authoritative picture of life in the USSR . . . VERA INBER . . . BORIS AGAPOV, noted Journalist, . . . AND MANY OTHER well-informed special writers and authorities on various subjects contribute to the pages . . . April 20, 1938, p. 22.

The self-advertisements appearing in the *Moscow News* between October 5, 1930, and August 2, 1938, were examined. During this period there were 473 issues of the *News,* of which 48 issues were missing in the collection studied (43 of the missing issues being prior to January, 1932). In the 425 issues that were examined, 243 self-advertisements were found. Of these, 107 referred to the authoritativeness of the *Moscow News;* that is, in almost half of the advertisements in the paper it was recommended to readers as an authoritative source regarding the USSR.

Between August 2, 1938, and March 10, 1939, there were 33 issues of the *Moscow News;* 14 self-advertisements were published during this period. Of these 14 ads, 12 referred to the alleged authoritativeness of the publication.

For the entire period, therefore, between October 1930 and March 1939, 458 issues of the *News* were examined (48 issues missing); 243 self-advertisements were found and described; 119 referred to the authoritativeness of the publication.

2. The Parallel Test

In the *Pelley* case the parallel test was applied to the contents of the periodical for which the defendants were responsible. The problem was to determine the degree to which the contents of the *Galilean* ran parallel with the contents of channels known to be under the control of enemy propaganda. The Federal Communications Commission testified to the classification of Nazi propaganda themes used by the monitoring service of the Commission.[14] The duty of the monitoring service was to record and analyze the short-wave broadcasts directed to this country (and other places in this Hemisphere). In connection with their regular course of business, the Nazi propaganda material was grouped into 14 themes. (Number 14 has three sub-themes.)

An investigation was made of the relationship between what was published in *The Galilean* and the 14 Nazi themes. The method was statement analysis, which is somewhat more intensive than item classification. In illustrating the themes, however, certain extracts were taken, without breaking them down into detailed statements. The examples (in some instances contradictions are practically zero and no examples are given):

Nazi Propaganda Theme 1

The United States is internally corrupt. (e.g., There are political and economic injustice, war profiteering, plutocratic exploitation, Communist sedition, Jewish conspiracy, and spiritual decay within the United States.)

Consistency

"In other words, the spiritual status of America is not only being ignored; it is being torpedoed, in the interest of Luciferian cliques and blocs that want to work their crackpot caprices on the whole body politic."

—*The Galilean*, January 26, 1942, p. 9.

Contradiction

"As this war goes into reverse upon reverse, the men responsible for starting it, are going to get the odium. Inefficiency, politics, wastralism (sic), patronage, profligacy, nepotism—these must encounter the mounting wrath of Gentiles. New-Dealism is DONE!" *

—*The Galilean*, December 29, 1941, p. 6.

Nazi Propaganda Theme 2

The foreign policies of the United States are morally unjustifiable. (e.g., They are selfish, bullying, imperialistic, hypocritical and predatory.)

Consistency

"It is futile to plead that American territory and property were wantonly attacked in the Hawaiias. The attack obviously resulted from a baleful and provocative diplomacy which appeared to neglect no opportunity to make actionist enemies of all major countries on the globe but England."

—*The Galilean*, January 5, 1942, p. 1.

Nazi Propaganda Theme 3

The President of the United States is reprehensible. (e.g., He is a warmonger and a liar, unscrupulous, responsible for suffering, and a pawn of Jews, Communists or Plutocrats.)

Consistency

"Mr. President, at any time within the past year, might easily, by the turn of a phrase or the erasure of a word, have prevented the attack on Pearl Harbor (sic), Sunday morning, December 7."

—*The Galilean*, January 5, 1942, p. 4.

Nazi Propaganda Theme 4

Great Britain is internally corrupt. (e.g., There are political and economic injustice, war profiteering, plutocratic exploitation, Communist sedition, Jewish conspiracy, and spiritual decay within Great Britain.)

Consistency

"England flourished for a thousand years under Nordic jurisdiction, crude as it may have been in its sophistries. But the moment that Nordic England permitted the Luci-

---

* Unless there is a forecast of violence, or an appeal to violence, a statement that the government can be changed puts our political institutions in a favorable light and contradicts the corruption theme.

ferian Israelites jurisdiction over its financial and political affairs, its degeneracy set in."

—The Galilean, February 2, 1942, p. 30.

Nazi Propaganda Theme 5

The foreign policies of Great Britain are morally unjustifiable. (e.g., They are selfish, bullying, imperialistic, hypocritical and predatory.)

Consistency

"England has held us up to ridicule and contempt. She has sought to smash the sovereignty of America on three occasions."

—The Galilean, January 26, 1942, p. 10.

Nazi Propaganda Theme 6

Prime Minister Churchill is reprehensible. (e.g., He is a warmonger and a liar, unscrupulous, responsible for suffering, and a pawn of Jews, Communists or Plutocrats.)

Consistency

"Mr. Churchill concedes—even brags—that he has been for thirty-one months assiduously plotting and finagling to drag our Republic into the British cataclysm, and that our Administration and propagandized masses eventually succumbed to his strategizings and blandishments."

—The Galilean, February 23, 1942, p. 6.

Nazi Propaganda Theme 7

Nazi Germany is just and virtuous. (e.g., Its aims are justifiable and noble; it is truthful, considerate and benevolent.)

Consistency

". . . Looked at with utter dispassion, however, what Hitler and his Nazi Party truly did was to challenge and vanquish the Luciferian * aspects of apostate Jewry, cleanse the German Fatherland of them, and strengthen the incarnatory racial walls around the Teutonic elements in the race of 'fair whites.' "

---

* *The Galilean* often makes use of mystical language. The term "Luciferian" is a word of unfavorable reference in this vocabulary.

Nazi Propaganda Theme 8

The foreign policies of Japan are morally justifiable. (e.g., Japan has been patient, longsuffering; it is not responsible for the war.)

Consistency

"It should be regarded as childish to seem appalled at the onslaught when it came. Rather we ought to be astonished that it was so long delayed. Japan 'was' the Axis, to all intents and purposes, in the Orient. We have, by every act and deed performable, aggressively solicited war with the Axis.

"The Axis, in the agency of Japan, has responded. Why not?

"Nothing is remarkable about such dénouement."

—*The Galilean,* December 22, 1941, p. 3.

Contradiction

". . . the real megalomania to order the world stems not out of Berlin but out of Tokio."

—*The Galilean,* January 26, 1942, p. 3.

Nazi Propaganda Theme 9

Nazi Germany is powerful. (e.g., Germany has the support of Europe; it possesses the manpower, armaments, materials and morale essential for victory.)

Consistency

". . . On the other hand, even the most biased observer is forced to admit that strange new energies and capabilities have come to demonstration in Germany and Japan— Germany in Europe and Japan in Asia."

—*The Galilean,* February 2, 1942, p. 6.

Nazi Propaganda Theme 10

Japan is powerful. (e.g., It possesses the manpower, armaments, materials and morale essential for victory.)

Consistency

"That is to say, taking Nippon proper, Korea, and Manchukuo, and supplementing these with territorial gains in China, the Philippines, Siamese Thailand, Guam, Wake Island, and the East Indies, the military geographist beholds the Mikado's empire suddenly swollen to an expanse bigger than the forty-eight States of the American Union. If you doubt it, get out your pencil and war maps and do a little elemental arithmetic.

"Moreover, some of these territorial gains happen to be among the richest on earth.

"The Japanese, of course, are quite aware of it."

—*The Galilean,* January 12, 1942, p. 4.

Contradiction

"Japan is overreaching herself, in that it is doubtful if she has nationals enough to occupy the territories she has seized throughout the Orient."

—*The Galilean,* February 2, 1942, p. 13.

Nazi Propaganda Theme 11

The United States is weak. (e.g., It lacks the materials, manpower, armaments and morale.)

Consistency

"Meanwhile, fighting the whole universe goes on, and the morale of the American people threatens to go so low that they must stand on a sheet of paper to look into the eyes of a mouse."

—*The Galilean,* January 12, 1942, p. 7.

Contradiction

"This Republic, barricaded and defended behind her own stupendous resources, could ignore the balance of the Universe for a thousand years."

—*The Galilean,* February 16, 1942, pp. 8-9.

Nazi Propaganda Theme 12

Great Britain is weak. (e.g., The British Empire is collapsing; and it lacks the materials, manpower, armaments and morale.)

Consistency

"Britain, as Britain, is indicated by compounding defeats as ceasing to exist after the current year is out. It has befouled its own nationalistic and racial household, therefore will it sink to nonentity among the world's controlling sovereignties."

—*The Galilean,* March 2, 1942, p. 23.

Nazi Propaganda Theme 13

The United Nations are disunited. (e.g., They distrust, deceive, envy and suspect each other.)

Consistency

"Poking between the lines of dispatch after dispatch that is coming from Europe by short-wave or the reports of returned travelers, is the ugly insinuation that Stalin is already so badly mauled that he may arrive at an 'understanding' with Hitler before renewed fighting on the eastern front takes serious aspect after the melting of the present winter's snows. Stalin—in other words—may 'dump' Britain and the United States and arrive at a liaison with the Axis."

—*The Galilean*, February 2, 1942, p. 12.

Nazi Propaganda Theme 14-A

The United States and the world are menaced by Communists.

Consistency

"January 24, in Washington, Secretary of Labor Frances Perkins said that by 1943 'it will be necessary to mobilize young women for factory workers.' She indicated plainly that women would be drafted. That has been done in England—with disastrous results—and it is a part of the communistic scheme of sovietizing America."

—*The Galilean*, February 16, 1942, p. 11.

Nazi Propaganda Theme 14-B

The United States and the world are menaced by Jews.

Consistency

"The year 1933 closed a definite sequence in the Republic's expansion and wholesome maturity.

"In that year some ten million Mongolic Israelites who had infiltrated among all migrations suddenly manipulated to political and economic control, subtly 'took over' and injected mischief, bedlam and spoliation into this strangely distinctive State as an organism."

—*The Galilean*, March 2, 1942, p. 20.

Nazi Propaganda Theme 14-C
The United States and the world are menaced by Plutocrats.

Consistency

"Working best through their political influence in the United States and Great Britain, international financiers wished to keep the Philippines under political domination of a nation friendly to their great financial interests in the Far East. That is, as one of the two richest spots on earth, they wanted to exploit the great resources of the Islands as they have those in India, southeastern Asia and the Dutch East Indies."

—*The Galilean,* January 12, 1942, pp. 14-15.

A statement analysis was made of 157 articles appearing in *The Galilean* from December 22, 1941, to March 2, 1942. All told, 183 articles were published in this period.

The 26 articles which were excluded consisted almost entirely of, (a) features made up of quotations from specified other sources, and (b) purely theological features. Among the excluded theological articles were:

"The Cover"—a description of the biblical scene illustrated on the cover of the issue. This feature appears in most issues of *The Galilean.* The tenor of the description may be judged from the following quotation in the issue of December 22, 1941:

"The picture offered on this, the first front cover of the *Galilean Weekly,* depicts a home of the average resident of Galilee not only today but in the times of Christ. It is, in fact, a reproduction of the type of home to which Joseph and Mary brought the infant Jesus on their return from the tax registration at Bethlehem. In such a domicile, Our Lord grew to manhood. . . ."

"Significant Golden Scripts"—material written in a biblical style, perhaps actual quotations from one of the esoteric translations of the Bible. This feature appears in about half of the issues. An example from the first issue in the series (December 22, 1941):

"*Chapter X: 'Gather Ye and Prepare a Place for Me'*
"And now, my beloved, I bequeath you a silence.
"2 I say it shall be with you as it hath been with the

table **1** "THE GALILEAN" (December 22, 1941 — March 2, 1942)

STATEMENTS IN "THE GALILEAN" CONSISTENT WITH AND CONTRADICTORY TO NAZI PROPAGANDA THEMES

	Consistent	Contradictory
1. The United States is internally corrupt	279	26
2. The foreign policies of the United States are morally unjustifiable	39	0
3. The President of the United States is reprehensible	70	0
4. Great Britain is internally corrupt	28	0
5. The foreign policies of Great Britain are morally unjustifiable	23	0
6. Prime Minister Churchill is reprehensible	16	0
7. Nazi Germany is just and virtuous	12	2
8. The foreign policies of Japan are morally justifiable	15	5
9. Nazi Germany is powerful	19	2
10. Japan is powerful	79	2
11. The United States is weak	317	5
12. Great Britain is weak	113	3
13. The United Nations are disunited	29	0
14. The United States and the world are menaced by: **a.** Communists	43	0
b. Jews	112	0
c. Plutocrats	1	0
Total	1195	45

prophets throughout all the ages: many shall be called, few shall be chosen. . . ."

Table No. 1, page 187, gives the results of statement analysis in relation to Nazi propaganda themes. "The United States is weak" (11) has the most frequent mention 317, followed by "The United States is internally corrupt" (1), with 279 references. "Great Britain is weak" (12), "The United States and the world are menaced by Jews" (14b), "Japan is powerful" (10), and "The President of the United States is reprehensible" (3), follow in order (113, 112, 79 and no mentions, respectively). The table shows the number of contradictions, which are very few, the largest frequency being 26 in relation to the first theme.

Figure 4, page 189, summarizes the findings in two bars, one depicting consistencies and the other contradictions (1195 to 45).

Table No. 2, page 190, answers the question whether the unbalance has persisted throughout the period under investigation, or whether it was found during only part of the time. The period is divided into two equal parts, and the consistencies and contradictions are reported for each half. The result is to show the great similarity between the two subdivisions, and to justify the assertion that the state of unbalance was persistent. In the first half there were 627 consistencies and 19 contradictions; in the second half, 568 consistencies and 26 contradictions.

Figure 5, page 191, brings out certain significant features of the data by grouping together some of the separate categories. The treatment of the United States and Great Britain is contrasted with the treatment of Germany and Japan. The tall column at the left shows the number of unfavorable references to the United States and Great Britain (914). Pro-references number 34. The number of pro-mentions of Nazi Germany and Japan is 125; negative references total 11. (The tall column combines the consistencies for all themes except 7, 8, 9, 10 and 13. The Pro-U.S.-Britain column includes the noted contradictions to Themes 1, 11 and 12. The pro-Nazi bar summarizes the consistencies with Themes 7, 8, 9 and 10. The anti-Nazi column includes the contradictions of these four themes.)

figure **4**

STATEMENTS IN "THE GALILEAN" CONSISTENT WITH AND CONTRADICTORY TO NAZI PROPAGANDA THEMES

THE GALILEAN (December 22, 1941-March 2, 1942)

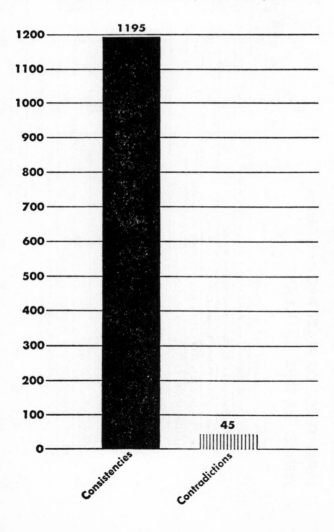

table 2 "THE GALILEAN" (December 22, 1941 — March 2, 1942)

PERSISTENCE OF NAZI PROPAGANDA THEMES IN "THE GALILEAN"

	Dec. 22, 1941-Jan. 26, 1942		Feb. 2, 1942-Mar. 2, 1942	
	Consistent	Contradictory	Consistent	Contradictory
1. The United States is internally corrupt	155	8	124	18
2. The foreign policies of the United States are morally unjustifiable	23	0	16	0
3. The President of the United States is reprehensible	53	0	17	0
4. Great Britain is internally corrupt	9	0	19	0
5. The foreign policies of Great Britain are morally unjustifiable	12	0	11	0
6. Prime Minister Churchill is reprehensible	7	0	9	0
7. Nazi Germany is just and virtuous	2	2	10	0
8. The foreign policies of Japan are morally justifiable	11	4	4	1
9. Nazi Germany is powerful	7	1	12	1
10. Japan is powerful	41	0	38	2
11. The United States is weak	197	2	120	3
12. Great Britain is weak	42	2	71	1
13. The United Nations are disunited	9	0	20	0
14. The United States and the world are menaced by: **a.** Communists	11	0	32	0
b. Jews	47	0	65	0
c. Plutocrats	1	0	0	0
Total	627	19	568	26

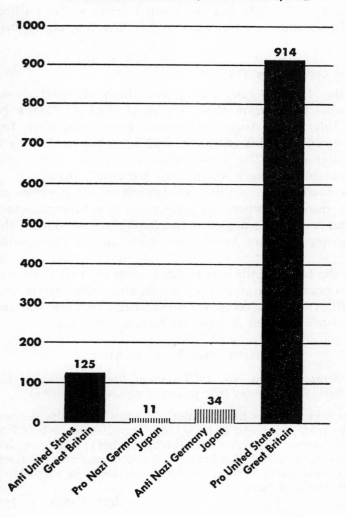

TREATMENT OF NAZI GERMANY-JAPAN VS. TREATMENT OF UNITED STATES-GREAT BRITAIN "THE GALILEAN"

THE GALILEAN (December 22, 1941 — March 2, 1942)

Figure 6, page 193, presents the "menaces" to the United States and the world as they were depicted since the United States entered the war against the Axis. The columns for the Jews, the chief "menace," and for Communists and Plutocrats are the same as reported before. The other columns are the result of retabulating all the mentions of Great Britain, Japan and Germany to determine if they are expressly said to be "menaces." It would be difficult to infer from what was said in *The Galilean* that the United States was not allied with Japan and Nazi Germany, rather than fighting against them.

3. *The Consistency Test*

In the *Auhagen* case, only a small body of material was analyzed. There were three copies of *Today's Challenge* (June-July, 1939; August-September, 1939; November- December, 1939). This magazine had been superseded by a newsletter called *The Forum Observer*, whose issues were also studied (February 29, 1940, to August 28, 1940).

The final results of this investigation were not presented to the court, but experience was gained in applying a standard that had not been used in the *Bookniga* case. This is the *consistency standard*—consistency with known propaganda aims.

On the basis of public pronouncements by Nazi Party and government officials, four propaganda aims were determined. The four were not taken as an exhaustive list; nor was any significance attached to the order from one to four.

Declared Nazi Strategic Aims:

Nazi Strategic Aim No. 1: To show the war guilt of the enemies of Germany (the peaceful aims of Germany)

Hitler says: "It was fundamentally wrong to discuss the war guilt from the point of view that Germany alone could be made responsible for the outbreak of this catastrophe, but it would have been far better to burden the enemy entirely with this guilt, even if this had not been in accordance with the real facts. . . ."

—*Mein Kampf*, p. 236.

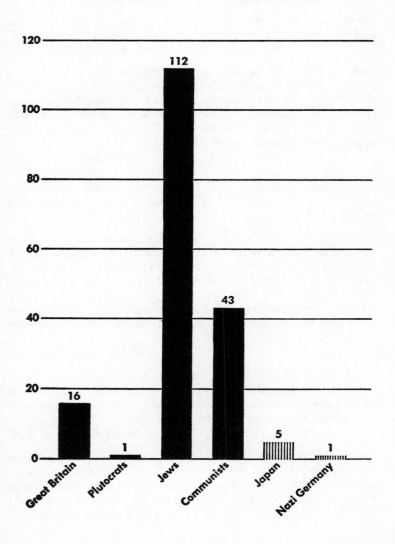

figure **6**

"MENACES" TO THE UNITED STATES AND THE WORLD ACCORDING TO "THE GALILEAN"

THE GALILEAN (December 22, 1941-March 2, 1942)

Nazi Strategic Aim No. 2: To expose the lying propaganda of the enemies of Germany (the truthfulness of Germany).

An official decree of the German Government states:

"In modern war the enemy fights not only with military weapons, but also with means which are designed to influence and undermine the people spiritually. One such weapon is the Radio.

"Every word that the Enemy broadcasts is obviously a lie and is designed to bring detriment to the German people."
                                    —*Voelkischer Beobachter*, September 2, 1939.

Hitler says: "As soon as by one's own propaganda even a glimpse of right on the other side is admitted, the cause of doubting one's own right is laid. (The masses) become uncertain and mistrusting, especially if the enemy does not produce the same nonsense, but in turn, burdens their enemy with all and the whole guilt."
                                    —*Mein Kampf*, p. 237.

Nazi Strategic Aim No. 3: To expose the weakness and decadence of the enemies of Germany (the strength and morality of Germany).

Hitler says: ". . . our German people . . . need that suggestive force that lies in self-confidence. But this self-confidence has to be instilled into the young fellow-citizen from childhood on. His entire education and development has to be directed at giving him the conviction of being absolutely superior to the others. With his physical force and skill, he has again to win the belief in the invincibility of his entire nationality.
                                    —*Mein Kampf*, p. 618.

". . . democratic majority rule has not always dominated mankind, but on the contrary it can be found only in very small periods of history which, however, have always been periods of decline of nations and states."
                                    —*Mein Kampf*, p. 672.

"It shows little insight into historical developments if today people who call themselves folkish emphatically assure again and again that by no means they wish to be active in *negative criticism* but in *constructive* work; a genuinely folkish stammering that is equally childishly stupid . . .

Marxism has a goal . . . but previously it nevertheless exercised criticism for seventy years; and at that ruinous and destructive criticism, until by this continuously corroding acid the old State was undermined and brought to collapse."

—*Mein Kampf*, p. 674.

Nazi Strategic Aim No. 4: To show the world menace of the Jews and plutocrats (the benefit of NSDAP).

Hitler says: "The struggle against this Jewish world danger will, moreover, start at this point.

". . . the National Socialist movement has its mightiest tasks to fulfill: It must . . . over and over again recall who is the real enemy of our present world . . . it must condemn to general wrath the evil enemy of humanity (the Jews) as the true creator of all suffering."

—*Mein Kampf*, p. 931.

Gottfried Feder, Secretary of State in the German Reich, states:

". . . the power of the financiers, who know no fatherland, no homeland, is becoming ever more sinister, as they sit in their modern robber-baron castles, the banks, and plunder the people.

—*Hitler's Official Programme*, p. 90.

"Antisemitism is in a sense the emotional foundation of our movement."

—*Hitler's Official Programme*, p. 56.

Illustrations of conformity to Nazi strategic aims in *Today's Challenge:*

Nazi Aim No.1

"If the disarmament pledges had been carried out by the Allies, there would be no armament race today. By 1926 —according to the report of the Inter-Allied Control Commission—Germany had fulfilled her disarmament obligations to the last blank cartridge. . . . However, instead of beginning to reduce armaments, some nations actually continued to increase them. In other words, the former Allies made it plain enough that, once all power was on their side, they did not care to relinquish it in favor of a new order of justice and equality."

—"*The New Europe*," p. 24, F. E. Auhagen.

Nazi Aim No. 2

"And did we learn nothing of the wily ways of propaganda in those dreadful days of twenty years ago when we spat out what tasted poisonous but swallowed no less noxious pills because they were alluringly sugar-coated?"

—"Speaking as an American," p. 22-23,
H. S. Adams (June-July, 1939).

Nazi Aim No. 3

". . . under the influence of a vague doctrine, reinforced by a primitive Christian zeal for equality, it (equality) developed into the idle dream of actual equality of all mankind. The perversion of the intrinsic meaning of equality thus becomes the source of that insidious process of levelling which is the curse of modern democracies."

—"The Crisis of Democracy," p. 5, Hans Zbinden
(November-December, 1939).

Nazi Aim No. 4

"Another serious split in French opinion is that caused by the Jewish question, a problem much aggravated just at present by the multitude of émigrés in Paris. Even I, as a stranger in the city, could not help noticing how much German is being spoken, especially in the better restaurants. Such an influx naturally makes the French wonder, not only about these incoming Jews, but also about their co-religionists who live and work here and call themselves French. The facts that there are two Jews in the present cabinet, Messrs. Zay and Mandel, and that the Jewish bankers Mannheimer, de Rothschild and Lazard Frères are known to stand behind the present government all complicate the situation."

—"London & Paris—Midsummer 1939," p. 26,
Philip Johnson (August-September, 1939).

As a means of estimating the relation between these publications and native American magazines, comparisons were made with the widely circulated *Reader's Digest* (June, July, August, December, 1939) and the *Saturday Evening Post*

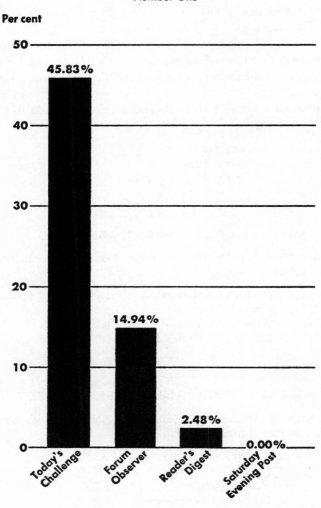

figure **7**

NAZI STRATEGIC AIM NUMBER ONE

**Percentage of Articles and Editorials
Consistent with Strategic Aim
Number One**

Per cent

50

45.83%

40

30

20

14.94%

10

2.48%

0.00%

0

Today's
Challenge

Forum
Observer

Reader's
Digest

Saturday
Evening Post

(July, August, September, November, December, 1939). *Today's Challenge* was said to have been modelled after the *Digest*. The *Post* was isolationist. Editorials and articles were analyzed (fictional material in the *Post* was omitted).

Figure 7, page 197, shows the percentage of articles and editorials consistent with strategic aim number one (guilt of enemy). *Today's Challenge* comes out with 45% of its editorials and articles containing material of this kind. *The Forum Observer* ranks next, with over 14%. The *Reader's Digest* and the *Post* are 2.48% and zero, respectively.

Tables 1, 2 and 3, pages 198 and 199, show the small number of consistent material appearing in the *Digest* and *Post*. The *Challenge* and *Observer* keep their high position, except on Theme 4.

The total number of editorials and articles referred to was:

Today's Challenge	24
Forum Observer	87
Reader's Digest	121
Saturday Evening Post	140

TABLE 1

NAZI STRATEGIC AIM NUMBER TWO

Percentages of Articles and Editorials Consistent with Strategic Aim Number Two:

Today's Challenge	25.00%
Forum Observer	12.64%
Reader's Digest	0.00%
Saturday Evening Post	0.71%

TABLE 2

NAZI STRATEGIC AIM NUMBER THREE

Percentage of Articles and Editorials Consistent with Strategic Aim Number Three:

Today's Challenge	70.83%
Forum Observer	57.47%
Reader's Digest	5.79%
Saturday Evening Post	0.71%

NAZI STRATEGIC AIM NUMBER FOUR

Percentage of Articles and Editorials Consistent with Strategic Aim Number Four:

Today's Challenge	20.83%
Forum Observer	1.15%
Reader's Digest	0.00%
Saturday Evening Post	0.00%

4. The Presentation Test

A.

In the *Bookniga* case, content analyses were made of certain periodicals and books. During the period investigated, the *Moscow News* was a weekly tabloid-sized newspaper, printed in English in the Soviet Union. According to the masthead, the paper is "For English-speaking people in the Soviet Union and throughout the world." *Sovietland* was a monthly magazine published and printed in Moscow, carrying articles on "topics of current interest in the U.S.S.R." and devoting half its pages to pictorial presentation. *International Literature* was a monthly literary magazine published by the State Literary Publishing House in four editions—English, French, German and Russian. *U.S.S.R. in Construction* was a monthly illustrated magazine published and printed in Moscow, and issued in five languages—Russian, English, French, Spanish and German. The books included 76 in the English language and 132 in Russian. From a scientific point of view, the purpose of the investigation was to determine whether these periodicals and books could correctly be called political propaganda. Political propaganda is the dissemination of words (and word-equivalents, like pictures) as means of influencing attitudes on controversial matters.

The purpose of the presentation test is to show the degree in which controversial questions are given balanced or unbalanced treatment in a particular channel of communication. An unbalanced presentation may be taken to indicate an intention to influence opinion in a certain direction, thus justifying inferences about the presence or absence of propaganda.

At the time of the litigation, one of the most controversial questions in world politics was the philosophy of Communism and the success or failure of the Soviet Union. The purpose of the analysis of the publications specified by the government was to determine the degree in which these controversial matters were given balanced or unbalanced treatment.

In the books and periodicals studied, the two most general themes were: (1) The Soviet Union is a success; (2) Communist doctrines are correct. These two themes support each other, since it is asserted that the Soviet Union is an example of Communist doctrine in practice. If the Soviet Union is favorably presented in non-Communist countries, or favorably depicted, Communist doctrine is apparently vindicated. These master themes were developed in several ways, and fifteen sub-themes were found.

Since a detailed classification of the books called for more time than was available, the court was given the results of a quantitative survey of periodicals. In order, however, to illustrate the meaning of the principal sub-themes each one was illustrated with a quotation. In the following list, the source of the quotation is given and the affiliations of the author, if important, are stated. The source of information about the author is cited. (Data as of trial year.)

THEME 1

The U.S.S.R. is strong and successful.

". . . the national economy of the Soviet Union will steadily continue to advance so that, in a few years' time, after surpassing the United States of America technically and economically, it will occupy first place in the world in all respects."

> Varga, E.," Two Decades of Capitalist and Socialist Economy," from *The World Hails the 20th Anniversary of the Soviet Union* (p. 80) Moscow; Cooperative Publishing Society of Foreign Workers in the USSR, 1938. Printed in Soviet Union. 247 pp.
> Varga, E., Director, Institute for World Economics and World Politics, Academy of Science, USSR. This Acad-

emy is subsidized by, and is a branch of, the Government of the USSR. Editor, *World Economics and World Politics*, an authoritative Soviet Journal dealing with topics of current interest in these fields. At present, Varga is unofficial economist and economic statistician for Stalin. (O.Yu. Shmidt (Editor), *Bol'-shaya Sovetskaya Entsiklopediya* (Great Soviet Encyclopedia), Vol. 8, pp. 791-792, Moscow, 1931.)

(*Mirovoe Khozyaistvo i Mirovoe Politika* (World Economics and World Politics), Moscow, 1938.)

(E. Gurvich, *Poslevoennaya Amerika* (Post-war America), Moscow; State Social-Economic Publishing House, 1937, p. xi.)

THEME 2

The U.S.S.R. is the home of happy, prosperous, cultured people.

"The USSR is the only country in the world where every toiler cheerfully and confidently regards his own future. The toilers of our country know nothing of fear and trepidation about the morrow. For them there is no dark perspective of unemployment and poverty. The Stalinist Constitution guarantees to all citizens of the USSR the right to work; the right to relaxation; the right to material security in their old age; the right to education."

(The preceding is an excerpt from the Soviet publication *Za Kommunisticheskoe Prosveshchenie* (For Communist Education), August 4, 1932.)

Sorokin, N. (Editor): *Zabota o Sovetskom Sluzhaschem* (The Care of the Soviet Employees), Moscow; Publishing House of the Trade Unions, 1937. 60 pp. Price: 4 cents.

THEME 3

Exploitation is ended in the Soviet Union.

"In our Soviet country we have no exploitation of man by man."

Krupskaya, N. K.: "Soviet Woman, A Citizen with Equal Rights." A collection of articles and speeches.

Pamphlet 76 pp. Moscow; Cooperative Publishing Society of Foreign Workers in the USSR, 1937. Printed in the Soviet Union. Translator, M. Jochel; Editor, Elizabeth Donnelly; Technical Editor, H. J. Canter. Translated from Russian. Edition issued by *Partizdat*, 1937. Printed by "Iskra Revolutsii," Printing Shop No. 7, Moscow.

Krupskaya, Nadejda K., Lenin's widow (died March 1939); Assistant Commissar of Education, RSFSR; Member Presidium, Supreme Soviet of the USSR Central Committee of the CPSU (b). *(Moscow News,* February 27, 1939, p. 5.)

THEME 4

The only true democracy is the Soviet Union.

"The Soviet system is more impregnated with democracy than any other system."

Molotov, V. M.:"The Constitution of Socialism." Speech delivered at the Extraordinary Eighth Congress of Soviets of the USSR, November 25, 1936. (p. 9) Moscow; Cooperative Publishing Society of Foreign Workers in the USSR, 1937. Printed in the Soviet Union. Translated by J. Fineberg. 31 pp.

Molotov, V. M., Chairman of Council of People's Commissars of the USSR. *(Moscow News,* January 26, 1938, p. 6.)Served both as Chairman of Council of People's Commissars of the USSR and Foreign Commissar. Still retains post of Foreign Commissar and became Vice-Chairman of the Council of People's Commissars of the USSR. *(New York Times,* May 7, 1941, p. 1.)

THEME 5

The highest morality is found in the Soviet Union.

"Against the barbarian, bloody, manhating 'morality' of the present-day cannibals-fascists, who divide people according to so-called 'racial' designations, we counterpoise our customs of socialist living together, the morality of genuine humanitarianism, which raises the dignity of men, irrespective of their social and national distinctions."

Kosarev, A. V.: *Stalinskaya Konstitutsiya i Sovetskaya Molodezh* (The Stalinist Constitution and Soviet Youth),

Moscow; Young Guard Publishing House, 1937. 224 pp. Price: 2.50. Report given at the Komsomol section of the Superior School for Propagandists in the name of Y. M. Sverdlov, November 19, 1937.

Kosarev, A., General Secretary of the Central Committee of the Young Communist League of the USSR (from title page of pamphlet). Member, Presidium Supreme Soviet of USSR. (*Moscow News*, January 26, 1938, p. 7.)

THEME 6

The Soviet Union is free from religion and the church.

"Our country is justly proud of its successes in the matter of the conquest of religion—one of the most despicable and harmful survivals of capitalism in the consciousness of the people."

Kogan, Yu, and Megruzhan, F.: *O Svobode Sovesti* (On the Freedom of Conscience), Moscow; State Antireligious Society Publishing House, 1938. 68 pp. Price: 35 k. Edited by P. A. Krasikova.

THEME 7

Capitalism oppresses people.

"Labour in capitalist society kills the worker . . . . the worker's leisure time in the capitalist world is either nightmare oblivion after exhausting toil, or rest tainted with the poison of bourgeois propaganda."

Semashko, N. A.: "The Right to Rest and Leisure." Pamphlet 32 pp. Moscow; Cooperative Publishing Society of Foreign Workers in the USSR, 1937. Printed in the Soviet Union.

Semashko, N. A., Chairman of the Children's Commission under the All-Union Executive Committee; Head of DETGIZ, the Children's Publishing House. (*Moscow News*, May 1, 1935, p. 23.) Member All-Russian Central Executive Committee. (Book Cover: "Right to Rest and Leisure.")

THEME 8

Capitalism includes Fascism and bourgeois democracy.

"Fascism is the offspring of bourgeois culture and its state of putrefaction and disintegration, its cancerous tumor. The theoreticians and practitioners of fascism are adventurers, brought forward by the bourgeoisie from its midst. In Italy and Germany the bourgeoisie handed over the political, physical, power into the hands of the fascists, manipulating them with the Machiavellian skill with which the bourgeoisie of the medieval Italian cities commanded the condottiere."

Gorki, Maxim: *Esli Vrag Ne Sdaetsya Ego Unichtozhayut* (If the Enemy Will Not Submit, He is to Be Destroyed), Moscow; State Publishing House of Belles Lettres, 1938. 344 pp. Price: 4.25. Subtitle: "A Collection of Articles." Introduction by I. Luppol.

Gorki (Gorky), Maxim M., the most famous of Soviet writers, now a revered martyr. Sometime member of the Central Executive Committee of the USSR. President of the Union of Soviet Writers. (*USSR Handbook*, London; Victor Gollancz, Ltd., 1936, p. 610.) (Communist Academy, *Literaturnaya Entsiklopediya* (Literary Encyclopedia), Publishing House of the Communist Academy, 1939, Vol. II, pp. 643-655.)

THEME 9

The weakness and collapse of capitalism is inevitable.

"We comrades know what contradictions are gnawing at bourgeois society. These contradictions not only cannot be eliminated, but they inevitably grow and multiply. They became particularly acute as a result of the World War, and they found striking expression in the economic crisis which began in 1929."

Litvinov, Maxim M.: *Protiv Agressii* (Against Aggression), Moscow; State Publishing House for Political Literature, 1938. 109 pp. Price: 1 ruble, 25 kopecks. The above quotation (p. 31) was made by Maxim Litvinov in a speech to the VIII Extraordinary All-Union Congress of Soviets on November 28, 1936.

Litvinov, Maxim M., Bolshevik for many years; Delegate to many international congresses; Representative of USSR at The Hague, Genoa, Locarno Disarmament Conferences; People's Commissar of Foreign Affairs (appointed 1929); Member, Council League of Nations, 1934-38. (*International Who's Who,* 1939). Resigned as

People's Commissar of Foreign Affairs, May 1939. (*New York Times*, May 4, 1939.)

THEME 10

The weakness and collapse of capitalism in the United States is inevitable.

"The rapid growth of inner contradictions of American monopolistic capital leads to a tremendous exacerbation of foreign contradictions: increases the export of capital, sharpens the struggle for markets, ruins the countries of South and Central America, prepares the way for war with Japan, and with England, makes inevitable a new division of the world, and puts a new imperialistic war on the order of the day."

Gurvich, E.: *Poslevoennaya Amerika* (Post-war America), Moscow State Social and Economic Press, 1937. Subtitle: "The Decay of American Capitalism." xxii, 479 pp. Issued by The Institute of World Economics and World Politics, Academy of Science of the USSR. Book contains a short foreword by E. Varga, Director of the Institute, who assisted in editing the book itself. The Academy is subsidized by, and is a branch of, the Government of the USSR.

Gurvich, E., Member of the Institute of Economics and Politics, Academy of Sciences of USSR. The Academy is subsidized by, and is a branch of, the Government of the USSR.

THEME 11

Revolutionary violence is justified.

"Lenin and Stalin incessantly taught the youth that the only true means for the discontinuing of imperialistic war is the proletarian revolution, the armed overthrow of the bourgeoisie, and the establishment of the power of the working class."

Ostryakov, S.: *20 Let VLKSM* (20 Years of the All-Union Leninist Communist Union of Youth), Moscow; The Young Guard Printing House of the Central Committee of the VLKSM, 1938. 124 pp. Price: 2 rubles. Subtitle: "An Historic Reference Book."

THEME 12

For true theoretical understanding, study Marx and Lenin.

"*The conduct of a fighter, his fighting capacity, his stamina in every battle, and particularly in the coming war, will depend on how well he is armed not only technically, but above all ideologically.* . . .Our slogan in work and political education must be: study Marx—from Marx, Lenin—from Lenin, and study Stalin—from Stalin."

Kossarev, A.: "On Reorganizing the Work of the Young Communist League." Pamphlet, 52 pp. Moscow; Cooperative Publishing Society of Foreign Workers in the USSR, 1935. Printed in the Soviet Union.

Kossarev, A. V., *vide supra.*

THEME 13

For proper method of action, support the Communist Party.

"The working people of the capitalist countries see that the working class in the U.S.S.R. has been victorious because it has been led by the Party of Lenin and Stalin. Hence the steady growth of the prestige of this Party in the eyes of the working people of the whole world. And this means the growth of the influence of Communism, it means that the workers of the capitalist countries are adopting an attitude of increasing respect for the Communist Parties of their various countries."

Manuilsky, D. Z.: "The Victory of Socialism in the U.S.S.R. and the People's Front Movement," from *The World Hails the Twentieth Anniversary of the Soviet Union* (p. 55), Moscow; Cooperative Publishing Society of Foreign Workers in the USSR, 1938. 247 pp. Printed in the Soviet Union.

Manuilsky, D. Z., Member of the Central Committee of the Communist Party of the Soviet Union; Member of the Presidium of the Communist International; Chairman of the delegation of the Communist Party of the Soviet Union to the Comintern. (*International Who's Who*, Europa Publications Ltd., London, 1939. pp.793-794.) (Moscow *Pravda*, March 12, 1939, p. 3.)

THEME 14

For proper leadership and training, follow Stalin.

"All our successes are tied to the name of comrade Stalin, as the mouthpiece of the great ideological aspirations of the whole population of the Soviet Union, and not only of the Soviet Union, but of the toilers throughout the world."

Kalinin, M. I.: *Stati i Rechi, 1936-1937* (Articles and Speeches, 1936-1937), Moscow; Party Publishing House, 1938. 180 pp. Price: 1.25.

THEME 15

For a Fatherland, be loyal to the Soviet Union.

"Never before has there been a state like the U.S.S.R., a state which millions of people in all parts of the globe, regardless of nationality or race, cherish as their own fatherland, feeling that they themselves, their lives, their destinies and hopes are closely linked with it."

Dimitrov, Georgi: "The Soviet Union and the Working Class of the Capitalist Countries." Pamphlet, 12 pp. Moscow; Cooperative Publishing Society of Foreign Workers in the USSR, 1937. Printed in the Soviet Union. (Also reprinted in *The World Hails the Twentieth Anniversary of the Soviet Union.*)

Dimitrov, Georgi, General Secretary of the Comitern during this period. Was acquitted at the famous German trial on burning of the Reichstag. (Albert Rhys Williams: *The Soviets*, 1937, p. 466.)

The content of periodicals was classified according to favorable and unfavorable items. By the term "item" is meant any material with a caption. This means that each article, editorial, picture or advertisement counts as an item. Only a few parts of each issue of a periodical are not items. In every case, non-item material included the masthead on the editorial page, the box entitled "Table of Contents," and the name of the publication. Almost all the items were found to be composed of uniformly favorable or unfavorable material. In a few instances, the same item contained both favorable and unfavorable references. In such cases, the item was classified according to *dominant* theme.

In making the item-count, the Soviet Union or another country is considered to be favorably presented when it is shown as strong, cultured, considerate or moral. Conversely, the USSR or another country is considered to be presented unfavorably whenever it is shown as weak, uncultured, inconsiderate or immoral.[15]

The items were summarized by number of favorable and unfavorable items, and also by column inches.

Charts were introduced in evidence, summarizing the contents of the *Moscow News, Sovietland, International Literature,* and *USSR In Construction.* In every case, the periodicals devoted most of their space to the Soviet Union and gave an overwhelmingly favorable presentation of the USSR. In general, other countries were presented more unfavorably than favorably. Figure 8, page 209, is representative of the findings. It summarizes the favorable and unfavorable articles and pictures referring to the USSR and other countries and published in the *Moscow News* between August 2, 1938, and March 10, 1939. No fewer than 1903 articles and pictures were favorable to the USSR; only 3 were unfavorable; 397 articles and pictures referred to other countries, and 328 items presented these countries unfavorably, only 69 items being favorable. Hence, 82% of all the items referring to other countries put them in an unfavorable light, while 18% presented favorably. In terms of column inches, 36,757 column inches put the USSR in a favorable light; only 57½ column inches were unfavorable; 7,043½ column inches depicted other countries unfavorably, while 1,590 column inches presented them favorably. It is obvious that the presentation test left no doubt about the way in which the balance was inclined.

B.

The presentation test was also applied to the material transmitted by the *Transocean* agency. This agency cabled news gathered in the United States to Germany and also to South America. (In the terminology used, the former was called "cables" and the latter "transmissions.") *Transocean* also received news in German and English from Germany,

figure **8**

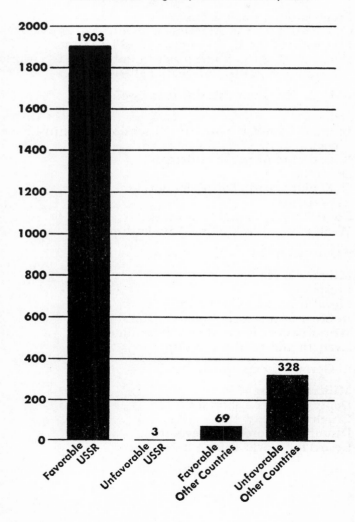

FAVORABLE AND UNFAVORABLE ARTICLES AND PICTURES ABOUT THE U.S.S.R. AND OTHER COUNTRIES

Moscow News (August 2, 1938 — March 10, 1939)

and prepared a "news letter" that was distributed daily in both languages to American publications.

The first step in the analysis was to examine the balance of favorable and unfavorable presentations of the United States and Germany in the outgoing news.

Pro- and Anti-Judgments

Pro-U. S. (or Great Britain) items would be:

Progress of national defense
Cooperation of the Americas and internal unity
Prosperity of the U. S.—industrial achievements
Praise of U. S. or leaders, as a country and as a world force for morality—international friendliness

Anti-U. S. (or Great Britain) items would be:

Strikes
Internal conflict—political dissension—disunity—inefficiency
Retardation of national defense
Depression
U. S. immorality—lynching—rioting
Imperialism
Control by Jews and plutocrats
Weakness and lack of good leadership

Pro-German items would be:

Military success
Prosperity
Moral behavior—kindliness
Internal unity—racial unity—cultural unity
World power—international friendliness
Strength and good leadership

Anti-German items would be:

Military failure
Depression—food shortage
Cruelty—atrocity
Disunity and probable revolution
Desire for world conquest

Examples:

Pro-USA

TRANSMISSION 6:30 PM EST DECEMBER 10, 1940, 145, WASHINGTON. — USAMEXVERHAND-LUNGEN UEBER VERTEIDIGUNGSFRAGEN WERDEN NACH ANDEUTUNGEN UNTERRICH-TETER MIT NAECHSTTAGE ERWARTETER RUECKKEHR MEXBOTSCHAFTER NAJERA SCHNELLEN FORTGANG VERZEICHNEN WO-BEI ALS ERSTE FRUCHT USAMEX ZUSAMMEN-ARBEIT REGELUNG OELFRAGE ERWARTET.

Transmission, 6:30 PM, December 10, 1940, 145, Washington. — According to hints of informed persons, U.S.A.— Mexican negotiations about defense questions will show speedy progress at the return of Mexican Ambassador Najera, which is expected within the next few days. As first fruit of U.S.A.—Mexican cooperation, regulation of the oil question is expected.

Pro-USA

TRANSMISSION 00:30 AM EST FEBRUARY 14, 1941, 214, NEW YORK. — UEBERTRUMPFUNG SELBST WELTKRIEG ENTWICKELTEN SCHIFFS-BAU TEMPOS PROPHEZEIT NEWYORK HER-ALD TRIBUNE IN UMFASSENDER UEBERSICHT UEBER GEGENWAERTIGES UND FUER ZU-KUNFT GEPLANTES FRACHTER BAUPRO-GRAMM.

Transmission, 00:30 AM, February 14, 1941, 214, New York: The New York *Herald Tribune* prophesies the surpassing even of the shipbuilding tempo developed during the World War in an inclusive survey of the program of freighter construction for the present and the future.

Anti-USA

TRANSMISSION 2:15 PM EST FEBRUARY 7, 1941, 90, WASHINGTON. — EXMARINEFLIEGER UND WEITHIN BEKANNTER LUFTSACHVERSTAEN-

DIGER MAJOR AL WILLIAMS BESCHULDIGTE IN AUSSAGEN VOR SENATS AUSSCHUSS BETREFFS LENDLEASE ROOSEVELT REGIERUNG MODERNE USAFLUGZEUGE ENGLAND ZU UEBEREIGNEN UND SICH AUSLAENDISCHE ANGELEGENHEITEN EINZUMISCHEN.

Transmission, 2:15 PM, February 7, 1941, 90 Washington. — Former navy flyer and widely known air expert Major Al Williams, in testimony before the Senate Committee with regard to the Lend Lease Bill, accused the Roosevelt government of handing modern planes over to England and of mixing in European affairs.

Anti-USA

TRANSMISSION 6:30 PM EST FEBRUARY 8, 1941, 122, NEW YORK. — REPFUEHRERS LANDON SCHARFE KRITIK AN LENDLEASE VORLAGE SOWIE ROOSEVELTS TAKTIK ZUR MUNDTOTMACHUNG OPPOSITION ABENDPRESSE AUSFUEHRLICHST WIEDERGEGEBEN ABER SPAERLICHST KOMMENTIERT.

Transmission, 6:30 PM, February 8, 1941, New York: The sharp criticism of Republican Leader Landon directed against the Lend Lease Bill, as well as Roosevelt's tactics of muzzling the opposition, were given in great detail by the evening press, but commented on very little.

Pro-German

TRANSMISSION 6:30 PM EST DECEMBER 7, 1940, 111, NEW YORK. — VERSUCHE VERHAFTUNG PARISER USA-BOTSCHAFTS SEKRETAERIN ELISABETH DEEGAN DURCH DEUTMILITAERPOLIZEI ZWECKS ANTIDEUTSCHER PROPAGANDA AUFZUBLASEN ZUSAMMENFIELEN MIT VEROEFFENTLICHUNG STAATSDEPARTMENTS MELDUNG WONACH DEEGAN LEDIGLICH PRIVATHOTEL INTERNIERT UND AUSGEZEICHNET BEHANDELT.

Transmission, 6:30 PM, December 7, 1940, 111, New York: Attempts to puff up for anti-German propaganda purposes the arrest of Elizabeth Deegan, the secretary of the U. S. embassy in Paris, by German military police, fell through with the release of a State Department report according to which Deegan was merely interned in a private hotel, and very well treated.

Pro-German

TO CABLE DECEMBER 10, 1940 TRANSFER ACCOUNT TRANSOCEAN BERLIN (GERMANY) 10005 EXLONDON MELDET NYTIMES EINZELHEITEN BERICHT SZWEIER ALS ROTKREUZDELEGIERTE TAETIGER SCHWEIZER AERZTE UEBER LEBENSBEDINGUNGEN IN HOSPITAELERN UND GEFANGENENLAGERN BESETZTEN FRANKREICHS BELGIENS UNTERGEBRACHTER BRITGEFANGENER STOP DEMZUFOLGE LASSE BEHANDLUNG WIE VERPFLEGUNG BRITKRIEGS GEFANGENER ZIVIL-GEFANGENER NICHTSWUENSCHEN UEBRIG STOP

Cable, December 10, 1940, 10005
The New York Times reports the details of information received in London, from two Swiss doctors who are serving as Red Cross delegates, about the living conditions of British prisoners in hospitals and prison camps of Belgium and occupied France. According to these reports, the treatment and food of the British military and civil prisoners leaves nothing to be desired.

Anti-German

TO CABLE DECEMBER 11, 1940 TRANSFER ACCOUNT URGENT TRANSOCEAN BERLIN (GERMANY) 11230 WASHINGTON EXMARINEDEPARTMENT VERLAUTET DASS DEUTSCHDAMPFER RHEIN CUBANAEHE VON HOLLAND-ZERSTOERER AUFGEBRACHT

Cable, December 11, 1940, 11230
Washington: It was reported by the Navy Department

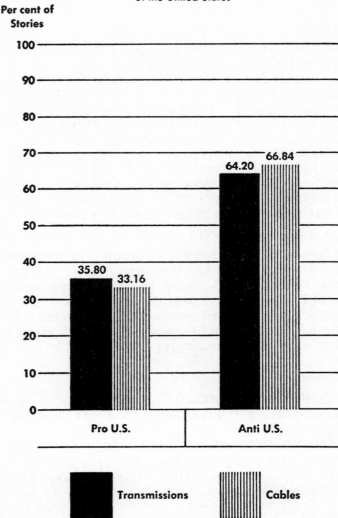

figure **9**

TRANSOCEAN NEWS SERVICE FROM AMERICA

Favorable and Unfavorable Presentation
of the United States

Per cent of
Stories

Pro U.S. Anti U.S.

35.80 33.16 64.20 66.84

Transmissions Cables

figure **10**

TRANSOCEAN NEWS SERVICE FROM AMERICA

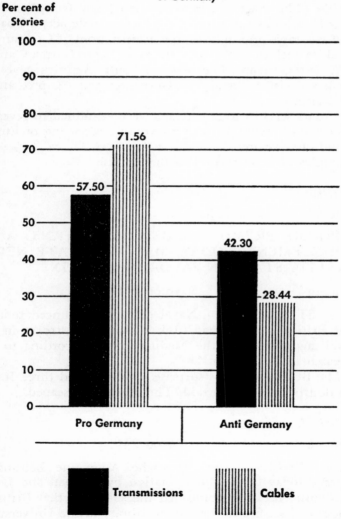

Favorable and Unfavorable Presentation
of Germany

Per cent of
Stories

Pro Germany — Transmissions 57.50, Cables 71.56

Anti Germany — Transmissions 42.30, Cables 28.44

Transmissions Cables

that the German ship "Rhein" was stopped by a Dutch destroyer in the neighborhood of Cuba.

The results of the investigation of outgoing news are given in Figures 9 and 10, pages 214 and 215. Figure 9 shows that, of all the news stories involving the United States, two-thirds put this country in an unfavorable light, and one-third were favorable. (The exact figures were 64.20% and 66.84% anti-U.S.; 35.80% and 33.16% pro-U.S.) Figure 10 depicts the balance of favorable and unfavorable presentations of Germany. The cables back to Germany were 71.56% pro-German, and 28.44% anti-German. The news to South America gave a much less decisive "break" to Germany: 57.50% pro, and 42.50% anti.

The news services to Americans were examined to reveal the balance of favorable and unfavorable reporting of England and of Germany.

Examples of news related to the English:

Pro-British

June 26   Noon   9.

TURKISH PREMIER MAKES IMPORTANT AN-
NOUNCEMENT TODAY; MAY MODERATE NEU-
TRALITY STAND IN FAVOR OF BRITAIN

June 29   10:00 PM

32. — STOCKHOLM— Naval officials announced today that British warships had sunk an Italian destroyer in a naval engagement in the Mediterranean, according to a dispatch from London.

The British warships surprised and attacked three Italian destroyers, London said. The other two escaped.

Anti-British

June 26   2:00 PM

16. — BERLIN— The "Deutsche Allgmeine Zeitung" charged today that an investigation by German and Belgian authorities had confirmed the suspicion that British troops had set fire to the famous library of the University of Louvain. . . .

figure **11**

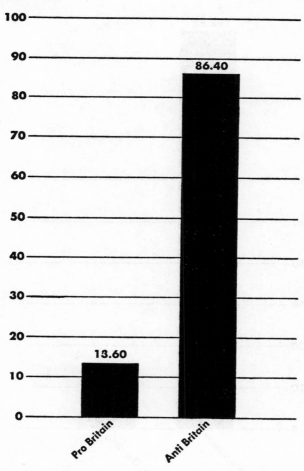

TRANSOCEAN NEWS SERVICE TO AMERICANS

(in English)

**Favorable and Unfavorable Presentation
of Great Britain**

Per Cent of Stories

100 ⎯⎯⎯⎯⎯⎯⎯⎯⎯⎯⎯⎯

90 ⎯⎯⎯⎯⎯⎯⎯⎯⎯⎯

86.40

80 ⎯⎯

70 ⎯⎯

60 ⎯⎯

50 ⎯⎯

40 ⎯⎯

30 ⎯⎯

20 ⎯⎯

13.60

10 ⎯⎯

0 ⎯⎯

Pro Britain   Anti Britain

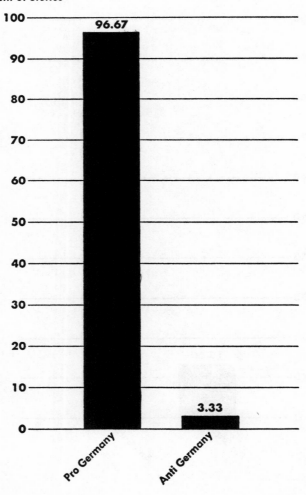

figure **12**

TRANSOCEAN NEWS SERVICE TO AMERICANS
(in English)

Favorable and Unfavorable Presentation
of Germany

Per Cent of Stories

100 — 96.67

90 —

80 —

70 —

60 —

50 —

40 —

30 —

20 —

10 —

0 —

3.33

Pro Germany   Anti Germany

It had been previously charged that the British wished the library destroyed so it would be blamed on the Germans and thus prejudice the United States against the Reich.

The results of the investigation are summarized in Figures 11 and 12, pages 217 and 218. The news to Americans was 86.40% anti-British, 13.60% pro-British. The news of Germany, on the contrary, was 96.67% pro, and 3.33% anti.

The English-language service was only slightly less pro-German than the German-language service (see *Table 1*, page 219). However, the English service was noticeably more pro-English than the German service (see *Table 2*, page 220).

TABLE 1

TRANSOCEAN NEWS SERVICE TO AMERICANS

June, 1939
October, 1939
July, 1940
December, 1940

	English Service	German Service	Combined English and German Service
Pro-German	378	911	1289
	96.67%	97.23%	97.06%
Anti-German	13	26	39
	3.33%	2.77%	2.94%
Total	391	937	1328
	100%	100%	100%

In order to provide a basis of comparison with the treatment of news in the American press during the time period in question, analyses were made of certain American newspapers. The *New York Times* is notable for its news coverage. The *New York Post* was pro-interventionist and reached a lower income group than the *Times*. The *New York Journal-American* was regarded as an isolationist organ.

Table 3, page 220, compares the balance of favorable and unfavorable treatment of Germany.

The *Times* and *Post* were close together, the German-favorable news being 52% in the former and 49% in the

TABLE 2

TRANSOCEAN NEWS SERVICE TO AMERICANS

June, 1939
October, 1939
July, 1940
December, 1940

	English Service	German Service	English and German Service
Pro-Great Britain	62	51	113
	13.60%	6.95%	9.50%
Anti-Great Britain	394	683	1077
	86.40%	93.05%	90.50%
Total	456	734	1190
	100%	100%	100%

latter, and the anti-German news being 48% and 51%, respectively. The balance in the *Journal-American* was 61% pro- and 39% anti-Germany. *Transocean* was 97% favorable and 3% unfavorable to Germany.

The handling of Britain was also compared in the various channels. Britain was most favorably presented in the *Journal-American* (74)%, followed by the *Times* (63%), and the *Post* (54%). *Transocean* was 14% favorable. Anti-British

TABLE 3

NEWS SERVICE TO AMERICANS

June, 1939
October, 1939
July, 1940
December, 1940

	Transocean (in English)	New York Times	New York Post	New York Journal-American (except June 1939)
Pro-Germany	378	663	211	118
	96.67%	52.08%	49.30%	61.46%
Anti-Germany	13	610	217	74
	3.33%	47.92%	50.70%	38.54%
Total	391	1273	428	192
	100%	100%	100%	100%

items were most numerous in the *Post* (46%), the *Times* (37%), followed by the *Journal-American* (26%). *Transocean* items were 86% unfavorable to Britain.

TABLE 4

NEWS SERVICE TO AMERICANS

June, 1939
October, 1939
July, 1940
December, 1940

	Transocean (in English)	New York Times	New York Post	New York Journal-American (except June 1939)
Pro-Great Britain	62	1003	274	157
	13.60%	62.88%	54.15%	74.05%
Anti-Great Britain	394	592	232	55
	86.40%	37.12%	45.85%	25.95%
Total	456	1595	506	212
	100%	100%	100%	100%

The sample dates were selected by taking the same months previously used for Figures 9 to 12 and spacing the days through these months, approximately one day each week. The actual dates:

1939 — June 5, 12, 19, 26
October 2, 9, 16, 23, 30
1940 — July 1, 24, 27, 30
December 2, 9, 16, 23, 30

On these sample days, *Transocean* disseminated through its English news service to Americans a total of 533 stories. The results of a statement analysis of these stories were compared with the results of a statement analysis of the same stories appearing in the *Times*. (Only a few stories did not appear at all in the *Times*.)

The following are examples of news items broken up into statements:

Pro-German (October 9, 1939)

   —DNB announced that the British blockade has had no effect on German trade. (This statement was not in the *Times*.)

Pro-German (June 19, 1939)

   —German newspapers today described as a "true plebiscite" the German demonstrations in Danzig.

   —After Goebbels had told them that no power in the world would prevent Danzig's reunion with the German Reich.

   —"This demonstration of true national feeling . . . is stronger and more effective than all the intrigues and maneuvers of the encirclement powers."

(The first two statements were in the *Times*.)

Anti-German (December 30, 1940)

   —Five were killed and seven were badly injured in a German train wreck, Berlin reports.

(This statement was not in the *Times*.)

Non-relevant (October 2, 1939)

   —Ciano left for Rome this noon.

(This statement was in the *Times* (and the *Post*).)

   —Chinese quarters report the evacuation of Changsha, Hunan, by Chinese troops.

(This statement was in the *Times*.)

Figure 13, page 224, summarizes the relationship between news items appearing in *Transocean* and the *Times*. About nine out of ten statements in *Transocean* that presented Germany as strong or weak said that Germany was strong. The outcome of statement-by-statement analysis gives results substantially similar to item analysis, but the pro-German balance is somewhat less extreme. In Figure 12, page 218, the results were 97 to 3, not 90 to 10.

Certain details are given in *Table 5*, page 223.

5. *Source Test*

Another possible test of propaganda is the balance of sources relied upon in furnishing news or comments on controversial matters. Figure 14, page 225, shows the amount of space in the *Moscow News* acknowledged to be from official Soviet sources. These acknowledged sources fall into three

TABLE 5

CONTROVERSIAL THEME: "GERMANY IS STRONG."

533 News Stories in *Transocean* and the *New York Times*

	Transocean	*New York Times*
Pro-German	872	462
	89.53%	64.17%
Anti-German	102	258
	10.47%	35.83%
Total	974	720
	100%	100%

groups: (a) articles by government and party officials; (b) acknowledged translations of articles from government and party sources; (c) acknowledged translations of official documents.

The signed articles account for 38541½ column-inches; the acknowledged articles amount to 22551½ column-inches. The official documents come to 1617 column-inches. The total number of column-inches in the *Moscow News* was 37,778, of which 7727 column-inches were acknowledged governmental and party material. Hence between 20% and 21%, respectively of the space in the *Moscow News* during the period came from acknowledged governmental and party sources. No government other than the USSR is used as a source, nor is any party other than the Communist Party relied upon.

The type of material referred to in this connection includes the text of speeches by Stalin, the text of laws passed by the government organs of the USSR, articles signed by office-holders of the government or of the party, articles reprinted or abstracted from official newspapers (*Pravda, Izvestia*) for which credit is given, and editorials in the *Moscow News,* for which the *Moscow News* itself assumes responsibility.

6. *Concealed-Source Test*

Another useful test in detecting propaganda is the use of unacknowledged sources of news and comment on controversial matters. If the choice of source is heavily balanced on

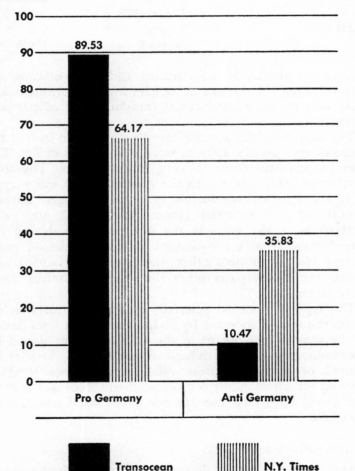

figure **13**

CONTROVERSIAL THEME: "GERMANY IS STRONG"

533 News Stories in Transocean
and the New York Times

Per cent
of Statements
in Stories

Transocean

N.Y. Times

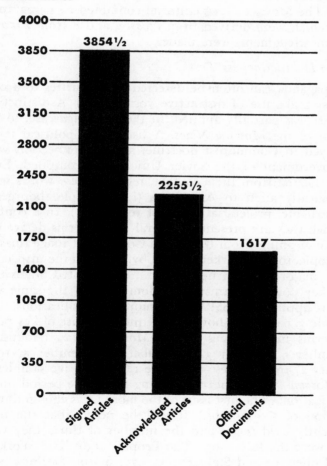

figure **14**

SPACE IN THE 'MOSCOW NEWS' DEVOTED TO:

(A) Signed articles by government and party officials
(B) Acknowledged translations of articles from
    governmental and party sources
(C) Acknowledged translations of official documents

Column Inches

4000
3850 — 3854½
3500
3150
2800
2450
2100 — 2255½
1750
1400 — 1617
1050
700
350
0

Signed Articles   Acknowledged Articles   Official Documents one side, this increases our confidence that we are correctly describing the channel as an instrument of propaganda. It is evident that the test can be applied only when several different media are investigated. In many cases, the amount of research required to locate original sources is great. The concealed-source test was utilized on a very limited scale in connection with the *Moscow News*. It was noted, for example, that on February 6, 1939, an editorial was published as an original contribution that was actually a combination of an editorial from *Izvestia*, the leading governmental organ of the USSR, and *Pravda*, the chief organ of the Communist Party. The *Moscow News* editorial contained 22 paragraphs, 13 of which were derived from *Izvestia* and 8 from *Pravda*; no acknowledgments were made.

7. *The Distinctiveness Test*

Propaganda can often be detected when parties to a controversy make use of distinctive vocabularies. A distinctiveness test was partially applied, in the *Bookniga* case, to the content of the *Moscow News*. A list of key political terms employed in Communist doctrine, and in connection with the government of the Soviet Union, was compiled. Even when isolated from their context, most of these words seem ideologically alien to Americans (for example, bourgeois, class struggle, proletariat, socialist revolution). In a context in which they are presented, several of the terms derive distinctive meanings from USSR and Communist usage (masses, the people, toilers, workers). It is obvious from the inspection of any major national newspaper in the United States that these key political terms are seldom used in the same way they are applied in USSR and Communist publications.

Table 3, page 227, shows the frequency of use of key political terms in six issues of the *Moscow News* (August 2, September 5, October 3, November 7, December 5, 1938, January 2, 1939). These issues are representative samples of the *Moscow News* appearing during the entire period under investigation. (The first issue of the month was chosen during a period of six months.) It will be noted that the most frequently used terms and the number of times they were used, were the following: The People, 1136; The Workers, 633; Collective and State Farms, 378; Stalin, Stalinist, 280;

table **3**

FREQUENCY OF USE OF KEY POLITICAL TERMS

MOSCOW NEWS 6 Issues

August 2, 1938;
September 5, 1938;
October 3, 1938;
November 7, 1938;
December 5, 1938;
January 2, 1939.

BOURGEOIS	61
CLASS	92
CLASS STRUGGLE	97
COLLECTIVISM	56
COLLECTIVE AND STATE FARMS	378
COMMISSARIAT	187
COMRADE	78
SOVIETS (COUNCILS)	270
DIVERSIONISM	25
EXPLOITATION	54
FIVE-YEAR PLAN, PLAN	217
LENIN, LENINIST	243
MASSES	146
THE PARTY (COMMUNIST)	172
PROLETARIAT	45
RED ARMY	162
REVOLUTION	217
SOCIALIST CONSTRUCTION AND/OR RECONSTRUCTION	62
SOCIALIST COMPETITION	29
SOCIALIST LABOR	23
SOCIALIST REVOLUTION	34
STAKHANOVISM	165
STALIN, STALINIST	280
THE TASK	62
THE PEOPLE	1136
TOILERS	35
WORKERS	633

Soviets (Councils), 270; Lenin, Leninist, 243; Revolution, 217; Five-Year Plan, 217.

8. *The Distortion Test*

The distortion test is a more refined method of detecting propaganda than the simple presentation test. During a period in which Germany is winning, for example, realistic reporting will tilt the balance of favorable references to German strength in Germany's favor. It is obvious that realistic reporting and critical comment will not always result in a 50-50 balance. Hence, degrees of unbalance will be significant.

The purpose of a distortion test is to show the direction in which dissimilar statements about the same topic are slanted. Similar statements about a given topic may appear in two channels. By disregarding the statements common to both channels, and examining statements that differ, we may learn something about the persisting bias (distortion) of the channel. The dissimilar statements may be compared with the propaganda aims of the parties to a controversy, or they may be reported according to the degree of favorable or unfavorable presentation of the parties to the controversy. In the former case, the dissimilar statements are summarized by the consistency test; in the latter, by the presentation test. It is apparent that the distinctiveness test is a more technical form of the tests previously described. The distinctiveness test was applied, in part, to the handling of news stories in *Transocean*. One of the Nazi propaganda aims was to emphasize the strength of Germany (for authoritative quotations see the report of the *Auhagen* case). The degree of Germany's strength was a matter of continuous controversy during the period in question. The procedure was to classify the same news stories appearing in *Transocean,* the *New York Times,* and the *New York Post,* on sample days. Similar statements were cancelled out, but all other statements were classified as consistent with, contradictory of, or nonrelevant to, the theme "Germany is Strong."

The statements appearing in the same news stories in two channels obviously fall into three classes: (1) statements parallel in both stories; (2) statements in channel (a) and not in channel (b); (3) statements in channel (b) and not in channel (a). In a comparison involving *Transocean* and the *Times,* we may speak of parallels, additions (appearing in *Transocean* alone), and omissions (appearing in the *Times* alone). The following brief item in *Transocean* and in the *Times* concerning German nationals will serve as a concise example:

> *Statement 1*: A Latvian government announcement disclosed today that German nationals evacuated from Latvia will be settled in the former Polish Corridor.

> *Statement 2*: Settlers will replace the Poles moved out by Germany.

Both of these statements occur in the *New York Times.* Consequently, there are two parallels and no additions. On the other hand, there were two additional statements to the *Transocean* account in the *New York Times*:

> *Statement 1*: Germany is hastening those evacuated minorities from the Baltic States,

> *Statement 2*: presumably because Russia's army is marching in.

The total score, then, on the story is: no additions, two parallels, and two omissions. The question now to be asked is: To what extent is this distortion meaningful? This can be answered by classifying the statements according to German propaganda intent (Nazi strategic aims). When such a classification is effected, it becomes readily apparent that both of the statements in the *Transocean* account are consistent with the theme "Germany is Strong." On the other hand, both statements in the *New York Times,* which were omitted from the *Transocean* account, contradict this theme. According to our method of analysis, then, there will be no additions in the story, two parallels consistent with the Nazi theme, and two omissions contradictory to it. A general analysis of all statements in all stories results in showing the direction of the systematic distortion.

Table 6, page 231, gives the results of applying the distortion test to *Transocean,* the *Times* and the *Post*: 58% of the additions in *Transocean* (to the *Times* account) were consistent with Nazi aims; 3% of the additions contradicted them. About the same differences were found with reference to the *Post. Post* and *Times* additions to the *Transocean* news reports were 25% consistent with and 27% contradictory of Nazi aims. Of *Transocean* omissions, 48% was material that contradicted Nazi aims, and 16% was consistent with them. (Results were about the same when comparisons were made with *Times* or *Post*.) *Post* and *Times* omissions were 26% contradictory of Nazi aims, and 34% consistent with them. (Table 7, page 232, shows the details for each of four Nazi aims; see the *Auhagen* case for details of each aim.) [16]

TABLE 6

STATEMENTS COMPARISON

June 5, 12, 19, 26, 1939
Oct. 2, 9, 16, 23, 30, 1939
July 1, 24, 27, 30, 1940
Dec. 2, 9, 16, 23, 30, 1940

	Transocean and Times			Transocean and Post			Post and Times		
	Additions	Parallels	Omissions	Additions	Parallels	Omissions	Additions	Parallels	Omissions
Consistent with Nazi aims	735 57.78%	520 50.34%	92 16.40%	1079 55.22%	176 50.00%	49 17.95%	242 24.90%	254 29.88%	349 34.38%
Contradictory to Nazi Aims	44 3.46%	73 7.07%	268 47.77%	94 4.81%	23 6.53%	127 46.52%	267 27.47%	179 21.06%	260 25.62%
Nonrelevant to Nazi Aims	494 38.84%	440 42.59%	201 35.83%	781 39.97%	153 43.47%	97 35.53%	463 47.63%	417 49.06%	406 40.00%
Total	1273 100%	1033 100%	561 100%	1954 100%	352 100%	273 100%	972 100%	850 100%	1015 100%

TABLE 7

STATEMENTS COMPARISON

June 5, 12, 19, 26, 1939
Oct. 2, 9, 16, 23, 30, 1939
July 1, 24, 27, 30, 1940
Dec. 2, 9, 16, 23, 30, 1940

	Transocean and Times			Transocean and Post			Post and Times		
	Additions	Parallels	Omissions	Additions	Parallels	Omissions	Additions	Parallels	Omissions
Plus Nazi Aim 1	136 10.68%	83 8.23%	13 2.32%	197 10.08%	24 6.82%	7 2.56%	22 2.26%	38 4.47%	44 4.33%
Minus Nazi Aim 1	9 0.71%	1 0.10%	40 7.13%	9 0.46%	1 0.28%	16 5.86%	29 2.98%	18 2.12%	28 2.76%
Plus Nazi Aim 2	102 8.01%	30 2.90%	8 1.43%	120 6.14%	12 3.41%	3 1.10%	15 1.54%	11 1.29%	28 2.76%
Minus Nazi Aim 2	0 0.00%	4 0.39%	38 6.77%	2 0.10%	2 0.57%	4 1.47%	3 0.31%	5 0.59%	20 1.97%
Plus Nazi Aim 3	476 37.39%	396 38.33%	66 11.76%	736 37.67%	136 38.64%	35 12.82%	180 18.52%	198 23.29%	268 26.40%
Minus Nazi Aim 3	34 2.67%	68 6.58%	190 33.87%	82 4.20%	20 5.68%	106 38.83%	229 23.56%	147 17.29%	206 20.30%
Plus Nazi Aim 4	21 1.65%	9 0.87%	5 0.89%	26 1.33%	4 1.14%	4 1.47%	25 2.57%	7 0.82%	9 0.89%
Minus Nazi Aim 4	1 0.08%	0 0.00%	0 0.00%	1 0.05%	0 0.00%	1 0.37%	6 0.62%	9 1.06%	6 0.59%
Non-relevant to Nazi Aims	494 38.81%	440 42.59%	201 35.83%	781 39.97%	153 43.47%	97 35.52%	463 47.63%	417 49.06%	406 40.00%
Total	1273 100%	1033 100%	561 100%	1954 100%	352 100%	273 100%	972 100%	850 100%	1015 100%

Chapter **10**

TREND: MAY DAY SLOGANS IN SOVIET RUSSIA, 1918-1943 *

As PART of the observance of May Day, the Communist Party of the Soviet Union issues a list of slogans to the public as a guide for the interpretation of politics. These slogans are authoritative, rich in key political symbols, and widely disseminated. They are connecting links between party theorists, decision-makers, and the rank and file of party and community. For all these reasons, they are among the significant streams of regular communication in modern politics.

Our analysis deals with the purport and style of these slogans, from the first year of their appearance after the Revolution. We center upon the key symbols. We are especially interested in the function they perform as links between the doctrinal subtleties of the theorists, the action language of the decision-makers, and the everyday speech of the common citizen.

The importance of slogans has been a long-standing tradition in the Russian revolutionary movement that culminated in the seizure of power in 1917. As early as 1894, Lenin accepted, as a slogan for both theoretical and practical activities of Russian Socialists in their fight against the "class en-

*The authors acknowledge the kind technical assistance of Joseph M. Goldsen.

emy," the memorable words of Liebknecht, *"Studieren, propagandieren, organisieren"* (Study! Propagandize! Organize!).

The occasion we have selected, May Day, likewise has a long revolutionary background. The organization, on the first of May, of international demonstrations by workers in the cities of the world was decided upon for the first time at the Congress of the Second International held in Paris in July, 1889. Besides the Belgian representatives, the delegate who voted against the innovation was the Russian social democrat, Plekhanov. As he saw it, local political conditions in czarist Russia did not augur well for the feasibility and the success of such an undertaking. However, since the early 90's of the last century, strikes and demonstrations have marked the observance of May Day in Russia. Until 1895, May Day slogans in Russia were purely economic in nature; but later, definite political demands were included. May Day became a day of struggle "against capitalism and czarism" as the Russian proletariat asked for economic and political freedom. "The demand for an eight-hour day," wrote Lenin in 1900, "has its peculiar significance: it is a declaration of solidarity with the International Socialist movement. We must see to it that the workers understand this difference, so they will not put the demand for an eight-hour day on the level of a demand for free railroad tickets or the dismissal of a foreman."

During World War I, on the eve of the Russian Revolution, the May Day slogans put out by the Bolshevists preached revolutionary action to the Russian workers. They urged the Russian proletariat to strike, to demonstrate and, above all, to realize Lenin's slogan of the transformation of the imperialist war into civil war. The liquidation of absolutism, the establishment of a democratic republic in Russia, the eight-hour day, the abolition of private ownership of the instruments of production, and especially the immediate cessation of hostilities were among the most popular demands.

The first May Day slogans after the seizure of power by the Communists were circulated by the Central Committee of the party in April 1918. They were signed by Ia. Sverdlov, Chairman of the committee, and were addressed to all local party committees and communist groups in the Soviets. The list was remarkably short. Most of the slogans were taken over from days preceding victory, and were of a rather general character. Conspicuous was the effort to defend the young Soviet Republic and the idea of Socialism against foes at home and abroad. Following previous practice, the slogans were addressed to Russian workers and peasants—the word "proletariat" was mentioned only twice. On the other hand, solidarity between the various "proletarian" groups inside Russia—urban workers, agricultural toilers, and Cossacks—was particularly stressed.

Our aim in examining the symbols and slogans of May Day, from 1918 on, is to register the relative strength of tendencies to repeat and to modify the original slogan list. In the beginning, "revolutionary" symbols were prominent. Would they continue to occupy the same position in later years? At the start, symbols were "universal." After a brief lag, the slogans spoke in the name of the world, not only of Russia. In the course of time, did "national" symbols rise in frequency, and did the slogans become more preoccupied with "domestic" policy than "foreign" policy?

Another set of questions is related to the vocabulary of traditional "liberalism" and "morality." At first, there was a tendency to revive "sentimental" terms of the "bourgeoisie" revolution, and we want to know to what extent this original line was adhered to. Socialist theories exalted "material" or "impersonal" factors over "personal" factors in social development. What do the slogans reveal about the relative weight of such factors in communications addressed to large audiences?

There is also the question of how groups are identified in society. As the new order is established, do "class" names decrease in relation to the mention of more restricted social formations?

With these problems in mind, we use eleven categories for the classification of key symbols: (for important slogans, see *pp. 285ff.*)

I. The *revolutionary* symbols are the key terms in statements endorsing or predicting revolution. They include:

Revolutionary
Communist International
Socialism, Socialist

World Revolution, World Revolt, World October, etc.
Communism, Commune, Bolshevist, etc.
Revolutionary United Front
October Revolution
Red
Proletarians
Class, Class-less
Working People, Toiling Masses
Proletarian Dictatorship
Comrades
Soviet, Soviets, Soviet Power
Communist Party, Communist Youth, Pioneers, V.K.P., Central Committee

II. The *anti-revolutionary* terms designate enemies of the Revolution, or directly imply the existence of enemies:

Fascist, Fascism
Capital, Capitalism, Capitalist
Dictatorship
Imperialism, Imperialist
Imperialist United Front
Counter-Revolution
Anti-Soviet
Defense
Resistance of the U.S.S.R. against foreign aggression
Social Democrats, Menshevists, Social Fascists, Social Imperialists
Bourgeoisie, Nep-men, Profiteers, etc.
Second International
Bourgeois Democracy
Reaction
Militarism
Clergy, Orthodox Priests, Catholic Priests, Rabbis
The Pope
God
Church
Feudalism
Appeasers
The Wealthy
Attack on the U.S.S.R.
Intervention
Kulaks
Saboteurs
Landowners

Liberals
Generals
Civil War

III. The *national* symbol list is composed of words that are used to speak of the U.S.S.R. as a "national" entity, rather than as a state with distinctive doctrines and institutions. Most of these symbols are used by "bourgeois," as well as by "socialist" powers. Some of the terms are used in statements of self-praise:

Fatherland
Our land
Patriotism
Defense
Resistance of the U.S.S.R. against foreign aggression
Security
Enemy
Aggression
Intervention
Encirclement of the U.S.S.R.
Attack on the U.S.S.R.
Soviet frontiers
Peace, peace policy
Easy, prosperous life in U.S.S.R.
Joy, cheerfulness
Watchfulness

IV. The *universal* symbols occur in statements of demand for the completion of revolution on a world scale, and in statements referring to the world as a whole, or to internationalism. Some of the most prominent symbols also appear in the "Revolutionary" list:

International
Internationalism
All countries, whole universe, all nations, mankind, globe
World Revolution, World Revolt, World October, etc.
Communist International

V. The *Domestic Policy* symbols are used in statements of demand for action inside the U.S.S.R., or in slogans that mention internal conditions. The list is peculiarly dependent upon the problems current at any given time, and at first sight appears quite heterogeneous:

Communal
Culture, cultural
Plan, planning, Five-Year Plan, etc.
Technique
Production, productivity
Labor
Collective farms, collective farmers, etc.
State farms
Factories, coal mines, power stations
Motor-tractor stations
Science, art, literature
Industrial nation
Self-criticism
Bureaucracy, red tape
Industry, and various branches of industry
Transport
Government
Agriculture
Trade
Constitution
Cooperatives
Government offices
Laws, decrees
Collectivization
Stakhanovism
Unemployment
Material
Competition
May 1
Internal Enemy
Trade unions
Private
State
Society
People
Progressive
Front
Rear

VI. The *Foreign Policy* symbols are found in statements describing or endorsing the official acts of the U.S.S.R. in foreign relations. The list duplicates most of the terms in the

National Symbol list, and adds the names of all countries and regions that figure in foreign-policy slogans.

VII. The *Social Group* symbols are the identifying terms employed in referring to social formations inside Russia and other countries:

Cossacks of proletarian origin
Proletariat, proletarians
Workers, working women, city
Peasants (except Kulaks), village
Red Army, Red Navy, Red soldiers. Various units like artillerymen, tank men, air force, etc.
Communist Party, Communist Youth, Pioneers, V.K.P., Central Committee
Workers by profession, like coal miners, metal workers, etc.
Collective farmers, etc.
Individual peasants
Intelligentsia, Soviet specialists, scholars, technicians, teachers, etc.
Peoples of the U.S.S.R., Nationality policy, minorities
Various (children, students, members of sport organizations, civilian flyers, etc.)
Non-Party men
Elite, illustrious people
Youth
Stakhanovists
Intelligence service, secret police
Employers
Partisans, guerillas
Bourgeoisie, Nep-men, profiteers, etc.
Clergy, orthodox priests, Catholic priests, Rabbis
The wealthy
Church
Kulaks
Landowners
Liberals
Social Democrats, Menshevists, Social Fascists, Social Imperialists
Generals
Trade unions
Women

VIII. The list of *Persons* contains the names of all who were singled out for separate mention in the slogans of the entire period:

Lenin, Leninism
Marx, Marxism
Engels
Liebknecht
Luxemburg
Stalin
Kolchak
Denikin
Sinoviev
Trotsky
Hitler
Bukharin
Poincaré
Thälmann
Uritzky
Chiang Kai-shek
Shaumyan
Dzhaparidze
Arizbegor
Baginsky
Vechorkevich

IX. The *Old Liberal* symbols were prominent in pre-proletarian ideologies of freedom:

Sons
Brethren, fraternity, sisters
Liberty, freedom, free
Citizen
Patriotism
Ideal
Honor
Loyalty
Honesty
Heroic, heroes
Individual
Responsibility
Democracy, democratic
Progressive
Duty
Moral

People
Justice
Blood
Death
Pacifism
Self-determination

X. The *Moral* symbol list is the preceding one, minus those with an explicit political tinge, like "citizen" or "progressive." The Moral symbols are usable in more doctrinal systems than the "Old Liberal," and hence are among the least distinctive terms appearing in Communist slogans:

Solidarity
Discipline
Heroic, heroes
Honor
Opportunism
Loyalty
Honesty
Model, exemplary
Joy, cheerfulness
Responsibility
Irreconcilability, incompatibility
Watchfulness
Duty
Moral
Justice

XI. The *Action* symbols are the verbs and expressions used in statements referring to, or demanding, audience participation:

Fight, struggle, fighters; activity, initiative, creative, enthusiasm, etc.
Victory, victorious
Success
Long live . . . !
Down with . . . !

As a further means of revealing trend, we selected some categories with stylistic considerations chiefly in mind. Slogans are "synoptic statements submitted to the public for guidance," * and style is the way the component parts are ar-

* Harold D. Lasswell and Dorothy Blumenstock (Jones), *World Revolutionary Propaganda; A Chicago Study*, Knopf, New York, 1939, p. 107.

ranged. Some slogans are specifically addressed to groups, a device that presumably increases audience impact ("address"). Another "intensity" device is the use of "admonition," "denunciation" or "endorsement," rather than "fact-form" statements ("expectations"). Finally, we note the explicit mention of symbols referring to the speaker, in this case the Communist Party ("self-identification"). The six categories are:

A. Expectation (descriptions)
"May First is a festival of Labor."
B. Endorsement
"Long live the Russian Communist Party."
C. Denunciation
"Down with the Armies of Imperialism."
D. Admonition
"Watch carefully the plots of our enemies."
E. Address
"Workers, peasants, Red Army men . . ."
F. Self-identification
". . . the Russian Communist Party—the Party of the working class, the Party of Lenin."

Looking at the results as a whole, we find that certain patterns stand out. There has been a pronounced drop in "universal-revolutionary" symbols (Figure 15, page 243). Expressed as a ratio of their frequency of occurrence to the total word count of the slogans, such symbols fell from a high point of over 12 in 1919 to less than 1 in 1943. At the same time, the trend of "national" terms has been upward, from the low point in 1920 of less than 1, to the high point of over 7 in 1940 and 1942.

A further confirmation of the tendency to become more self-preoccupied is the record of symbols referring to "domestic policy" (Figure 16, page 244). Despite sharp ups and downs, it is evident from the graph that the trend for the whole period is upward. The same relationship is shown by the withdrawal of attention to symbols of reference to the enemies of revolution ("antirevolutionary").

Some of the categories do not have high enough frequencies to give wholly unambiguous curves for the period, but after the low point of 1924, there is a steady if slight

figure **15**

'NATIONAL' AND 'UNIVERSAL-REVOLUTIONARY' SYMBOLS IN MAY-DAY SLOGANS OF THE COMMUNIST PARTY (S.U.)

Symbol Groupings

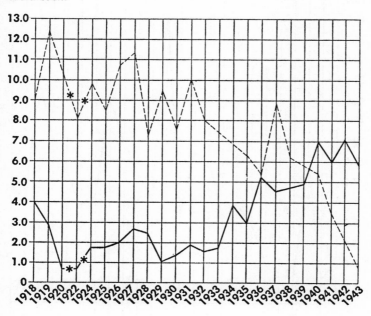

Ratio of
frequency to total
Word-count

National
Universal-Revolutionary

*No slogans issued in 1921 and 1923

figure **16**

"DOMESTIC POLICY," "ANTI-REVOLUTIONARY," AND "UNIVERSAL" SYMBOLS IN MAY-DAY SLOGANS OF THE COMMUNIST PARTY (S.U.)

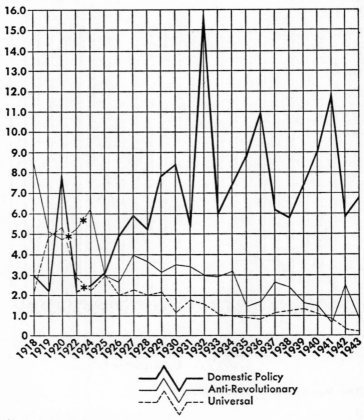

Ratio of Symbols to Word-total

Domestic Policy
Anti-Revolutionary
Universal

*No slogans issued in 1921 and 1923

increase in "old liberal" symbols (Table I, page 246). The "moral" terms follow the same pattern, though less distinctly (some categories remain at constant levels: "persons," "groups," "active").

The special style categories reveal a pronounced rise in symbols of address. (Figure 17, page 247). The low in 1925 was less than 1, while in recent years the figure is over 8.

Symbols of admonition display the same upward movement, beginning at 1 in 1918 and reaching high points in 1942 and 1943, around 7 (Figure 18, page 248).

The "endorsement" symbols vary, but the trend is not too evident. Between 1937 and 1940 there was a bunching of high points between 5 and 6 (Table II, page 249).

"Denunciation" terms show low frequencies, moving downward from the 1918 peak of 3. "Expectation" symbols show a broadly similar tendency (high point over 12 in 1920). "Identifications" reached a high point in 1926 of nearly 5, and then diminished. A special study of the mentions of "Communist Party (S.U.)" and "Soviet Power" shows a clear upswing of the latter and a drop of the former after 1926.

Considering the overall picture as a whole, what does it suggest? In general there has been a movement away from the pattern of world revolution toward "parochialism" ("nationalism"). We speak of this modification as "restriction from within" of the orginal symbol pattern in the name of which the revolutionary élite seized power. The departures have been toward the "revival" of terms connected with previous political attitudes.

What are the main factors that account for this general transformation? No doubt, the outstanding element is changed expectations regarding the imminence of world revolution, and the resulting change in the relationship of the ruling élite to the world balance of power. So long as the hope of world revolution was vivid, the rulers of Russia could hope to defend themselves by appealing over the heads of established governments to the masses. But after the prospect of world revolution diminished, the maintenance of power began plainly to depend upon cooperating with one set of governments against another, which is the characteristic balance of power process in world politics. Obviously, if the cooperation of a foreign élite is to be obtained, doctrinal

TABLE 1

FREQUENCIES OF SYMBOL-GROUPS

Year	I	II	III	IV	V	VI	VII	VIII	IX	X	XI	Total
							Symbol-Group					
1918	8	9	3	2	3	4	12	0	2	2	6	51
1919	22	12	3	11	5	5	34	6	2	1	9	110
1920	7	7	1	8	12	2	9	2	3	1	3	55
1922	16	15	1	8	6	10	29	7	5	0	18	115
1924	22	17	4	6	7	21	43	3	0	0	19	142
1925	39	18	5	18	19	24	76	5	6	2	32	244
1926	43	12	4	9	22	19	62	6	4	2	18	201
1927	45	19	11	11	28	32	43	5	3	2	25	224
1928	38	24	11	13	34	21	74	4	5	2	19	245
1929	79	32	7	22	80	17	112	11	2	4	36	402
1930	81	39	7	12	93	17	117	10	9	8	39	432
1931	65	24	7	12	38	15	63	9	8	7	28	274
1932	69	24	8	12	122	20	64	13	7	6	32	377
1933	90	38	17	13	77	23	104	12	11	17	50	452
1934	60	27	25	8	63	29	102	10	11	10	44	391
1935	93	19	25	11	119	17	161	24	19	21	46	555
1936	79	21	45	9	135	29	159	10	20	21	50	578
1937	53	15	17	6	35	19	53	9	16	8	32	263
1938	53	18	23	9	44	20	82	17	21	10	41	338
1939	37	10	23	8	46	15	62	12	16	5	43	277
1940	38	8	27	6	52	14	84	10	11	6	38	294
1941	36	4	22	5	78	6	83	10	8	6	43	301
1942	35	24	52	3	55	81	120	11	30	8	44	493
1943	34	22	49	2	84	81	133	13	16	11	48	493

figure **17**

MAY-DAY SLOGANS
COMMUNIST PARTY: SOVIET UNION

Symbols of ADDRESS (E)

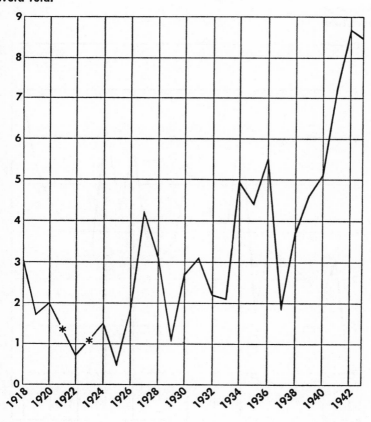

Per cent of
Word Total

*No slogans issued in 1921 and 1923

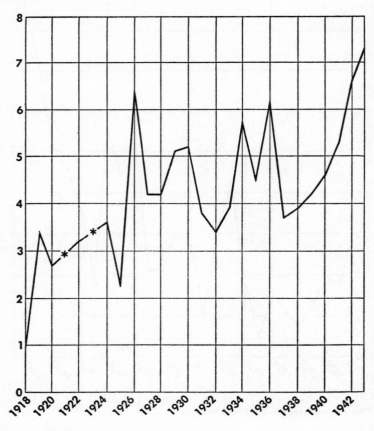

figure **18**

MAY-DAY SLOGANS
COMMUNIST PARTY: SOVIET UNION

Symbols of ADMONITION (D)

Per cent of
Word Total

*No slogans issued in 1921 and 1923

TABLE II

A. Expectations (Descriptions)
B. Endorsement
C. Denunciation
D. Admonition
E. Address
F. Self-Identification

	A	B	C	D	E	F
1918	6.0%	4.0%	3.0%	1.0%	3.0%	2.0%
1919	9.4	2.6	.9	3.4	1.7	1.7
1920	12.7	.7	0	2.7	2.0	3.3
1922	4.2	3.9	1.8	3.2	.7	2.1
1924	2.6	5.5	1.5	3.6	1.5	2.6
1925	1.5	3.6	1.5	2.3	.5	2.5
1926	3.8	3.3	1.8	6.4	1.8	4.7
1927	4.8	2.9	1.2	4.2	4.2	1.2
1928	4.0	1.5	.5	4.2	3.1	1.4
1929	3.3	2.1	.2	5.1	1.1	1.1
1930	2.0	2.7	1.2	5.2	2.7	1.1
1931	1.1	4.3	.9	3.8	3.1	.7
1932	2.1	2.1	.8	3.4	2.2	1.2
1933	1.9	2.7	.6	3.9	2.1	.2
1934	1.7	3.4	.5	5.7	4.9	.3
1935	1.1	4.3	.2	4.5	4.4	.4
1936	1.2	3.8	.2	6.1	5.5	.2
1937	1.1	5.7	.4	3.7	1.9	.7
1938	1.4	4.8	.1	3.9	3.7	.4
1939	.8	5.9	0	4.2	4.5	.3
1940	.4	5.5	0	4.6	5.1	.7
1941	.6	4.3	0	5.3	7.1	.6
1942	.9	2.6	.5	6.6	8.6	.2
1943	.6	2.2	.4	7.3	8.5	.1

differences must be de-emphasized. At the same time, internal solidarity may be heightened by emphasizing territorially distinctive symbols, such as those connected with land, country, nation, economic achievements and local history.

It must not be assumed that the readjustments to which we have referred went forward in a straight line. Indeed, the "zig-zag" of political development is notorious, and is once again exemplified by the ups and downs of the symbols appearing in Communist slogans.

In order to bring out these short-term variations in more detail, we have examined significant subperiods. These subdivisions are as follows:

   I. 1918-1920 Revolution, intervention, civil war
  II. 1921-1925 Reconstruction
 III. 1926-1929 Industrialization
 IV. 1930-1934 Collectivization of agriculture
  V. 1935-1938 "Established Socialism," new constitution
 VI. 1939-1943 Vigilance and war

Already, in the second period, we observe certain significant changes in the rank order of symbol categories (Table III, page 251). The "national" symbols begin their gradual upward climb, moving from the tenth rank into a tie for the next highest position. "Universal" and "antirevolutionary" symbols drop off, although the urgency of "foreign policy" is such that it actually moves up. In the third period, "domestic policy" comes into third place, and the "national" symbols climb another step. During the 1930-1934 years, the picture remains much the same. In 1935-1938, the upward movement of "old liberal" and "national" is worthy of observation. It is during the final period of acute uncertainty and crisis that the greatest degree of internal preoccupation is revealed. Both the "domestic policy" and "national" symbols outrank "revolutionary" and "foreign policy" terms. Close statistical analysis shows that the first four periods are quite similar in make-up. The figures emphasize the relatively sharper break between IV and V than between previous intervals. The rank-order correlations for successive pairs of time and periods are:

Periods I and II	.88
Periods II and III	.92
Periods III and IV	.96
Periods IV and V	.76
Periods V and VI	.94

The first four periods show, as we have remarked, a high degree of interchangeability.

TABLE III

(1) 1918-1920

1. Social groups
2.5. Revolutionary
2.5. Antirevolutionary
4. Domestic policy
5. Action
6. Universal
7. Foreign policy
8.5. Persons
8.5. Old liberal
10. National
11. Moral

(2) 1921-1925

1. Social groups
2. Revolutionary
3. Action
4. Foreign policy
5. Antirevolutionary
6. Domestic policy
7. Universal
8. Persons
9.5. National
9.5. Old liberal
11. Moral

(3) 1926-1929

1. Social groups
2. Revolutionary
3. Domestic policy
4. Foreign policy
5. Action
6. Antirevolutionary
7. Universal
8. National
9. Persons
10. Old liberal
11. Moral

(4) 1930-1934

1. Social groups
2.5. Revolutionary
2.5. Domestic policy
4. Action
5. Antirevolutionary
6. Foreign policy
7. Universal
8. Persons
9. National
10. Old liberal
11. Moral

(5) 1935-1938

1. Social groups
2. Revolutionary
3. Domestic policy
4. Action
5. National
6. Foreign policy
7. Old liberal
8. Antirevolutionary
9. Persons
10. Moral
11. Universal

(6) 1939-1943

1. Social groups
2. Domestic policy
3. Action
4. National
5. Revolutionary
6. Foreign policy
7. Old liberal
8. Persons
9. Antirevolutionary
10. Moral
11. Universal

TABLE IV

INTERPERIOD RANK-ORDER CORRELATIONS

	(1)	*(2)*	*(3)*	*(4)*	*(5)*	*(6)*
(1)	X					
(2)	.88	X				
(3)	.86	.92	X			
(4)	.93	.92	.96	X		
(5)	.60	.70	.80	.76	X	
(6)	.45	.55	.68	.66	.94	X

It is worth noticing that Period V is more similar to the first four periods than is Period VI (the correlations of Period V are higher). Moreover, the correlations of Period V with the first four periods, and of Period VI with the same intervals, tend to increase in value as the time interval is reduced. This progression reflects the basic transformations occurring in the total value of symbols.

When we examine in more detail the graphs and tables displaying the variations in slogan style (Figures 17 and 18 and Table II, pages 247 to 249), a number of significant points emerge. At first, it seems that few groups are addressed directly. At the beginning, the ruling élite was made apprehensive by the overt and covert opposition of many elements inside Russia. Hence, a limited number of major group symbols were invoked, and the audience was kept aware of class affiliations. Later on, however, production was stimulated by direct recognition of constituent elements in Russian life, in which differentiation by skill is taking the place of the prominence formerly taken by the classes.[1]

When we examine the symbols of admonition, two interesting explanatory possibilities suggest themselves. Are we to account for the rise in certain symbols by regarding them as a reaction against increasing apathy? Or is there evidence that

[1] This does not necessarily imply that "classes" have been abolished, if we use the term to refer to the major groupings of the population by basic social values, like power, income, or respect. But it recognizes the possibility that attitude formation in politics may be more significantly affected by occupation than by class position as thus defined. Hence "skill" analysis becomes more important than "class" categories of analysis. For a more detailed discussion of these distinctions, see the forthcoming volume of basic political categories by Harold D. Lasswell and Abraham Kaplan, *Power and Society.*

such appeals are substituted for peremptory modes of address? It is not possible to give a conclusive solution to this problem, although the very great prominence of "action" symbols in certain periods does point to the substitutive hypothesis.

Denunciations multiply in the immediate presence of danger. The general lack of prominence of such appeals suggests that the problems of Russia passed from negative to positive goals and that, as opportunities for effective action multiplied, merely negative symbols were deemed less effective.

In connection with the endorsement symbols, it is notable that in extreme crises of action, as in 1941, endorsements are taken for granted and not increased. The low points in the use of endorsement symbols are evidently connected with the expectation of immediate danger in reality (e.g., 1920, 1928, 1932). Nineteen hundred and twenty was a time of acute peril for the revolutionary regime. In 1928, the factional struggle was at its height. In 1932 the internal difficulties connected with the first Five-Year Plan were exceedingly acute.

Expectations and identifications appear to behave in a similar way. When there is need to enhance the sense of self, as in the early days, self-identifications are frequent. Fact-form statements (expectations) appear to be related to new situations that call for explanation. Over the long term there is better knowledge of the context and more can be taken for granted.

After this preliminary view of the slogan history of the 25-year period from 1918 to 1943, it will be productive to focus more intensively upon details. The year 1920 was one of Soviet victory over the White counter-revolutionary movement. As the Red Army defeated the forces of General Denikin and Admiral Kolchak the Soviet state—temporarily reduced to the size of medieval Muscovy—gradually reconquered and reunited lost territory. The festive character of the time and occasion was reflected in the May Day slogans. Although the struggle against hunger and other privations was still a major disturbing factor, new hope and confidence prevailed. Most of the slogans were terse and general. Several of them juxtaposed policies and attitudes imputed to the capitalist world with those appropriate to the proletariat. In the main, the slogans were devoted to domestic issues, the outside world being mentioned but twice, in connection with the western front against Poland. An innovation is a slogan hailing locomotives, rehabilitated through May Day labor—the earliest referring to the period of reconstruction and the idolatry of machinery.

The years 1921-1925 were the period of reconstruction. The slogans for 1922 presented an entirely new picture compared to those of preceding years. (These slogans were the only ones which have been signed personally by Stalin as Secretary of the Central Committee of the Party.)

No longer was the emphasis on questions of home policies. Nearly half of the slogans were devoted to foreign issues. The land of victorious Socialism now took an active interest in the revolutionary struggle of the European proletariat, but, significantly, mainly of neighboring countries: Germany, Hungary, Georgia, Azerbaidzhan, (the latter two still preserved their independence), Finland, Latvia, and Esthonia (which broke away from Russia after the October Revolution). The slogans declared war, in alliance with the international proletariat, on aggressive capitalism, imperialism, bourgeois democracy and the Social Democrats. For the first time, we find celebrated in the slogans the Communist International, the proletarian world revolution, and the Red Army as the army of Socialism and—as far as this can be deduced from the text of the slogans—the executor of the war waged by the working class against world capitalism. Continuous support and care by the whole of the Russian masses were pledged to the Red Army. Simultaneously, the sovereignty and the borders of the Soviet Republics were declared to be inviolable. On the home front, the alliance of workers and peasants were emphasized, as well as the brotherhood of Soviet Republics, which was to be tended until total victory of the working class was achieved. For the first time the Red youth, the working youth of Soviet Russia, was especially mentioned and honored by a slogan. Significant was a special attack directed against "reactionary" clergymen for hiding church treasures from sequestration; the party professed to utilize them in the fight against famine.

The slogans for 1924 were signed by Andreev, the new

Secretary of the Central Committee of the Party. Once more, the attention of the parading Soviet masses was focused on different aspects of the international proletarian struggle. The U.S.S.R. was now openly referred to as the fortress of international proletarian revolution. However, there was one distinct difference in comparison with the slogans of 1922. The circle of attention given by Moscow to the revolutionary struggle abroad was widened. The struggle of the French proletariat against Poincaré was acclaimed, along with that of the Polish proletariat, alleged defenders of the pacification of eastern Europe. The Romanians were warned to give up Bessarabia. Greetings were extended to the Ukrainian and White Russian peasants fighting the Polish land lords. All victims of international capital, as well as subjugated peoples in general, were honored; and the struggle of the working masses against capital was acclaimed. The broadening of the Communist International was recommended as an execution of one provision of Lenin's will and testament.

For the first time, the word "Fascism" was used in the slogans of 1924, but the struggle of the world proletariat against Fascism was recommended by the Party simultaneously with that against the Social Democrats, who were denounced as servants of international Fascism. Thus, the Bulgarian Social Democrats were accused of assisting the Bulgarian Fascists in the annihilation of revolutionary fighters, and the German Social Democrats were brought to account for camouflaging a dictatorial regime of generals in Germany. Consequently, the Soviet working class was admonished to remember, on May 1, 1924, the workers of Saxony and Hamburg who lost their lives in the fight against reaction, along with all the other prisoners of capitalism and of the Social Democrats in Germany, Hungary, Poland, Latvia and Romania. Thus, in 1924 and in the years to come, the edge of Communist attacks was and will be directed against the competitors of Communism in the political leadership of the proletarian masses—the orthodox Marxist Social Democrats— as against the avowed foes of the working class, the capitalists.

The international character of the May First celebration in 1924 was further stressed by the effort of Moscow to promote, for the first and only time, an international peasant council next to the international alliance of workers and peasants. The few domestic slogans of 1924 mainly propagated the defense of the Soviet Union against the increasing danger of enemy attack from outside. Others celebrated the Communist Party, the proletarian dictatorship, the working youth and the Soviet woman. As in 1922, the fight against illiteracy was given prominence in Soviet reconstruction work.

The 1925 May Day slogans were again signed by Andreev, but this time attention was more evenly divided between domestic and international issues, between the major task of selling the idea of Communism to the Soviet Russian peasantry and the expression of solidarity, even if merely moral, with the revolutionary struggle of the world proletariat.

The First of May was declared by Moscow in 1925 to be simultaneously a day of fighting solidarity among workers of all countries and a day of close unity between the urban and rural working masses. The leading part in this alliance was, however, reserved to the factory worker, who was regarded as guarantor of the victory of Communism.

During 1925, the May First slogans acquired a definitely militant character. They were phrased in military terms. The international proletariat was referred to as a world "army" of workers. The united "front" of the entire proletariat against capital was celebrated. The Soviet Union was proclaimed an "advanced position" of world Communism. The Communist International was hailed as the "headquarters" organizing the "leading troops" of the international proletariat. Similarly, other terms were taken from the military vocabulary.

The slogans of 1925 reflected the interest Moscow was taking, and the hopes it placed at the time, in a victorious world revolution. Several slogans speak of world Communism. World revolution is now explicitly mentioned in the introductory statement. One slogan advocates the necessity of a united world trade-union movement. The Russian Communist Party not only gives its support and identifies itself with the struggle of the workers of Poland, Esthonia, and now also those of England, but it transcends Europe and takes the rôle of coordinator and leader of the world proletariat's revolutionary masses. Moscow now favors the alliance of the European, and, for the first time, American proletarians with the subjugated peoples of the East. China, Egypt, Persia, Turkey are placed under the patronage of the international proletariat against exploitation through world imperialism. The Soviet working class offers its fraternal help to the millions of "slaves" in Asia and Africa. Simultaneously, the counterpart and enemy of the proletariat, the bourgeoisie, is now also treated specifically as an international body. It is an exponent of world imperialism, of world capital, of the international stock exchange, etc. Yet all the slogans dealing with proletarian cooperation are still worded in very vague, unspecific terms. They stress only fraternal feelings, extend greetings, offer handshakes. One slogan mentions the names of two Polish Communists, victims of the White terror.

In contrast, domestic slogans in 1925 were definite and precise. The leitmotif is the desired and advocated rapprochement between factory worker and peasant. The support of the Soviet Government by the peasant class, so conspicuously lacking, was to be secured by all possible means, the lowering of prices for retail goods, by credits, better land utilization, an improved supply of agricultural tools and machines, tax exemption, expert agricultural advice, and more efficient organization of village Soviets in which red tape and corruption would be eradicated. A further step toward workers' and peasants' cooperation, toward the realization of Socialism was the encouragement of the cooperative movement.

Next to the proposed unification of town and village in the Soviet Union, the slogans of 1925 presented the defense preparations of the Soviet Union as a most urgent and vital task facing the country—the only proletarian state in the world. And, as before, women and youth were played up in the slogans as all-important segments of the anticapitalist front.

A new Secretary of the Party Central Committee, Kosior, signed the May First slogans of 1926. The First of May of that year coincided with Easter Eve. It is significant as an example of the still impressive strength of religious feeling in atheistic Soviet Russia that the Party organizations were strictly admonished by Moscow to relinquish, or at least to reduce, antireligious propaganda on this particular day. Moscow considered it essential—especially in the countryside—to avoid all antireligious demonstrations "able to provoke the

religious fanaticism of the believers among the population."
The fight for the soul of the Russian village was still going
on.

The slogans for 1926 did not differ in general very much
from those of 1925, although their wording was shortened
considerably. The slogans paying homage to the Communist
International had been promoted to a more dignified place,
and appeared as second on the list. The denunciation slogans
indicated the stand taken by Moscow on international issues.
The Russian Communist Party was against aggressive capitalism, against new wars (but also against bourgeois and
socialist pseudopacifism), against the League of Nations,
against Locarno, and against intervention in China, in Mor-
occo, and in Syria. Help was promised by the Russian Communist Party to the workers of China; and simultaneously
the workers of Great Britain, Japan, and the United States
were also called upon to assist revolutionary China. Greetings were extended that year to all the Communist Parties of
the world—the deadly enemy of the bourgoisie.

After the defeat of Trotsky, and the acceptance of the
theory of "Socialism in one single country" formulated by
Stalin, the proud and omnipotent term "world revolution"
did not appear in the 1926 slogans; it was replaced by less
ambiguous catch words, as "world proletarian-unity", "united
front of workers of all countries"; and by old slogans, such
as "world trade-union movement" and "the union of European and American proletariat with the subjugated peoples
of the East."

On the domestic front, in 1926, the consolidation and
success of Socialism in Soviet Russia was the predominant
theme. The road to victorious Socialism led—according to the
slogans—by way of strengthening the Soviets, trade unions
and cooperatives; and especially by way of the industrialization of the country, and Socialist accumulation. The strictest
economy and avoidance of all extravagance and waste in industry, as well as in state administration, were prerequisites
of a successful industrial development of the country. And
again the economic and cultural progress of the Union was
said to depend on close collaboration between the urban
proletariat and the peasantry,—which, judging by the promi-

nence given to these objectives in the slogans, was still far from being achieved.

On the other hand, not the whole of the peasantry was now regarded as worthy of becoming an ally of the factory worker. The struggle of the village poor against the Kulaks was for the first time (1926) mentioned and sponsored in slogans. Thus, the 1926 slogans and propaganda were based on the idea of three circles of gravitation and action: the Soviet workers were united in and by the Party, the continuity of which was guaranteed by the Komsomol and the Young Pioneers; the Soviet peasants lent their support to the urban proletariat and the Soviet Government; and all the exploited and persecuted in the world were led and taken care of by the Communist International.

A new partly line in relation to the world proletariat was laid down in the 1927 May slogans, signed by the Party Central Committee Secretary, Kubiak. This time, Moscow expected to get its help and cooperation: First, because the world proletariat had a direct interest in successful socialist construction in the U.S.S.R., the workers of the world were called upon to facilitate the progress of the Soviet Union's socialist revolution; secondly, in view of the British endeavor to destroy the Soviet Union, the proletarians of all countries were asked to give their protection to the "land of the Soviets". The Soviet Union was presented in the slogans as a guarantor of world peace. (In spite of numerous "provocations," the Soviet land had refused to be provoked and to accept the challenge.)

The hopes of Moscow were still directed toward world revolution. The Communists were encouraged to penetrate deeper into the workers' and peasant masses, under the banner of the Communist International. No less than four slogans were devoted to China, in which Moscow celebrated the Chinese revolution, the revolutionary Kuomintang, the Chinese proletariat, and the Chinese Communist Party, and called upon the workers of England, the United States, Italy and Japan to insist on the recall of "imperialist" troops and warships from China. Moscow wanted to oppose "imperialism" by means of an international class solidarity of the workers of the world, and thought of overcoming Fascism through the establishment of a dictatorship of the proletariat all over the world.

The domestic slogans in 1927 dealt mainly with the same topics as those of 1926: building of Socialism; industrialization of the U.S.S.R.; the rapprochement between the industrial proletariat and the peasantry; the class struggle in villages; and defense of the Soviet Union. But the economic propaganda of this year was especially focused on the lowering of prices—the sorest point in Soviet economics of that period. For the first time, the slogans celebrated the Soviet Union as a fraternal union of the various nationalities of the U.S.S.R. For the first time, also, a lengthy citation from Lenin was added to the list of slogans.

The May Day slogans of 1928, signed that year by V. Molotov, brought a number of innovations. First, the number of slogans representing direct quotations from Lenin rose to three. Second, the Communist International was mentioned twice in the slogans: as "the revolutionary headquarters of the proletarian struggle for the destruction of capitalism in the world," and then as a revolutionary banner in the fight "against the White terror, against Fascism, against worldwide reaction." But although the world proletarian revolution remained, as before, the goal, all direct references to the active struggle of the proletariat in various countries disappeared from the slogans, except for China. But even here, the wording was changed. This time, neither the solidarity of the Russian working people with the Chinese proletariat was advertised, nor was its help offered to the Chinese "class brethren." On the contrary, the slogan simply registered the "call of the thousands of fighters of the Chinese proletariat, who sacrificed their lives in the interest of the Soviets in Canton, to continue the struggle for the liberation of millions of workers and peasants of the oppressed East."

The slogans of 1928 clearly put the Soviet Union in a defensive position. Greetings were now extended to the workers of all countries, to the oppressed colonial peoples, and to the prisoners of capital in the entire world. But the slogans reflected the chief concern of the Party with a threatening world conflagration, allegedly prepared by the imperialists with the help of the social democrats, and especially concern with the menacing imperialistic attack on the Soviet land. Moscow still had no confidence in the League of Nations, which it considered a camouflage for the armament race and new wars. As before, the Soviets alone were played up as advocates and protagonists of general disarmament; the Red Army was now introduced as the defender not only of the Soviet Union, but of the interests of the proletariat and the "oppressed" peoples of the world.

The slogans of 1928, the first year of the first Five-Year Plan, showed an extremely wide range of domestic appeals; these, somehow, were not systematized. Still conspicuous among the more than thirty domestic slogans were those dealing with the activization of Soviet masses, with the economic problems of industrialization and of the beginnings of agricultural collectivization, with an all-front attack against the Kulaks, and with questions of cultural life.

From 1929 onward, the May First slogans of the Communist Party ceased to be signed by the Secretary of the Central Party Committee, and were presented in the name of the Central Committee as a body. The first effect of this change was, in 1929, an unprecedented increase in the number of slogans. Once more prominence was given on the "International Red Day," to international revolutionary slogans, to propaganda of the "World October." The Communist International, with headquarters in Moscow, now five times mentioned in the slogans, was in 1929 at last openly declared to be "organizer and leader of the proletarian revolution." The Soviet State was introduced as the "fatherland of the international proletariat and the stronghold of world revolution," and the Red Army and the Red Fleet were now characterized as the "armed battalions of world revolution."

According to the Party slogans, the world proletarian revolution alone could put an end to the armament race and to war. Correspondingly, the proletariat of all countries was admonished to fight for the destruction of the bourgeoisie. For the first time, in 1929, the Soviet system was suggested as the best form of government for the entire world. For the first time, also in 1929, the establishment of a Soviet India was foreseen and recommended in the May First slogans. Finally, corresponding to the old Lenin conception, the working class was expected to transform the "imperialist war, sponsored and fostered by the bourgeoisie," into a civil war

with the definite aim of establishing a proletarian dictatorship all over the world.

Was this war a certainty? The Kellogg Pact was denounced
as a camouflage for the preparation of new wars. New battles
were foreseen and, of course, the subject of the forthcoming
attack on the U.S.S.R.—the natural enemy of the international bourgeoisie and the liberator of all the oppressed
nationalities of the world—was again taken up in the slogans.
Simultaneously, greater tribute than ever before was paid in
them to the Red Army, which was now lauded as a guarantor
of peace, and protector of the achievements of the October
Revolution, as well as the promoter of Socialism in towns and
villages. For the first time, the internal difficulties through
which the Commintern was passing were reflected in the
slogans. The weaklings or, more correctly, the men of little
faith, were accused of leaving the ranks of the fighting International, and a merciless war was declared upon the Rightists
and the Trotskyists.

In the domestic slogans, preference was again given to
those dealing with the industrialization of the country, the
collectivization of agriculture, and the fight against bureaucracy. A seven-hour working day was promised in 1929 to the
workers of the U.S.S.R., but without any letdown in the accelerated tempo of industrialization nor lowering of output
norms. The retarding factors and shortcomings in the industrial program, such as loafing and drunkenness, mentioned
again and again in the slogans, were violently attacked, and
were to be removed through Socialist competition, rationali-
zation of production, creation of shock brigades, self-criticism
fostered by the trade unions, strengthened labor discipline
and other devices. The pattern of life in the villages was also
supposed to change entirely through the collectivization of
agriculture, the extension of which seemed now to be especially entrusted to the Communist youth. Next to the collective farms, the State farms—the agricultural Socialist factories
—were now introduced as the most effective weapon in the
dislocation of the Kulaks. The idea of a more outspoken
participation of workers in the administration of State and
industry was further played up in the slogans. This obviously
reflected the desire of the Party to meet the accusation of a
growing cleavage between the bureaucratic machine and the

working masses of the Union. For the first time, anti-Semitism—apparently still rampant in the Soviet Union—was denounced in the 1929 slogans, along with the activities of orthodox clergymen, Catholic priests, rabbis, and members of the still existing religious sects. The desired but lacking unity in the Party was specially stressed in the slogans, but under explicit exclusion of "opportunists," "rightists," and "appeasers," and especially Trotskyists, who were now accused of having deliberately betrayed the Revolution by openly joining forces with the counter-revolutionary camp.

A considerable shift in the focus of attention can be observed in the May First slogans of the year 1930. The considerable reduction in the number of slogans on international and revolutionary topics is striking. The mentioning of a "World October," of the Soviet Union as the "fatherland of the international proletariat" was merely a legacy of the past. Although the Communist International is still recommended as *the* leader—not only of the international proletariat, but also of the oppressed peoples of the colonies—the fear of a rift in its midst is clearly reflected in the slogans. The revolutionary storm subsided. Economic crises in the capitalist West, with the possible subsequent radicalization of the masses, were closely watched in Moscow but, for the time being, a workers' and peasants' revolution seemed to be a practical possibility only in China and other countries of the East.

On the other side, the Soviet working masses were still left to believe that the Soviet Union was in danger of being attacked from abroad. The Holy See now came for the first time under direct attack as an active opponent of the Soviet regime and as the spiritual leader of the crusade against Red Moscow. And the social democrats, who already before had been referred to as protagonists of imperialism, were now additionally accused of plotting with Rome new wars and an attack on Soviet Russia. Unity and increased industrial assistance to the Red Army, now even more emphatically stressed in the slogans, was the answer of Soviet workers and peasants to the "manipulations of greedy capital."

The slogan of the Five-Year Plan in four years was, however, the real link between the propaganda for a greater effort on the industrial front and that for a timely "frontal attack on capitalistic enemies." The idea of the Five-Year Plan predominated in the domestic slogans of 1930. Although those referring to industrialization were still mainly the same as in 1929, some grew more precise and specific. Some of the larger plants then under construction (which subsequently became famous in the Soviet war effort against Nazi-Germany) were played up and referred to by name. The necessity of adopting the standard of American technical processes was driven home. Unexpectedly, Socialist competition, though further recommended, was simultaneously accused of being overadvertised, thus defeating its original purpose.

The slogans dealing with Soviet agrarian problems, and primarily with the collectivization of agriculture, produced no new ideas in 1930, in spite of their great number. Only excesses in carrying out collectivization brought forward several slogans professing the integrity of the middle peasantry as a social class. Well-known slogans criticizing the shortcomings of the Soviet state machine, the lagging struggle against illiteracy, anti-Semitism, drunkenness, and counter-revolutionary activities of the Trotskyists and other dissidents inside the Party, made up the rest of the list of domestic slogans. Self-criticism was proclaimed to be healthful and invigorating to Soviet security. "All revolutionary parties which perished until now did so"—according to Lenin's words quoted in one of the slogans—"because they became overconfident and feared to speak about their weaknesses, but we shall not perish, because we do not fear to discuss these weaknesses and we shall learn to overcome our shortcomings."

In 1931, the subject of a disintegrating capitalist society and of the imperiled Soviet Union was again taken up in the May First slogans. Unemployment, famine and the very high death rate in capitalist countries were contrasted with the flourishing life in the Soviet Union. The international proletariat was urged to follow the path of the working masses of the Soviet Union. The accusations of dumping and forced labor in the Soviet Union were rejected as a slander and an invention put out and spread by capitalists and Social Fascists.

Still, in spite of the assertion of a new outburst of revolutionary activities in the world, only two concrete examples could be cited in the 1931 slogans. The Chinese Red Army and the Soviets in China were toasted as liberators of the Chinese people from the yoke of foreign imperialists, Chinese generals, landlords and the bourgeoisie. Also, the Spanish Communist Party, together with the workers of Spain, were congratulated upon their heroic fight for the overthrow of feudalism and capitalism.

Nevertheless, no active help, except for sheer oratory and invitations to follow the lead of the Lenin International, was offered by the Moscow Communist leaders to the struggling international proletariat. On the contrary, the workers of the world were now implored to defend the Soviet Union against the coming intervention, and the imperialist war was supposed to be turned into a civil war between the exploited and the exploiters. Thus, the defense of the Soviet Union—"the fatherland of the whole proletariat"—by each individual worker was now put first and before any independent revolutionary uprising.

The world revolution was projected into the distant future. It was now anticipated that only the youngest group in the Party, the pioneers, would accomplish Lenin's bequest, the instigation of a world October. Thus, the threat of intervention in Soviet Russia appeared in these years as a real bogey on the Communist horizon. In 1931, it was to be fought off by the Red Army, sworn to remain faithful to the proletarian dictatorship and, incidentally, the world proletarian revolution, by accelerated Socialist industrial construction, i.e., industrialization, and by progressive and intensified collectivization. The fear of intervention served as a whip. The Soviet Union was—we read in the slogans—technically fifty years behind the advanced countries in the West, and there were only ten years granted by Moscow to the working masses of the U.S.S.R. for catching up and eliminating this painful discrepancy.

The remaining domestic slogans in 1931 repeated the catch words of previous years—which may be explained either by the pressure to fulfill the third year of the first Five-Year Plan, or to reestablish the crumbling unity of a Party suffering from the dissension of Rightist and Leftist "renegades of Communism."

The May First slogans of 1932 show remarkable stagnation

in political thinking and the complete drying up of imagination in regard to revolutionary or international, as well as domestic, slogans. With only a few exceptions, there is practically no slogan which we do not already know as a cliché from previous years, and especially from the immediately preceding year of 1931. Even the wording of the slogan is, in very many cases, practically the same. Still, when changes occur, they are significant. Thus, for instance, the Red Army no longer was swearing its allegiance to the "world proletarian revolution," but only to the "working class of the whole world." Each factory, state farm and collective farm was now openly declared to be an impregnable fortress for the defense of the country. For the first time, Stalin's words were cited which in the years to come became a stereotyped May Day slogan: "We don't want a single strip of foreign land. But we shall not give away to anyone our own land, not a single inch of it." Thus, the phantom of war was casting its shadow well ahead of events, forcing on Russia and her watchful government in Moscow not only a state of technical preparedness, but psychological readjustment as well.

On May 1, 1933, the Soviet Union was confronted with a new political situation—the rise of Hitler to power in January of that year. The diminishing number of May Day slogans in 1931 and 1932 now jumped to 47. Also, the slogans dealing with international affairs increased substantially. The slogan of world Socialist revolution reappeared in 1933. The international proletariat was now incited to revolutionary struggle against imperialists, to fight against capitalism and Fascist dictatorship and for Communism. The success of the first Five-Year Plan was now regarded as a particular stimulus to the overthrow of capitalism and the emulation of the Soviet example. Faced with an aggressive "Fascist counter-revolution," Moscow now for the first time accepted and propagated the idea of a united anticapitalist front of Communist and social democratic workers. But what this union would amount to in practice was clearly shown by another slogan which, accusing the social democrats of giving help to the bourgeoisie and the Fascists, invited the workers to leave the social democratic camp by joining the fighting anti-Fascist Communist International.

Three countries, significantly enough, were selected for

direct reference in the 1933 slogans. Next to China—the victim of domestic and foreign exploiters—came Germany and Great Britain. In the case of Germany, references were limited to praise of her "heroic" Communist Party and of its leader, Comrade Thälmann. More attention, however, was given to England by Moscow as late as 1933. Here, the "obstinate slave owners" were accused of preparing a united imperialist attack on the U.S.S.R. The bill forbidding the import of Soviet goods to England was quoted as the opening phase of this attack.

As in the preceding years, the Soviet Union was praised in 1933 as the only genuine protagonist of peace. Its defense was entrusted by Moscow both to the Red Army and the International proletariat. A quotation from Stalin denying Soviet lust for annexation was meant to persuade even the most doubtful and skeptical mind, in regard to Soviet intentions. The Red Army continued in 1933 to be sworn to remain faithful to the international proletariat.

The domestic slogans of 1933 did not show much change. The second Five-Year Plan had taken the place of the first. However, there was one important innovation. To a larger extent than before the slogans were directing appeals for better labor and output to various social groups, such as the metallurgical workers, the coal miners, the railroad workers, etc. The increased number of direct quotations used as slogans—and this time exclusively from Stalin—was also remarkable. Not a single reference to the writings of Lenin can be found, though every Communist was still supposed to "gather strength" from intimate knowledge of Marxist-Leninism. For the first time, the ideal of a "comfortable" life found its way into the slogans. The greater number of slogans dealing with the deepening of class struggle in the Soviet villages is striking—this, obviously, in direct response to the intensified collectivization of Soviet agriculture in the early '30's. And in 1933, the purity of the Party ranks remained still an unachieved goal—the recommendation for iron proletarian discipline inside the Party was tied up with an open demand for further purges.

Nineteen hundred and thirty-four was the second year of the second Five-Year Plan, and also the second year of Hitler's rule over Germany. The May First slogans of that year contrasted the Soviet Eldorado, the happy life of workers and peasants under the Soviets, with the appalling economic conditions under "bloody" Fascism.

The Party advised that the fight for the world Socialist revolution should proceed along the following moderate lines: first, by promotion of the idea of proletarian internationalism, and secondly, by elimination of the traitors in the working class, the leaders of the Second International, who were accused of aligning themselves with the henchmen of Fascism. But what about the underdogs in Fascist Europe, what about Japan? To both the working class of Austria and the revolutionary proletarians of Germany the Soviet proletariat extended on this day of "battle rally of the revolutionary forces of the world proletariat," its brotherly greetings. It reiterated its admiration for the Communist Parties of both countries. But any practical action was boiled down, at least so far as the slogans were concerned, to the proclaimed determination of liberating the German Communist leader Thälmann from his internment in a Nazi concentration camp. The anti-Soviet provocations of the warlords of Japan were supposed to be confronted by detachments of the Far Eastern Red Army and by the pointed declaration of Stalin, which was stressing both Soviet Russia's desire for peace and her preparedness to fight, if provoked. Incidentally, in 1934 the Red Army was no longer sworn to be faithful to the international proletariat, but to its Fatherland—a symbol which from then on played an ever-growing rôle in the May First slogans. Moreover, next to the Red Army, the protection of the Socialist Fatherland was assigned to the millions of Soviet workers and peasants—the members of the Osoviakhim.

The domestic May Day slogans in 1934 were primarily meant to serve the propaganda for the fulfillment of the second Five-Year Plan in town and country. The plan was interpreted as being dedicated to the strengthening of the "Fatherland," as well as to the establishment of a classless Socialist society. However, the prospect of a "comfortable" life, promised them by the slogans for the end of the second Five-Year Plan, must have been especially appealing to Soviet workers and collective farmers. A promise of greater and more individualized differentiation of wages was another attraction in the slogans of 1934. In return, the Party expected from the rank and file of the Soviet workers greater activity, creative enthusiasm, and initiative in production. In 1935, the May First slogans had no less than eight quotations from Stalin. But, so far as international issues were involved, the slogans remained essentially the same as those of 1934. In fact, even the wording was little changed. The Red Army was from now on referred to as "our beloved invincible Red Army," and the symbol of "our Fatherland" received an additional honorary adjective, "great"—"our Great Fatherland."

The international ties uniting the working class of the U.S.S.R. with the proletariat of the capitalist countries was, however, still regarded, at least officially, as one of the main pillars of the greatness and fortitude of the Soviet Union. Correspondingly, the idea of international proletarian solidarity was once more stressed in the slogans. This seemed, as before, to guarantee the universal victory of Socialism and the establishment of a Soviet pattern of government all over the world. This, it was proudly asserted, had opened to all workers the path toward a comfortable, civilized and happy life. The Soviet Government proudly claimed credit for the liquidation of unemployment in the U.S.S.R.

Another change occurred with reference to China. While, in the preceding years, the Chinese Red Army and the Soviets in China were feted, the place of honor was now given to the heroic Communist Party of China.

The second Five-Year Plan still dominated domestic slogans for 1935. But its interpretation received a new and more human touch. Stress was laid on the "people who have mastered the technique," on the protection and encouragement of every capable and intelligent worker. Simultaneously each group of workers, technicians, and engineers were separately called upon to live up to its duty and thus to contribute to the plan's success. In the field of agriculture, attention was given in 1935 to the burning problem of increasing livestock reserves, once the grain problem had been cared for. Harmonizing the personal interest of collective farmers with the interest of the collective farm as such, was the other big topic. The Party had to make concessions to the property sentiment of the peasant, be he of Russian or other descent.

Remarkable, finally, was the effort of the Party to play up the accomplishments of proletarian democracy in the U.S.S.R.—a new tune among the old familiar slogans. The greetings extended to the Red Army of the Soviet Union were termed "battle" greetings. Other slogans, also, emphasized the growing concern of Soviet leadership with the state of military preparedness of the Union.

In 1936, the May First slogans offered the masses of the Soviet Union for the first time, in addition to well-known clichés, a more specific description of Fascist ideology. Previous general references to Fascism were replaced with an appeal directed to the international proletariat to close ranks and to establish a united front against Fascism and the danger of war. Fascism was, according to Moscow, "a capitalist offensive against the working class." Further, it meant an aggressive war; it amounted to starvation, poverty. War could break out quite unexpectedly; the international proletariat should not be found napping. Peace and Socialism were the battle cries.

In spite of this theoretical reasoning, however, Moscow apparently was on guard against jeopardizing relations with Nazi Germany. The "heroic" Communist Party of Germany was no longer mentioned in the slogans; nor was the "revolutionary" proletariat of Germany. Only Thälmann was, as before, acclaimed as a leader of the German working class. The place of distinction was given to Spain, to the heroic Spanish Communist Party, and to the Spanish workers fighting both Fascism and reaction. Nor did China reappear in the 1936 slogans. The Far East was only twice mentioned—first, greetings were extended to the Mongolian People's Republic fighting for its independence and liberty; secondly, the peoples of the Soviet Union were again warned to be on guard against the provocations of Japanese militarists endangering the safety of the "Fatherland's frontiers." Independence of the homeland took precedence over revolutionary exploits. And, significantly, even the Soviet Red Army was no longer fêted as the "faithful guardian of the achievements of the October Socialist Revolution," but as the "faithful guardian of Soviet frontiers." The Red Army men were giving their oath not to the "workers' and peasant Government" but to the "Soviet Power." For the first time, the frontier guards were especially mentioned in the slogans. The general militarization of life in the Soviet Union was further expressed in the growing number of slogans devoted to the Army, to the building up of morale and skill among the armed forces; and in terminological changes. The civilian leaders were called "captains of industry," "captains of metallurgy," "captains of railway transport," etc.

In 1936, the second Five-Year Plan was well on its way to fulfillment. The workers were now admonished to overfulfill the norms laid down for 1936. The slogans sponsored complete technological mobilization of the country for the sake of the Fatherland, and continuous Stakhanov production in the factories, plants, mines, and in transportation. The improvement of standards in the technical training of the workers was another slogan. The goal was clear. The Soviet industry was to lead the world, first in output of blast furnaces, metallurgical equipment and the exploitation of oil wells.

Simultaneously, the slogans admitted a wider circle of persons to the ranks of the new Soviet élite. To the town nobility, Stakhanovites ("the heroes of Socialist labor") were added now the new country noblemen—the tractorists (male and female), the harvesters (male and female), and the chairmen of the collective farms, again of both sexes.

The theory that Socialism was an accomplished fact in the Soviet Union finds documentation in the slogans of 1936. The U.S.S.R., formerly the "land of the Soviets," is now referred to (in slogans otherwise repeated verbatim) as "the land of Socialism," and the Soviet state as "our Socialist State." Incidentally, the idea of Socialism received a new interpretation. In the slogans of 1936, it meant "liquidation of the shortage of living quarters and overcrowding."

The appeal to finish off the dying class enemy is combined, in the 1936 slogans, with warmer references to national minority groups and to the equal position of women in the U.S.S.R. Significant of the effort of Moscow to organize the Soviet populace into one single-minded, single-purposed community was the occasional telescoping of references to workers and collective farmers into one symbol, "the working people," and the change from the term "working people" to the "whole working people." Greetings were extended, on

May 1, 1936, to the "whole working youth" of the Soviet Union and not, as before, exclusively to the Communist Youth League. The importance attached to gaining the confidence of the entire younger generation was further revealed by special mention of the Soviet teacher, responsible for the upbringing and education of new generations of Soviet citizens.

The international slogans of 1937 followed in their general pattern those of 1936, but they sharpened in tone, became more aggressive and, also, in a way, more definite. The old revolutionary battle cry, "proletarians of all countries unite," reappeared once more. A fighting note was added to the definition of Fascism.

Fascism was presented as a "terrorist policy of capitalists and landlords directed against the workers and peasants" and as an "instigation of one nation against another." Recommended as remedies against this evil were the mobilization of all available forces for the fight against Fascism, and an appeal to the workers and peasants of the entire world to strengthen and widen the anti-Fascist front. The fight was to be, as before, in the name and in defense of peace and Socialism. But this time, in 1937, one more aim was significantly added—"for the democratic freedoms," but without further specification.

Once accepted, the idea of a united anti-Fascist front led logically to significant changes, as in reference to Spain. In 1936 the Spanish Communist Party was the hero of the anti-reactionary struggle. In 1937, the hero was the righteous *front populaire*. All the open and hidden enemies of the people's front were anthematized. All available forces were now to be utilized in the fight. In Germany, once more, the "revolutionary" workers and the "heroic" German Communist Party took the place of honor next to Comrade Thälmann in the Moscow slogans. And the Red Army became once again the "protector of the great October Revolution," though the defense of the Fatherland was declared to be a sacred duty of each citizen of the Union. Incidentally, the Fatherland was constantly referred to as a "Socialist Fatherland," and the new Stalin constitution of 1936 was celebrated as the "constitution of victorious socialism and of true democracy."

Moscow wanted to appear as an adherent of democratic ideas. But there was still no sign in the slogans of a weakening or abating of the nineteen-year-old dictatorship of the Soviet proletariat or, rather, the Communist Party. As before, its preservation was regarded as necessary to secure for the working class a leading rôle in Soviet society. Nothing shows, however, more clearly the new trend in Soviet ideology than the effort to recognize "faithfulness to the Fatherland" as the highest virtue in the new Soviet State. The intelligentsia gets a good mark because it honorably fulfills its obligations toward the Fatherland. Soviet children are expected to be healthy, gay and, of course, faithful to the Fatherland.

The realization of Communism even in Soviet Russia becomes a distant dream. This is now recognized or, rather, indirectly admitted. That the execution of Lenin's ideas would take more time than previously anticipated might perhaps be deduced from a change made in the slogan referring to the pioneers—the Party members of school age. If, before, they were expected to carry on and finish Lenin's work, now they are only urged to become fighters for his ideas.

Things were not developing too smoothly inside the Soviet Union, to judge by the considerable number of slogans dealing in 1937 with the struggle against the internal enemy. Political "carelessness" was to be banned and abolished, once and for all, from Soviet society. Revolutionary watchfulness was the slogan of the day. All political double-dealers were to be detected and brought to book. The Party, which was modestly referred to only as "the vanguard of the Soviet workers," was expected to be converted into an unassailable fortress of Bolshevism. All people's enemies—the Japanese-German Trotskyist wreckers and spies—were to be exterminated, and the traitors of the Fatherland condemned to death. Once more the Soviet masses were given to understand that the Communist International was their saviour, leader and organizer in the fight against war, Fascism and capitalism.

The international May First slogans in 1938 again showed important changes in wording and order. The Fascist stream was rapidly rising. Its dangerous aspects had to be emphasized and brought closer home. Fascism, represented before in the slogans as a threat to the workers and peasants, was now characterized as endangering also the working intelligentsia. In references to Fascist terror, the adjective "bloody" was added. Fascism was treated as the worst enemy of international order and of existing friendships among the nations of the world.

The struggle of the Spanish people against domestic and foreign Fascism was now declared to be a common cause of progressively minded humanity as a whole. Moscow regarded this heroic struggle not as before, as a fight of the Spanish worker alone, but of the whole Spanish people for independence and freedom. Correspondingly, no longer the Chinese workers—not to speak of the Chinese Communist Party—but the "great Chinese people" were fêted and congratulated upon their struggle against encroachments by Japanese, and other peoples left unnamed.

The Fascist danger required the mobilization of all moral and material resources. A special slogan stressed the necessity of fostering and strengthening the international ties linking the proletariat of the U.S.S.R. with the working class of the capitalist countries. International proletarian solidariy thus appeared to be prerequisite for the struggle. However, the slogan praising the Socialist world revolution was dropped completely in 1938. The change with reference to the united fight against Fascism was also significant. The international proletariat was not asked as before to place itself under the banner of the Communist International, but under the international banner of Marx, Engels and Lenin. The reference to the Communist International as the leader and organizer of the struggle against war, Fascism and capitalism remained in the slogans. But mention of the International was removed from its place of honor at the top of the list.

Other changes are highly revealing of the technique of writing May First slogans. The Bolshevist Revolution was called not the "great October Revolution" but the "great October Socialist Revolution". There seemed to be a conscious desire to have a certain frequency of the words Socialism, Socialist, etc. While, in one slogan, the word "Socialist" with reference to the Fatherland was dropped, the next one restored the equilibrium by replacing the words "sentries of Soviet frontiers" with "sentries of the land of Socialism."

Great efforts were made in 1938 by the Party to promote by means of new slogans community feeling, fighting spirit and the sentiment of equality among Soviet citizens. One new slogan praised the moral and political unity of the Soviet people, who gained freedom and independence under the guidance of the Bolshevist party. The idea of the U.S.S.R. as the union of equal peoples was played up in contrast to Czarist Russia, "prison of peoples." For the first time, the Red Fleet was celebrated as a separate unit, the guardian of the maritime borders of the Fatherland. The three largest units of the Soviet armed forces—the Red Army, the Red Navy, and the Red Air Force—were thus mentioned singly and in their own right in the slogans. And if, in 1937, the aim was to convert the Party into an unassailable camp of Bolshevism, in 1938 not alone the Party but the whole of the U.S.S.R. was to become such a fortress.

Other innovations are also noteworthy. The term "citizens of the Soviet land" appeared for the first time in the slogans of 1938; they were promised more cotton, silk, clothes, knitted fabrics and footwear. A "comfortable" life became the ideal for today and tomorrow. Other long-forgotten terms of a somewhat archaic nature appeared in 1938 slogans. The heroic Papanintsy—the daring conquerors of the North Pole —were celebrated, for instance, as "worthy sons of the Socialist Fatherland." Finally, it is worth mentioning that the appeal to the youth to learn, in order to be able to continue Lenin's work, was addressed in 1938 no longer only to the Pioneers of the Party, but to all Soviet school children. And for the first time Lenin's work was introduced as the combined deeds of Lenin and Stalin.

Of particular interest also was the advice given by the Party to the Soviet workers and peasants how to behave and vote at the coming elections to the Supreme Council of the Soviet Union and the individual Union Republics. They were expected to elect as delegates people who were one hundred per cent faithful to the work of Lenin and Stalin, who were unyielding fighters for the happiness of the workers and peasants and for Socialism, but who were also—and this is revealing—"valiant patriots of the Fatherland." Particular stress was further laid on the cooperation of Communists with non-Party masses.

That the internal situation in the Soviet Fatherland—and the Fatherland symbol was given predominance over that of the Communist International—was not altogether satisfactory, was again revealed by an even greater number of slogans than before dealing with the alleged activities of Trotsky-Bukharin wreckers and spies. But apparently, in order not to offend or to create bad feelings in Berlin and Tokyo, the wreckers were no longer, as before, openly accused of being in the pay of Germany and Japan, but rather of mysterious foreign intelligence services.

The May Day slogans of 1939 revealed a further decrease of world revolutionary proletarian clichés and a slowing up of active revolutionary struggle. The May First festival was no longer called the "battle rally," but simply the "rally day" of the revolutionary forces of the international proletariat. The former appeal directed to the international proletariat to follow the banner of Marx, Engels and Lenin was dropped. No longer "proletarian" greetings, but rather "brotherly" greetings, were extended to the working masses and the revolutionary fighters outside Russia. Moreover, although one of the slogans continued to speak explicitly of the victory of the working class in the entire world, much more attention was given to the home slogans. One new quotation from Stalin advocating assistance to nations who are victims of aggression, and who fight for the independence of their Fatherland, seemed to take care of the deteriorating international situation. All credit was given to Soviet foreign policy for the preservation of peace, all honor to the Red Army, though this was no longer toasted as a "faithful guardian of the achievements of the great October Socialist Revolution" but, significantly, as a "guardian of the freedom and independence of the Fatherland." Incidentally, the frontier guards were no longer protecting the borders of the "land of Socialism," but of the "Fatherland."

The Soviet Union seemed or pretended to expect an attack on its territories and lands. The prospective aggressor was warned that the Soviet people would answer the attack not with an ordinary counterattack, but with one of extraordinary strength. The frontier guards became "brave and fearless." The slogans enumerated the various branches of the armed forces in a new order closer to war realities—first the frontier guards, then the Air Force, and last, the Navy; the slogans for 1938 had the reverse order. Increasing danger seemed to require greater unity. It was no longer the alliance of workers and peasants that was celebrated, but the united front of workers, peasants, and—a newcomer—the Soviet intelligentsia. As in 1938, the moral and political unity of the whole Soviet society was acclaimed, the former bourgeois and "feudal" classes having ceased to exist. But the Communist Party was still claiming leadership—its ranks were called, in a new slogan, the "gold reserve of Party and State," who deserved care, honor and special treatment, but who themselves had to strive for better theoretical equipment and political tempering.

The immediate task facing the Soviet people was proclaimed and believed to be one of equaling and surpassing—in the course of the next ten to fifteen years, with the help of the Stakhanovite movement—the economically progressive capitalist countries. This goal was at once a reiteration and a new manifestation of Soviet neonationalism. The Soviet economy was ambitious to lead the world. For this purpose, the Socialist state of workers and peasants had to be not only strengthened, but first of all, better organized. For the first time, the slogans urged the working people of the Soviet Union to strengthen the Socialist intelligence service (meaning the secret police), in order to destroy the people's enemies. The members of the Komsomol were at last added to the list of people who were supposed to increase their knowledge.

Finally, nowhere had the proud national self-appraisal so characteristic of the Soviet Russia of the Thirties found such unmistakable expression as in the new 1939 slogan celebrating the "free, powerful, talented Soviet people, the people of heroes, the people of creators." Simultaneously, the slogan acclaiming Communism was silently dropped from the list. On the other hand, Stalin's name in 1939 was added to those of Marx, Engels and Lenin as a symbol of victory.

The year 1940 brought vital changes in the May First slogans. Even the definition of the meaning of the holiday was changed. The European war had begun. The Soviet-German pact of friendship was signed in August 1939, in

Moscow. The Soviet Government was on its guard not to antagonize the masters of Nazi Germany.

The May Day became a "battle rally" of revolutionary forces, but this time of the "working class" and no longer of the "international proletariat." No longer were greetings extended to the "victims of Fascist terror" or to the "fighters for the victory of the working class in the entire world," but only to the "fighters for the liberation of the working class in the entire world." Moscow was careful in the selection of terms, as well as of slogans. The appeal to the working masses of the world to establish an anti-Fascist front in the name of liberty, democratic freedom, Socialism, was significantly removed from the 1940 slogan list. Even the quotation from Stalin in favor of giving help to the nations that were considered victims of aggression, and of repudiating the work of war instigators directed against the security of Soviet frontiers, was now sacrificed. Moreover, the Communist International was no longer praised as a "leader and organizer of the struggle against imperialist war and against capitalism." Thus the mention of Fascism was left out here also.

The foreign policy of the "land of Socialism"—incidentally, in 1940 consistently called "Soviet Union"—which guaranteed international peace and the security of the Fatherland, was now glorified even more than previously. The Soviet Government knew, however, the value of appeasing Hitler. Special attention was given in the slogans to the uninterrupted strengthening of the defenses of the country. In the slogans, the troops and the Navy units who were protecting the security of Leningrad and of the northwestern Fatherland frontiers were celebrated separately. The danger of "imperialist encirclement" seemed more acute than ever. The Soviet Air Force was twice honored.

The domestic slogans of 1940 underwent further changes, of which the following are worth mentioning: The newly liberated peoples of western Ukraine and western White Russia, as well as the citizens of the new Karelian-Finnish Soviet Socialist Republic, were welcomed as new members of the "brotherly" family of the peoples of the Soviet Union. A new task was assigned to Soviet trade unions—they were to become a school of Communism and were especially instructed to educate all members in the spirit of Leninism.

But, most conspicuously, the slogans of the first year of the European war turned toward the Soviet young generation—the future of the Fatherland. "The children," said one of the slogans, "are our future, so let us rear the Soviet children as patriots of our Fatherland prepared to carry on the fight for the cause of Lenin-Stalin."

The May First slogans in 1941 followed closely the pattern of 1940. It was the period of the "phony" war, and the Soviet Government was anxious not to affect adversely, by any hasty or unfriendly word, the established understanding with Berlin. Nor were there in the May Day slogans any signs of the coming rupture with Nazi Germany, on June 22. On the contrary, much seemed to point to the readiness of Moscow to refrain from displeasing Hitler. The greatest modesty was shown even in the use of the symbol of victory. The formerly celebrated "victorious working class" was called simply "our working class"; the word "victorious" was also dropped, with reference to the collectivized peasantry. Significant was the rewriting of the words describing the Communist International—in 1940 "organizer of the struggle against imperialist war and against capitalism," it became in 1941 the "organizer of the struggle for the victory of the working masses."

Nevertheless, the slogans carried a few changes signifying greater watchfulness on the part of the Soviet State. In the presence of world conflagration, the foreign policy of the Soviet Union could no longer be appraised and applauded as one guaranteeing the preservation of peace between nations. The wording of this particular slogan was correspondingly changed, and replaced with the identification of Soviet foreign policy with peace policy. The danger of capitalist encirclement—a theme on which Moscow was never tired of speaking—was now, in 1941, supposed to be repelled not only by the Red Army, but also by a strengthened Socialist intelligence service. Incidentally, Moscow preferred to use in the slogans the old name of the institution, the VCHK, familiar and dreaded from the time of the first revolutionary days, and not the new one of the OGPU. Simultaneously, an appeal was directed to every worker, male or female, to every engineer and technician, to guarantee the fulfillment of the third Five-Year Plan in each workshop and brigade, by every shift and by every bench. Work had to be carried out in

Bolshevist fashion and with Bolshevist tempo. In addition to increased output, the quality of production, the application of progressive technique, and the installation of new technical devices had to be taken care of. Workers in the building industry and transport workers were added to the list of the various skilled groups that were especially called upon to fulfill their professional tasks and obligations toward the Fatherland. The industrial effort was an integral part of the total mobilization of the country. Loafing and inefficiency in the industrial setup were openly criticized as impeding the growth of the military strength of the Fatherland and the Red Army. In case of real war, manpower was another question which needed attention. Several new slogans propagated the development of local industries and the building up of larger skilled labor reserves for industry and transport.

Hitler's attack on Soviet Russia on June 22, 1941, gave the May First slogans the former vitality, color and independence of action. The days of political bondage were over, in spite of the serious military situation. In 1942, the First of May was restored to its former position. The proletarians of all countries were now called upon to fight unitedly the German-Fascist aggression. The Nazis became "Hitlerite imperialist bandits" who had upset world peace and had thrown millions of workers into the misery of war. Other slogans called them "German-Fascist robbers and aggressors," "bloody enslavers of the peoples of Europe," "avowed enemies of freedom-loving peoples of the world." Greetings were extended by Moscow to all the nations of Europe who were fighting Hitler's imperialism. Not only were the workers of Germany encouraged to overthrow Hitler and his clique and thus free themselves, but all Europe's patriots were incited to fight for their liberation from the Fascist yoke and against Hitlerite tyranny. And next to the German workers and European patriots, the oppressed "Slav brethren" were given by Moscow a special place of honor. They were moved to rise in a "sacred people's war" against the Hitlerite imperialists —the deadly enemies of Slavdom," and the slogans celebrated the "fighting unity of the Slavic peoples." A more cautiously worded slogan referred finally to the United Nations. It acclaimed the "fighting alliance of the military forces of the Soviet Union, Great Britain, the United States of America, and the freedom-loving peoples who carry out a just war of liberation against the German and Italian bandit imperialism."

War against Nazi Germany was, for the Soviet Union, a total affair. It was, first of all, a Fatherland's war of all the peoples of the Soviet Union. Correspondingly, the slogans spoke of the Red Army as the army "of brotherhood and friendship among the peoples of the U.S.S.R." Secondly, the enemy had to be met by the "brotherly alliance of workers, collective farmers and Soviet intelligentsia." Each professional and social group, each Soviet citizen had to participate in the fight and to play his part. Thus most of the May First slogans addressed to the officers, soldiers, and the political workers of the Red Army, to the officers, sailors, and the political workers of the Red Fleet, to the Soviet airmen, to the tank formations, to the artillerymen, to the infantrymen, to the cavalrymen and frontier troops, to the Soviet guards, to the heroic defenders of Leningrad, to the guerillas; to the engineers, technicians and workers of the munitions, tank and aircraft factories, of oil, coal and metallurgical industries, and of railway and water transport; to collective farmers, agronomists, to women and girls, to the Soviet intelligentsia —all these slogans specified the part to be played and the contributions to be made by each of these groups in the nation's effort to protect the "freedom and independence of the glorious Fatherland."

But, conspicuously, one body failed to appear in the slogans of 1942, the Communist International. The All-Union Communist Party was acclaimed as the "organizer of the struggle for victory over the German Fascist trespassers." The leading part in the fight was assigned to the Komsomol, the "true assistant of the Bolshevist party." Under the "banner of Lenin and Stalin," victory was to be achieved. The name of the Communist International, however, was dropped in 1942 from the slogans, well in advance of its official liquidation in 1943—either by reason of obsolescence or in an effort to appease the new democratic allies.

Stalin declared the war to be a "Fatherland war," a "just one and a war of liberation." The slogans taught the Soviet people revenge—"blood for blood," "death for death." They praised the great mission of liberation confronting the Red

Army, the Red Fleet and the guerillas. But thus far in 1942 this mission seemed to be limited to the liberation of the Nazi-occupied Soviet land and of millions of Soviet citizens suffering from German-Fascist rule.

The year 1943 was the year of Stalingrad. The military situation had changed in favor of Russia. But the outcome of the war was far from being decided. Unity at home remained the prerequisite of victory.

The May First slogans of 1943 were for the first time officially referred to as "appeals" of the Central Committee of the Communist Party. The peoples of the Union were now called "brethren and sisters." The First of May, formerly the "rally day of the fighting forces of the workers," became now the "rally day of the fighting forces of the working masses." Correspondingly, no longer exclusively the urban workers but the working masses of all countries were supposed to unite for the anti-Nazi fight. The words "proletariat," "proletarian," etc. were no longer used in the appeals.

It was a foregone conclusion that the Red Army would be particularly mentioned in the 1943 slogans. The prosecution of the war and the annihilation of the Nazis were the major, or rather the only, topics of the May First propaganda effort. But the wording of the slogans had become more businesslike and to the point. The preceding May victory was foreseen before the end of the year—in 1943, only "decisive battles." As a result of experiences gained on the battlefield, particular stress was laid on adequate military training. The Red Army commanders had to learn the art of warfare; the tank troops, how to attack the enemy formations skilfully; and the cavalry, how to pursue them courageously and decisively. Personal bravery, of which there was no lack in the Red Army, had to be matched by military efficiency. The strengthening of military discipline was another requirement.

As before, particular appeals were directed to single groups, military and civilian. The infantry who, perhaps contrary to expectations, still had to continue to carry the burden of the fighting in this war, was placed at the top of the list, ahead of airmen, tank formations, and artillery. Other army groups were added to the list of all who had to contribute their share of sweat and blood for the defeat of the hated enemy. It was characteristic of the intensity of the struggle that the medical personnel in Soviet Russia were made responsible not only for the saving of lives, but for the return of the wounded to the front after recuperation. On the other hand, "half of the care" and attention given to the army was pledged in 1943 to the families of the defenders of the Fatherland and the front fighters. Victory was further to be achieved, or rather accelerated, by the work of the rear. The new professional groups who were specifically mentioned in the 1943 slogans were the workers in light, textile and food industries, and the workers in machine and tractor stations, and on the state farms. A special appeal was directed to Soviet youth, male and female.

The Communist International was again absent from the list. The hailing of the Komsomol as such was also omitted in 1943, though, as before, its members were expected to be among the top fighters against the Nazi invader. The Communist Party was now supposed—not only as before—to be the organizer, but also the inspirer of the fight until victory was achieved. For the first time, Stalin's rôle and position in the Soviet state was specifically acknowledged by the slogans. The march to victory was to take place under the "leadership" of Stalin. The war aim of 1942—the defeat of the German occupation—received in 1943 an additional interpretation, "the expulsion of the German intruders from the confines of the Fatherland." The name of Hitler appeared in the appeals exclusively as an adjective—the Hitlerite robber-imperialists, the Hitlerite tyranny, etc.

The struggle against Nazism was to be carried out by the "patriots of the European countries" and the Slav brethren, besides the Soviet Union. Moscow had apparently lost faith in a domestic revolution in Germany. German workers who, in 1942, were incited to rise against Hitler did not reappear in the slogans of 1943. And, in regard to the Western Allies and the United Nations, the slogans celebrated "the valiant Anglo-American troops who were defeating the German-Italian Fascists in North Africa." The 1943 slogans lauded further the "victory of the Anglo-Soviet-American fighting alliance over the enemies of humanity, the German-Fascist enslavers." These references to the Anglo-Saxon Allies were still rather restrained, but nevertheless their wording showed a remarkable change in a friendly direction. The former qualification, "the fighting alliance of the *military forces* of the Soviet Union, Great Britain and the United States of America," was now significantly dropped and did not reoccur. And the Soviet Union became voluntarily and somewhat informally hyphenated between Great Britain and the United States.

The analysis of May First slogans makes an interesting and important study. The history of the Soviet Union could be easily written in terms of changing slogans. In a totalitarian state—and Soviet Russia is one of them—the population is constantly and consciously kept on the alert by all kinds of artificial means. Propaganda through slogans is an important part of it.

Nothing is here left to chance—neither the selection of slogans nor the choice of words; neither the order of slogans, nor the additions or omissions; neither the temper of their composition nor the range of attention. Audience, occasion, general situation and current aims are all taken into account. A detailed analysis of the changing trends in slogans could occasionally even facilitate the making of political weather forecasts.

As years went by, a definite pattern of May First slogans evolved in the Soviet Union. The slogans were not worked out anew by the Party on each May Day celebration. On the contrary, the list for the preceding year was obviously taken from the files and carefully re-edited, rewritten, and rearranged, but hardly ever remodelled. This procedure is an art in itself, in which the sense of balance and proportion affects failure or success.

Taken as a whole, the May First slogans are in the last analysis mainly variations on a single theme. That leitmotif is the security of the Soviet regime. Even the interest Moscow takes, or pretends to take, in revolutionary activities abroad is subordinated to this main concern. The blending of international with patriotic slogans and the changes, in the course of years, in their mutual relationship are also primarily dependent upon survival considerations.

References to World Revolution

1918 None

1919 World Revolution has begun; let's finish it, proletarians!

1920 None

1922 Long live the world proletarian revolution.

1924 Long live the U.S.S.R., fortress of the international proletarian revolution! Long live the war of the working class against capital!

1925 Long live the united front of the proletarians of the whole world against capital. Long live international cooperation of workers and peasants against capitalism.

1926 Let us establish a united front of workers of all countries against the capitalists' offensive, against new wars.

1927 Proletarians of all countries, raise the banner of world revolution. Long live international class solidarity of the workers.

1928 Workers and peasants! Forward to the victory of the world proletarian revolution.

1929 Long live the international proletarian revolution! Only an international proletarian revolution will end the growth of armaments, and wars. Long live the Soviet power in the whole world. (Also referred to: Red Army, armed battalion of world revolution; U.S.S.R., pillar of world revolution.)

1930 (Referred to: World October.) Long live the workers' and peasants' revolution in the colonies. The construction of Socialism in the U.S.S.R. is the basis of international proletarian revolution.

1931 (Referred to: World October.) Soldiers of Red Army . . . pledge allegiance to world proletarian revolution.

1932 Long live the victorious offensive of the proletarian revolution in the whole world. Long live the Communist International—the fighting headquarters of the world proletarian revolution. (Referred to: World October.)

1933 Long live the world socialist revolution. (Referred to: World October.)

1934 Long live the world socialist revolution.

1935 Long live the world socialist revolution. Up with the banner of international proletarian solidarity. For the victory of socialism in the whole world.

1936 Proletarians of all countries, strengthen the cause of proletarian internationalism. Follow the banner of the Communist International.

Onward to new struggles and victories. Long live the world socialist revolution!

Proletarians and peasants of the whole world, follow the path of workers and peasants of the Soviet Union. Down with Fascism! Down with capitalism. Long live the Soviet power in the whole world!

Up with the banner of international proletarian solidarity!

1937   Long live the Socialist revolution in the whole world.

1938   Proletarians of all countries unite! Follow the international banner of Marx-Engels-Lenin.

Let us strengthen and fortify the international ties between the working class of the U.S.S.R. and the working class of capitalist countries.

Up with the banner of international proletarian solidarity! Men and women workers, peasants, and working masses of all countries, expand and strengthen the peoples' front in the fight against Fascism and war. For peace, for democratic liberty, for socialism!

1939   (Reference to victory of the working class in the whole world.) Workers, men and women, peasants and working masses of all countries, expand and strengthen the peoples' front in the fight against Fascism, against war. For peace, for democratic liberties, for socialism!

Let us strengthen and fortify the international ties between the working class of the U.S.S.R. and the working class of capitalistic states. Up with the banner of international proletarian solidarity!

1940   Up with the banner of international proletarian solidarity!

1941   Same

1942   Long live the fighting unity of Slavic peoples. Long live our glorious Fatherland; its freedom; its independence.

1943   Long live the fighting unity of Slavic peoples. Long live the freedom, the independence of our glorious Soviet fatherland.

References to the U.S.S.R.

1918   The defense of the Soviet Republic by arms is a solemn duty of every worker and peasant.

1919   None

1920 None

1922 The Union of Soviet Republics is a sure weapon against imperialist attack; let us strengthen and extend this union for the total victory of the working masses.

1924 Long live the U.S.S.R.—fortress of the international proletarian revolution.

1925 The Union of Soviet Republics, the outpost of world communism, the banner of liberation for the workers of all countries, should grow and strengthen (sic!).

1926 Proletarians of the world!   Steadfastly defend the first land of the workers—the Union of Soviet Socialist Republics.

1927 Long live the U.S.S.R., the stronghold of peace in the whole world.

1928 Proletarians of the world! U.S.S.R. is your fatherland and the genuine stronghold of peace among peoples. Defend the U.S.S.R. against imperialist attack.
The Soviet Union is the banner of liberation for the oppressed nationalities of the whole world.

1929 Long live the Soviet Union, the fatherland of the international proletariat. The U.S.S.R.—stronghold of world revolution.
(Also referred to: U.S.S.R.—banner of liberation for the oppressed nationalities of the whole world.)

1930 Long live the Soviet Union, fatherland of the international proletariat.

1931 (Referred to: U.S.S.R.—fatherland of the workers of all countries.)

1932 (Referred to: Land of the Soviets—fatherland of the workers of the whole world.)

1933 Defend the land of the Soviets—fatherland of the workers of the entire world.

1934 For the defense of the Soviet Union—fatherland of all workers.

1935 None

1936 None

1937 None

1938 Long live our mighty fatherland and may it grow more powerful—the Union of the Soviet Socialist Republics.

1939 Same

1940 Same

1941 Same

1942 Long live our glorious fatherland; its freedom; its independence.

1943 Long live the liberty and independence of our glorious Soviet fatherland.

References to May First

1918 None

1919 May First is a festival of labor. Long live the fellowship of labor, long live labor discipline. May First is rally day for the shock battalions of world revolution.

1920 None

1922 Long live May First, the festival of proletarian struggle and victory.

1924 Same

1925 Long live May First, the day of fighting solidarity for the workers of all countries, the rallying day of the urban and rural working masses around the toilers.

1926 Long live May First, the day of world proletarian unity, the day of battle call to struggle for Communism.

1927 None

1928 Long live May First, the rally day of the revolutionary forces of the world proletariat.

1929 Same

1930 Long live May First, the battle rally of the revolutionary forces of the international proletariat.

1932 Same
1933 Same
1934 Same
1935 Same
1936 Same
1937 Same
1938 Same

1939 Long live May First, the rally day of the revolutionary forces of the international proletariat. Proletarians of all countries, unite!

1940 Long live May First, the battle rally of the revolutionary forces of the working class. Proletarians of all countries, unite!

1941 Same

1942 Long live May First, the rally day of the fighting forces of the working class. Proletarians of all countries, unite for the struggle against the German-Fascist trespassers!

1943   Long live May First, the rally day of the fighting
forces of the workers. Workers of all countries unite
for the struggle against German-Fascist trespassers.

References to Communist International

1918   None
1919   Long live the Communist International, the fighting
headquarters of world workers' revolution.
1920   None
1922   Long live the Communist International.
1924   Let us fulfill the legacy of Vladimir Il'ich—let us
strengthen and extend the union of the workers of
the whole world, the Communist International.
1925   Long live the Communist International, leader of millions of the oppressed, headquarters for the vanguard
of the working class of all countries.
1926   Long live the Communist International—leader of the
world proletariat.
1927   Proletarians of all countries, up with the banners
of world revolution! Communists of the whole world,
penetrate deeper into the masses of workers and peasants! Everyone under the banner of the Communist
International.
1928   Long live the Communist International—revolutionary headquarters of the proletarian struggle for the
destruction of capitalism in the world.
Let us unite the revolutionary workers of all countries
for the struggle against the white terror, against
Fascism, against world-wide reaction under the banner of the Communist International.
1929   Long live the Comintern—organizer and leader of proletarian revolution, Lenin headquarters of the world
proletariat. Long live the Lenin Comintern, fulfilling
the legacy of Marx and Engels.
1930   Proletarians of all countries and oppressed peoples
of the colonies, join the ranks of fighters against imperialism under the banner of the Comintern. Let us
fight the rightists of opportunism—the main danger
in the ranks of the Comintern. Long live the Lenin
unity in the Communist International.
1931   Proletarians of the whole world, class brethren, follow
the banner of the Lenin Comintern.
1932   Proletarians of all countries! Follow the fighting banner of the Lenin Communist International.

Long live the Communist International—the fighting headquarters of the world proletarian revolution.

1933   Proletarians of all countries! Follow the banner of the Lenin Communist International! Forward to new struggles and victories! Long live the World Socialist Revolution!
Long live the Communist International, the fighting vanguard of the struggle against Fascism.

1934   Proletarians of all countries! Strengthen the cause of the Proletarian Internationalism. Follow the banner of the Communist International. Forward to new struggles and victories!
Long live the World Socialist Revolution!

1935   Same

1936   Follow the banner of the Communist International.

1937   Proletarians of all countries, unite! Follow the banner of Communist International. Long live the Communist International—leader and organizer of the fight against war, Fascism and capitalism.

1938   Long live the Communist International, leader and organizer of the fight against war, fascism and capitalism. Long live Communism!

1939   Long live the Communist International, leader and organizer of the fight against war, against fascism, against capitalism.

1940   Long live the Communist International—organizer of the struggle against imperialist war, against capitalism.

1941   Long live the Communist International—organizer of the struggle for the victory of the working masses.

1942   None

1943   None

References to the Communist Party

1918   Long live the Russian Communist Party.

1919   None

1920   None

1922   None

1924   Long live R.C.P. (Russian Communist Party), leader of the working class. Let us strengthen the R.C.P.— the pillar of proletarian dictatorship.

1925   Long live the R.C.P.—the party of the working class, the party of Lenin.

1926   Same

1927 None

1928 All the best and active forces of the working class join the ranks of the V.C.P. (All-Union Communist Party).

Workers and peasants—under the leadership of V.C.P.—forward to new achievements of socialism in our country; to the victory of world proletarian revolution.

1929 Long live the Lenin unity in the ranks of the V.C.P. Progressive workers—men and women—join the ranks of the V.C.P. Up with the banner of V.C.P., the organizers of October. Workers and working masses unite around V.C.P., the leader of Socialist construction.

1930 Proletarians—fighters for the Five-Year Plan, record-makers of Socialist construction, join the ranks of V.C.P.

For the general party line.

Close the ranks of the working class around the Bolshevist vanguard.

1931 Workers, collective farmers, poor peasants and individual middle farmers, close your ranks around the V.C.P.

For the general Party line.

Best record-makers, join the ranks of V.C.P. Best proletarians, collective farmers, poor peasants and land workers, join the ranks of the Lenin party.

Long live the Lenin unity in the Bolshevist ranks. Under the leadership of the Lenin party and its central committee—to new victories.

Up with the banner of V.C.P.—organizer of the October revolution.

1932 Long live the V.C.P.—organizer of victorious socialist construction. Workers, collective farmers, all working people, close your ranks around V.C.P. For the general party line.

Best record-makers, progressive proletarians, and collective farmers, join the ranks of the Lenin party.

Long live the Lenin unity of the Bolshevist ranks. Under the banner of the Bolshevist party, its Lenin central committee—forward to new victories. Up with the banner of V.C.P.—organizer of the October Revolution.

1933 Long live the V.C.P.—leader and organizer of the victorious construction of Socialism. Let us equip each communist with Lenin-Marxist theory! For the ideological steadfastness of the members of the Communist party, let us clear the ranks of the Bolshevist party of all unreliable, unsteady, hypocritical elements! Down with the helpers of the class enemy, the "right" and "left" opportunists.

Long live iron proletarian discipline within the party. Long live the unity of Bolshevist ranks. Under the banner of the Bolshevist party and its Lenin central committee, forward to new victories! Up with the banner of the V.C.P.—organizer of the October Revolution.

1934 Long live the All-Union Communist Party, leader and organizer of the victorious construction of socialism. Under the banner of the Bolshevist party and the Lenin central committee, forward to new victories. Long live the great, unconquerable banner of Marx, Engels and Lenin.

1935 Men and women workers, men and women collective farmers, workers of the Soviet Union! Let us tighten our ranks around the Lenin party.

Onward to the fight for the general party line! Onward to the victory of Communism! Let us make the history of the Lenin party a possession of each Communist, of each member of the Komsomol, of each fighter for Socialism.

For the ideological equipment of each communist with the theory of Marx, Engels, Lenin!

Long live the All-Union Communist Party—leader and organizer of the victorious construction of Socialism!

Long live the great, unconquerable banner of Marx, Engels and Lenin! Long live Leninism!

1936 Men and women workers, collective farmers, all working masses of the Soviet Union! Let us tighten the ranks around the Lenin party; onward to the fight for the general party line, to the victory of communism! Long live the All-Union Communist Party of the Bolshevists—leader and organizer of the victorious construction of socialism!

Long live the great, unconquerable banner of Marx-Engels-Lenin!

Long live Leninism!

1937 Let us make our party into an unconquerable fortress of Bolshevism. Long live the All-Union Communist

Party— the vanguard of the workers of the U.S.S.R.!
Long live the great, unconquerable banner of Marx,
Engels and Lenin! Long live Leninism!

1938 Long live the All-Union Communist Party of the
Bolshevists—advanced vanguard of the working masses
of the U.S.S.R.! Long live the great, unconquerable
banner of Marx-Engels-Lenin! Long live Leninism!

1939 The Bolshevist cadres are the gold reserve of party
and state. Nurture these cadres, honor them, cherish
them.

For the improvement of theoretical level and for the
political tempering of our cadres. For the mastering
of Marxism-Leninism. Long live the All-Union Communist Party of the Bolshevists! Long live the great,
unconquerable banner of Marx-Engels-Lenin-Stalin!
Long live Leninism!

1940 Long live the All-Union Communist Party—vanguard
of the workers of the Soviet Union. Long live the
great, unconquerable banner of Marx, Engels, Lenin
and Stalin. Long live Leninism!

1941 Same

1942 Long live the All-Union Communist Party, party of
Lenin-Stalin, organizer of the struggle for victory over
the German-Fascist trespassers.

1943 Long live the all-Union Communist Party—party of
Lenin-Stalin—inspirer and organizer of the struggle
for victory over the German-Fascist trespassers. Under
the banner of Lenin, under the leadership of Stalin,
forward toward the destruction of the German in-
vaders, and their expulsion from the territories of our
fatherland.

Appeals to the Red Army

1918 None

1919 Cherish and protect your arms, proletarians! Cherish
and protect your Red Army!

1920 None

1922 Down with the armies of imperialism, down with the
robbery of imperialistic wars. Long live the Red
Army, the army of Socialism. Long live the war of the
working class against world capital. The workers' and
peasants' army should be given ample sustenance, continuing support, and watchful care by the land of
labor.

1924   Down with the armies of imperialism. Down with predatory wars; long live the Red Army of Socialism—the stronghold of peaceful labor. Long live the war of the working class against capital.

1925   On May First, brotherly greetings of the workers and peasants to the gallant and victorious workers' and peasants' Red Army and Fleet.

1926   May First greetings to the workers' and peasants' Red Army.

1927   Red Army! Watch carefully the plots of our enemies! Increase your might—the stronghold of peaceful labor of the peoples of the U.S.S.R. On May First, the Red Army will show once more its readiness to defend the dictatorship of the proletariat.

1928   On May First, the Red Army swears to defend firmly the interest of the proletariat, and of the oppressed of all countries.

1929   May First greetings to the Red Army and the Red Fleet—the permanent sentries of the Soviet frontiers, the armed battalions of world revolution. On May First, the young Red Army men swear before the workers of the entire world to defend firmly the U.S.S.R.—the stronghold of world revolution.
         The Red Army is a protector of peace, it will protect the achievements of the October revolution. The Red Army prepares conscientious fighters and builders of Socialism in the towns and villages.

1930   Workers, peasants, Red Army men, watch carefully the enemy's plots, increase the might of the Red Army —the stronghold of peaceful labor in the U.S.S.R.
         Greetings to the fighters of the Red Army and Fleet, the faithful sentries of the Soviet frontiers, the watchmen of socialist construction.

1931   Long live the Red Army, stronghold of the peaceful policy of Soviet power, faithful guardian of Soviet frontiers. Greetings to the young fighters of the Red Army, who on May First swear allegiance to the proletarian dictatorship and the World Proletarian Revolution.

1932   Long live the Red Army, stronghold of the peaceful policy of Soviet power, keen-eyed sentries of Soviet frontiers, faithful guardian of October.
         Greetings to the young fighters of the Red Army, who on May First swear allegiance to the workers' and

peasants' government, to the working class of the whole world.

1933 Long live the Red Army—stronghold of the peaceful policy of Soviet power, keen-eyed sentry of Soviet frontiers, faithful guardian of the achievements of October.

Greetings to the young fighters of the Red Army, who on May First swear allegiance to the workers' and peasants' government; to the working class of the whole world.

1934 Long live the Red Army, stronghold of the peaceful policy of Soviet power, keen-eyed sentry of Soviet frontiers, faithful guardian of the achievements of the October Revolution. Greetings to the young fighters of the Red Army, who on May First swear allegiance to the workers' and peasants' government; allegiance to our Fatherland.

1935 Long live our beloved, invincible Red Army—powerful stronghold for the peaceful labor of the peoples of the U.S.S.R., faithful guardian of the achievements of the October Socialist Revolution. Battle greetings to the Young Fighters of the Red Army, who on May First swear allegiance to the workers' and peasants' government; allegiance to our great Fatherland.

Our beloved, mighty Red Army should grow and strengthen, mastering technique, and making itself fit.

1936 Long live our beloved, invincible Red Army—the mighty stronghold of peaceful labor of the peoples of the U.S.S.R., the faithful guardian of the frontier of the U.S.S.R. Battle greetings to the young fighters of the Red Army, who on May First swear to be faithful to Soviet power; to our Great Fatherland. May First greetings to the fighters of the border patrol, the keen-eyed sentries of the Soviet frontiers. (Here begins the singling out of elements in the Red Army for special appeals, which is accentuated in 1942 and 1943.)

1937 Long live our beloved, invincible Red Army—mighty stronghold for the peaceful labor of the peoples of the U.S.S.R.; faithful guardian of the achievements of the Great October Revolution—defense of the Fatherland is a holy duty of every citizen of the U.S.S.R.

Battle greetings to the young fighters of the Red Army, who on May First swear allegiance to the Soviet power, allegiance to our Great Socialist Fatherland.

Greetings to the fighting border guards, to the keen-eyed sentries of Soviet frontiers. Our beloved, mighty Red Army should grow and strengthen, mastering technique, and making itself fit.

1938   Long live our beloved, invincible Red Army, mighty stronghold for the peaceful labor of the peoples of the U.S.S.R.; faithful guardian of the achievements of the Great October Socialist Revolution. The defense of the Fatherland is a holy duty of every citizen of the U.S.S.R.

Battle greetings to the young fighters of the Red Army, who swear on May First to be faithful to Soviet power; to be faithful to our Great Socialist Fatherland.

1939   Long live our beloved, invincible Red Army, mighty stronghold for the peaceful labor of the peoples of the U.S.S.R; faithful guardian of the freedom and independence of our Fatherland.

Greetings to the brave and fearless fighters—the border guards, the keen-eyed sentries of the frontier of our Fatherland.

1940   Long live our beloved Red Army, mighty stronghold for the peaceful labor of the peoples of the Soviet Union; faithful guardian of the achievements of the Great October Socialist Revolution.

Brotherly greetings to the gallant fighters, commanders and political workers of the Red Army and Navy who guarantee the security of Leningrad and of the Northwestern Frontiers of our Fatherland.

1941   Long live our beloved Red Army, mighty stronghold for the peaceful labor of the peoples of the U.S.S.R.; faithful guardian of the achievements of the Great October Revolution.

1942   Long live the Red Army of brotherhood and friendship of the peoples of the U.S.S.R.

1943   Long live our gallant Red Army—heroically fighting for the honor, freedom and independence of our Fatherland against German-Fascist trespassers.

Appeals to Soviet Children

None before 1930.

1930   Children of the revolution, young pioneers, be prepared to carry on and carry out the task of Il'ich.

1931   Young pioneers, children of October, be prepared to

carry on and carry out Lenin's great cause, the cause of World October.

1932 Same

1933 Same

1934 Young pioneers! Strengthen school discipline; get acquainted with the fundamentals of science. Be prepared to carry on and carry out Lenin's great task.

1935 Pioneers and pupils! Get acquainted with the fundamentals of knowledge. Strengthen school discipline. Be prepared to carry on and carry out Lenin's great task. Long live our Soviet children.

1936 Same

1937 Pioneer boys and girls! Get knowledge, and learn how to become fighters for Lenin's cause.

1938 Pioneer boys and girls, pupils of Soviet schools, get knowledge, learn how to become fighters for the cause of Lenin-Stalin.

1939 Pupils of Soviet schools! Komsomol boys and girls! Pioneer boys and girls! Get knowledge, learn how to become fighters for the cause of Lenin-Stalin.

1940 Children are our future. Let us rear Soviet children as patriots of our fatherland, prepared to carry on the struggle for the cause of Lenin-Stalin.

1941 Same

1942 None

1943 None

Chapter 11

INTERACTION: THE THIRD INTERNATIONAL ON ITS CHANGES OF POLICY *

Introduction

THE PRESENT study[1] sets itself the task of analyzing those symbols of the Communist International [2] which are dealing with its own symbol-practice variations through time. To use the terminology of certain recent epistemological trends: It is proposed to investigate the "meta-language" of the Comintern about the changes of its own "object-language." The ulterior aims of this research are twofold. First, it is intended to be a contribution to the study of the symbolic aspects of revolutionary techniques since World War I. Secondly, the analysis to follow may be relevant for the construction of a more general theory concerned with the dynamics of dogmas, political and other.

For the study of these dynamics in contemporary politics, the Comintern seems to present perhaps the most important single case. This may be asserted for a number of reasons, among which the following are conspicuous: (1) The political dogma of the Comintern possesses a higher degree of elaborateness than that of any other major political movement of

---

* Revised from Document 25, *Experimental Division for the Study of Wartime Communications*, Library of Congress, May 1, 1942.

our time. (2) This dogma has been subjected to variations through time which in frequency and amplitude excelled those of its competitors. (3) These variations found a degree of acceptance on the part of affiliates of the Comintern which probably also excelled that shown in comparable situations in rival movements. In this connection, the present study can be envisaged as a consideration of *some* of the "techniques" used by the élite of the Comintern to produce assent to "changes of line."

The sources used were, for 1919-1935, the verbatim reports of the extant seven world congresses of the CI [3,4] and, for the period since 1935, the *International Press Correspondence* (*Inprecorr*)—since 1938 renamed *World News and Views*—a weekly publication of the CI. For the shift in policy accompanying the outbreak of the Russo-German war in 1941, the *New York Daily Worker* was also taken into account. As to the dissolution of the Comintern in 1943, the May 15 resolution of the Presidium of its Executive Committee was taken as the text.

The following major policy changes of the CI were investigated: [5]

(1) *The turn to the right of 1921.* This was a turn, from a policy oriented on the immediacy of revolution and exhibiting extreme forms of aggression against other labor organizations, to a policy related to the diagnosis of an "ebb" in the revolutionary process; maintaining relative legality; and offering, as well as practicing, collaboration with other labor organizations in a "united front from above," as well as "from below," and in "workers' governments."

(2) *The turn to the left of 1924.* This was a turn toward a refusal of collaboration with other labor organizations under the symbol of the "united front from below" and to the reinstatement of the "dictatorship of the proletariat" as an ostensibly immediate goal.

(3) *The turn to the left of 1927-1928.* After the intervening period of 1925-1927, with its relaxation of aggression against other labor organizations—expressed most sharply in the Anglo-Russian trade-union alliance and the "Farmer Labor Party" policy of the Communist Party of the USA—this was again a turn toward a refusal of collaboration with

"social fascists," toward "dual unionism" and insurrection-ary gestures.

(4) *The turn to the right of 1934-1935.* This was a turn toward a "proletarian united front from above," "organic unity of the workers' parties" and a "people's front."

(5) *The turn to the left after August 23, 1939,* coincided with the codification of a change in relationships between the Soviet Union and Germany.

(6) *The turn to the right after June 22, 1941,* coincided with the outbreak of the Soviet-German war.

This study will deal with typical symbolic structures of admissions and denials of these changes of line, as exhibited in the sources mentioned. It should be added, however, that there is plainly a third method of "referring" to such changes, which is silence.

If G. B. Shaw asserted that Stalin "has acted in every military crisis as if the German army and its present owner did not exist" (letter to the *New Statesman and Nation,* May 31, 1941, p. 555), one may perhaps with more justification claim that the Stalinist Comintern increasingly tended to treat policy changes as so entirely nonexistent as not even to bother to deny their occurrence. More and more the Comintern came to "live in the moment." If a policy change occurred, most attention was concentrated on proving why the new policy was correct, and not on whether, and if so why, it was new. The factors influencing the incidence of *denials* of policy changes (which will be dealt with below) were presumably also operative here.

Part I DENIALS OF CHANGE

Section 1—Forms of Denial

Denials of change may be classified according to certain *formal* characteristics. Thus, it is possible—and for some analytic purposes presumably significant—to distinguish *negations* of change from *affirmations* of constancy.

Such affirmations are to be found in all the cases studied. This, however, does not imply that the magnitude of the rôle of this theme as against other simultaneously occurring, and often contradictory, themes remained constant. Affirmations of this kind were typically, for obvious reasons, made by that nucleus of the dominant faction of the Comintern which had been responsible for the old policy, and which remained in power under the new dispensation.

The frequency and prominence of the use of this device seems to have shown an ascending trend during Comintern history. This could be related to a number of factors, among which we may mention: the trend toward elimination of internal dissent; the presumably decreasing trend of intensity of allegiance to their exoteric ideology on the part of the Comintern élite; the presumably decreasing "realism" of that élite.

Direct affirmations of constancy of policy may be supplemented by assertions of invariance, not in reference to the immediately preceding period, but a more remote period. Insofar as the history of the CI shows an alternation between right and left turns, the policy adopted at a turn in one of those directions may be alleged—and frequently with considerable truth value—to be identical with the policy adopted at the previous turn in the same direction. This, of course, does not prove the ostensible *thema probandum;* but it constitutes an *ignoratio elenchi* which presumably contributes to the illusion of the audience that the constancy of policy of the present with the *immediate* past has been demonstrated.

Thus, to give an example, Dimitrov at the Seventh Congress, in 1935, evoked the ghosts of the Fourth and Fifth Congresses (1922 and 1924) where "the issue turned essentially upon a question (sc.: that of the 'workers' government') which was almost analogous to the one we are discussing today (sc.: that of the 'government of the united front'). The debates that took place at that time in the Communist International concerning this question . . . have to this day retained their importance . . ." (*VII, p. 972.*) The reference of Dimitrov to the authority of the Fifth Congress (performing a turn to the left), and not only to that of the Fourh Congress (performing a turn to the right), was probably intended to serve a major aim of Dimitrov's speech: that of counteracting the correct belief that the Seventh Congress was a new (and much more extreme) edition of the right Fourth Congress. Similarly, but in a more overt fashion, denials of a change of policy after the outbreak of the Russo-German war in 1941 were frequently buttressed by references to specific policies of 1934-1939 rather than of 1939-1941.

As was indicated above, one finds—apart from affirmations of constancy of policy, which have been dealt with so far—negations of change. These negations, in their turn, either are negations of the fact itself, or they assert the falsity of assertions of others, that a change is taking place.

So long as overt dissent was possible in the CI, such statements pointing to the change in process were typical, and for evident reasons were made by the minority factions of the moment, whether they had belonged to the dominant group under the old policy or not. Thus, at the Fifth Congress, the occurrence of a turn to the left was pointed out by the two extreme wings of the CI at the time: on the one hand, by the extreme right group of Radek-Brandler (which had belonged to the dominant faction for most of the period between the Fourth and Fifth Congresses); on the other hand, by the ultra-left group, headed by Bordiga, which had belonged to the opposition ever since the Second Congress of 1920. Contrariwise, the moderate rights (such as a part of the leadership of the Czechoslovak party) and the moderate lefts (such as the new leadership of the German party) tended, in varying degrees, to accept the denials of change put forward by the persisting dominant nucleus represented by Sinoviev. These intermediate factions were those who had made their peace with the Sinoviev group, or wanted to make it. The acceptance of the invariance-myth by these groups amounted to a price exacted by the Soviet leadership of the CI, or to a token of good will offered to it. At the Seventh Congress, however, all such bargaining possibilities had vanished, by virtue of the stricter interpretation of the postulate of ideological "monolithism." The dominant faction could therefore direct negations of assertions of change only against persons and organizations outside of the CI, or against unnamed addressees within it. (Naming would be practically tantamount to expelling.) Thus, Dimitrov was restricted to asserting that *"there are wiseacres* who will sense in all this (sc.: the new policy proclaimed at the Congress) . . . some sort of turn to the Right . . ." (*VII, p. 977,* underlining supplied.)

Apart from these changes in the nature of the objectors referred to, certain symbolic ways of dealing with them remained constant.

A major mode consisted in supplementing a direct refutation of the assertion that the CI was changing its line with an inquiry into the motives of those who made this assertion. (The close relationship of this procedure—which, of course, is far from unused outside of the CI—to the general structure of "dialectical materialism" is evident.) The allegation of "bad" motives was presumably intended either to disprove the assertions directly (in which case the "genetic fallacy" would be involved) or to diminish, extralogically, the chances of their acceptance. Thus, at the Fifth Congress, Sinoviev exclaimed: "How can one (sc.: Radek) . . . say that we are performing a revision (sc.: of the theses of the Fourth Congress)? No, comrades, this is merely an 'agitational slogan' of Radek directed against the CI, nothing more than that!" (*V, p. 485.*) And again, with reference to the same "reproach" of Radek: "Comrades, you certainly understand which specific undertone there is in this reproach just now, when we have to work for the first time without comrade Lenin, when we have all these severe crises in the various countries." (*V, p. 467.*)

In an identical vein, Dimitrov at the Seventh Congress clinched his reference (cited above) to the "wiseacres," who pointed to the occurrence of a turn to the right, by continuing: "Well, in my country, Bulgaria, they say that a hungry chicken always dreams of millet. Let these political chickens think so." (*VII, p. 977.*) Similarly, in his press conference of August 24, 1939, Earl Browder referred to the fact that "there is a great deal of newspaper comment that this (sc.: the Russo-German pact) represents a change of policy of the Soviet Union . . . All that is, of course, nonsense, although a kind of nonsense which is very plausible for Berlin." (*World News and Views,* August 26, 1939, p. 914.)

Once, however, the proposition that the pointing out of policy changes has "opportunistic roots" is well established, it is possible to reverse the sentential chain and to infer the presence of "opportunism" from the presence of assertions that the policy of the CI has changed. A clear example of this technique is given in the elaborate Fifth Congress statement of Wenzel, a Czechoslovak delegate belonging to the Sinoviev group. (Cf. *V*, *pp. 209-210*.) In his endeavor to prove the commission of a "right deviation" by the majority of his delegation, he cites a declaration of this majority envisaging the mere possibility of the expediency of a change of line by the Fifth Congress. Without any intermediary links, he uses this passage as one of his major proofs for the existence of "opportunist tendencies" in the group involved. Of course, the same symbolic technique is also used to corroborate the dogma that "ultra-left" deviations are "really" of a right nature. Thus, Sinoviev can not abstain from remarking at the Fifth Congress upon the agreement of the right Radek and the left Bordiga that a change of line is taking place, and he adds significantly: "That happens in the case of ultraleft deviations: the ultralefts and the ultrarights meet." (*V*, *p. 504*.)

If one way of discrediting allegations of policy change is to impute negatively preferred motives to their authors, another way consists in "turning the tables" against them. One motto here is: "Not we, but you, are changing." (In such cases we may or may not find ourselves in the presence of "projection," in the strict psychological sense of the term.) Thus, Sinoviev states at the Fifth Congress: "I think I can assert and prove that it is not we who propose to revise the resolutions of the Third and Fourth Congresses, but precisely Radek and the other Rights." (*V*, *p. 467*.) In a similar fashion, an article in the *Daily Worker*, after the outbreak of the Russo-German war, stated: "Many of those who have been shouting about a war against Hitlerism to forward the game of Empire are now hard pressed to explain their inconsistency when a real war against Hitlerite aggression is being waged by the Soviet Union . . . To hide such inconsistencies . . . these people turn around and try to twit the Communists for their 'inconsistency.'" (L. Budenz, *Daily Worker*, June 26, 1941.)

Another motto, related to the one just discussed, asserts—apropos of those who allege that "we have changed"—this: "we haven't changed, but we would have changed, now or earlier, if we had acted as you asked us to act." Thus, an article in the *Daily Worker*, after the outbreak of the Russo-German war, addresses itself to those who allege that the

Comintern performed "flipflops" after August 23, 1939, and June 22, 1941: "You expected the Communists (sc.: at the outbreak of the war in September 1939) to perform a real 'flip-flop' . . . to endorse your imperialist war aims." (L. Budenz, *Daily Worker,* June 26, 1941.)

Among the factors making for a high level of denials of policy change throughout Comintern history, the most obvious, and probably also the most important one, is this: the degree of *"subjective* elasticity" of Comintern affiliates in the various levels of the hierarchy probably fell far short of the very high measure of *"symbolic* elasticity" provided by the structure of the ideology of the CI. That is, the nuclear symbols of Comintern ideology were such as to permit of the derivation of a large range of policy changes; but at the same time actualizations of this symbolic flexibility, *if recognized as such,* were apt to call forth negative subjective reactions of adherents, ranging from slight bewilderment to outright shock. (We have no reason to assume that the Comintern in this respect furnished an exception from a very widely diffused pattern of social behavior; but the particularly high ideological elaboration of Comintern strategy and tactics tended to enhance the degree of subjective [as distinguished from symbolic] rigidity of its adherents. This was often taken for granted by those groups within the Comintern who defended a denial of a policy change [which had actually taken place] against others who proclaimed its occurrence.)

Evidently, the degree of subjective rigidity to be found differed between various strata of adherents at any given time, and varied through time. The extreme scarcity of evidence on these matters does not permit us to go beyond plausible guesses.

One would expect, at a given moment in time, an inverse relationship between the altitude of the position of persons within the Comintern hierarchy and the degree of their subjective rigidity in the sense alluded to above. (However, one might want to qualify this, in so far as the lowest levels of the hierarchy, i.e., the more or less inactive sector of the simple party members, were involved: their only slight degree of politization would seem to make for a rather low subjective rigidity in relation to policy changes.) Furthermore, for any given policy change one would expect an inverse relationship between the degree of subjective rigidity and the time which had already elapsed since the moment the policy change "broke." This would be one of the main factors making for the typical concentration of denials of policy change immediately after such a change became apparent. Thus, to mention only one instance, in the first days after August 23, 1939, denials predominated; as the days passed, admissions increased.

Through time, we may surmise a declining trend of the phenomenon discussed. A number of factors probably played a rôle in bringing this about. In this connection, one could cite: the accumulating impact of the lengthening series of ever more violent policy changes; the declining depth of beliefs and of interest in beliefs (at least in regard to "substantive" tenets, as against the "formal" dogma that the directing organs of the movement are always right); and, in the upper and middle levels of the hierarchy, a selection of personnel with the maximization of subjective flexibility as one of the major goals in view. This decline of subjective rigidity tended to diminish the *incentives* for denying policy changes. But counteracting factors were present. On the one hand, the increasing amplitude of policy fluctuations tended to increase these incentives; on the other hand, the trend toward disappearance of intraparty criticism on major points of policy, and toward the consolidation of an unwritten infallibility-dogma in favor of the Comintern leadership, tended to *facilitate* denial operations.

If one investigates the *differences* in the relative rôle of denials of policy changes in the various instances at hand, the most important relationship to come into sight is that between the *direction* of the change and its denial: at least up to 1939 turns toward the right were more intensely denied than turns toward the left. Although it is not proposed to go all the way to quantification in this report, it seems safe to say that denials played the smallest rôle in the Sixth Congress (which codified the sharpest turn toward the left) and the largest rôle in the Seventh Congress (enacting the biggest turn toward the right). The explanation for this is not far to seek: while the predispositions toward the term "left"—and towards the types of behavior to which it ambiguously alludes—were on the whole positive within the Comintern up to 1934-1935, the contrary was true for "right." [6] Thus, the incentive to deny was stronger in the case of right, than in that of left, turns. After the protracted impact of the unprecedently right policy initiated in 1934, this situation was probably reversed. Presumably, the predispositions toward rightness and leftness changed and, as a consequence, the turn to the left in 1939 was much more denied than the 1941 turn in the opposite direction.

Section 2—Derivations of Denial

In the case of a denial of a policy change, the denial may or may not be derived from other assertions made.

It is possible to observe, through time, an increasing rôle of *"flat"* as against *"derived"* denials in Comintern symbolism; and also a decreasing trend in the *elaborateness* of derivations, so far as they were used. The difference, in both these respects, between 1924 (the Fifth Congress) and 1935 (the Seventh Congress) is striking. It goes without saying that these trends are sensitive indicators of the "totalitarianization" process which the Comintern was undergoing.

What were the prominent types of derivations of denials of policy change?

The following discussion will be organized around an investigation of the rôle of certain sets of sentences in these derivations, namely, the fact-sentences referring to: (1) the "new" symbols and practices toward which a transition is made, and (2) the "old" symbols and practices away from which it proceeds. The symbolic device which is typically used in this connection is one which may be designated as "the technique of *symbolic assimilation* between the old and the new." That is: the old and/or the new symbols and practices involved are falsely presented in such a fashion as to minimize the differences between them. We may speak of *"total assimilation"* if these differences are entirely obliterated, and of *"partial* assimilation" if they are merely minimized without being altogether denied. We may also speak of *"unilateral* assimilation" if only one of the two "lines" in question is being presented in a distorted fashion, and of *"bilateral* assimilation" if they are both so presented. In the case of "unilateral assimilation," we may further distinguish between cases of *assimilation of the old to the new* and cases of *assimilation of the new to the old,* according to which policy is symbolically distorted. If symbolic assimilation, as here defined, was introduced above as the major basis of denials of policy change, it is possible, and relevant, to investigate in their turn the typical bases of symbolic assimilation itself. By what devices does Comintern ideology attempt to blur apparent discrepancies between the old and the new?

Among the variety of procedures which were employed in this connection, the most elementary—but not the least important—may be called *assimilation by simple affirmation.* That is, it may be flatly, and falsely, asserted that the Comintern had "always" followed a certain line which in reality was introduced only recently. In other cases, however, the symbolic assimilation is "derived" rather than "flat."

Sub-section 1 —Symbolic Assimilation by Redefinition of Terms

The new "line" may be expressed by the old formulae, and at the same time the redefinition of terms which is implicit in this procedure may be an unavowed one; i.e., it may be explicitly asserted, or implicitly taken for granted, that the definitions involved have remained constant through time. This technique has been very frequently and intensely used in the domestic ideology of the Bolshevik élite. Changes in agrarian policy, for example, have frequently been accompanied by surreptitious redefinitions of such terms as "kulak," "middle farmer," "poor farmer."

The same technique has figured with equal prominence in the symbol manipulations of the Comintern. Thus, F. Borkenau states, with reference to the term "workers' aristocracy": "At times the concept . . . was narrowed down until it became coincident with . . . the paid personnel of the socialist parties and the trade unions. At other times, it was extended so as to include . . . every man in employment." (*The Communist International,* London, 1939, p. 83.) Similar observations could be made about the "harmonica rhythm" of the history of such terms as "avant-garde of the proletariat" and "the majority of the decisive strata of the proletariat," to quote a famous coinage of the Third Congress.

A. *The Transition Between the Fourth and the Fifth Congress*

The most important, and also the most instructive, use of this technique occurred at the Fifth Congress of the Comintern, with special reference to the two key terms "workers' government" and "united front tactics." What happened was that the Fifth Congress preserved the central formulae of the Fourth Congress (according to which Communist parties ought to "apply" the tactics of the united front and demand a "workers' government"), but changed their meanings by covertly redefining the key terms quoted. (The evidence can not be presented here, for reasons of space.)

It may be reëmphasized that these redefinitions were un-avowed, so far as the dominating group in the International was concerned. "We continue to be in favor of a workers' and farmers' government," declared Sinoviev. (*V, p. 87*). "The tactics of the united front remain correct," the assembly was assured. (Sinoviev, *V, p. 77*). More directly it was asserted that the definitions of the key terms involved, given at the Fifth Congress, were identical with the orthodox definitions of the previous period. By and large, only the extreme right (which wanted to prevent the change of line) and the extreme left (which wanted to go still further left than the dominant faction and which distrusted the new-found leftness of that faction) took the trouble of exploding—as could be done so easily—this official myth.[7] But already, at that early date, nobody dared to point explicitly to the symbolic techniques by which that myth was constructed; only Clara Zetkin referred in a general way to the exegetic exertions of Sinoviev. (*V, p. 335*).

B. *The Transition Between the Fifth and the Sixth Congress*

In the preceding instance, the device of symbolic assimilation by redefinition was applied to terms which refer to policies of the self. We may now sketch an instance of the same mechanism used in connection with a term of reference to the environment rather than to the self, but reference to such aspects of the environment as are held to determine the behavior of the self.

The dominant group in the Comintern asserted, both at the Fifth and at the Sixth Congress, that a "crisis of capitalism" existed.

At the Fifth Congress, the term "crisis" was used—so far as the economic sector of its meaning was concerned—approximately as a synonym for "economic depression." A diagnosis and prognosis of such a state of affairs for the whole "capitalist world" was given, qualified only by the admission of "partial," as well as "provisional," "stabilizations."

At the Sixth Congress, Bucharin's estimate of the economic situation, which had the same official character as Sinoviev's appraisal in 1924, was a rather different one. The term "third period" (sc.: of the development of post-war capitalism) which was the key term of this estimate, referred to the situation about which Bucharin bluntly asserted: ". . . the economy of Europe is making rapid progress." *(VI, p. 865.)* And the term itself was defined by the same speaker, in his central report to the Congress, in the following way: "From the economic point of view the second period (sc.: of post-war development) can be regarded as the period of the *reconstruction of the productive forces of capitalism. . . .* This period was followed by the third stage, the *period of capitalist construction* which expresses itself by a quantitative and qualitative progress beyond the prewar level. . . ." *(VI, p. 10.)* It was thus consistent with Bucharin's general estimate to rebuke, in his report, as alarmist a "bourgeois" economist who asserted that "the breakdown of the world credit system has become an imminent danger." *(Cf. VI, p. 13.)*[8]

Despite this sharp change of economic diagnoses and prognoses, the Sixth Congress retained the by then traditional assertion concerning the "crisis of capitalism." This was made possible by a redefinition of the term "crisis of capitalism," which was unavowed and "projected" back upon the Fifth Congress.

That the new definition of "crisis" diverged significantly from the previously adopted one, becomes rather apparent in the rhetorical question which Bucharin addressed to his audience: "If all these facts (sc.: the economic stabilization of the middle twenties) are correct . . . what then becomes of the question of the *general crisis of the capitalist world system?* . . . Can we, if these facts are correct, say that they signify the liquidation of the crisis of capitalism?" (*VI, pp. 11-12.*) The contents of Bucharin's negative answer to this question make it clear that he unavowedly *extended* the implicit definition of the key term involved, "crisis," so as to make the implicit definition of the Fifth Congress constitute merely a part of the new definition, i.e.—to speak in the "material" rather than in the "formal mode"—to transform into one special "form of crisis" what had hitherto alone been understood by "crisis": "This is the right answer: *the general crisis of capitalism continues,* it even becomes *intensified, although* the present form of the crisis is *different.* . . . At present, the old form of the crisis has been replaced by another form—that is all. . . . One should not believe that the general crisis of capitalism . . . consists in the ruin of capitalism in almost all, or in most, countries. The situation is different. The crisis of capitalism consists in the fact that *radical modifications of the structure* of the whole world economy are now in process, modifications which *aggravate* enormously and inevitably *every contradiction within the capitalist system, and which finally lead to its downfall.* Let us take, for instance, a fact like the existence of the USSR. What does it signify? . . . it is the expression of the fact that the crisis continues. . . ." (*VI, pp. 11-12.*)

Bucharin had, it will be seen, a choice between two formulations. On the one hand, he could maintain the previous definition of "crisis" and then assert that crisis: (1) had subsided for the time being, (2) was going to attain as yet unrealized magnitudes in the near future. Or, he could change the definition of "crisis" and then simply reiterate the text of the old formula. As we have seen, the latter alternative was chosen, in the main, although the first-mentioned "way out" was at least alluded to when Bucharin asserted that the crisis of capitalism, although it had not "disappeared," was in a state of "latency." (*VI, p. 12.*) This is, then, an example of the frequent use of a plurality of contradictory themes in the ideology we are studying.

Sub-Section 2—Symbolic Assimilation by Modification of the Presentation of the Old Dogma

If modifying the definition of terms contained in dogmatic texts constitutes one major device of doctrinal change, modifying the presentation of these dogmatic texts constitutes another.

A. *Changes of Emphasis*

"Changes of emphasis" may, in their turn, be classified according to whether they do or do not imply the complete omission of reference to, and/or the radical negation of, the existence of certain texts unfavorable to the new line. In the case where no such complete elimination takes place, various subcategories may further be distinguished.

Thus, certain texts may be emphasized by appropriate voice modulations of the speaker who quotes them; and these voice qualities may leave a trace in the use of *italics* in the printed records of the quotations involved. (In printed matter without oral antecedents, italics may, of course, directly be used in the same fashion.) This procedure was extensively adopted at the Fifth Congress in quoting from the texts of the Fourth Congress. It was used both by those who advocated and by those who opposed the change of line with reference to the "workers' government" and the "united front."

For reasons of space, we shall not stop in this study to illustrate other methods of change of emphasis as between different sectors of the extant dogma, which fall short of complete silence about, and/or negation of, the existence of "unfavorable" sectors. The latter devices were adopted after August 23, 1939, by giving retrospectively an almost exclusive prominence to Stalin's speech to the Eighteenth Congress of the CP of the Soviet Union, on March 10, 1939. This speech, which already significantly departed from the "collective security" and "anti-Fascist" line of 1934-1938, was retrospectively presented as the epitome of the central symbolism of those years, and was asserted to be identical in content with line at and after the Russo-German Pact.

The possibility of the use of the various devices indicated presupposes the presence of antagonistic components in the extant dogma, i.e., of statements going in opposite directions and thus qualifying one another. The "dialectic" structure of the basic ideology of the Comintern enhanced the feasibility of dogmatic texts of the kind to which French political vocabulary used to refer as a "nègre blanc." This phrase also connotes the presence of an intention to fashion dogmatic texts in the manner indicated, in order to be able subsequently to apply to them the symbolic devices which were just discussed. It does not fall within the purview of this paper to discuss to what extent such intentions were present in the cases here treated. That they were, is at least in some cases extremely plausible. Consider, for instance, the Seventh Congress resolution on the international situation: "Should a new imperialist war break out . . . the Communists will strive to lead the opponents of war . . . to the struggle for the *transformation of the imperialist war into civil war.* . . . If the commencement of . . . war forces the Soviet Union to set the Workers' and Peasants' Red Army in motion . . . the Communists will call upon all toilers *to work with all means at their disposal* and *at any price* for the victory of the Red Army. . . ." (*VII, p. 1184,* underlinings supplied.) "All means" and "at any price," however, presumably included the "means" of supporting "one's own bourgeoisie"—if it happened to be allied with the Soviet Union—and the "price" of enhancing the chances of its victory. The divergence between the two sentences quoted is further intensified by the fact that an allusion to the second sentence is incorporated into the first one: in a part omitted in the preceding quotation it mentions, as the target of the civil war demanded, not only the "bourgeoisie" but also "the fascist instigators of war."

B. *Direct Falsification*

A prominent case of the device of direct falsification consists of Sinoviev's Fifth Congress quotations of the Fourth Congress decisions on the "workers' government." Sinoviev quoted texts adopted by the latter Congress, with the avowed aim of buttressing his assertion that the position he advocated in 1924 was identical with that of the majority of 1922. He did this by fabrication and misquotation. (The evidence can not be presented here, for reasons of space.)

PART II

ADMISSIONS OF CHANGE

*Section 1—Admissions of Change at the Center of the
Comintern*

Admissions of change may refer to the center or to the
"sections" of the Comintern. Admissions of change at the
center may be investigated with a view to ascertaining, in
the first place, the factors which are advanced to justify it.
The following discussion will, for the sake of convenience,
be organized around the Comintern's treatment of its admitted *symbol* changes; it will be seen that, *mutatis mutandis,*
the same considerations can be made with reference to the
practice changes involved.

*Sub-section 1—Allegations of an Identity of Meaning of the
New ond the Old Symbols*

The admittedly new symbols may be asserted either to
coincide in their meaning with the old symbols or to diverge
from them. In the first case, one is dealing with a situation
bordering on a denial of change: it is only a difference in
"formulations," not in "purport," which is admitted. Various types of alleged differences in formulation may be distinguished here.

It is often asserted, in such a connection, that the new
symbols merely express more "precisely" the meanings of
their predecessors.

In this connection, explanations are often advanced as
to the causes of the low precision of the old symbols, neces-
sitating their supersession by the new formulae. Thus, Sinoviev maintained at the Fifth Congress that the high ambiguity
of the Fourth Congress resolution on the "workers' government" had been caused by the deceptive behavior of the
right wing.

Assertions were also frequently advanced about causes
and consequences of the high precision of the new symbols
adopted. Such causes were often generally referred to as the
"experience" acquired through the passage of time. Or,
more specifically, violations—in symbols and/or acts—of the

old symbols were alleged to be among the causes involved. As Sinoviev stated at the Fifth Congress: "After the speech of Comrade Radek (sc.: representing the right wing) . . . a revision by the congress of the wording of the resolution (sc.: of the Fourth Congress) on the workers' government has become unavoidable." (*V, p. 363*.) In such a case, the higher precision of the new symbols is typically presented as having been adopted with the motive of rendering future " deviations" less easy.

In other cases, the new symbols (the meaning of which was supposedly identical with that of the old ones) were asserted to have more favorable relationships to the attitudinal predispositions of the targets of the propaganda, and to have been introduced with this in mind. Radek referred to such an instance in talking about those for whom "workers' government" was a synonym for "dictatorship of the proletariat," but who were at the same time in favor of the introduction (or retention) of the former term: ". . . many comrades . . . say: . . . it is very difficult to agitate with the slogan of the dictatorship of the proletariat; let us rather say workers' government, that sounds very sweet and innocent . . ." (*IV, p. 101*); or, as the Fifth Congress theses on tactics put it: "The watchword of the Workers' and Peasants' Government was, and is, the formula most easily understood by the masses of the toilers." (Cf. the English edition of the *Inprecorr*, August 29, 1924, p. 652.) The emergence of such motives on the part of the propagandists may, in its turn, be related to changes in the environment: "The slogan 'workers' and farmers' government' originated just because of the fact that we had to proceed in some parties from the ordinary propaganda for communism to mass agitation . . . and to the preparation of the struggle for power. When we put the question of power, we must . . . issue . . . this slogan which is popular and attractive." (Sinoviev, *V, p. 92*.)

Sub-section 2—Admissions of a Difference of Meanings Between the New and the Old Symbols

If, thus, in a number of cases, the admittedly new symbols were presented as identical in meaning with their predecessors, there were other instances in which this was not the case. In these latter instances, two further sets of cases may be distinguished: those in which the new meaning was asserted to be compatible with the old, and those in which it was not.

A. *Allegations of a Compatibility of the Meanings of the New and the Old Symbols*

A typical instance of this category is presented when the new symbols are merely asserted to be more specific than the old ones.[9] Thus, Trotsky veiled the sharp change of line between the Second and the Third Congress by affirming that, at the former occasion, "we have established *the large perspective* and outlined *trends*. . . . Have they proved to be correct? Completely so! . . . But we did not then outline the *fluctuations around these trends,* and we become aware of them now." (*III, p. 89,* underlinings supplied.) At the Fourth Congress, Sinoviev veiled the trend to the right, since the Third Congress by asserting that "the tactical resolution (sc.: on the united front), which we have accepted today, has merely the modest function to adapt the directives of the Second and particularly the Third Congress *in a concrete fashion* to the political tasks of the present situation." (*IV, p. 973,* underlinings supplied.) In a similar fashion, Pieck at the Seventh Congress veiled the sharp change of line to be codified, by asserting: "Laying down a sharp line of demarcation between the reformist and communist policies, which is . . . one of the . . . foundations of our tactics of 'class against class,' by no means precludes Communists . . . from undertaking at elections—for instance, in Great Britain—to support the labour candidates who vote in favour of the urgent demands of the working class or, in France, concluding, in special cases, election agreements with the socialists. . . ." (*VII, p. 897.*) Thus, the *"tactical"* symbols of the *Right* period since 1934 were presented as mere specifications of the "strategic" symbols of the Left period of 1927-1934, whereas the "tactical" symbols of the Left period were not mentioned at all, and for good reasons. As in the previously discussed cases in which the new symbols are presented as merely the old symbols restated in a more precise form, additional assertions were frequently advanced about causes and consequences of the alleged rise in specificity. "The situation" at large was in this connection often referred to.

B. *Admissions of Incompatibility of the Meanings of the New and the Old Symbols*

In a further set of cases, the meanings of the new symbols are asserted to be not only different from those of the old ones, but even—at least partially—incompatible with them. Such admissions were, however, typically accompanied by assertions about causes, characteristics and consequences of this incompatibility which presumably tended to diminish the dysphoria aroused by the admission itself.

(1) Alleged types of incompatibility

In a number of cases, the symbol variations—and hence the ensuing incompatibilities—were presented as *small*. Subcategories of this theme are the assertions that only a small number of the old symbols have been changed; that those which have been changed have not been changed sharply; and that the symbol changes which have taken place have affected only symbols occupying a rather subordinate position within the whole system of the Comintern, but have not touched its supreme layers. Thus, it may be asserted that only very specific "tactical" symbols have changed, while those concerned with "tactical principles" and "strategy" remain untouched. For instance, Sinoviev at the Fifth Congress alluded to the necessity "of modifying in some respects our ways of putting the united front into operation" *(V, p. 88)*, which was rather an understatement. In an almost identical fashion, Bucharin at the Sixth Congress maintained, with reference to the new left line—liquidating in fact the "united front policy"—that "these tactics . . . while changing the *form* do not in any way change the principal *content* of the tactics of the united front." *(VI, p. 1573.)* At the Seventh Congress, Ercoli stated that "our whole struggle against war must take on a completely different character from the one it has had up to the present . . . we are not altering one whit our fundamental Marxist attitude toward the problem of war and peace." *(Inprecorr, 1936, p. 133.)* After August 23, 1939, Dimitrov declared that "the united proletarian and People's Front tactics . . . *in the form* in which they were conducted before the present war, are no longer suitable for other countries (sc.: than 'colonial and dependent countries')." (*World News and Views,* November 11, 1939, p. 1081, underlinings supplied.) In its May 15, 1943, resolution recommending the dissolution of the CI, the ECCI Presidium recalled: "Already the Seventh Congress of the CI . . . emphasized the necessity for the ECCI . . . to make a rule of avoiding interference in the internal affairs of the Communist Parties. These same considerations guided the CI in considering the resolution of the CPUSA . . . on its withdrawal from . . . the CI."

The importance of such allegedly mainly "tactical" changes could be further minimized by explicit reference to the "short run" character of their validity and/or to the "exceptional" character of their application. Thus Pieck, at the Seventh Congress, merely stated that *"in special cases"* the French CP was permitted to enter into the election agreements with the Socialists. (*Cf. VII, p. 897.*)

The importance of the admitted symbol change was also minimized by affirmations that it touched only "exoteric" rather than "esoteric" symbols. If Sinoviev stated that "our *agitation* must be changed in many respects" (*V, p. 62,* underlinings supplied), the implication is that propaganda— "many ideas into one head" as against "one idea into many heads"—will remain unchanged.

(2) *Alleged causes of incompatibility*

If admissions of the category here treated occurred—i.e., if the new symbols were conceded to be incompatible with some of the old ones—the elaboration of the admission usually did not stop with the allegation of such mitigating characteristics as we have surveyed. To them were almost always joined allegations about changing context factors implicitly or explicitly justifying the admitted symbol change.

These factors can plainly be of two kinds: either changes of "the situation"—i.e., of certain features of the environment and/or of the self—or changes of one's insight into the situation.

(a) "Conditions have changed."

The justification of an admitted symbol change by reference to changes in "the situation" was the vastly more popular one of the two symbolic patterns just mentioned—so much so that Radek, in a late and daring exercise of his buffoon function could jest: "Even if Comrade Sinoviev were to sign a thousand times the undertaking never to enter into a bloc with the social democrats, he is going to do so the day it becomes necessary; he will only declare that the situation has changed." (*V, p. 189.*)

The theme here involved occupied, within the sphere of admissions, an important place at the sharpest turn toward the left (1928), as well as at the sharpest veering toward the right (1935), and also at the occasion of the 1943 dissolution. On the former occasion, Bucharin explicity rejected the justification of the policy change by insight augmentation (". . . why have we modified our estimate of the general situation? Not because we are cleverer than we were, but because the situation has changed" *VI, p. 865*); and he emphatically declared in his report that "the change in the objective situation is the only important cause which determines our tactics." (*VI, p. 16.*)[10] Dimitrov affirmed that the new policy inaugurated was caused by the "new . . . questions which life itself and the development of the class struggle present us." (*VII, p. 1650.*) The theme we are treating was, for obvious reasons, the one adopted almost to the exclusion of all others after June 22, 1941. An editorial of the *Daily Worker* of July 1, 1941, states, with reference to the manifesto issued June 29 by the National Committee of the CPUSA, and formulating the new line: "The manifesto begins: 'The people of our country face a new world situation.' From this it derives all the necessary conclusions for the people's guidance." As W. Z. Foster put it, in his speech to the National Committee: "Hitler's attack upon the Soviet Union changes the character of the war, and thereby makes necessary changes in our Party's attitude towards that war." (*Daily Worker,* July 1, 1941, p. 6.)

(i) Alleged interconnections between changes of conditions and changes of line.

The adoption, in a particular case, of the pattern here discussed was usually accompanied by enunciations of the universal proposition that "correct" political behavior differs and varies with differences and variations of the "concrete" context in which it occurs. This proposition could in its turn be related to the basic Marxist position in favor of "dialectical" flexibility as against "metaphysical" rigidity. All the tendencies within the Comintern outside of an ultra-left fringe—which was half-hearted in its deviation—concurred in this. Because of the factors which were already alluded to (cf. p. 306), the incidence of this theme was higher in the case of turns to the right than on the occasion of turns to the left. Thus, the highest point of its use was reached on the occasion of the largest turn to the right, i.e., the Seventh Congress. Time and again, Dimitrov and the other official speakers emphasized that "we would not be . . . worthy pupils of Marx, Engels, Lenin and Stalin, if we did not reconstruct our politics and tactics in accordance with the changing situation. . . ." (*VII, p. 977*.) In its May 15, 1943, proposal to dissolve the CI, the ECCI Presidium declared: " . . . Communists . . . have always subordinated forms of organization . . . to the fundamental . . . interest of the working-class movement . . ., to peculiarities of the concrete historical situation. . . ."

Sometimes the universal proposition affirming the dependence of the "correct line" on the context was expressed by affirming the dependence on the context of meanings of the terms used in formulating a given line: a way of expression which is plainly related to the uncritical Comintern attitude toward language. A probable instance of this was the following remark in Molotov's speech to the Supreme Council of the Soviet Union on October 31, 1939: "In connection with these important changes in the international situation (sc.: since August 23, 1939) certain old formulas, formulas which we employed but recently, . . . are now obviously out of date and inapplicable. We know, for example, that in the past few months such concepts as 'aggression' and 'aggressor' *have acquired a new concrete connotation, a new meaning.* It is not hard to understand that we can no longer employ these concepts in the sense we did, say, three or four months ago. Today . . . Germany . . . is striving for peace, while Britain and France . . . are opposed to the conclusion of peace. Rôles, as you see, are changing. . . . This war promises nothing to the working class but bloody sacrifice and hardships. Well, now judge for yourself, *whether the meaning of such concepts* as 'aggression' and 'aggressor' *has changed* recently *or not."* (Molotov, Speech to the Supreme Council of the Soviet Union, October 31, 1939, *World News and Views,* November 4, 1939, pp. 6-7, underlinings supplied.)

The universal proposition just discussed (affirming a dependence of the "correct" line on the "context") was typically —and again, most heavily on the occasion of turns toward the right—accompanied by another universal proposition to the effect that the function of interrelating correct policy and total context can not be specifically described at any given moment, except for the neighborhood of the context of that moment. As Dimitrov put it, with reference to the prerequisites for the entrance of Communist parties into governments of the "united front" or of the "People's front": "The question of whether the Communists will . . . enter such a government depends for its solution on a given situation. Questions of this sort can be settled only in relation to given circumstances." (*VII, p. 1653.*) (A statement to the same effect was incorporated into the resolutions of the Congress.)

It may be presumed that the incidence of this subsidiary universal proposition also varied directly as the magnitude of the turn to the right which was occurring; for any higher specification of the prerequisites for a certain right move would be apt to create a left reaction against their insufficiency.

It was thus, by implication, the prevailing assertion that the new symbols could be presented as the consequences of syllogisms into which entered certain new premises—referring to changing situational aspects—and certain unchanged premises, namely, those referring to the invariant ulterior aims of the movement. The adoption of the pattern here discussed was often accompanied by emphasis on the invariance of the latter, and on the necessity of the admitted changes of line in view of these invariant premises.

To the foregoing emphasis was sometimes added stress upon the constancy of the interconnection between certain changes in the situation and certain policy changes. A special form of this was references to the past of the movement in which similar changes in the situation had allegedly been responded to by similar changes of policy. Thus. Dimitrov's Seventh Congress introduction of the policy of entry into coalition governments under certain circumstances was buttressed by the speaker—more implicitly than explicitly—by statements that the "worker's government" policy of 1922-1924 had been a similar reaction to similar conditions. Similarly, the May 15, 1943, resolution of the ECCI Presidium, recommending the dissolution of the CI stated: "Communists . . . remember the example of the great Marx who . . . when the First International had fulfilled its historical task, and, as a result of the matured situation . . . dissolved the First International, in as much as this form of organization already no longer corresponded to the demands confronting it."

The pattern which we are examining is compatible with the assertion that the older, now discarded symbols were "correct" before the alleged situational change. Such an assertion evidently facilitated the acceptance of innovation by those connected with the previous line. Hence, this tended to be the universal pattern of those who were already "in," and who remained actual or aspiring élite members after the policy shift. There seems to have been an ascending trend of such assertions of "non-retroactiveness" of line changes as their frequency and depth increased.

(ii) Types of alleged changes of conditions.

For various purposes, it is relevant to subclassify the pattern here discussed, according to the characteristics of the situation which are alleged to have changed.

In an important set of cases, the new features were presented as related to the line now to be superseded: these new features were frequently described as consequences of the "application" of the old line. In this case, they were presented either as desired or as undesired effects. An instance of the first category is provided by the Fourth Congress theses on the "united front," in which it was asserted: (1) that the previous line had made possible the consolidation of communist parties, and (2) that this very consolidation now made the new united front line expedient. (Cf. IV, pp. 1020-1021.) An argument of this kind was at least suggested in the May 15, 1943, resolution of the ECCI Presidium, recommending the dissolution of the CI: "The whole development of events in the last quarter of a century . . . convincingly showed that the organizational form of uniting workers chosen by the First Congress of the CI answered conditions of the first stages of the working-class movement, but [that] it had been outgrown by the growth of this movement [presumably made possible by the CI] . . . and has even become a drag on the further strengthening of the national working-class parties."

In other cases, the allegedly new features of the situation which justify the change were presented as negative rather than positive effects of the application of the old line. In this context, the euphemism "experiences" or "lessons of our struggle" was typically used. Thus, Sinoviev affirmed, at the Fifth Congress, with reference to the 'worker's government": "We have now acquired experience. Now we must say directly that the slogan of the 'workers' government' and of the 'workers' and farmers' government' has its main importance for us as a method of agitation and of the organization of the masses for revolutionary struggle (sc.: rather than as a serious policy aim)." (*V, p. 89.*) And the same theme was used with greater emphasis at the Seventh Congress: ". . . we must now adapt our policy and tactics to the newly created situation on the basis of the deeply instructive and far-reaching experiences of the past few years." (*Dimitrov, VII, p. 1649.*) "The experience accumulated by the CI" was also adduced as a reason for dissolving it, in the May 15, 1943, resolution of the ECCI Presidium.

The alleged effects of the old line which were said to constitute new features in the situation were not always asserted to be effects of its "application"; in some cases, they were said to be effects of its "violation." Thus, "right deviations" from the old line were mentioned in justifying a turn to the "left," and vice versa.

In the hitherto treated categories, the allegedly new aspects of the situation were presented as *effects* of the old line. In other cases, the new aspects are affirmed to be at variance with those—hitherto realized—conditions for which alone the old line had been intended during its existence. Thus, the Fifth Congress majority maintained that the transformation of the socialist parties into "third parties of the bourgeoisie"

eliminated that situation for which alone the previously
adopted form of the "united front" policy had been intended.
If, thus, in many cases, the new aspects of the situation
were characterized in relation to the old line, they were in
other cases related to other elements of the total system of
symbol and practice. The other elements were previous predictions—"we have at the time of the old line foreseen the
change in the situation which requires its abandonment"—or
statements about the positive or negative relevance of the
new aspects for the realization of the movement's major
goals. Two major themes appear here: According to one, the
alleged changes in the situation constitute advances; according to the other, they portend threats which can be combated
(by a change of policy). It is the first of these themes which
appeared much more frequently and emphatically than the
latter.

It was plainly the dominant symbol pattern, in the case
of turns to the *left,* which was justified by references to a
change in the situation; for such a change was then almost
always one or another form of the "intensification of the
crisis of capitalism." In cases of a turn to the *right,* this symbol pattern was found to be less frequent and prominent,
but still playing a very important rôle. It is true that it was
only of minor significance on the occasion of the first important turn to the right, which was codified by the Third
Congress. That turn was related to alleged setbacks—the end
of the revolutionary wave lasting from March 1917 to March
1921—rather than to advances; it was, as Lenin put it, a question of "adapting our tactics to the zigzag course of history."
(*III, p. 749.*)The symbol pattern in question did, on the other
hand, play a predominant rôle at the Seventh Congress. With
reference to the Third Congress, it may be debated whether
its estimate of the revolutionary ebb was realistic, as Franz
Borkenau assumes,—or overpessimistic, as Arthur Rosenberg
maintains. But there would be little disagreement among
specialists as to the diagnostic overoptimism (from the Comintern's point of view) of the passage in the Seventh Congress
resolutions in which one of the "basic changes in the world
situation" by which "the tasks facing the labor movement of
the world are determined" is described as follows: "The relationship of class forces on a world scale is changing more

and more in the direction of a *growth of the forces of revolution.*" (*VII, p. 1177.*) Finally, the May 15, 1943, resolution of the ECCI Presidium recommended the dissolution of the CI "in consideration of the above [the neutrally presented factor of a growing divergence between conditions in the different areas] and taking into account the growth and political maturity of Communist Parties and their leading cadres in separate (sic) countries. . . ."

In most of the cases in which changes in line were shown to be justified by changes in the situation which were desirable (from the point of view of the movement's aims), the latter changes were endowed with further characteristics relevant to our discussion.

In the first place, there were apt to be shifts outside the movement rather than within it. The self could thus be presented as essentially invariant, and responding by a modification of policy only to environmental variations beyond its control, to the "new . . . questions which life itself and the development of the class struggle present us. . . ." (*Dimitrov, VII, p. 1650*); for "time does not stand still." (*Dimitrov, VII, p. 970.*)

Thus, the CP of Great Britain could, in referring to August, 1939, speak of "the significance of *this change in Nazi policy* . . ." (statement of the Central Committee of the CPGB of August 22, 1939; *World News and Views,* August 26, 1939, p. 916, underlinings supplied); and it could be declared that "the pact deals solely with the undertaking not to take part in aggressive action against one of the two contracting parties. For the USSR . . . this represents a complete reversal on Nazi Germany's part." (*World News and Views,* September 2, 1939, p. 951.) In view of the "psychological rigidity" tendencies mentioned above (cf. p. 305), such a presentation was presumably quite skillful.

If one compares allegations of the type just mentioned with "objective" estimates of the situation, one will often find rather high discrepancies. In some circumstances it was the *self* which took the initiative in introducing the change; *others* merely responded.

Such would, for instance, be the estimate of many specialists with regard to the situations confronting the Fifth, the Sixth and the Seventh Congress: In all these cases the Comin-

tern alleged itself to be adjusting to changes—among others—
in the socialist camp, whereas it would seem more accurate to
describe the situation in the inverse fashion. (The evidence
can not be presented here, for reasons of space.)

Favorable changes in the situation which were taken to
justify policy innovations were not only asserted to be
changes of the environment rather than of the self; they were
also often affirmed to have been *demanded* by the self from
the environment for some time past. Thus the environment
was presented as at last "coming around" to a higher degree
of conformity with demands which had for a longer or
shorter time been made by the self. The classical instance of
this is furnished by the assertions concerning the socialist
parties when turns were toward the right. Thus, at the
Seventh Congress it was asserted: (1) that the Comintern had
long since desired more positive relations with the socialists
who had, however, up till recently refused (cf. *Dimitrov,
VII, p. 960; Pieck, VII, p. 912*); and (2) that finally the socialist parties seemed to show a greater willingness for cooperation under the "pressure of the masses." (*Cf. Pieck, VII, p.
855.*)

The characterization of relevant situational changes not
as advances, but as threats—huge but not overwhelming—was
no less prominent at the Seventh Congress. The twin threats
of "fascism" and war were referred to as grounds for the new
line.

Finally, in presenting situational changes, they may be related not to the obsolete or invariant parts of the old dogma,
but rather to the new symbols which are at the point of being, or have just been, dogmatized. It may thus be asserted
that the new symbols do nothing but *"codify"* and *"systema-
tize"* changes in practice which have already sprung up.
Thus Hoernle (Germany) affirmed at the Fourth Congress
with reference to the prehistory of the Third Congress: "The
offensive of capital in Germany has begun . . . in the spring
of 1920. . . . In the summer of 1920 . . . we had as yet no
theory of the united front, but instinctively our party organizations . . . have adopted this tactic. . . . I remind you
further of the winter 1920-1921, when for the first time four
or five demands were raised spontaneously by the Stuttgart
metal workers, upon which then . . . the Open Letter (sc.:

of the Communist Party to the workers' parties and trade unions) of January 1921, followed. . . . *The Third World Congress has therefore created no new tactics. It has only systematized this tactic. . . ."* (IV, p. 384.)

(b) Augmentation of insight.

If the justification of a policy change by a situation change was an almost universal pattern, justification by an increase of insight into an invariant situation—implying the erroneousness of the old policy—was quite rare. An approximation to it was found in Sinoviev's Fifth Congress assertions (note the delay between the events and their treatment) about the change of line between the Second Congress, on the one hand, and the Third and Fourth Congresses on the other. He referred to the period 1919-1921 as a "period in which we were essentially merely a propaganda organization without knowing it. After the first battles the real relationship of forces and also our consciousness of it, were clarified. . . ." (*V, pp. 77-78.*) Perhaps this theme was suggested when the May 15, 1943, resolution of the ECCI Presidium, recommending the dissolution of the CI, stated: ". . . the war of liberation of freedom-loving peoples against the Hitlerite tyranny . . . has demonstrated with still greater clarity that the . . . uprising and mobiliaztion . . . for the speediest victory . . . can be best of all and most fruitfully carried out by the vanguard of the working-class movement of each separate country, working within the framework of its own country." (The relationship of this discovery to "Marxism-Leninism" was not gone into.)

In this instance, one of the themes which typically accompany the central theme here studied is apparent: the assertion that the accretion of insight is an effect of a change in the situation, and more specifically of the old policy. The implication is that an earlier acquisition of the new insight would have been "impossible": "one learns only through experience." The past error appears as the necessary instrument for the present illumination.

Conjointly with this, the past error may be laid at the door of certain sectors of the self toward which the symbol manipulators and/or their audience have negative attitudes. Thus, Sinoviev at the Fifth Congress, (*V, p. 86*) charged Radek with having introduced "right deviations" into the Fourth Congress resolutions. (It may be added that if Radek was guilty, Sinoviev was also.)

Section 2—Admissions of Change Outside the Center of the Comintern

After having discussed the center's admisison of its own changes in symbol and practice, we now proceed to deal with the center's admissions of variations occurring in other parts of the movement.

Here we encounter the following typical theme: the admitted symbol-practice changes outside the center were presented as rectifications of previous (intentional or unintentional) "deviations" from the invariant center line. That is, the existence of deviations *at* the center was denied, that of past deviations *from* the center affirmed.

Sub-section 1—Allegations about the Rôle of the Center

The denial of deviations at the center was an invariant element of the more ceremonial parts of the symbolism of every one of the congresses. One of its typical forms was the assertion that the permanent organs of the Comintern, particularly the Executive Committe, have "correctly executed the line" laid down by the preceding congress. There are exceptions to the pattern; but these exceptions are unvaryingly of a rather harmless sort; and their frequency and importance declined steadily. In the first place, admitted center mistakes were apt to be minor mistakes, either in terms of their alleged effects or in terms of their nature. Thus, the most frequently admitted center mistake was in the mere *timing* and, less frequently, in the *quantity* of action rather than its direction. The main "self-criticism" of the ECCI by the president of the Comintern in his report to the Sixth Congress was that "almost all parties (of the Comintern) react *too slowly* to changes in the situation. . . . It seems to me that this is also true for the Comintern itself and its leadership" *(Bucharin, VI, p. 22,* underlinings supplied), and that there was "an *insufficient* degree of execution of our decisions" *(loc. cit.).* And at the Seventh Congress Pieck summed up the discussions on the report of the ECCI by stating that "a number of important shortcomings were mentioned in the report of the ECCI pertaining not only to the work of individual sections, but also to that of the Executive Committee of the Communist International. . . . It is no serious matter, of course, if in some instances the Executive Committee did not *answer in time* some of the letters which did not relate to fundamental questions of our movement. . . . But far more important are those cases in which the Executive Committee was *late in giving assistance* on important issues to this or that Party . . . it is possible that the Executive Committee has in fact in some cases *not interfered immediately and with sufficient energy* against sectarian tendencies (of the sections) . . ." (*VII, pp. 1351-1352,* underlinings supplied.)

Another type of reference mitigating the admission of center deviations was that of alleging their causation by the sections. Thus Pieck at the Seventh Congress explained "the big shortcoming that the Executive Committe was not sufficiently supported in its work by the sections. The mistakes and the shortcomings in our work can be overcome only if the best representatives of the sections constantly cooperate with the Executive Committee. . . ." (*VII, p. 1351.*)

Sub-section 2—Allegations About "Deviations" Outside the Center

The pendants to the denials of change at the center in the cases studied were the admissions of change for parts of the movements outside it. Such admissions in their turn entail two allegations: that of the past existence of "deviations"— without the collusion of the center, on the one hand; and that of their present rectification, typically presented as occurring by influences from the center, on the other hand. In the case of a turn toward the left, there will thus be allegations of right deviations, and a concentration of "fire" against them as the "main danger"; and at the occasion of a turn toward the right, there will be affirmations about the existence of "ultra-leftism," and a direction of "struggle" against them as "the biggest hindrance to the carrying out of a really bolshevist policy."

In such cases, certain subsidiary themes were frequently

introduced to elucidate the genesis of such deviations. One set of such themes which was predominant at the Fifth Congress revolved around the alleged "mimicry" behavior of the deviationists. It was said that they slyly presented their early symbolic deviations as differences of style rather than of content, and thus were able for a time to deceive the good-natured and unsuspecting center, the vices of which are here, as elsewhere, but the excesses of its virtues. Thus, Sinoviev is able to plead guilty merely to a rather attractive fault: too great conciliatoriness in matters of form. Needless to say, here again the assertions of the historian would be of a rather different tenor.

A. *The Truth Value of Allegations About Deviations*

If one confronts these assertions with those of objective observers, one will again frequently encounter sharp divergences between the two sets of sentences.

Those behaviors outside the center which are presented as deviations from the old line have, in fact, quite frequently been applications of it, undertaken with the consent and even at the behest of the center.

Prior to the complete abolition in the Comintern of the expression of symbols substantially diverging from those of the ECCI, the extreme wings of the movement tended themselves to make the point just alluded to. (Again, no evidence can be given, for reasons of space.)

Sometimes a given set of assertions about past deviations outside the center constituted, to speak in the language which the Comintern inherited from the French Revolution, an "amalgam": the assertions involved refer partially to behaviors which, if they had taken place, would have been deviations from the old line then existing, and partially to behaviors which would have been deviations only from the new line and not from the old one. Thus, a Seventh Congress resolution "notes the serious shortcomings in the work of a number of sections of the Communist International: (1) the belated carrying out of the tactics of the united front, (2) the inability to mobilize the masses around partial demands, (3) the failure to realize the necessity of struggle in defense of the remnants of bourgeois democracy, (4) the failure to realize the necessity for creating an anti-imperialist

People's Front in the colonial and dependent countries, (5) neglect of work in reformist and fascist trade unions and in the mass organizations of toilers formed by bourgeois parties, (6) underestimation of the importance of work among the toiling women, the peasantry and the petty bourgeois masses in the towns. . . ." (*VII, pp. 1157-1176,* numberings supplied.) In this instance, at least factors (1), (3) and (4) seem to imply "projections backward" of the new line inaugurated in 1934.

B. *The Term Structure of Allegations About Deviations*

The proposition which was discussed above—implying the high frequency with which a given behavior was presented at one moment as conforming to the "line," and as deviating from it at a later moment—has certain implications for the technical terminology of the Comintern.

For a number of types of political actions the Comintern has evolved sets of three standardized terms or term compounds (for each of which there may be synonyms). One refers to the "correct" ("bolshevik", "marxist-leninist-stalinist") action, whereas the two others designate opposite kinds of deviations. Each of these may or may not be distinctively ultra-left ("sectarian," "doctrinaire," "formalist") or right ("opportunist," "liquidationist," "reformist"). Thus, the "correct" behavior of the party towards the "masses" is flanked by the "divorcement from the real life of the masses" (the "unwillingness to learn from them" and "to make it easier for them to come over to the positions of Communism"), on the one hand; and it is threatened by the "reliance on the spontaneity of the masses" and the "lack of a sufficiently distinct Communist line," on the other hand. That is, besides the "correct" line there is a certain manifestation of "sectarianism" on the one hand, and of "chvostism" ("tail-end-ism") on the other. Or, so far as the mixture of propaganda content between manifestly revolutionary symbols and others is concerned, the correct position is to be distinguished, on the one hand, from a neglect of, and, on the other hand, from an overemphasis on, "partial demands." Or, with reference to the relationship of action to "principles," the correct behavior again lies between an "opportunist lack of principles" and "sectarian simplified methods of solving the most complex problems on the basis of stereotyped schemes." If it is a right deviation to "give communism a Western haircut" (as Ruth Fischer said at the Fifth Congress), it is a "left deviation" to "lose the specific features of the specific conditions in each individual country out of account." (Cf. Dimitrov, as stated at the Seventh Congress.) In these cases, the "correct" action can be represented as occupying a *middle* position on a continuum between hypo-quantities and hyper-quantities. In other cases, the "correct" action is located at the *extreme* of a continuum, and there are two standardized terms or term compounds present, one referring to the correct extreme, the other to the rest of the continuum. Thus, there can not be too much of a "taking advantage of the difficulties of the class enemy."

What happens, then, in the situation described above is that at one moment one term out of a set of two or three is applied to a given behavior, and that the other term, or one of the two other terms, is applied to the same behavior at a later moment. This is, in its turn, made possible by the absence of precise definitional delimitations of the terms involved against each other—a linguistic situation which is significantly implied in a commonplace 1925 remark of Stalin, quoted by Dimitrov at the Seventh Congress: "It is necessary that the Party be able to combine in its work the greatest adhesion to principle (not to be confused with sectarianism) with a maximum of contacts and connections with the masses (not to be confused with tailism)." (*VII, p. 976*.)

If, thus, the symbolic devices adopted imply high ambiguity of the terms referring to correct and incorrect shapes of various kinds of political actions—an ambiguity which is, in its turn, enhanced by the use of such terms in the fashion depicted—they have plainly the same implications for the terms of which those sentences are composed which state "the line" itself. As we have surveyed a number of them in our previous discussions, further corroborations seem at this point hardly necessary.[11]

We may only add here that the degree of ambiguity to be adopted for the formulation of a "line" was apt to become an object of contention between the center—interested in the maximization of that ambiguity as a factor facilitating the employment of the symbolic devices just discussed—and oppositionist groups outside of the center who regarded higher precision as safeguards against "arbitrary" actions of the center against them; actions which could and did present them with a trap of the "If-it's-not-one-thing-it's-another" variety. Thus, at the Fifth Congress the right Clara Zetkin deplored that "sufficient clarity has not yet been achieved as to this question: How shall the various sections . . . execute the united front policy? . . . The resolutions of the world congresses must be able to be directive for us without explanations, without commentaries." (*V, pp. 335-336.*) In the same vein, the "ultra-left" Bordiga states: "We demand . . . a clear and precise fixation of the tactics of the Comintern. Even if its contents will be other than those which we demand, . . . they ought to be clear. We want to know where we are going." (*V, p. 402.*)

But in the case of the right, as well as the left, the demand for more precision (the presumable motive for the demand which we alluded to above) was not overtly stated. Whereas that motive was one of delimiting the power position of the center, the oppositionists claimed—with real or feigned naïveté—that their motive ran exactly in the contrary direction. Bordiga's colleague Rossi explained: "It is . . . necessary . . . to say in which form these tactics (sc.: the united front) ought to be applied; otherwise, it will not be possible to condemn a party which on its own initiative . . . has found an application of the united front which it deems correct." (*V, p. 156.*) As if Rossi did not know, or could not have known, that it had just then proved "possible," "despite" the vagueness of the Comintern formulations, to condemn the Brandler-Radek leadership of the German Communist Party for a certain "application of the United front" tactics which it had not even developed "on its own initiative," but rather on the behest of the center!

In the same ostensibly naïve fashion, Clara Zetkin pointed out: "If we give the president of the Executive Committee the right to elucidate what a resolution of the world congress really means . . . , then we give the same right of interpretation to any other member. The monolithism of our discipline and action will thereby be broken." (*V, p. 336.*) Certainly the Fifth Congress was the last at which these words could have been spoken!

Chapter **12**

INTERACTION: THE RESPONSE OF COMMUNIST PROPAGANDA TO FRUSTRATION

1. *Introduction*

A. *The Problem*

THE HISTORY of the Communist International is a history of defeats. It was brought to life in 1919 by the sole great victory of the Communist movement, the Russian Revolution. From then on, its major sections were destroyed, or became shells of their former selves, in one country after another. Those that remained abandoned their more ambitious revolutionary objectives in favor of restricted ones connected with Russian foreign policy. Finally, in 1943, the Comintern was liquidated. It was liquidated, it is true, during a resurgence of Russian power and influence, but a resurgence with which the International had little to do. It is important to distinguish clearly between successes of Russia and successes of the Communist International. The victories of the Red Army were won not under the slogans of Communist revolution, but under the traditional slogans of nationalism. Communists throughout the rest of the world likewise sought support for one objective—the military defeat of Germany—an objective which in most cases was best served by losing their distinctiveness, and was only hindered by the International which was, consequently, abandoned. Defeats, in fact, continued to plague the Comintern even in this period of Russian success.

Both the loyalty and the number of followers of a political movement ordinarily rise when it succeeds, and fall when it fails. Now, this is in general true of the Communist movement as it is of others. However, the Communist movement seemed to be exceptionally resilient in the face of frustration. Non-communists have, in general, erred in predicting far greater effects for each setback than actually were recorded. After each one, an intensely loyal group of followers remained.

A full explanation of the limited impact of Comintern defeats on the behavior of its followers would take us far beyond the scope of this paper. One factor, however, is undoubtedly the elaborate propaganda which the International addressed to its supporters. Whether the treatment given to its own difficulties in this propaganda should be assigned a large or small causal rôle in maintaining loyalty is open to question, but there can be no doubt that, in either case, it is an important object of investigation.

It was with this in mind that Comintern defeat propaganda was chosen for the study. The primary objective is to ascertain the relation between this propaganda and the conditions under which it was emitted. Insofar as this objective has been achieved, the study also serves to illustrate the applicability of quantitative method (content analysis) to the study of communications.[1]

In order to analyze propaganda content, it was necessary to construct a typology of the modes of treating setbacks symbolically. It might seem impracticable to enumerate *all* the relevant kinds of statements; nevertheless, the authors feel that the goal was at least approached. An outline was constructed consisting of approximately 1000 statements (formulated in general terms) which might be made in such a situation, and most of which presumably would have the effect of mitigating the impact of a setback upon a sympathetic audience.[2] The opposites of these statements were also listed. (Parts of this outline are reproduced in Appendix II.) A count was then made of the frequency with which statements corresponding to each category of the outline actually occurred in the sample of Comintern propaganda analyzed.

B. *The Sample*

The source studied was the English edition of the Communist weekly, the *International Press Correspondence* (the title of which was changed in 1938 to *World News and Views*). This was one of the two official periodical publications of the Communist International, the other being the *Communist International*. While this latter was a monthly, primarily devoted to "theoretical" matter, the *Inprecorr* provided a running commentary on current affairs. Among its major functions were "feeding" Communist newspapers, and providing information for the élite of the active party members.[3]

It was decided to concentrate on electoral defeats and strike defeats. Defeats of each type are frequent and homogeneous enough to provide a group of events suitable for statistical treatment. On the other hand, the two types are quite different, in regard to both the situations in which they occur and the political methods used. They are sufficiently different to permit us to assume that characteristics found in the treatment of both types are fairly characteristic of Communist defeat propaganda in general.

An *electoral defeat* was defined as an election outcome in which the percentage of the total vote received by the Communist Party was smaller than in the previous election. (As a matter of fact, all such defeats also involved a decline in the absolute number of Communist votes.) An attempt was made to gather election statistics for all European countries and for the United States. With the exception of certain of the smaller Eastern European states the requisite data were obtained. All national parliamentary (in the U.S., presidential) elections which were defeats for the Communists were studied.[4]

All strikes were listed which were mentioned in the *Inprecorr*, and which were also characterized by the New York *Times* as Communist-dominated and as resulting in defeats. This selection is, of course, far from satisfactory; many Communist-strike defeats were not so reported in the New York *Times*; and conceivably the *Times* might have designated as

Communist or as a defeat a strike which, on further investigation, might not have been either one. However, the authors, on guard for this possibility, did not come across any cases which seemed to be open to the latter objection. It should be noted that those cases were rejected in which the *Times* simply quoted an interested party as asserting that the strike was Communist-inspired or a defeat. All strikes satisfying the conditions stated above were studied, up to three in any given year (except that strikes in countries Axis-occupied since Pearl Harbor were not included, because of technical difficulties in getting information). In the few cases in which more than three a year were eligible the selection was made on the basis of magnitude. (Of course, strikes of little importance do not usually "make" the *Times*.)

The application of these rules resulted in a sample consisting of 33 strikes and 30 elections. Their distribution through time is a matter of considerable importance. The history of the Communist International breaks up into a number of well-defined and universally recognized periods marked by sharply diverging "lines".[5] For our purposes, we have considered the years from the beginning of our sample up to the late summer of 1927 as a single period which shall be called the "early years." It is true that within this period there were fluctuations from left to right to left and then to right again; the amplitudes of these fluctuations were, however, smaller than those shown subsequently. This period is here regarded as a "right" period, a classification which is not unreasonable, in view of the fact that the first case of the kind we are studying occurred in 1921, after the initial left subperiod. Starting in the late summer of 1927, after the Austrian uprising of July 15, a sharp turn to the left took place, codified by the Sixth World Congress of the Communist International in the summer of 1928, and inaugurating a period which we call "Third Period" (Stalin's and Bucharin's term for the new world situation).

The Seventh Congress of the Communist International, in 1935, marked the culmination of an extreme turn to the right, which had first become visible in the spring of 1934. The period thus inaugurated we call the "People's Front Period." In August 1939, the signing of the Stalin-Hitler pact precipitated a new, somewhat left period which we name after the pact. It continued until the invasion of Russia, on June 22, 1941. Finally, the period ending with the liquidation of the Comintern we call the "War Period." It was, of course, an extreme right period.

The number of events studied falling into each of these periods was as follows:

	Elections	Strikes
1. Early years (1919-1927):	8	11
2. Third Period (1927-1934):	14	11
3. People's Front Period (1934-1939):	7	9
4. Stalin-Hitler Pact Period (1939-1941):	1	2
5. War Period (1941-1943):	—	—
Total in left years (2 and 4):	15	13
Total in right years (1 and 3):	15	20

The absence, during the last period, of setbacks falling within our sample is hardly surprising. Communists were not conducting strikes except in Axis territory, and elections were not commonly held in Europe.

Five election defeats and 6 strike defeats were disposed of by silence. Three of these election setbacks and 5 of these strike failures occurred in "right" years. Since these cases of silence obviously can not be subjected to content analysis, the analyzed sample consists of 12 right elections, 13 left elections, 15 right strikes, and 12 left strikes.

As will be seen below, the left and right periods differed in a number of respects in the propaganda devices used. It should therefore be made clear that the devices did not enter into the definitions of these periods. They were defined on the basis of other political characteristics. Reference to any history of the Communist International, except one by a loyal Communist, will reveal agreement upon the major periods.[6] However, as one would expect, a certain lag can usually be observed between the date of the political event (declaration of policy, etc.) marking a change of line and the full emergence of the propaganda technique characteristic of the new line. A defeat occurring in such an interval is called "transitional." That is, a defeat near the beginning of a new period of the Comintern's history is "transitional" if its treatment conformed in many respects to the pattern of the previous period.

Where correlations are made, the regression lines of left

and right periods are frequently of opposite sign. Events occurring near the start of a new period are often found to cluster around the intersection of the regression lines. In such a case, or in cases in which they manifest the behavior of their actual period, they are treated with the other events in their period. If, however, they conform closely to the pattern of the period before, then in addition to the coefficients for the regular periods, correlations are computed grouping transitional cases with the preceding period. Of course, this was not done for each transitional case separately; all cases in the transitional interval were handled as a group. The use of this procedure is always clearly indicated in the text.

The number of cases during any transition varied, of course, with the accidental chronological distribution of elections and strikes. It varied also with the gradualness of a given change of line. In regard to the latter, it should be pointed out that, as the Comintern became more totalitarianized, changes of line became more abrupt. Hence, the number of transitional cases declined through time. The first four setbacks after the first change of line—all occurring during a period of just under two years—were transitional. Three events, during just over one year, are so regarded in the change from the Third Period to the People's Front. No events after that appear to be transitional.

All articles in the *Inprecorr* which fulfilled the following two conditions were analyzed:

(1) Containing at least one reference to the election or strike in question.

(2) Appearing after the date of the defeat, but not more than three months later in the case of elections, or one year later in case of strikes.

The date of the defeat of a strike was not always easy to determine. We took it as the date of the return to work, but often that is a gradual process of long duration. Here again, we had to rely to some extent on the non-Communist press; when it regarded a strike as definitely over, we took it to be so. Since sometimes the Communists would concur and write the autopsy some months later, we had to allow a longer period for the sample of strike articles than for the sample of election articles.

Within each eligible article, all statements were classified and tabulated that were *subsumable* under any outline heading (cf. Appendix II). The only exception was the outline section called "Statements about matters not connected with the setback." To have tabulated every pertinent statement would have meant the inclusion of much irrelevant material. Such assertions were therefore tabulated only when a statement coming under another section of the outline came in the same paragraph (or in the paragraph immediately preceding or following).

From the frequencies of statements fitting each category of the outline, indices of propaganda behavior were constructed. Each defeat ordinarily had a score on each index, summarizing the types of statement made about it. These indices are described in Appendix I. (The reader will need to make himself thoroughly familiar with the definitions, since the results of this study are reported in terms of the relations among the categories defined in Appendix I.)

Where less than ten classifiable statements were found, the authors excluded the case from computations. (All other exclusions are reported in the text.) In two instances, indices having statistical reliability could not be constructed since, although there was not silence about an event, there was great reticence.

Although the size of the sample is small, it consist of almost the total "population" involved. However, as the authors are less interested in establishing historical facts than in working toward the confirmation of general hypotheses, significance tests are applied for whatever they are worth. Our hope is that this study has succeeded in devising techniques whereby the formulation and confirmation of hypotheses about verbal social behavior will be facilitated. The full confirmation of the hypotheses advanced must await further research.

All significant correlations of the indices constructed have been reported—except in the case of alternative measures of "almost the same thing." Where a relationship is not reported, it lacked significance. For significance, the *t* test is generally applied and 2.0 is taken as the requisite critical value. The preceding indications imply that none of the results obtained has achieved a fully satisfactory degree of confirmation. The study, however, may show what might be done in improved researches of this kind.

II. *Cumulation*

One of the simplest devices of propaganda is to offset unfavorable statements with favorable ones. Thus, if "we have been forced to retreat," then "the enemy bought his gains dearly." This device is here called *compensation*. Many propagandas even offset good news. The propaganda of the Communist movement, on the other hand, is marked not by compensation but by *cumulation*. If it is decided to put a good face on a setback, almost all aspects of the situation are presented as favorable. If it is decided that the defeat should not be toned down, then "self-criticism" will be given free play over a large field.[7]

A considerable amount of evidence was found to confirm this hypothesis. A number of the indices described in Appendix I refer to kinds of symbolic behavior to which a sympathetic audience tends to respond by feeling more or less unhappy (dysphoric). When the self (of the sympathetic audience) is presented as suffering a setback, the symbolic behavior is said to be *self-deprivational*. Whatever dilutes this presentation is *self-indulgent*.[8] Relevant indices are of frankness, mitigation, retrospection and diversion. If these indices, in any case of defeat, all tend to be either self-deprivational or self-indulgent, we are in the presence of cumulation. If, on the other hand, some show self-deprivation and others self-indulgence, then we are in the presence of compensation.

What is the actual situation? There is between the frankness (B) indices [9] of the different defeats and their mitigation indices [10] a negative correlation amounting to $-.53$ ($t = 3.0$) for elections and to $-.47$ ($t = 2.7$) for strikes. Since high frankness presumably increases the negative impact of defeat, and propaganda with a low mitigation index does the same, these negative correlations reveal a clear case of cumulation.

In the case of elections, we find that frankness also correlates positively with retrospection, that is, with looking back to the antecedents of the setback, rather than turning attention away from it towards the future.[11] The correlation is $+ .67$ (t $= 4.0$),[12] again indicating cumulation. (The strike correlation is not significant.)

As one might expect from the preceding correlations, there is in the case of elections a negative correlation between mitigation and retrospection. The correlation is $- .54$ (t $= 2.9$). That is, the more the CI spokesmen looked back, the more upleasant the things they said about both the causes of the defeat and about other subjects—another instance of cumulation.

Although these two variables were not proved to be significantly related for strikes as a whole, we find a correlation which further confirms the hypothesis under discussion, if we consider only strikes occurring in left periods; it is $- .62$ (t $= 2.5$).

At this point it may be well to distinguish two types of self-deprivational and self-indulgent behavior. The impact of a setback on a sympathetic audience is affected, on the one hand, by the amount of attention given to a subject, and, on the other hand, by the character of the subtopics referred to. A large number of United Nations references to the Battle of Cassino would be highly self-deprivational. However, these references might contain more assertions than usual about individual heroism, etc., of our troops, in which case there would be high self-indulgence as to subtopic. This would be an instance of compensation. In the case of compensation, much attention to dysphoric topics *per se* would be accompanied by highly mitigating subtopical references; in the case of cumulation, the opposite would be true.

It is clear that of the symbolic indices used in this study frankness (A) and mitigation are subtopical indices. Diversion and retrospection, on the other hand, are indices of overall attention to a subject. Frankness (B), of course, is affected to some extent by the amount of material irrelevant to the question of frankness; that is, it not only refers to the ratio of admissions and denials, but also takes account of the specific weight of admissions in the whole. Applying this distinction, we can say that the correlations so far observed indicate that the propaganda studied manifests cumulation with regard to what is said, and also cumulation *between* what is said *and* attention to causes as against effects (i.e., retrospection). In other words, there is cumulation among the different subtopical indices, and there is also cumulation between them and one subject index.

The only compensation manifested is a slight tendency to balance off self-deprivational behavior (of either of the above two kinds) by devoting less attention to the setback itself and more attention to things unconnected with the setback (i.e., diversion).[13] This diversion of attention, although it does not conform to our hypothesis about cumulation, is quite significant in confirming an hypothesis discussed more fully below (p. 362) about the use of diversion. The compensatory pattern involved here is shown by correlations between diversion and two of the other variables, mitigation and retrospection. The only significant correlation between diversion and mitigation is manifested in Right-Period elections; it amounts to —.56 (t = 2.2). If to these right period elections are added the transitional (cf. p. 338) elections, the correlation is not greatly changed, although slightly diminished to —.47 (t = 2.0). However, the residual elections, that is, the pure-left elections, now manifest a pattern extremely suggestive of cumulation. The regression line is certainly positive and, if one case were disregarded, the correlation would be significant (+.76 = 2.9), even despite the small number of cases. However, the extreme selection of cases necessary to find this correlation casts doubt upon it. In summary we can say that there is, under certain conditions, a tendency toward compensation of aggravating assertions by the diverting of attention to unconnected matters. This tendency is, however, not as clear-cut as the cumulative ones noted above.

A similar situation exists in regard to diversion and retrospection. For strikes during the Third Period, there was a positive correlation between these two indices; that is, there was compensation. This correlation is +.59 (t = 2.2) with a transitional case, and almost identical without it. In contrast to the situation above, whatever correlation between these variables exists in relation to events other than Third Period strikes, it is certainly not cumulative (i.e., negative). That is to say, there are no signs of cumulation between these two variables, although the compensatory pattern can not be demonstrated, except for Third Period strikes.

In the light of this evidence, it seems fair to conclude that, in Communist defeat-propaganda, cumulation is the dominant pattern. To give to these results their fullest significance, it would of course be necessary to have comparative results for other political movements. Obviously, none such exist as yet. Nevertheless, the pattern described can, presumably, be related to the commonly recognized propensity of the Communist movement toward various forms of extreme behavior. Numerous cases may be cited to illustrate the apparent inability of the Comintern to assume an inbetween position on any question. Before June 22, 1941, the Communist Parties in all anti-Axis countries adopted a totally oppositional attitude toward the war. In the United States, the main line of the Communist Party centered around keeping out of war; in fact the Party went so far as to say, after Molotov,[14] that the Allies were primarily responsible for the war and that Germany was striving for peace. Yet, within a matter of weeks after the invasion of Russia, they were calling on the United States and Britain "to open up a Western Front." At that time, when eighty per cent of the American public was anxious to keep out of war, most political movements making such a shift would have denied any advocacy of an expeditionary force, calling only for "aid short of war."

Another clear-cut example of extremism was the Moscow trials. Not satisfied with simply purging the "old Bolsheviks," the defendants, who had distinguished records in the Communist movement, were made to confess to fantastic crimes.

That these examples of "going the whole hog" are glaring instances of a general pattern manifested also in the minutiae of propaganda technique, is shown by the predominance of the cumulative pattern in the material here analyzed. Another clear instance is the bimodal distribution of the values of the mitigation index. The number of events in each decile of the mitigation index is 0, 0, 3, 6, 11, 4, 7, 13, 4, 4. A similar pattern is found if strikes and elections, and left and right periods, are presented separately. The bimodality is therefore not due to the juxtaposing of two normal distributions. (The frankness (A) index has an even more markedly bimodal distribution, but this may well be due, at least in part, to its method of construction.)

III. *The Communist Party and the Masses*

The current "line" of the Comintern affects the scope of objects toward which favorable attitudes are taken. As one would expect, the scope of approval is broader in Right periods. This is indicated clearly by a number of results obtained in this study. In Communist propaganda, as in war propaganda, there is a very high degree of self-enemy polarization. Whoever the devils and angels may be at any given moment, a sharp dichotomy is drawn. The actors (and targets of action) referred to in the material studied were grouped as sectors of: (a) the Communist movement, (b) the non-Communist "masses," (c) opponents within the working class movement, and (d) the bourgeoisie and its supporters. Of course, very few favorable expressions toward any sectors of (c) or (d) were found.

In the treatment of *elections,* out of a total of 253 mentions of *rival working class* actors and targets, only 28 were favorable. Of a total of 438 mentions of *bourgeois* actors and targets only 4 were favorable. Most important of all, it should be noted that these few scattered favorable items were not evenly distributed over different periods. There was none in either of the Left periods. In the early years, there were four favorable references to the British Labor Party out of 54 references to rival working class actors and targets. All the remaining favorable references to these groups were in the extremely rightist People's Front Period. In the latter, 24 out of 55 references to rival working class movements, and 4 out of 137 references to bourgeois groups, were favorable. These results clearly reflect the differing electoral policies in these different periods. Until the People's Front Period, a "lesser evil" policy was by and large excluded at the polls, even though the Communists often could not count on securing a substantial parliamentary position for themselves. In the early years, however, support—critical support—of other labor parties was occasionally allowed. But in the People's Front Period this situation was completely reversed, and the Comintern relied on blocs with other, and even bourgeois, parties against "fascism." The scope of favorably mentioned symbols broadened correspondingly.[15]

Related differentials are found in the *distribution of attention* between the four above-mentioned classes of actors and targets. That is, there are differentials not only in the favorableness of the attitude expressed, but also in the total amount said about each set of objects. In part, the latter differentials may be related to differences in "interest" in the objects in question. In general, there is greater attention to the masses in Right periods. The masses account for 14 per cent of the references to all actors and targets in Left elections, and 19 per cent in Right elections. Similarly they accounted for 49 per cent in Left strikes and 55 per cent in Right strikes.[16] (A biserial correlation between *leftness* and attention to the *masses* confirms this result in the case of elections; it amounts to −.42 (+ = 1.9).[17] The big difference in the gross percentage between strikes and elections is to be expected from the nature of the subject matter. (In elections, the parties themselves appear as the main actors; in strikes, the striking non-party workers appear as the principal actors.) However, as in the previous results, the People's Front Period shows a shaper swing to the right than any preceding period; actors and targets from the masses were 20 per cent and 61 per cent respectively, of all actors and targets in elections and strikes. (Although a biserial correlation, comparing left and right periods as wholes—parallel to the one for elections reported above—is not significant, still there is a statistically significant difference between the People's Front Period and all other periods in the mean of the index of attention to the masses. The difference is 2.5 times its standard error.*)

Similar tendencies are to be observed in an examination of references to rival working class movements. In Left years,

* Although the number of statements from the Stalin-Hitler Pact Period is not sufficient to give reliable separate results, it is worth noting that, relative to the Third Period, and in some respects even relative to the early years, if not relative to the immediately preceding People's Front Period, the epoch of the Pact seems to show the "right" characteristics. This may indicate that, in addition to the zig-zag course between Left and Right, there may be a long-term trend toward the Right. The first Right period is not as far right as the second, nor the second as far right as the third; the first Left period is further to the left than the second.

there is a tendency to concentrate on Left opponents—that is, on opponents who approach the Communist Party in radicalism; while in Right years, there is a tendency to concentrate on enemies who stand far to the Right of the Communist Party.[18] Thus, more attention is paid in Right years to those whom the C.I. would have characterized as "reformists" (i.e., Right socialists), and less attention to those whom they would have characterized as "centrists" (i.e., Left socialists or dissident Communists). "Centrists" were 2 per cent of all actors and targets in Right elections, and 5 per cent in Left elections. Reformists, on the other hand, were 15 per cent of the actors in Right elections, but only 12 per cent in Left elections. (In the case of strikes, "centrists" accounted for less than 1 per cent of the references.)

All these changes in attention correlate highly, it may be presumed, with changes in "interest." We may guess that the expanded focus of attention in Right years is related to a broadened range of interest in groups on the part of the Communists. This, in turn, is related to the widening of the scope of favorable attention in Right years.

Finally, the greater identification of the self with the masses in Right than in Left years is indicated by the inelasticity of references to the party in Left years. In other terms: in those Left cases in which more of the total space was devoted to the enemy, and thus less remained for the self, a greater proportion of the cut in the material devoted to the self came from material devoted to the masses, rather than from material devoted to the party. If we correlate the index of attention to others (extraversion) and the index of attention to the *Communist Party as against the masses*,[19] we find in the case of strikes a negative regression in Right years and a positive regression in Left and transitional years. That is to say, in Left years, attention to the enemy rises with attention to the Communist Party *as against* the masses. In Right years, the situation was reversed and material about the party showed greater elasticity. The correlations above described were, in *Right* years, —.76 (t = 4.0), and in *Left* years, +.57 (t = 2.3).

IV. *Realism* [20]

A. *Realism Through Time*

During the past two decades, there has been a decline in the degree of realism with which the Comintern met defeats. Although this hypothesis is generally accepted, it is perhaps one of the most difficult to prove; for confirmation requires indices of occurrences with which to compare indices of symbolic treatment. A comparison of this sort is practicable in regard to the amount of strike activity, on the one hand, and the volume of symbols devoted to it, on the other. It is possible to use the Internationl Labor Office statistics on number of strikes, number of strikers, and number of man-days lost through strikes, for the years between 1922 and 1938. These statistics are, unfortunately, not uniformly collected in various countries; countries differ in the method of obtaining data, in the definition of strike, and in many other details. However, for a rough index, these differences can well be overlooked. There is, however, a more serious difficulty: not all countries reported for all years. In order to overcome this obstacle, it was necessary to estimate the volume of strike activity for certain countries for certain years. If no major political event intervened in a country, it was assumed that the strike trend would reflect the world trend, and the average for that country in the immediately preceding or following years, plus or minus a correction for the world trend, was inserted. If, however, a major political event intervened, such as the coming to power of a fascist government, allowance was made.

As mentioned above, all *Inprecorr* articles referring to specific strikes were tabulated. For any given year, the proportion which they formed of the total volume of material appearing in that year (as estimated from the number of pages) was computed. The resulting index was compared with the strike statistics. It was found that a closer relation existed between the number of man-days lost from strikes and *Inprecorr* space than between the latter and either the number of strikes or the number of strikers. We therefore concentrated on the statistics for man-days lost. There is certainly a positive relationship between the number of man-

figure 19

VOLUME OF, AND ATTENTION TO, STRIKES, 1922-1938

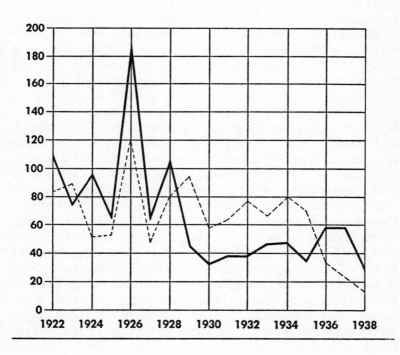

Number of man-days lost through strikes throughout the world. (In millions.)

Number of articles about strikes in the Inprecorr divided by the total number of pages. (Superimposed in the position of best fit.)

days lost in strikes and the amount of space devoted to them. What interests us, however, is not the absolute correlations, but the trend through time of deviations from the values that would exist if there were a perfect relationship. The Communists' interest in strikes is greater in Left than Right years. If, in the graph of the number of man-days lost, we superimpose in the position of best fit the graph of the number of articles devoted to strikes, we find that in Right years the symbol curve falls below the event curve, while in Left years it rises above it.[21] Only three years are exceptions to this rule, and two of them are transitional years. We may relate this differential between Left and Right periods to a difference in the importance attributed to strikes. In Left years they are presumably taken more seriously than in Right, since in Left periods there is more immediate expectation of revolutionary events which strikes are taken to herald. In Right years, the parliamentary arena is more highly valued, and consequently some attention is withdrawn from extra-political conflicts. It has often been observed that Communists tend to call strikes more hastily or, to use their own term, "adventuristically," in Left than in Right periods.

Further inspection of strike-attention curves will reveal that they are close to one another until 1928; that is, the space devoted to strikes depended, during the early years, very much on their actual volume. After 1928, the differences in both directions become much greater, indicating a decline of realism. The increasing totalitarianism of the Comintern affected this in two ways: In the first place, criticism "from below" was eliminated. In the second place, spontaneous reaction to events by the national leadership of the various Communist Parties—and indeed by all below the top leadership of the Comintern—was sharply reduced as stricter adherence was required to the "line." Whatever the causes, the fact remains that in the early years the number of man-days lost accounts for the mean ratio of the difference between the two curves to the amount of *Inprecorr* space (.40 to 1 in the early years, .69 to 1 in the Third Period, and 1.03 to 1 in the People's Front Period.) [22] This indicates that the space devoted to strikes in the International Press correspondence was decreasingly dependent on the actual number of strikes.

A decline in realism may also be indicated by a diminishing frequency of self-deprivational references (discussed below).[23] Since we are dealing exclusively with defeats, there is certainly a very close and direct relation between realism and self-deprivation. But it may be validly objected that simply to show an increase in symbolic behaviors tending to reduce dysphoria is not in itself a proof of declining realism. It is not such a proof *unless* it can also be shown that there has been no corresponding trend in the character of the defeats themselves. In the case of elections, no time trend is visible for the "severity" index.[24] In the case of strikes, however, there may be a trend toward decreasing severity of defeats,[25] although it is far from significant in our data. Some caution is indicated as to deciding whether the observed decrease in self-deprivation in regard to strikes indicates declining realism.

If we infer greater realism in Left than in Right years from the greater self-deprivation of Left years (cf. p. 357), similar reservations apply.

B. *Realism about Strikes and Elections*

The realism of Communist propaganda is higher in regard to strikes than with respect to elections. This stands out most clearly in the frankness index. For elections, there is no correlation at all between the severity of defeats and frankness about them. On the other hand, there is a biserial correlation of as high as $+.96$ ($t = 13.71$) between severity and frankness (A) in the case of strikes. (It amounts to $+.77$ ($t = 5.92$) for the frankness (B) index.)

In Appendix I, it is explained that serious strike defeats were divided into two groups, according to the severity of defeat. This gives us a total of three grades of severity. Computing the correlations with three categories, instead of two (by the usual techniques for correlating quantitative variables divided into unequally and indeterminately spaced intervals), we obtain the following results: There is a correlation of $+.51$ ($t = 3.6$) between severity of strike defeats and the frankness (A) index. There is a correlation of $+.71$ ($t = 6.7$) between severity and the frankness (B) index.

Correlating severity and mitigation we get results similar to, but less striking than, those for severity and frankness, above. For elections, there is no significant correlation. However, the presence of a negative correlation of $-.34$ (t $= 1.7$) probably indicates some measure of realism even for elections. The correlations in the case of strikes are, however, far more clear-cut, and support our hypothesis. The biserial correlation is $-.49$ (t $= 3.06$). The correlation using three grades of severity is $-.67$ (t $= 5.7$). Thus, although the degree of mitigation may be somewhat less in more severe defeats of both kinds, the extent of such realism is apparently greater after strikes.

Also, confirmatory of the hypothesis that there is greater realism in regard to strikes than with respect to elections is the positive correlation of $+.45$ (t $= 2.4$) between severity and diversion in the case of elections. The more severe the defeat, the greater the attention to matters not connected with it. In the case of strikes this tendency, if it existed at all, was certainly not of sufficient magnitude to be significantly established with this sample.

The only available evidence in the other direction is the relationship of severity to retrospection. There is no significant correlation between retrospection and severity in either strikes or elections as wholes, although in both cases there is a slight positive relationship between these variables. However, if one group of three cases clustered far from all others is eliminated, a just significant correlation of $+.45$ (t $= 2.1$) does exist in the case of elections. Such a correlation would not stand up as confirmatory evidence for the hypothesis under investigation, but should perhaps be reported as evidence to the contrary.

In addition to severity, other characteristics of defeats which might affect their treatment were considered. Among these was the amount of forceful repression engaged in by the enemy. That this variable had no ascertainable effect may perhaps be explained by the existence of counteracting tendencies.[26] Under conditions of much violence the propagandist may, on the one hand, believe that little dysphoria on the part of his audience is caused by frankness (and other self-deprivational behavior), since *force majeure* can plausibly be held responsible for the defeat. On the other hand, the presence of repression makes more plausible the claim that "we" have not lost strength, since repression makes political behavior more covert and more open to unverifiable assertions. Such counteracting tendencies tend to eliminate ascertainable effect on the variables studied.

Also without influence was the magnitude of the occurrences involved. The size of the country having an election, the number of men involved in a strike, or its length, might be expected to affect its treatment (at least the amount of space). However, within the limits set by the size of our sample and the types of events studied, this was not the case. Of course, this does not mean that no such tendencies exist; they undoubtedly do. We can be certain that silence is not as likely in regard to an election in the United States as in Luxembourg. However, such relationships were insufficiently strong to be revealed in this limited study. This may be partly explained by the hypothesis that, among the factors entering into the propagandist's use of any given event, its effect on the general political scene ranks below the facility with which it lends itself to an interpretation conforming to the aims of the propagandist. For this reason, great attention may be devoted to small events. Thus, in a number of Third Period election reports, as much (or more) attention was paid to a campaign meeting at which Social-Democratic workers expressed dissatisfaction with their own party (and approval of the Communists) as was devoted to the actual election returns.

There was an additional defeat characteristic, however, which did affect the treatment of strikes. The more hostile the attitude of the non-Communist labor movement toward a strike, the greater was the frankness in regard to its failure. This is obviously to be explained by the fact that the propagandist would feel less dsyphoria in making an admission, or would expect the admission to cause less dsyphoria in his audience, when it could be plausibly argued that a "betrayal" was responsible. (Propagandas of states defeated in war frequently manifest similar behavior. It is seldom conceded that the enemy won by virtue of greater strength; this is an extremely dysphoric theme. Rather, it is asserted that the defeat was the result of a stab in the back by some group of traitors who ought to have been on "our" side.) Thus, frankness was greater about Communist strike defeats in which the regular trade-union leadership fought the strike than about those in which the strike was supported by the non-Communist unionists: there is a negative biserial correlation of—.42 ($t = 2.2$) between frankness (A) and degree of support by non-Communists.

No comparable situation existed in the case of elections, since in the latter any kind of coalition was very rare.

Further evidence of greater realism about strike, than about election, defeats is the fact that the mean frankness (A) index is higher in the case of strikes than in the case of elections; the differences is 1.9 times the standard error of the difference.[27] This can hardly be explained as reflecting a difference in the average severity of strike defeats ahead of election defeats (as measured by an "objective" observer). It should be noted that a frankness (A) index below 50 indicates an actual predominance of denials over admissions. In view of the fact that we are dealing with defeats exclusively, and that all the indices are low—42 and 65 for elections and strikes, respectively—we may consider greater frankness as indicating greater realism.

It is not plausible, either, to assume that there is a constant difference in the Communist's own evaluation of the importance of strikes as against elections. (If this were true, one might explain the difference in realism observed by the greater importance attributed to elections.) As we mentioned above (p. 350), and as we shall further see below (p. 363), any such differential in evaluation is limited to Right years; in Left years, if anything, the opposite is true. Yet greater realism in regard to strikes was by no means limited to Right years. Two possible explanations, by no means mutually exclusive, come to mind. In the first place, election defeats are defeats of the party itself, whereas strike defeats, even when equally serious to the Communist Party, can be portrayed as caused by, and primarily affecting, the masses and the non-Communist element. Such a portrayal would, of course, reduce the negative impact of frankness. This, in turn, enables the propagandist to be more realistic.

The second explanation depends upon the hypothesis to be presented next: namely, that self-deprivation varies directly with leftness. If this is true, and if it is also true that elections are more highly evaluated in Right years, and strikes more highly in Left ones, then we may make the following surmise: In Right years, when self-indulgence prevails, elections, being more highly evaluated, are more indulgently (and therefore less realistically) treated than strikes. In Left years, strikes are more highly evaluated, but since self-deprivation prevails, they are not much more indulgently treated than elections. Presumably, one characteristic of a more self-negative propaganda is that the highly evaluated fields are not treated more indulgently than the less highly evaluated ones. Thus, the effect of the Right years on the total self-deprivation, in regard to strikes and elections combined, is not fully counteracted in Left years.[28] *

The low degree of realism of at least large sectors of Communist propaganda may be further explained by the "dogmatism" of the Comintern—the high degree of importance attached to conformity to accepted symbols, and reluctance on the part of leaders to change these symbols or to recognize their own fallibility. As a result, Comintern propagandists emitted statements that conformed closely to certain symbolic norms (the general "line" of the moment). Such high conformity leaves little scope for variations according to actual circumstances; at least, in the case of elections, this was observed to be the case.

V. *Self-indulgence Differentials*

A. *By Periods*

The statement that "one defeat propaganda is more (or less) self-indulgent than another" may refer to any one of at least four aspects of the propaganda involved.[29] We have already mentioned the distinction between "aggravating" assertions (measured by the frankness and mitigation indices), on the one hand, and the directing of attention to certain subtopics (measured by the diversion, and retrospection indices, and silence), on the other. In the third place, if aggravating assertions are made about actors belonging to the

---

* The above explanations are relevant only insofar as realism in regard to defeats is self-deprivational. This is generally so, but as we have seen it is certainly not true of all aspects of realism and illusionism. However, our own study uses indices referring to those kinds of realism which, as a matter of fact, are also self-deprivational. It is impossible, on the basis of the present results, to say whether the contrast also holds for kinds of realism which are independent of self-deprivational references.

figure **20**

EXAMPLE OF CORRELATION PROCEDURES

(Self-indulgence differentials between
Left years and Right and
Marginal Left years.)

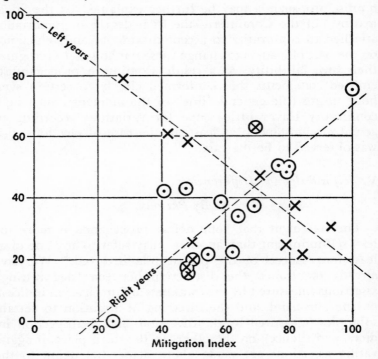

Introversion:
The Communist Party as
against the enemy

Mitigation Index

✕ Left years.
⊙ Right years
⊗ Marginal Left years (grouped with
Right years in this correlation)

nonfocal parts of the self (e.g., to the masses rather than the party) or to the enemy, and the assertions with regard to Communist actors are mitigating, then, in all probability, the negative impact of the assertions on a sympathetic audience will be smaller than if the ratio of mitigating and aggravating assertions remained the same but the actors mentioned were reversed. To call the same event "a defeat for the working class," or even "a victory for the bourgeoisie," is not as conducive to dysphoria by Communists as to call it "a defeat for the Communist party."

Fourthly, we may refer to certain relationships between the values of different indices. This may be illustrated with reference to the hypothesis already mentioned: that the symbolic behavior of Right years is more self-indulgent (less self-negative) than that of Left years. This is to some extent true for propaganda about both strike and election defeats, though to a greater extent in the case of the latter. In the case of elections, we find a difference between Left and Right years in the relationship between the diversion and mitigation indices. There is, in Right years, as we noted above (p. 343), a negative correlation between these variables of —.56 (t = 2.2), and in Right plus marginal left years a negative correlation of —.47 (t + 2.0). In other words, the more said about focal events, the more mitigation of what is said. This is self-indulgent behavior.

In pure Left years the opposite is true, but the relationship is not quite so clear, since it is necessary to exclude certain cases (which is hardly desirable, in view of the small number). Three of the Left election defeats were accompanied by the rather extensive use of forcible repression against the Communists. In these cases, there was somewhat less diversion and rather more mitigation than when relative freedom prevailed. To state the situation a little more accurately: With or without repressive measures against the Party, there is a positive correlation between diversion and mitigation in Left elections; the regression lines are roughly parallel, insofar as it is possible to tell with such small numbers. However, the "a" values are different in the two circumstances. Where repressive acts took place, a given amount of mitigation was accompanied by less diversion than when there were none. This can probably be attributed to the fact that such mitigatory themes as "the enemy used immoral methods" or "their methods show that they are really afraid of us" often are more plausible in the case of overt violence. There is therefore less need to divert attention.

If we exclude all the Left elections marked by repression, the correlation between mitigation and diversion amounts to +.94 (t = 5.3). If we exclude only the election most deviant from the usual pattern, the German election of March 1933 (after the Reichstag fire and the illegalization of the Communists by Hitler), the correlation is +.76 (t = 2.9). The relationship between Right and Left years may, in general, be described by saying that Left periods manifest less self-indulgence (more self-deprivation) than Right ones.

In case of strikes no relation exists between the above two variables. Furthermore, one of the instances of discomfirmatory evidence, in regard to the major hypothesis under consideration (that of higher self-deprivation in Left periods), appears in reference to strikes. There is in the extreme-Left Third Period a positive correlation, between diversion and retrospection, of +.59 (t = 2.7). In Left years, as a whole, a similar correlation is found, and is significant; however, it is exclusively due to the Third Period, which includes most Left strikes. In Right years, the same tendency operates to some extent, though not significantly. Thus, the qualifying hypothesis—about the lesser difference between Left and Right periods in the treatment of strikes than in the treatment of elections—is supported.

Let us summarize this illustration of the fourth kind of self-indulgence: The hypotheses, we repeat, are, (a) that the symbolic behavior of Right years is more self-indulgent, and (b) that this differential is clear-cut in the case of elections, but slight in the case of strikes. (1) A negative correlation between diversion and mitigation is self-indulgent. Such a correlation exists in Right elections; a positive correlation (self-deprivation) exists in Left elections. No significant correlations exist for strikes. (2) A positive correlation of diversion and retrospection is self-indulgent. There are no significant correlations of these for elections, but there is a positive (self-indulgent) one for Left-period strikes.

In the case of elections, Right years clearly manifest more self-indulgence of this form than Left. In the case of strikes, the major hypothesis is not confirmed; rather, the evidence points in the other direction, but not significantly.

Let us now see if our hypotheses are confirmed by the data about the third type of self-indulgence, that involving the degree of introversion (or extroversion). First, there is some reason to believe that in Right years attention to the enemy, as contrasted with the self, varies directly as the diversion index; whereas, in Left periods, it varies inversely to it. This is a case in which the hypothesis of greater self-deprivation in Left years seems to lack support, for it is in Left years that statements about relatively innocuous, unrelated events are centered around the self. Interestingly enough, the exception here, as in practically all exceptional cases,[30] involves a special pattern, a mode of diversion that apparently differs from other forms of self-indulgence. The exceptions themselves thus seem to provide the following suggestion for a further general hypothesis about this variable: Whenever the structure of a symbol system is such as to prohibit or reduce the use of appropriate *symbolic* devices to serve a given end, the chances are increased that the device of silence will be used.

It should, however, be noted that the evidence on the above relation between diversion and extraversion is only moderately substantial.[31] In the case of elections, a positive correlation of +.66 (t = 2.6) exists in Right years if one case is excluded (the German election of 1924), and its exclusion is not entirely arbitrary. As was mentioned in the Introduction, although we handle the early years as a single period on grounds of homogeneity, in comparison with subsequent periods, there were important zigzags within the early years also. The year marking the formation of the International (which occurred before any of the events here studied) and 1924 are the Left years. The latter was the year of the Fifth World Congress of the Comintern which took a sharp turn to the left.[32] This followed the 1923 débâcle of the German Communist Party, one immediate result of which was the ousting of the Right German Communist Party leadership and replacement with a Left one. For these reasons, the non-conformity of the treatment of the German election defeat of 1924 with the Right-period pattern is understandable. The Left elections showed no uniform pattern whatsoever.

In the case of strikes, there is a correlation of a self-indulgent character between diversion and extraversion only in Left years. This amounts to —.68 (t = 2.9), again if one case is excluded. But, this time, the only justification for exclusion is the relatively small number of statements involved. The Right years show no hint of any pattern.

Thus, while our hypothesis about diversion is somewhat supported, our hypotheses about self-indulgence in Right and Left periods, and strikes and elections, are by the same token contradicted. The only self-indulgent correlation occurred among Left-period strikes, the only self-deprivational one among Right-period elections.

Although these relationships between diversion and extraversion seem partly to contradict the main hypotheses of this section, the relationships between diversion and attention given to the masses confirm them. In the case of Right-year elections, again excluding Germany in May 1924, there is a negative correlation of —.80 (t = 4.0) between diversion and attention to the masses. On the other hand, for Left elections there is a positive correlation of +.55 (t = 2.2). Thus, in Right elections the smaller the degree of diversion, that is, the more references to the setback itself, the more of what was said was about the masses; in Left years, the opposite was true. The masses are a part of the self, but not the central part. Statements about the masses were an alternaive form of self-reference to statements about the Communist Party. That is, it is less humiliating to refer to a defeat for the working class than a defeat for the Communist Party. The data just mentioned show that in Right years this device was often used; not so, however, in Left years.

Bringing out the same point even more clearly, similar correlations exist between the index of attention to the Communist movement as against the masses (rather than simply attention to the masses) and diversion. In Right elections, excluding Germany in 1924, there is a positive correlation of +.79 (t = 3.6)); in Left elections (with one case excluded) there is a negative correlation of —.73 (t = 3.2). Thus, the smaller the degree of diversion in Right years, the more attention was shifted from focal to peripheral actors; *vice versa* in Left years.

Significantly, there is little confirming evidence on this

point as to strikes, implying again that the hypothesized relationship between leftness and self-deprivation is less marked for such defeats. Only in the Third Period does any correlation show up, and this one is somewhat questionable, as here again one case based on a small number of statements must be excluded. The correlation is between diversion and attention to the Communist movement as against the masses; it is, of course, negative, amounting to $-.67$ ($t = 2.6$). The inclusion or exclusion of a transitional case has no substantial effect.

Retrospection is related to extraversion in only one limited case and, there, contrary to the general rule. In Left-period strikes there is a positive correlation between retrospection and attention to other of $+.72$ ($t = 3.3$). This concentration on others, when engaged in the unpleasant task of retrospection, is self-indulgent behavior. (There is no discernible relationship between these variables under other conditions.) This exception may be explained in terms of a previously mentioned hypothesis. It was mentioned that in Left periods there is a narrower scope of identification than in Right ones. Correspondingly, in Right years, Communists work much more closely with the regular trade-union leadership than in Left years, when they often attack it sharply, even going so far at times as to form separate Communist unions. Thus, in Left strikes there was more of a tendency than in Right strikes to place the responsibility for causing the defeat on the trade-union bureaucracy, a fact which may explain the correlation just mentioned.

The behavior of the mitigation index, perhaps the most important of all, strikingly confirms the hypothesis that Left periods manifest greater self-deprivation than Right ones. In the case of elections in Right and marginal Left years, we find that there is a positive correlation of $+.80$ ($t = 5.0$) between mitigation and attention to the Communist movement as against attention to the enemy.[33] Thus, the more pleasant the things said, the more likely were they to be about the self rather than about the enemy. On the other hand, in pure Left years the correlation was negative, and amounted to $-.77$ ($t = 3.2$). Indeed, if one case based on relatively few statements is excluded, the value is $-.96$ ($t = 8.3$). Thus, in Left years the more unfavorable the things said, the more likely were they to be about the self. In the case of strikes the same tendency existed, but again on a lesser scale. There is a correlation in pure Right years of +.81 (t = 4.7) between the two variables under consideration. However, in Left years the expected relationship does not appear; the distribution is very much at random.

The differences in the distribution of attention between the self and the masses, under varying conditions of mitigation, parallel very closely the above differences in distribution of attention between the self and the enemy. Thus in pure Left elections there is a negative correlation (a self-deprivational relationship) between mitigation on the one hand, and the relative attention to the Communist Party as against attention to the masses, on the other, of —.82 (t = 3.7). This time, it is in the case of elections that the opposite trend for the other periods is not significant. In the case of strikes, however, we find a very clear-cut relationship. For Left and marginal strikes, there is a negative correlation between these variables of —.78 (t = 4.1), and in the case of pure Right strikes there is a positive correlation of +.67 (t = 3.1).

All in all, eleven correlations confirm the hypothesis that in Right years dysphoric symbolism was shifted from the Communist Party to the masses and the enemy, while in Left years the shift did not occur. Three correlations, however, point in the opposite direction. Two of these, it should be noted, involve diversion; also, two of them apply to strike situations.

Our general hypothesis that Communist propaganda is more self-deprivational in Left than in Right years is also confirmed by differences in the distribution of attention between subtopics connected and unconnected with defeats (i.e., the second above-mentioned aspect of propaganda relevant to self-indulgence). There is a biserial correlation of —.86 (t = 7.82) between leftness and diversion, in the case of elections. This is direct evidence for the greater self-indulgence of Right years. A related piece of evidence, which is, however, of dubious value, concerns the distribution of silence about defeat. There were five cases of silence about Right strikes, and only one about a Left strike. In the case of elections, Right silences outnumbered Left ones by only 3 to 2.

The numbers are too small to have any statistical significance; however, the strike figures would be suggestive, were
it not that they may be equally well explained as an aspect
of the lower attention to strikes (whether defeats or victories)
characteristic of Right years.[34]

Perhaps, before going on to discuss the significance of the
hypothesis we have been investigating, it would be well to
summarize briefly all evidence relevant to it. In regard to the
relationship between mitigation and diversion, there is considerable positive evidence for our hypothesis, in the case of
elections. In the case of strikes, what little evidence there is
runs rather in the other direction. Also, the centering of
dysphoric behavior around the most focal actor, the self, is
found to be more common in Left than in Right periods.
This is strikingly shown by the relationship between mitigation and introversion. The hypothesis holds up here for both
strikes and elections, and as regards both the enemy and the
masses. The relationship between diversion and extraversion
tends to disconfirm the hypothesis, but the relationship between diversion and attention to the masses supports it.
Retrospection shows a significant tendency in Third Period
strikes opposite to that predicted. Finally, the correlation
between diversion and leftness strongly supports the hypothesis.

The two most suggestive parts of the confirmatory evidence
are the evidence of the mitigation index, and the negative
correlation between leftness and diversion. The three pieces
of counterevidence, although all statistically more doubtful
than the important pieces of confirmatory evidence, force us
to modify the general hypothesis to the extent of recognizing
the lesser degree to which it applies to strikes, and the frequent occurrence of opposite behavior in connection with
diversion.

A number of explanations of greater self-deprivation in
Left periods suggest themselves. Among these we consider:
(1) the higher evaluation in Right periods than in Left of
immediate, partial objectives as against ultimate, total objectives; (2) the greater importance attached in Right periods
to mass support; (3) the prevalence, in Left periods, of the
belief that things must become worse before they can become

better; and (4) the greater "negativity" of Left-period propaganda. Let us consider these explanations in order:

(1) Perhaps the first thing that would come to most people's minds upon mention of the terms "Right" and "Left," in connection with the Comintern, is the proximate or ultimate character of the goals most emphasized. It is true that, while immediate goals are frequently changed, none of the ultimate objectives are ever formally taken off the books. However, the stress put on them changes markedly. Thus, in the Third Period, slogans embodying the full revolutionary goal were daily fare. Among these were such slogans as "For a Soviet U.S.A." and "Forward to the German October." In the People's Front Period, such goals were relegated to study classes, and mass propaganda called only for such ends as "An anti-fascist People's Front" and "collective security."

One factor which may have been a major cause of the Third Period Left turn, and which in any case reinforced its "ultimatistic" tendencies, was the lessened interest of the Soviet regime in foreign affairs during those years. Hence, the immediate tasks assigned to the Comintern by the Russian regime were reduced. Hope of effective relief by revolutions abroad, prevalent in the early years, had largely evaporated by 1928. Until the middle of the second Five-Year Plan, the regime turned its energies toward internal tasks. Only after the rise of Hitler to power, and the reëmergence of immediate danger of attack by foreign powers, did the Soviet élite again become intensely interested in foreign affairs; and the Comintern at once raised a number of immediate slogans to help realize the foreign policy aims of the Soviet Union.

(2) As more importance is attached to immediate aims in Right periods, more importance also attaches to large-scale mass support; in Left periods, the "vanguard" rôle of the Communist movement is stressed. Turns from Left to Right periods have been marked by such slogans as "To the masses," which heralded the first important turn to the right initiated at the Third World Congress in the summer of 1921.

Lesser attachment to immediate aims, and lower evaluation of mass support in Left periods, tend to reduce dysphoria about defeat. In themselves, the objectives lost appear to be of less value, and the decline in mass support, whether implied in the defeat (as in elections) or a likely concomitant of it, may even receive a positive interpretation as emphasizing the "vanguard" rôle of Communists.

(3) The Left variant of Communist ideology reinforces these tendencies by emphasizing the theme that things must get worse before they can get better, whereas the Right variant is characterized by at least a modicum of gradualist optimism. In Left periods, pessimism about the immediate future diminishes the dysphoria of the propagandist, or of his audience, where symbols are handled self-negatively. It would therefore be a contributing cause of such behavior.

(4) In addition, the familiar "down with" character of Communist propaganda is more marked in Left than in Right periods. This in part explains why, in Left periods, mitigating assertions tend to be about the enemy; they take the form of asserting deprivations suffered by the other, rather than indulgences enjoyed by the self. It may also partly explain the more abundant self-deprivations that appear in Left periods, since in these periods the negative, critical attitude of the Communist movement can be assimilated even to statements about the self. This would not be surprising, in view of the extreme uniformity of Communist propaganda at any given time.

The fact that the self-indulgence differential between Right and Left periods is larger in the treatment of elections than in the treatment of strikes, may be related to different evaluations of parliamentary and strike arenas. We noted above (p. 354) that strikes are more highly evaluated in Left than in Right years, and elections in Right than in Left years. It may be assumed that in most propaganda situations, other things being equal, the more highly a sphere is evaluated, the more self-indulgently it will be treated. At the same time, for the reasons just discussed, the propagandist is likely to be less sedulous in minimizing self-negative references, in regard to the favored field, in Left than in Right years. The result is that the difference between the treatment of elections as the less favored sphere in the less indulgent Left periods and their treatment as the more favored sphere in the more indulgent Right years, is greater than the difference between the treatment of strikes as the less favored sphere in the more indulgent Right years and their treatment as the more favored sphere in the less indulgent Left years.[35]

B. *Self-indulgence Differentials Through Time*

In addition to the alternations from period to period, there seems to have been a long-term trend toward decreasing self-deprivation. This may be related to the long-term trend toward the Right noted above (cf. p. 346). The present hypothesis would then be a corollary of the preceding one. The trend toward decreasing self-deprivation may also be related to a trend toward decreasing realism (cf. p. 348). These two variables are logically quite unrelated, but of course low realism more often takes the form of pro-self than anti-self illusions.

In addition to evidence which has been presented for the above associated trends, some of which indirectly confirms this hypothesis, there are two pieces of direct evidence. There is a markedly increasing trend in the number of silences about strike defeats. As noted before, silences occur almost exclusively in Right years; and within Right years, they are found in the People's Front Period rather than in the early years. In our sample, there was one silence for eleven strikes in the early years, and the same number in the Third Period; but four silences out of nine strikes occurred in the People's Front Period.

There also seems to have been a decline in the frankness index for strikes. The mean frankness (B) index is lower in the second decade studied than in the first, by 1.8 times the standard error of the difference between the means.[36]

VI. *Conclusion*

This study has to some degree confirmed the existence of several long-term trends in Communist propaganda in reaction to defeat, particularly the trend of decreasing realism and increasing self-indulgence.

Also observed were certain recurrent mechanisms. Among these is the pattern of cumulation, which probably contributes greatly to the extremist appearance of Communist propaganda activity. In situations in which other movements would attempt to present a balanced picture, counterposing the "good" to the "bad," Communist propagandists tend to present events as almost entirely favorable or almost entirely unfavorable.

We also found that, when the structure of a symbol system is such as to reduce the use of appropriate symbolic devices for a given end, the chances are increased that the device of silence will be used.

The third major pattern observed was the extreme divergence between the propagandas of Left and Right periods. The influence of such factors, taken together with the very small influence of "objective" variables, such as the magnitude of the defeat in question, is largely responsible for the usual characterization of Communist propaganda as "dogmatic."

The differences between Left and Right periods manifest themselves in a number of interrelated ways.

It was found that the scope of objects toward which favorable attitudes were taken was greater in Right than in Left periods.

It was found, too, that the treatment of defeats was less self-indulgent, and more realistic, in Left than in Right years. The same can be said about strikes as contrasted with elections.

Finally, it was found that the difference between Left and Right years was smaller in the treatment of strikes than in the treatment of elections (See above, page 354). In explanation of these facts, we adduced the hypothesis that Communists evaluate the importance of strike results more highly in Left years and election results more highly in Right years. Without the possibility of conducting psychological tests on the propagandists, this hypothesis can not be fully confirmed, and certainly we can not, without such additional experiments, measure *exactly* the differences involved.

In order to illustrate the relationships between some of the hypotheses listed above, we shall use some diagrams, even though we can not assign numerical values. Let us construct a graph, the x-axis of which represents the evaluation assigned by the propagandist to any class of events, and the y-axis of which represents self-deprivation. For the time being, no correct numerical values can be assigned along the two axes. However, we can utilize the "greater than"-"less than" relationships listed in the above hypotheses.[37] On the basis of these, we can place four points, approximately: Left strikes, Right strikes; Left elections, Right elections.

For Right years, it may be safely assumed that the greater the valuation of a sphere, the greater the self-indulgence in its treatment. Strikes (S) and elections (E) will therefore appear on the graph as follows:

Self-
indulgence   (E)
                (S)
            Evaluation

Left years are marked by less self-indulgence. This might imply either of two kinds of graph patterns: Conceivably a propaganda might be so "masochistic" that the higher the evaluation of a field, the less the self-indulgence in regard to it. This would give us a negative regression line:

Self-
indulgence   (E)
                    (S)
            Evaluation

There is no reason, however, to believe that even Left-period Communist propaganda is, as a whole, that extreme. Indeed, this assumption would fail to explain our results. The more moderate assumption that does explain them is this: There is a positive correlation in Left periods, too, between evaluation and self-indulgence of treatment, but the regression line is less steep than in Right periods. That is to say, a given increase in evaluation results in a smaller increase in self-indulgence in Left than in Right periods.[38]

Self-   Self-   (E)
indulgence   indulgence
                (S)   (S)
        (E)

    20   60   20   60
    Evaluation   Evaluation
      LEFT   RIGHT

It is assumed here that strikes are more highly evaluated than elections in Left years, and elections more highly than strikes in Right ones; and that the difference between their evaluations is constant.

An inspection of these graphs shows that greater self-indulgence would be associated with any given amount of evaluation in Right than in Left periods. However, one of the hypotheses above was that there is greater evaluation of immediate objectives, in general (including both strikes and elections), in Right than in Left years. Let us therefore move both strikes and elections, in Right years, say, 20 points on the evaluation scale. This would increase the self-indulgence with which they would be treated.

We now have a model which fits the hypothesis stated above. If this model represents the actual situation, then:

(1) The difference in the treatment of strikes, as between Right and Left years, would be smaller than the difference in the treatment of elections.

(2) There would be a higher average self-indulgence for elections than for strikes.

Both of these implications, as well as the assumptions upon which the model was constructed, correspond to generalizations derived from the data here studied.

The situation is, however, complex. Not all the observed interrelations of variables provide evidence for these hypotheses.[39] Furthermore, as noted above, no way has been indicated to generalize, from the different indices, a single composite self-indulgence index without introducing arbitrary elements. Consequently, the study must leave the above pattern as an hypothesis, suggested by, and explanatory of, our results, but far from adequately confirmed.

Self-
indulgence (E_r)

          (E_l) (S_r) (S_l)

          20   40   60   80   100
                      Evaluation

Appendices to Chapter 12

APPENDIX I

Definitions of Variables Studied

BELOW ARE the definitions of the indices used in this study. The values of each of these indices apply to the individual "setback" as a unit (e.g., a given setback may show a frankness /A/ of .70). The non-symbolic indices measure characteristics of the event and its conditions; the symbolic indices measure characteristics of the things said about the defeat within the sample studied. (For the reasons for applying the symbolic indices solely to the whole treatment of a given setback, see Note 17).

A. *Non-symbolic variables*

1. Severity of setback:

Elections: The severity index was defined as the difference between the following two sums: (1) the percentage which the vote received by the Communist Party formed of the total vote cast in the election involved, and (2) the corresponding percentage in the previous election for the same offices.

Strikes: An impressionistic characterization of each defeat as "very severe," "severe," or "slight" was made on the basis of information, from newspaper and other sources, about the terms of the settlement and the effects of the defeat upon the labor movement. For some purposes, the two grades of "severe" defeats were combined for comparison with the "slight" ones.

2. Repression:

An impressionistic characterization was made of the amount of violence used in the event. A dichotomous distinction was used for elections (much, little), a trichotomous one for strikes (much, medium, little).

3. Magnitude:

Elections: The population of the country involved was the index of magnitude.

Strikes: Three indices were used: (a) the number of strikers, (b) the duration of the strike, (c) the number of man-days lost. Estimates, rather than exact figures, were usually unavoidable.

4. Attitude of the non-Communist labor movement toward the strike:

An impressionistic characterization was made of the relations between Communists and non-Communists, according to the following typology: "Cooperation in a single union," "a single union with the non-Communists supporting the strike, but opposing the Communist leadership," "two unions, one Communist, the other not, but both striking together," "only one union in the field of the strike, but the non-Communists opposing both the Communist leadership and the strike itself," "two opposed unions in the field, one Communist and conducting the strike, the other non-Communist and opposing the strike." For some purposes, the last two cases in which the non-Communist unionists opposed the strikes were combined, as were the first three cases, in all of which the non-Communists supported the strike. (N.B. By "non-Communists" we refer to the regular leadership of the trade-union movement, particularly to the part of it directly concerned with the strike involved, but also to the leaders of national trade-union federations, etc.)

5. Leftness:
The periods described above (cf. p. 338) were separated into Left and Right years—the early years, the People's Front Period and the war period being classified as Right, and the Third Period and Stalin-Hitler Pact Period as Left.

B. *Symbolic variables*

1. Frankness:
Frankness (A): In the outline of symbols studied (cf. Appendix II) are contained, among others, the following classes of statements: "Advance asserted" (139), "Setback admitted" (2x), "Advance denied" (170x), and "Setback denied" (40). If these statements were explicit and applied to the whole situation, they were given a weight of 4. If they applied only to one locality (e.g., "In the town of X we gained a large number of votes"), they were given a weight of 1. If they were implicit, they were also given a weight of 1. Implicit assertions were not counted in this study, except for implicit admissions or denials of defeat, and even here only if necessary to maintain the coherence of the text analyzed. (An example of such a situation is the type of article which lists as causes of the "results" a set of adverse circumstances, but fails to say explicitly that the results were a setback.) The weighted sum of admissions of setback plus denials of advance was then divided by the weighted sum of all four of the above-mentioned categories, in order to define the Frankness (A) index.

Frankness (B): All statements under the section of the outline "about the setback itself" entered into this index. They were classified as admissions, denials or neutral. As in the Frankness (A) index, they were weighted for explicitness and geographic scope. These weightings were multiplied by another set of weightings, ranging from 4 to 0.5, according to the degree of frankness or unfrankness of that class of assertions. For example, items under the category "setback denied" were weighted 4, while assertions that the "setback is not important" or "of small magnitude" were rated as denials, with a weight of 1.

It was also desired to take account of the weight of admissions and denials in the text as a whole. The index was therefore obtained by dividing not only by the sum of the weighted statements entering it, but also by the total number of statements occurring. A number of formulae fulfilling this requirement might be suggested, but the best proved to be the Janis-Fadner "Coefficient of Imbalance." The equation for this coefficient is $f^2 = fu/rt$. In this equation, f stands for the number of statements (or other symbols) in one cell of a dichotomy (in this case admissions); u stands for the number of statements in its other cell (in this case denials); r stands for the number of relevant statements, that is, the sum of f and u and neutral statements; and t stands for the total number of statements, relevant or not. This formula was designed to meet a number of criteria, such that it fits closely the usual meaning of "partiality" or "imbalance" in everyday language. This formula is described by its inventors in *Psychometrika*, Vol. VIII (June, 1943), pp. 105-119. Reproduced as Chapter VIII of the present volume.

2. Mitigation:

All categories of the outline were divided into the following three groups: those the exposure to which, it was presumed, would ordinarily tend to *decrease* the dysphoria felt by a sympathetic audience about the defeat; those the exposure to which, it was presumed, would ordinarily tend to *increase* its dysphoria; and those not readily classifiable into either of the above groups. The index was defined by the percentages which statements in categories of the first of these groups formed of the total of statements in categories of both the first and second groups.

Modified mitigation index: For correlations of mitigation with frankness, a mitigation index was used, derived in the same way as above, except that statements from the section of the outline "about the setback itself" (on which the frankness index is based) were excluded.

3. Retrospection:

The percentage which statements under the outline section "about causes of the setback" formed of the total of these statements, plus statements under the outline section "about effects of the setback," determined the index of retrospection.

4. Diversion:

The percentage which statements under the outline section

"about matters not connected with the setback" formed of the total of these statements, plus statements under the outline section "about the setback itself," defined the index of diversion.

Modified diversion index: The percentage which statements in categories of the outline section "about matters not connected with the setback" formed of all statements was used instead of the above in those correlations in which the other variable was dependent on the frequency of statements "about the setback itself" (e.g., Frankness (B)).

5. Indices of attention to different actors:

a. Attention to the Communist Party (introversion)

b. Attention to the masses

c. Attention to the enemy (extraversion)

Each of these three indices is defined by the percentage of all statements formed by the statements having subjects of the kind in question, i.e., falling under the corresponding sections of the "actor code" in the outline.

d. Attention to the Communist Party as against attention to the masses: The percentage which statements in which Communist Party actors were the subjects formed of the total of these statements, plus statements in which actors of the masses were the subjects.

e. Attention to the Communist Party as against attention to the enemy: The percentage which statements in which Communist Party actors were the subjects formed of the total of these statements, plus statements in which enemy actors were the subjects.

APPENDIX II

Examples of Categories From Analysis Outline

Part 1. *Statements Made*

N.B. The serial numbers were the numbers entered in recording the occurrence of a statement. The outline letters and numbers simply serve to indicate the structure of the list. Thus, headings may occur, for structural reasons, to which no counted statements correspond, and which therefore have no marginal number. Aggravatory assertions are indicated by an *x*. A *v* or *w* means indeterminateness in this respect.

Section   I—Statements about the setback itself:
                 I Description of event
                 II Statements about the event

2x A Setback admitted

3   1. Setback affects only small sectors of the self. 3x Large.

5   3. Setback is not important. 5x is important.

9   4. Setback is of small magnitude. 9x Large.

10   5. Setback is corrigible. 10x Incorrigible.

6. Time characteristics of setback:
   a. Length
   b. Time location

29   A′ Most of setback is past. 29x Most yet to come.

40 B Setback denied

84v C Constancy asserted (without the implicit meaning being clearly a denial of a setback or a denial of an advance)

120v D Constancy denied (without the implicit meaning being clearly the assertion of a setback or the assertion of an advance)

139 E Advance asserted

170x F Advance denied

Section II—Statements about actions and conditions connected with the setback:

  I Antecedent to the setback:
    B Subjective states:
      4. Beliefs
        a. Type
          A′ Preferences

212   b′ The enemy wanted an outcome different from the actual one. 212x The enemy wanted just this outcome.

        b. Truth value:

222   A′ We correctly predicted this event. 222x Our predictions were wrong.

223   B′ The enemy did not predict this outcome. 223x Enemy predictions were correct.

  II Subsequent to the setback:
    B Subjective states
      2. Moods

240   a. We feel euphoric about the situation. 240x Dysphoric.

241   b. The enemy feels dysphoric about the situation. 241x Euphoric.

D   Constellations of attitudes and actions

    2. Unity

260   a. We are united in the face of the event. 260x Disunited.

261   b. The enemy is disunited. 261x United.

    3. Support

262   a. We have much support with regard to the event. 262x Little.

263   b. The enemy has little support. 263x Much.

Section   III—Relation of the setback to symbols:

    I To symbol system of self

292   A   The event confirms propositions accepted by us. (Exception: predictions of event itself classified above.) 292x Disconfirms.

    II To symbol system of enemy

298   A   The event disconfirms propositions accepted by enemy. (Cf. above exception) 298x Confirms.

Section   IV—Statements about actions and conditions *of actors* connected with the setback:

    I Antecedent to setback

    A By self

        1. In regard to the inflictors of the setback

        2. With regard to those who opposed the occurrence of the setback

        3. With regard to the victims of the setback

    B By enemy

    II Subsequent to the setback

Section   V—Statements about the causes of the setback:

    The causes were:

    I Subjective states:

    A Virtues

404a   1. Our great virtue. 404xa Our lack of virtue.

404b   2. The enemy's lack of virtue. 404xb Great virtue.

II Ability:

414a A Our great ability. 414xa Lack of ability.

414b B The enemy's lack of ability 414xb Great ability.

III Social values:

415a A Our high possession of social values. 415xa Low.

415b B The enemy's low possession of social values. 415xb High.

Section VI—Statements about matters not connected with the setback:

451   I Assertions of indulgences to self. 451x Deprivations.

467   II Assertions of deprivations to enemy. 467x Indulgences.

Section VII—Statements about the effects of the setback:

502   I The effects of the setback are an advance for the self. 502x A further setback.

A Premises:

504   1. The dialectical character of change

514   3. Previous setbacks were never so bad, therefore (sic) the effects will be proportionately good.

B Substantive characteristics of the effects:

2. Effects on subjective states of self

535   a. Increased virtue of self. 535x Decreased.

538   A' We have been steeled. 538x Made soft.

d. Beliefs:

A' By type

1' Preferences

577   a' Self intends to deprive other. 577x Indulge.

578   A' In vengeance

B' By truth value

586   2' Learned by experience. 568x Did not learn.

5. Effects on constellations of attitudes and actions of self

622   c. Support of self increased. 622x Decreased.

625   A' Support by good elements increased. 625x Decreased.

635   B' Support by bad elements decreased. 635x Increased.

641   2' Sloughing off of bad leaders by self. 641x Misleaders increased.

C Formal characteristics of the effects:

659   4. Advances will be of large magnitude. 659x Small.

5. Time characteristics of effects:
c. Proximity

677   1. Good effects will come soon. 677x Far in the future.

Section VIII—Statements about the acceptance of outline statements:

I Assertions of acceptance or rejection

II Statements about the effects of acceptance or rejection

3000 A Acceptance of outline statement is cause of preferred outcome. (N.B. The number of the statement in question goes in the place of the zeroes.)

III Statements about the causes of acceptance of outline statements

Part 2. *Codes for Modifiers of Statements*

In addition to the main classification above, statements were characterized by a number of other specifications. Each such additional outline for a particular characteristic of statements is called a "code." The more important of these will now be briefly described.

Section   I—Political Phenomena List:

It will have been noted that most of the previous chapters contained an identical typology, which included the following headings.

Actions
Conditions
     Subjective states:
       Virtues
       Moods

Attention
Beliefs
Abilities
Social values
Constellations of actions and conditions:
Policies
Unity
Support

The phenomena list added, for each of these headings, a large number of subheads. If, for example, a statement was "Actions of self caused setback," it was thus possible to specify which actions. The major headings of the breakdown of actions are: (1) Symbol use, (2) Violence, (3) Economic control, (4) Practices. Similarly, for a statement about social values, it would be specified whether the values was (1) Economic, (2) Safety, (3) Deference, or (4) Power.[40] In part, the subheads were based on special characteristics of elections and strikes. For example, actions by economic control included such subheads as "lockout," "sympathy strike," etc.

Section   II—Quantity Code:
   1 Absolute quantity:
       + + 1 Very much
       +   1 Much
       01 Medium
       −   1 Little
       − − 1 Very little
   2 Comparison with previous time:
       + + 2 Much or rapid increase, etc.
   3 Comparison with other defeats
   4 Comparison with a norm
   5 Proportion

Section   III—Fact-preference:
   I Fact statements
   II Preference
      +   Preference for
      −   Preference against
    D + Demand for
    D − Demand against

Section   IV—Geographical delimitation of assertion:

Section V—Time code:
    I Extension (long, short, etc., by combination with quantity code)
    II Position in series (early, late, before, after, etc., by combination with quantity code)
    III Relation to present:
      A Past
      B Present
      C Future
    IV Rate (by combination with quantity code)
    V Frequency (by combination with quantity code)

Section VI—Interstatement relations:
    (These were indicated by various kinds of arrows between the recordings of the statements.)
    I Causation
    II Indication
    III Proof
    IV Hypothecation
    V Conjunction, disjunction
    VI Comparison

Section VII—Actor list:
    I The self:

M	A The masses
1	Workers (proletariat)
2	Farmers
3	Unemployed
5	Women
6	Youth
9	Negroes
12	Anti-fascists
13	Progressive people
21	Pickets
22	Trade union
23	Rank-and-file unionists
27	Strike committee
	B The Communist Movement
	Individuals:
44	Zinoviev
46	Dimitrov
	Official bodies:
47	The Communist International
49	World Congress of the C.I.

APPENDIX III

Example of Application by Outline

"DESPITE ALL this crowing by the boss press, never has a Communist Party gained so much support so rapidly as we have now won by our vigorous propaganda."

(1) The enemy press is crowing:—Outline statement 241x (the enemy feels euphoric about the situation); a fact statement; time: IIIB (the present); actor: 138 (the press).

(2) We conducted vigorous propaganda:—Outline statement

201 (action by self, antecedent to setback, connected with setback); phenomena: propaganda (a subdivision of symbol use); quantity: + 1; fact statement; time: IIIA (past); actor: 50 (the Communist Party); interstatement relation: cause of referent of next meaning unit.

(3) The Communist Party has gained much support, etc.:— Outline statement 622 (support of self increased); quantity: + + 1 (very much), + + 2 (very rapidly), + + 3 (much more than other object; object is recorded as C.P. before); actor: 50 (the Communist Party).

NOTES

CHAPTER I

1. *Rhetorica* and *De Poetica*, Vol. IX of *The Works of Aristotle Translated into English* under the editorship of W. D. Ross, Clarendon Press, Oxford, 1924.

2. Available in the Loeb Classical Library, in two volumes, 1942, Harvard University Press, Cambridge.

3. Lynn Thorndike, *A History of Magic and Experimental Science During the First Thirteen Centuries of Our Era*. Macmillan, New York, 1929, Vol 1, p. 45.

4. Harry Caplan, "A Late Mediaeval Tractate on Preaching," in *Studies in Rhetoric and Public Speaking, In Honor of James Albert Winans*, by pupils and colleagues, Century, New York, 1925. See also Etienne Gilson, "Michel Monot et la technique du sermon médiaéval," *Les Idées et les lettres*, Paris, 1932, pp. 93-154; Th. M. Charland, *Artes Praedicandi, Contribution a l'histoire de la rhétorique au moyen age*, Paris, Ottawa, 1936 (Publications de l'Institut d'études mediaevales d'Ottawa, VII).

5. Sister Mary Catherine O'Connor, *The Art of Dying Well*, Columbia University Press, New York, 1942. The author notes, "In MS Modl. 423, f. 192, there is a poetical treatise called 'To lerne to wepe.' And Dale's *Index of British and Other Writers of 1548-51*, p. 480, mentions a *speculum de arte lachrimandi (opus a quodam Anglo editum)*," p. 1, footnote 1. We do not overlook Evelyn Waugh, *The Loved One*, Little, Brown, Boston, 1948.

6. An indication of the effect of words is the use of words to maintain defense against them. Frederick Douglas (Negro orator): "A gentleman will not insult me, and no man not a gentleman can insult me." "Oaths are but words, and words but wind." (Samuel Butler, *Hudibras*). Seneca long ago remarked that "To be able to endure odium is the first art to be learned by those who aspire to power."

7. The books of Jean Piaget are the most important guide to the growth of language in the individual. On the use of words in altercations, see Pierre Bovet, *The Fighting Instinct*, Allen and Unwin, London, 1923.

8. Thorndike, *op. cit.*, Vol. 1, p. 70.

9. Thorndike, *op. cit.*, Vol. 1, pp. 358-59.

10. See H. D. Griswold for a brief statement on "Brahmanism and Hinduism" in the *Encyclopaedia of the Social Sciences*.

11. Edward Sapir, "The Concept of Phonetic Law as Tested in Primitive Languages by Leonard Bloomfield," *Methods in Social Science; A Case Book,* University of Chicago Press, Chicago, 1931, pp. 297-306.

12. Pioneer work is reported by Stanley S. Newman in *Language, Culture, and Personality, Essays in Memory of Edward Sapir,* edited by Leslie Speier, A. Irving Hallowell, Stanley S. Newman, Sapir Memorial Publication Fund, Menasha, Wisconsin, 1941. An early attempt to delimit the field of "special languages" is by Arnold van Gennep, "Essai d'une théorie des langues spéciales," *Revue des études ethnographiques et sociologiques,* June-July, 1908, pp. 327-337. He distinguished between "sacred" and "profane" languages, and went on to suggest that special languages were formed of words composed of: (a) elements from the general language, or (b) elements absent from it. For a view of the present state of linguistic knowledge, consult Leonard Bloomfield, *Language,* New York, 1933; H. Pedersen, *Linguistic Science in the Nineteenth Century,* Harvard University Press, Cambridge, 1931. Sporadic studies have been made of language in politics, such as Uno N. Philipson, *Political Slang, 1750-1850* (Lund Studies in English, edited by Professor ·Eilert Ekwall, IX), C. W. K. Gleerup, Lund, 1941; the penetration of political language into other functional areas has been an occasional topic, as by A. Harnack, *Militia Christi. Die Christliche Religion u. der Soldatenstand in den ersten drei Jahrhunderten,* 1905. Political words and images have been investigated in many literary works, forms of literature, and other expressive media. Example: James Emerson Phillips, Jr., *The State in Shakespeare's Greek and Roman Plays,* Columbia University Press, New York, 1940; Robert Taylor, *The Political Prophecy in England,* Columbia University Press, New York, 1941; Richard Lattimore, *Themes in Greek and Latin Epitaphs,* University of Illinois Press, Urbana, 1942; Victor Ehrenberg, *The People of Aristophanes; A Sociology of Old Attic Comedy,* Blackwell, Oxford, 1943.

13. A. V. Dicey, *Lectures on the Relation Between Law and Public Opinion in England during the Nineteenth Century,* Macmillan & Company, Ltd., London, 1924, p. 20.

14. Charles E. Merriam, *New Aspects of Politics,* University of Chicago Press, Chicago, 1925, p. xiv.

15. Karl Mannheim, *Ideology and Utopia; An Introduction to the Sociology of Knowledge,* with a preface by Louis Wirth, Harcourt, Brace & Company, New York, 1936, p. xvii.

16. Franklin H. Giddings, *Inductive Sociology,* Macmillan Company, New York, 1901, p. 138.

17. Gaetano Mosca, *The Ruling Class,* McGraw-Hill, New York, 1939.

18. ". . . . if we take the statement of the 'law' at face value, we may find it ambiguous; and we call it *normative-ambiguous,* because the word 'law' is used, and 'law' is a word that refers to norms, even though it is unclear whether the norm in question pertains exclusively to the speaker, whether it is shared by the speaker with others, or whether, though a norm of others, it is not the norm of the speaker at all. Common-sense experience emphasizes the enormous role of such normative-ambiguous statements in the discourse that purports to expound 'law' or 'ethics' or 'Divine Will.' 'That is right (morally)' is a sentence open to all the doubts raised about the 'this is the law' sentence; and 'this is God's will' is no less ambiguous. By evoking such word sequences a speaker may conceal his own preference or volition on contentious matters and increase the attention paid to what he says by enunciating norms whose sponsor appears to transcend the speaker."
H. D. Lasswell and M. S. McDougal, "Legal Education and Public Policy; Professional Training in the Public Interest," *Yale Law Journal,* 52 (March, 1943), p. 267.

19. These distinctions are in Harold D. Lasswell, *World Politics and Personal Insecurity*, McGraw-Hill, New York, 1935. Sometimes the same author has used the term "acceptances" as a synonym for expectations.

20. These studies are part of the research program which included the work of Harold D. Lasswell and Dorothy Blumenstock (Jones), *World Revolutionary Propaganda; A Chicago Study*, Knopf, New York, 1939.

21. On the technical means of making such comparisons, consult Harold D. Lasswell, "Content Analysis," in B. L. Smith, H. D. Lasswell, and R. D. Casey, *Propaganda, Communication and Public Opinion*, Princeton University Press, Princeton, 1945.

22. The fact that such assertions are often based on the expediencies of propaganda, rather than on the probabilities of research, need not blind us to their possible truth, although the discovery of truth in such matters is among the most delicate acts of political judgment. For many purposes it is convenient to look at a political pattern not only with reference to the past, or to a theoretical standard; the pattern may be compared with contemporary political doctrines and institutions. There is "similarity" or "distinctiveness"; and when there is interaction, similarities are a matter of "total or partial incorporation" (otherwise, "paralleling"). When distinctiveness is coupled with interaction, "total or partial rejection" is implied (in the absence of mutual influence, there is "divergence").

23. See Harold D. Lasswell, *Power and Personality*, Norton, New York, 1948, and *The Analysis of Political Behaviour*, Kegan Paul, London, and Oxford, New York, 1948.

CHAPTER II

1. For studies of political speeches consult William Norwood Brigance, editor, *A History and Criticism of American Public Address*, McGraw-Hill, New York, 1943 (2 vols.).

2. An excellent review of the theory of literary style is given by William Kurtz Wimsatt, Jr., *The Prose Style of Samuel Johnson*, Yale University Press, New Haven, 1941 (Yale Studies in English, Volume 94). Introduction.

3. The distinction between pure and accessory sign is most difficult to establish in sculpture. In literature, however, it is not difficult to determine what sign-features are beyond the "minimum necessary for comprehension." A striking example of accessory sign use is in Nodier's *Le Roi de Bohême et ses sept Chateaux*, in which the author "exhausted the resources of the printing establishment. At his command, the letters become so long that they stretch from top to bottom of the page; he commands again, and they dwindle into the tiniest of the tiny; he screams, and they stand up on end in terror; he becomes melancholy, and they hang their heads all along the lines; they are inseparately mixed up with illustrations; Latin and Gothic groups alternate, according to the mood of the moment; sometimes they stand on their heads, so that we have to turn the book upside down to read them; sometimes they follow the narrative so closely that a descent of the stairs is printed thus:

> 'Hereupon
>   our
>   hero
>   went
>   dejectedly
>   down
>   the
>   stairs.' "

(Brandes, *The Main Currents of Nineteenth Century Literature*, Boni and Liveright, New York, 1924, Vol. V, pp. 40-41.)

4. Noted in Theodore Reik, *From Thirty Years with Freud*, London, Hogarth Press and the Institute of Psychoanalysis, 1942, p. 19.

5. A convenient guide is Part II of *Personality and the Behavior Disorders*, edited by J. McV. Hunt, New York, Ronald Press, 1944 (2 vols.)

6. *Coronation Durbar, Delhi, 1911, Official Directory with Maps*, Calcutta, India, Superintendent of Government Printing, 1911, pp. 1-3. In general, see Reginald Maxwell Woolley, *Coronation Rites*, Cambridge University Press, 1915 (The Cambridge Handbook of Liturgical Study).

7. In Zainul A. Ahmad, *National Language for India* (A Symposium), Kitabistan Series No. 1, Kitabistan, Allahabad Law Journal Press, Allahabad, 1941, pp. 32-35. The intimate relation of language and nationalism is shown wherever the phenomenon of nationalism is studied. See Hans Kohn, *The Idea of Nationalism; A Study in Its Origins and Background*, Macmillan, New York, 1944.

8. In Ahmad, *op. cit.*, pp. 48-49, 56, 60.

9. J. M. Thompson, *The French Revolution*, Oxford, New York, 1945, p. 428. The circular was addressed to the civil service by Robespierre's fellow townsman Herman, once judge of the Revolutionary Tribunal, when Commissioner of Civil Administration in May, 1794.

10. In connection with the language of politics, an important hypothesis has been proposed by Heinz Paechter. "In a society based on the proposition that all men are created equal, a language is likely to be favored which will express the sovereignty of the subject, the creative power of action, the spontaneity of thought, and the problems of interaction and reciprocity. Its grammar will tend to lay stress on predication, with the verb required to make the sentence meaningful. A society built on the idea of a hierarchic structure will, on the contrary, deny both interaction between subjects and the evolution of ideas and values. It will tend to depict all conditions as essentially static. Its grammar and syntax will be magical, its language evocative. The predicate will not be an answer to a question put by the subject, but will be a commentary upon it. Word symbols will not stand for things, but will tend to become things in their own right, with a well-defined place in the hierarchy of values, and participation in the ritual on their proper level." (Heinz Paechter, in association with Bertha Hellman, Hedwig Paechter, Karl O. Paetel, *Nazi-Deutsch; A Glossary of Contemporary German Usage*, Frederick Ungar Publishing Co., New York, 1944, p. 6.) Paechter is on sound ground in putting the interpersonal relationship—the boundaries of the self—in the center of his theory. As formulated, the theory calls for the consideration of more of the context—the purport—than we include in our discussion of style. It is probable that our hypotheses about uniformity are consistent with it; and very likely that our propositions about prolixity and effect-contrast can be correlated with it.

The patterns of style that we have discussed depend upon more factors than we have brought into the analysis. Besides intensity of crisis and degree of respect, style is deeply influenced by whatever forms are used by political enemies. Every revolution in the political sphere is intimately linked with other revolutionary innovations; our American Revolution is no exception. In the sphere of architecture, we turned from the styles favored by the British ruling class and supported a revival of Greek architecture. "This new cultural direction taken by American leaders—and especially by Thomas Jefferson—was the 'correct' turn; it was a turn in the direction which world sentiment and taste was pursuing." For details, refer to Talbot Hamlin, *Greek*

Revival Architecture in America; Being an Account of Important Trends in American Architecture and American Life Prior to the War Between the States, Oxford University Press, New York, 1944. On political anthems and other paraphernalia of politics, see Roberto Michels, *Der Patriotismus,* Duncker and Humblot, Munich, 1929.

11. Svend Ranulf has sought light on anti-democratic movements by quantitative semantics in *Hitler's Kampf gegen die Objektivität,* Munksgaard, Copenhagen, 1946. On the study of national character, see Paul Kecskemeti and Nathan Leites, "Some Psychological Hypotheses on Nazi Germany," *Experimental Division for the Study of War Time Communications,* Document No. 60 (1945). Republished in *Journal of Social Psychology,* XXVI (1947), 141-183; XXVII (1948), 91-117, 241-270; XXVIII (1948), 141-164.

12. *Op. cit.,* note 2, Introduction.

CHAPTER III

1. Kegan Paul, London, and Knopf, New York, 1927; reprinted by Peter Smith, New York, 1938.

2. See Ralph Haswell Lutz, "Studies of War Propaganda, 1914-33," *Journal of Modern History,* 5: 496-516 (December, 1933).

3. Cotta'sche Buchhandlung Nachfolger, Stuttgart and Berlin.

4. Stanford University Press, Stanford.

5. *Die Englishe Presse zum Ausbruch des Weltkrieges,* Verlag "Hochschule und Ausland," Charlottenburg, 1928.

6. *Kriegsziele und öffentliche Meinung Englands,* 1914-16, W. Köhlhammer, Stuttgart, 1929.

7. Macmillan, London, 2 vols., 1886.

8. "The American Newspaper," *Annals of the American Academy of Political and Social Science,* 16: 56-92 (1900).

9. *Foreign News in American Morning Newspapers,* Columbia University Press, New York, 1930.

10. "How America Became Belligerent: A Quantitative Study of War-News, 1914-17," *American Journal of Sociology,* 40: 464-76 (January, 1935). See also studies summarized in Quincy Wright, *A Study of War,* University of Chicago Press, Chicago, 2 vols., 1942. Note especially Chapter XXX.

11. See Harold D. Lasswell, "Communications Research and Politics," in *Print, Radio, and Film in a Democracy,* edited by Douglas Waples, University of Chicago, Chicago, 1942, pp. 101-117.

12. For a review of the research situation at the outbreak of the war (1939), consult Douglas Waples, Bernard Berelson, and Franklyn R. Bradshaw, *What Reading Does to People,* University of Chicago Press, Chicago, 1940. More recent developments are noted in Harold D. Lasswell, "Content Analysis," in Bruce L. Smith, Harold D. Lasswell, and Ralph D. Casey, *Propaganda, Communication and Public Opinion.* Princeton University Press, Princeton, 1946. (Modified from *Document 11,* Experimental Division for the Study of Wartime Communications, Library of Congress, 1942.)

13. Ernst Kris, Hans Speier and Associates, *German Radio Propaganda; Report on Home Broadcasts During the War,* Oxford University Press, New York, 1944. See also *Propaganda by Short Wave,* edited by Harwood L. Childs and John B. Whitton, Princeton University Press, Princeton, 1942; and the valuable essay by Charles Siepmann, *Radio in Wartime,* Oxford University Press, Oxford, 1942. A survey of the situation in 1939 is by Thomas Grandin, *The Political Use of Radio,* Geneva Research Centre, Geneva, 1939; for a later period, Arno Huth, *Radio Today; The Present State of Broadcasting in*

the World, Geneva Research Centre, Geneva, 1942. Concerning the news and documentary film, the most penetrating inquiry to date, is by Siegfried Kracauer, *Propaganda and the Nazi War Film*, Museum of Modern Art Film Library, New York, 1942.

14. *United States of America* vs. *William Dudley Pelley* (and others), tried in the U. S. District Court for the Southern District of Indiana, Indianapolis Division, summer, 1942; conviction affirmed on appeal to the U. S. Circuit Court of Appeals, Southern Circuit, October Term, 1942. A writ of certiorari denied by the U. S. Supreme Court. Government witnesses included Harold N. Graves, Jr., of the Federal Communications Commission, and Harold D. Lasswell.

15. The historians of literature have relied upon quantitative analysis as one of the chief means at their disposal in the many "detection" problems that confront them. They must detect corrupt texts, decide among competing attributions of authorship, arrive at the true order in which works were composed, determine the sources relied upon by the author and the influences affecting authorship. As Yule points out, the technique of word-counting goes back many centuries, at least to the "Masoretes," who, after the destruction of the Jewish state, A.D. 70, devoted themselves to preserving the text of the Bible and the correct manner of pronunciation. It is curious to see that, despite the ease and amount of word-counting, first-class statisticians have only begun to concern themselves with the problems involved—notably G. Udny Yule, *The Statistical Study of Literary Vocabulary*, Cambridge University Press, Cambridge, Eng., 1944. Although word-counting is involved in the study of communication, not all quantitative procedures are necessarily "content analysis." This term can legitimately be applied only when "counts" are undertaken with reference to a general theory of the communication process. In this sense, "content analysis" is quite recent.

The literary historians have occasionally been stimulated by the methods of cryptography, and they have also made direct contributions to the subject. One example of the influence of this art is Edith Rickert, long associated with J. M. Manly in Chaucerian research, who worked in the "Black Chamber" during World War I, and subsequently devised new ways of studying style: *New Methods for the Study of Literature*, University of Chicago Press, Chicago, 1926. A brief example of differences in the handling of political material by different authors is revealed by a simple study of Scipio's alleged speech to the mutineers in 206 B.C. In Polybius "The speech contains 520 words, in which pronouns or verbal forms of the first person singular occur 14 times—i.e., once in every 37 words. In Livy the speech occupies about 1025 words, and there are no less than 64 occurrences of *ego* or *meus* or verbs in the first person singular—i.e., one word in every 16—a frequency of more than double." (R. S. Conway, *The Portrait of a Roman Gentleman, from Livy, Bull. of the John Rylands Library*, Manchester, 7 (1922-23): 8-22.)

An absorbing mystery story has been written in which detection depends upon content analysis and engineering: Brett Rutledge [pseud. of Elliott Paul], *The Death of Lord Haw Haw*, Random House, New York, 1940. On certain problems see Wladimir Eliasberg, "Linguistics and Political Criminology," *Journal of Criminal Psychopathology*, 5 (1944): 769-774.

16. Hypotheses or assumptions about skill have been stated or implied in quantitative studies of many channels of expression. Special attention has been given to oratory, from this point of view, and especially to such quantifiable characteristics as length of sentence. The language of Rufus Choate so greatly impressed his contemporaries that the chief justice of the highest court in Massachusetts, Joseph Neilson, was among those who gave it special

study (Memoirs of Rufus Choate, Houghton, Mifflin, 1884). Choate was given to long sentences, averaging no fewer than 37 words in one of his most famous cases. Nearly an eighth of all his sentences, in this instance, contained more than 80 words. Consult John W. Black, "Rufus Choate," in A History and Criticism of American Public Address, prepared under the auspices of The National Association of Teachers of Speech, William Norwood Brigance, Editor, McGraw-Hill, New York, 1943, Vol. 1, pp. 455-456. More technical investigations are conducted by modern specialists on public speaking. Howard L. Runion, for example, concentrated on fifty speeches by Woodrow Wilson, and counted many features, including the use of figures of speech. (Unpublished dissertation, University of Wisconsin, 1932. For more detail see Dayton David McKean, "Woodrow Wilson," in op. cit., Vol. 2, pp. 968-992, Brigance, editor.) It is perhaps unnecessary to remark that studies of classical orators are researches into the style of classical historians. See, for instance, Grover Cleveland Kenyan, Antithesis in the Speeches of Greek Historians, University of Chicago Libraries, Chicago, 1941.

17. See Harold D. Lasswell in Lyman Bryson (ed.) The Communication of Ideas, Harpers, New York, 1948, Chapters IV and XV.

18. The use of key symbols in quantitative analysis of comparative literature is exemplified by Josephine Miles, "Some Major Poetic Words," Essays and Studies (by members of the Department of English, University of California), University of California Publications in English, Vol. XIV, University of California Press, Berkeley and Los Angeles, 1943, pp. 233-239. ". . . the trend of change through five hundred years of main consistencies may be justly observed, and may be summarized in these three ways: First, in terms of parts of speech, it may be said that all the verbs to be stressed by more than one poet were established by Donne or sooner; the adjectives, by Burns, or sooner; the last noun, not until Poe. Second, in terms of new subject matter, the direction is clear from making to thinking, from good and great to high and sweet and wild, and from heaven and man to soul and heart, to eye and hand, and then to day, sun, dream, night; it is the direction from action to thought, and from conceived to sensed. Third, in terms of contrast between first and last, the prevailing strength of the three main words, man, love, and see, stands out, mainly the simple verbs are lost, and heart, day, and night are the fresher forces. These three views, as we have seen, add up strongly to one: the view of a general stability in the language of major English poetry, tempered by the shift, gradual in all save Collins, from action and concept toward feeling and sensing."

Expertly conducted studies in expressive media other than literature can throw a light on the changing outlook of peoples. The ruling classes of Delft, for instance, early retired from the brewing industry to live upon investments in the East India Company, and remained retired generation after generation. As they shrank from all forms of commercial activity, no other outgoing mode of life attracted them. Max Eisler has been able to demonstrate a remarkable parallel between Delft's paintings and the quietism of Delft life. First, they found landscapes too breezy and, withdrawing indoors, bought church interiors. Presently these seemed too expansive, and they took to cozy home interiors. Vermeer was the culminating artist in this development, and we see in his paintings the citizens of Delft in unvarying sunshine lounging at table, staring at their reflections in a mirror, or at their jewels; sometimes they have passed from lethargy to sleep. And in these paintings the walls are seen coming closer and closer. Year by year, the world of the Delft rentiers grows narrower and narrower, though always in perpetual sunshine. (Max Eisler, *Alt-Delft,* Vienna, 1923. Put in perspective by Miriam Beard, *A History of the Business Man,* Macmillan, New York, 1938, p. 306.)

19. Special studies eventually to be made public have been completed by some of our associates in the World Attention Survey: Professor Richard Burks, Wayne University; Dr. Heinz H. F. Eulau; Dr. Bruno Foa, formerly University of Turin; Doris Lewis; Dean James J. Robbins, Graduate School, American University; Professor David N. Rowe, Yale University; Professor Douglas Waples, University of Chicago.

CHAPTER V

1. The following instructions were used in # II:

NOTE: Distinctions *within* any category are made only for convenience in presenting and applying the rules; no attempt need be made to give them an exact or sharp interpretation.

I. STRENGTH—WEAKNESS
  A. Military.
    1. Direct military actions.
    Bombings, attacks, raids, capture of prisoners or supplies, military troop movements, casualties, sinkings of ships, downed planes, etc.
    2. General military situation or affairs.
    Tactics and strategy, comparative strengths of military units, predictions of military success or failure, preparedness, etc.
    3. Materiel and personnel (with direct military relevance).
    Equipment, skill or training of troops, troop morale, supplies, military transport and communication facilities, esprit de corps, production and distribution with direct military relevance, etc.
    Ex: GENERAL ACCLAIMS VALUE OF USO   but *not*
        (MARINES FETED AT USO DANCE)
        US TANKS ON ALL WAR FRONTS   but *not*
        (PRODUCTION STOPPED ON SPORTING GOODS)
    4. Civilian activities of direct military relevance.
    Civilian defense, selective service, enlistments, civilian air patrol, etc.
    Ex: PRACTICE BLACKOUT "HIGHLY SATISFACTORY"
                                  but *not*
        (CIVILIAN DEFENSE WORKERS
        GUESTS AT JACK BENNY SHOW)
  B. Political.
    1. Direction of military affairs.
    Grand strategy, conduct of the war, national defense legislation, etc.
    2. Non-military political activity of national leaders and agencies, of clear national significance.
    National elections, demonstrations, petitions, political movements, national programs or policies on farm, labor, industry, etc., "crises" or "emergencies," activities of national political figures in line of duty or ex officio, etc.
    The qualifications "of national significance" and "in line of duty" are especially important. Thus, *exclude* local elections or purely personal activities of political leaders.
  C. Diplomatic.
    1. Military international relations.
    Breaking diplomatic relations, non-military assistance for military purposes (lend-lease, convoying), peace feelers, mediations, ultima-

tums, threats, military "incidents" between non-warring nations, etc.
2. Non-military international relations.
Pacts, treaties, alignments, commercial agreements, sending envoys, etc.
D. Economic.
Of national or clear military significance.
Resources, finances, taxation, wealth, production, unemployment, manpower, transport and communication facilities, basic industries (coal, steel, etc.), standard of living and general working conditions, foreign trade, strikes of national significance, etc.
E. Morale.
Of national significance.
Loyalties of national groups, strikes at defense plants, standard of living and working conditions, social services, education, health, housing, food, rationing (all of national significance), enthusiasm of civilian population, their endurance, determination, etc.

II. MORALITY-IMMORALITY.
A. Keeping or breaking promises, agreements, understandings.
Violating or keeping pacts, treaties, international contracts; keeping or breaking faith; loyalty, treachery, treason, "stab in the back," "quisling," betrayal, sedition, subversive, slacker, shirk, evade; lying, cheating, fraud, deceit, insidious, under-handed, honesty; desertion; "black markets"; etc.
B. Unwarranted or extreme injury or kindness.
Injury of the innocent or helpless: women, children, prisoners, wounded, survivors, hostages; excessive reprisals; mistreatment of neutrals; extending mercy, sympathy, charity, relief, and aid (except to allies *for military, economic, or political reasons*), e.g., Red Cross; enslave, exploit, persecute, oppress, grind, trample; viciousness, ferocity, cold-bloodedness, infamy, "iron heel," brutality, flagrancy, atrocity, loot, rape; intolerance, bigotry; aggressor; terrorism, assassination; etc.
C. Principles and ideals.
Glory, heroism, extreme courage or cowardice; awards (except for efficiency), decorations, citations, medals, paying honor and tribute to heroes and holidays (on a national scale), extremely high or low morale, sacrifice (non-strategic); religiosity, desecrate, defile; democracy (not: democra*cies*), freedom, liberty, tyranny, equality, human rights, democratic rights; justice, distributive justice (extremely low wages or high profits), fairness, honor; virtue, vice, unprincipled, unscrupulous, shameful, depraved, degenerate, decadent, idealistic, corruption, lawlessness; patriotism; charity, generosity; etc.

III. BOTH STRENGTH-WEAKNESS AND MORALITY-IMMORALITY.
Clear elements of both these categories.
Several statements, each concerning a different standard; or the use of moralistic language concerning strength subject-matter; or combined subject-matters within a single statement.
The *indirect* strength implications of moral subject-matter are excluded. The subject-matter must involve strength-weakness independently of the morality reference. That churches are hit during an air raid would be classified BOTH; that the Nazis slaughter all the inhabitants of a Czech village would be M alone, even though they must obviously have "strength" (e.g., military advantage) to carry out such an act.

Desertion and draft-dodging involve both S and M, and are therefore coded B.

If the analyst is doubtful whether the caption is S or M, and no other categories are in question, code B.

IV. NEITHER STRENGTH-WEAKNESS NOR MORALITY-IMMORAL-ITY.

A. Non-political.

Crime without national-political significance (whether or not a Federal law is involved), weather, civilian accidents, human interest stories, society news (without political implications of a clear nature), vice (erotic), etc.

B. Political, diplomatic, and economic.

Local politics and social problems without clear and explicit national significance; similarly for education, science, invention, etc.; personal affairs or non-official acts of political or military leaders, without any clear political or military significance; etc.

C. Military.

News concerning the military in any of its aspects without any clear military bearing. Thus, that half the graduating class at West Point will be married immediately after the exercises is classified NEITHER; but that 500 officers will be commissioned at those ceremonies is STRENGTH.

V. UNINTELLIGIBLE.

Code U only those headlines which are so completely obscure that it cannot be determined to which of the other categories it belongs. A headline may be partially obscure, but still clear enough to classify.

Ex: SNOODS SAVE HAIR FOR WOMEN WAR WORKERS
which is clearly N, even though the analyst is not sure what "snoods" are.

CHAPTER IX

1. Amended and approved August 7, 1939, 53 Stat. 1244. In 1942, the administration of the Act was transferred from the Department of State to the Department of Justice. June 1, 1942, 22 U. S. C. A., 611 *et seq.*

2. See Bruce Lannes Smith, "Democratic Control of Propaganda Through Registration and Disclosure," *Public Opinion Quarterly*, 6 (1942), 27-40.

3. Approved October 17, 1940, 54 Stat., 1201, U. S. Code, Title 18, Sections 14-17.

4. Consult G. E. G. Catlin, "Propaganda as a Function of Democratic Government," in *Propaganda and Dictatorship*, H. L. Childs, Editor, Princeton Univ. Press, Princeton, 1936. But on the technical problems, see Zechariah Chafee, Jr., *Free Speech in the United States*, Harvard Univ. Press, Cambridge, 1941; David Riesman, Jr., "Civil Liberties in a Period of Transition," *Public Policy*, 3 (1942), 33-96; Karl Lowenstein, "Legislative Control of Political Extremism in European Democracies," *Columbia Law Review*, 38 (1938), 591-622, 725-74; "Militant Democracy and Fundamental Rights," *American Political Science Review*, 31 (1937), 417-32, 638-58; Carl Brent Swisher, "Civil Liberties in War Time," *Political Science Quarterly*, LV (1940), 321-47; Harold L. Elsten, "Mass Communication and American Democracy," in *Print, Radio, and Film in a Democracy*, Douglas Waples, Editor (3-13), University of Chicago Press, Chicago, 1942.

5. For more detail, consult Harold D. Lasswell, "Free Speech, Yes; Free Incitement, No," Chapter 8 in *Democracy Through Public Opinion*, Chi

Omega Service Fund Studies, George Banta Publishing Company, 1941. For additional suggestions, see Max Lerner, "Freedom in the Opinion Industries," in *Ideas Are Weapons*, Viking, New York, 1939; Morris Ernst, *Proceedings of the National Conference on Civil Liberties in the Present Emergency*, 1939, p. 16.

6. An introduction is Douglas Waples, Bernard Berelson, Franklyn R. Bradshaw, *What Reading Does to People*, University of Chicago Press, Chicago, 1940, Chapter 4.

7. See Edith Rickert, *New Methods for the Study of Literature*, University of Chicago Press, Chicago, 1926.

8. As in the report of President Hoover's Commission: Hornell Hart, "Changing Social Attitudes and Interests," Chapter 8 in *Recent Social Trends*, McGraw-Hill, New York, 1934.

9. The first three cases were tried in Washington, D. C. Verdicts for the government were not appealed by defendants. The last case was tried in a United States District Court for the Southern District of Indiana, Indianapolis Division, during the summer of 1942. Verdicts against the defendants were taken on appeal to the United States Circuit Court of Appeals, Southern Circuit, October term, in session 1942. Judge Evans wrote the opinion affirming the action of the lower court, Judge Major concurring, December 17, 1942. (United States of America vs. William Dudley Pelley . . . Lawrence A. Brown . . . Fellowship Press, Inc.) Wrote Judge Evans: "Objections were made to the admissibility of . . . the testimony of Dr. Lasswell, that the *Galilean* contained statements unanimously in accord with the present German propaganda themes—which conclusion he reached after extensive search, and preparation of charts. . . . We have no doubt as to the admissibility of all this evidence, if only to show the background from which the intent might be better judged. While we do not believe the utterances to have even a glimmer of ambiguity which might redeem their obvious connotation, still it is not amiss, in a trial before a jury, to bring home to them the real and undoubted intent of the maker of their pronouncements and his wilfulness in making them. Moreover, they were admissible because 'the character of every act depends upon the circumstances in which it is done.'" A writ of certiorari was denied by the United States Supreme Court.

10. Each item classified was offered and made available to the court.

11. For the relation of propaganda to the general field of public opinion study, the best textbooks are by William Albig and Leonard Doob. See also Harold D. Lasswell, R. D. Casey and B. L. Smith, *Propaganda and Promotional Activities: An Annotated Bibliography*, University of Minnesota Press, Minneapolis, 1935; B. L. Smith, H. D. Lasswell, R. D. Casey, *Propaganda, Communication and Public Opinion*, Princeton University Press, Princeton, 1946.

12. Most of these are stated in Harold D. Lasswell, "Communications Research and Politics," in Douglas Waples, Editor, *Print, Radio and Film in a Democracy*, University of Chicago Press, Chicago, 1942.

13. I want to express my appreciation to several members of the Department of Justice who were sympathetically interested in the use of quantitative content analysis. Benjamin Parker first saw the possibilities and pressed ahead with characteristic energy in the Bookniga case. George McNulty and Albert Arent were in charge of the Transocean and Auhagen cases. Henry Schweinhaut and Oscar Ewing handled the Pelley prosecution. The legal technicalities involved have been explored with utmost thoroughness, especially by Schweinhaut, who, I hope, will eventually summarize his contributions in print. Among research associates, the following should be given special mention: Jesse MacKnight; Charles A. H. Thomson; Louis Nemzer;

Paul Lewis; Huntington Harris; W. Phillips Davison; William Cherin; Irving Janis; and Morris Janowitz. Harold L. Elsten made the original contact between the lawyers and social scientists.

14. Harold Graves, Jr., Acting Head of the Foreign Broadcast Monitoring Service.

15. Reliability in this investigation among independent classifiers is exceedingly high—no less than 99 out of every 100 items were classified the same way.

16. The development of the distortion analysis is chiefly the work of Paul Lewis and Huntington Harris. Because of the exploratory character of the investigation and the order of complexity, the results of the distortion test were not presented to the court.

CHAPTER XI

1. The author is indebted to Ithiel Pool for a number of suggestions and criticisms.

2. To which we shall refer by the customary abbreviation "CI" or "Comintern." Other customary abbreviations which will be used are "ECCI" for "Executive Committee of the Communist International" and "CP" for "Communist Party."

3. The world congresses of the CI were held in 1919, 1920, 1921, 1922, 1924, 1928, and 1935.

4. In quotations from these reports, the congress involved will be referred to by its Roman numeral. For the first five congresses the reports in German —published by Carl Hoym Nachfolger Louis Cahnbley in Hamburg, 1921 (I, II, III), 1923 (IV), without year (V)—were used (and translated by the author), unless otherwise indicated. For the last two congresses the reports published in English were adduced from the edition of the "International Press Correspondence," with the exception of Bucharin's Sixth Congress report on behalf of the Executive Committee, for which the French edition of the *Inprecorr* was consulted and translated. The page references concerning the Sixth Congress all refer to the 1928 volume of the *Inprecorr;* those concerning the Seventh Congress refer to the 1935 volume, unless the 1936 volume is indicated.

5. Cf. for the context: H. D. Lasswell and D. Blumenstock (Jones), *World Revolutionary Propaganda* (New York, 1939); F. Borkenau, *The Communist International* (London, 1939); A. Rosenberg, *A History of Bolshevism* (London, 1934).

6. One conclusive indicator of this, among many others, is the following: the technical language of the Comintern with reference to "deviations" permits the use of the term "left" as signifying "ultra-left" *almost only in quotation marks,* whereas the term "right" can be used only as signifying a "deviation" and is *practically never used with quotation marks* in this (or in any other) context. (Cf. however, curious exceptions in the Fifth Congress theses on the report of the ECCI: cf. the English edition of the *Inprecorr* of August 29, 1924, p. 646.) The implications—which are often made explicit— are, of course: (1) that the Comintern policy of the moment is such that there can be no more "genuinely left" one than it; (2) that the "left" deviationists are "really" "rights."

7. There was, however, a "moderate" right-wing group composed of deposed leaders of the Czechoslovak and German parties, which at least ostensibly agreed with the new line, but also maintained its newness, which they justified by alleging certain changes in the political situation. (Cf. the

references of Smeral, V, p. 162. Cf. the discussion of this symbol pattern in this paper, p. 318.) This anomalous behavior was related to the fact that these elements were charged with having committed right deviations in the past period: their emphasis on the existence of a change of line in the Comintern at large was thus a necessary link in their attempted self-exculpation.

Cf. the references of Kreibich (Czechoslovakia), V, p. 389; of Bordiga (Italy), V, pp. 399-400; and of Radek, V, p. 162.

8. It may be noted here that, after the Sixth Congress, the term "third period" itself was subject to the kind of symbolic manipulation which we are studying here. The ground for this was laid by the fact that at the Sixth Congress "Stalin and Bucharin . . . (both) accepted the formula of the 'third period,' but put on it two mutually exclusive interpretations. To Bucharin . . . (it) meant that capitalism was in a process of expansion . . . To the left wing it meant the approach of a new revolutionary era." (F. Borkenau, loc. cit., pp. 336-337.)

9. In discussing precision—ambiguity in separation from specificity—generality, one should not overlook how very infrequently this distinction is neatly made in the symbol output studied.

10. Bucharin's intensity of emphasis was presumably polemically directed against those who regarded the turn to the left as a partial incorporation of the political line of the 1927 opposition in the USSR. Bucharin—despite the almost absolute ban of silence on "Trotskyism" in the central reports delivered to the Sixth Congress—could not refrain from mentioning that "certain comrades establish a correlation between the change of our line and certain secondary factors. . . . It would be childish to think that we try to 'radicalize' ourselves because of the reproaches of the opposition. These arguments do not even merit an answer." (VI, p. 16.)

11. We may note that to the resources implicit in the ambiguity of the formulations of the "line" of the moment could be added those created by the distinction between overt and covert violations of this line. Thus, at the Seventh Congress Dimitrov asserted that, in the latter years, "sectarianism" manifested itself no longer "in primitive, open forms as in the first years of the existence of the Communist International," but rather "under cover of a formal recognition of the Bolshevist theses. . . ." (VII, p. 975.) There has been an ascending trend of such allegations in Comintern history: a trend which contributed to the flexibility of the center.

CHAPTER XII

1. For a fuller discussion of content analysis methodology see N. Leites and I. de Sola Pool, *On Content Analysis*, Document No. 26, Experimental Division for the Study of Wartime Communications, Library of Congress, September 1, 1942.

2. Note that these presumable responses of certain "propagandees" to certain propaganda contents do not enter into the definitions of the "content analytic" categories referring to these contents (cf. N. Leites and I. Pool, *op. cit.*).

3. In its own words, it is "an organ for information on foreign affairs, economics and the Labor Movement, providing material for journalists, politicians, scholars, workers' officials, etc." Vol. XVIII, No. 33, p. 775, July 2, 1938.

4. The Danish election of 1943, held under Nazi occupation, in which the Communists were of course not allowed to run, was so noncomparable to the previous election that it was excluded.

5. Cf. N. Leites, *The Third International on its Changes of Policy,* Document No. 25, Experimental Division for the Study of Wartime Communications, Library of Congress, May 1, 1942. (Chapter XI of this book.)

6. Franz Borkenau, *The Communist International,* London, 1938; C. L. R. James, *World Revolution, 1917-1936,* Pioneer Publishers, New York, 1937; Arthur Rosenberg, *A History of Bolshevism,* London, 1939.

7. More accurately, cumulation may be defined in terms of correlations between indices of forms of behavior presumably tending to affect the dysphoria felt about a setback, or the euphoria felt about an advance. The indices may be classified as follows:

A. When applying to a setback:
    1. Indices a higher value of which indicates behavior which presumably results in greater dysphoria.
    2. Indices a lower value of which indicates such behavior.
B. When applying to an advance:
    1. Indices a higher value of which indicates behavior which presumably results in greater euphoria.
    2. Indices a lower value of which indicates such behavior.

Cumulation exists when there is a positive correlation between indices both of which are of any one of the four types; or when there is a negative correlation between indices both of which belong to the same type (A or B), but one is Type 1 and the other is Type 2.

Compensation exists in the same set of circumstances but when the sign is opposite to that specified above.

8. The *secondary* effects of self-indulgent symbols may, of course, be an increase of the dysphoria in regard to a setback. This is so, for example, in the case where self-indulgent symbols turn out to be grossly at variance with the "facts."

9. This index is an application of the Janis-Fadner coefficient of imbalance to statements admitting and denying the setback. Cf. I. Janis and R. Fadner, "A Coefficient of Imbalance for Content Analysis," *Psychometrika,* Vol. VIII (June, 1943), pp. 105-119. (Chapter VIII, this volume.)

10. This index is determined by the percentage of all classified statements which are classified under categories of statements tending (presumably) to reduce the dysphoria felt about the setback. The mitigation index used for this correlation is, of course, modified to exclude such categories as "admissions" and "denials" which enter into the frankness index, and which would create a spurious correlation with the mitigation index.

11. This index is defined as the percentage which statements about the causes of the setback are of the sum of these statements, plus the statements about the effects of the setback.

12. For the frankness (A) index; with the (B) index the figure is $+.48$ ($t = 2.4$).

13. This index is defined as the percentage which matters unconnected with the setback form of the total of these statements, plus statements about the setback itself.

14. Speech to Supreme Council of the Soviet Union, October 31, 1939.

15. The strike data on this point have not been computed; the frequencies would be smaller, if anything, and therefore hardly usable.

16. The abbreviation "left election," etc., is used for "election during a left period."

17. The percentage results have only a suggestive value, since, dealing as they do with nonindependent units, they can not be tested for significance. Terms, whether they be names or otherwise, do not occur independ-

ently of each other. For a further discussion of this point, see Leites and Pool, *op. cit.* To overcome this difficulty the correlations—of which most of the results consist—used as units not single symbols but all symbols about a given event (strike or election defeat). Taken as a whole each of these patterns is, of course, relatively independent. These results can therefore be tested for significance.

A few of the variables studied had to be cut, for convenience, into arbitrary segments. In these cases, biserial correlations were generally used. The main variables of this character are leftness-rightness of the period involved, degree of repression involved in the defeat, the seriousness of the strike defeat, and the degree of hostility of the non-Communist labor movement toward the strike. The assumption of a biserial correlation, that these variates are normally distributed, obviously, can not be proved, or it would probably not have been necessary to use this form of correlation. However, the assumption seems reasonable in each case, and certainly the authors know no reason for expecting any of these variates to be distributed in a skewed or plurimodal fashion.

The significance of the difference between means was used to test differences between strikes and elections, and between *one* period and other periods, since in these cases we are dealing with qualitative differences.

18. It is open to question whether this hypothesis would apply to references to groups actually to the left of the Communists (e.g., anarchists, Trotskyites, etc.). The latter did not have sufficient mass support to figure in the discussions of the election and strike situations studied. We have evidence only in regard to groups at greater or smaller distances to the right of the Communists.

19. Extraversion is defined as the percentage which statements about "enemies" form of all statements. The index of attention to the Communist Party *as against* the masses is defined by the proportion which statements about the former are of all statements about both sets of objects. The difference in the methods of computing the two indices is necessary in order to minimize the danger of a spurious correlation. Since the enemy, the masses and the self make up all actors and targets, a correlation between the percentage formed by any two of these would tend to be negative and fairly large. Consequently the expedient is used of correlating the percentage formed by one with the *ratio* between the other two.

20. Symbols emitted are called realistic if there is a correlation between some variable characteristic of them and some variable characteristic of their environment, the correlation being in the direction generally regarded as realistic. If there is no significant correlation, we characterize the symbols as "unrealistic." If there is a correlation, but in the opposite direction, we characterize them as "illusionistic."

21. Cf. Figure 19.

22. To state the same thing in somewhat different terms: The mean difference between the two indices was .149 in the early years, .223 in the Third Period, and .315 in the People's Front Period.

23. Cf. p. 355.

24. This index is defined as the difference between the percentage of the total vote received by the Communist Party in the previous comparable election and in the election in question.

25. Strikes are impressionistically classified into three groups, according to severity.

26. But, for one limited group of cases, cf. p. 358.

27. The A index for strikes is 64.6, for elections 41.8. (The difference be-

tween the B indices is 1.8 times the standard error.) Corrections have been made for the smallness of the sample.

28. Cf. p. 368 *infra* for a diagrammatic explanation of this and related points.

29. A formal definition would have to take account of those situations in which one propaganda is more self-indulgent than another in one respect, but less so in another. This would require the assignment of arbitrary weights. However, such a definition seems unnecessary for the purposes at hand.

30. Cf. p. 363.

31. In all correlations of extraversion (introversion) and diversion, the modified indices described in Appendix II must be used to avoid a spurious correlation, owing to the fact that almost all statements in the section of the outline "About the setback itself" are about the self.

32. Cf. Leites, *op. cit.*

33. Cf. Figure 20.

34. Cf. p. 354.

35. Cf. p. 368, for a diagrammatic explanation of this point.

36. Corrected for small samples.

37. It should be noted that, in the above discussion of self-indulgence differentials (p. 355), no attempt was made to assign absolute values on a self-indulgence scale. This would have required the weighting of the various elements of which this complex variable consists. We have, however, no basis for assigning appropriate weights. The above statements were therefore limited to assertions that one propaganda was more, or less, self-indulgent than another in a given respect.

38. At 0 evaluation there is no motivation for any self-indulgence. In the graphs, therefore, the regression lines go through the origin. The argument in the text is, however, not dependent on this.

If total self-deprivation sets in somewhere above 0 evaluation, and continues down to the latter point, a linear regression would not cover the situation at the extremes of the distribution. But, for our diagrammatic purposes, this difficulty may well be disregarded.

Of greater seriousness is the fact that the regression lines in point are in all probability not linear at all. But we have, of course, no information about their real shape, and so, for the present, must limit ourselves to the simplest assumptions.

39. However, a rough measurement of the degree of conformity can be made. In a perfect case, the following relationships would hold true:

(1) Right elections would be more indulgently treated than Right strikes.

(2) Left strikes would be more indulgently treated than Left elections.

(3) Right elections would be more indulgently treated than Left elections.

(4) Right elections would be more indulgently treated than Left strikes.

(5) Right strikes would be more indulgently treated than Left elections.

The remaining relationship, that between Left and Right strikes, is left indeterminate.

We can check these hypotheses with the facts by calculating for each of the four relevant indices the mean value for Right elections, Right strikes, Left elections, Left strikes. We find that, for both the retrospection and diversion indices, all five of the above statements hold true. For both frankness and mitigation, three of the five hold true. (The other kinds of self-indulgence differentials referring to combinations of indices can not be compared in this simple way.) If the small quantities with which we are dealing did not make it impossible to hold constant the effect of other observed relations (e.g., cumulation, realism, etc.), the hypothesis under consideration might have been more fully confirmed. Thus, for example, the difference in actors talked about in strikes and elections, coupled with the difference in the impact of parallel statements about different actors (cf. p. 366 *supra*), partly accounts for the lack of full conformity of mitigation to our model. Separate consideration of mitigation about each major group of actors results in a substantial increase in the degree of conformity of this aspect of propaganda to the pattern.

40. Cf. H. D. Lasswell, *Politics: Who Gets What, When, How*, New York, 1936.